Linda Gordon was educated at Swarthmore College and Yale University. From 1968 to 1984 she taught history at the University of Massachusetts, Boston. She is now Professor of History at the University of Wisconsin. An author of books and articles on social history and feminism, her highly acclaimed book *Woman's Body, Woman's Right*, a study of the politics of birth control in America, was nominated for the National Book Award in 1976. She lives in Madison, Wisconsin.

Heroes of Their Own Lives is a history of family violence from the point of view of its victims. Covering child abuse, child neglect, wife-beating and incest throughout the period 1880-1960, it is based on a new source for historians – the case records of social work agencies. Linda Gordon puts contemporary family violence into a new perspective, drawing out the ways in which wife-beating and child abuse must be seen as issues of power and domination, and holding up a mirror to present social policy. Moving, provocative and meticulously researched, it is a unique social document and an invaluable contribution to current debate.

HEROES OF
THEIR OWN LIVES

THE POLITICS AND HISTORY
OF FAMILY VIOLENCE

BOSTON 1880-1960

Linda Gordon

VIRAGO

Published by VIRAGO PRESS Limited 1989
20-23 Mandela Street, Camden Town, London NW1 0HQ

First published in 1988 by Viking Penguin Inc. Published simultaneously in Canada

Portions of this book first appeared, some in different form, in the following
publications.
American Quarterly, volume 37, no. 2, Summer 1985, under the title "Single Mothers
and Child Neglect, 1880-1920." Copyright 1985, American Studies Association.
Published by American Studies Association.
Feminist Studies, volume 12, no. 3, Fall 1986 under the title "Family Violence,
Feminism and Social Control."
Journal of Marriage and the Family, volume 46, no. 1, February 1984 under the title
"Incest as a Form of Family Violence."
Social Problems, volume 33, no. 4, April 1986, under the title "Incest and Resistance:
Patterns of Father-Daughter Incest, 1880-1930." © 1986 by The Society for the Study
of Social Problems, Inc. Used by permission.

British Library Cataloguing in Publication Data

Gordon, Linda, 1940-
Heroes of their own lives: the politics and history of family
violence.
1. Families. Violence
I. Title
306.8'7

ISBN 1-85381-039-8

Printed in Great Britain by Billings & Sons Ltd

PREFACE AND ACKNOWLEDGMENTS

A book that consumes as much time as this one did accumulates many meanings and lessons for its author as well as its readers. Doubting that any scholar can achieve "objectivity," if that means detachment from prevailing cultural norms, I think one can move closer to that goal by consciousness of what one's own values and biases are. Here are some of mine.

In positing the family as a subject of study, some historians have conceptualized it as a homogeneous unit. This mistake not only masks intrafamily conflicts of interests, and particularly the interests of women and children, but it stands in the way of a good understanding of family change and relations between family and the larger society. The topic of family violence provides a case in point for the necessity of seeing families as conflictual as well as harmonious. Moreover, much family history has been based exclusively on objective and quantifiable sources, such as censuses and employment records, which can yield information on the more public aspects of the lives of the poor—income levels, transience, jobs, family size—but little about their private lives. Too often these subjects have appeared only as aggregates, without individuality or subjectivity. It would appear that only the privileged had personalities. My focus on family violence and use of social-work case records are attempts to create a social history that does not erase personality.

I found also that this topic suggests a better conception of how "patriarchy" or male supremacy works than that now predominating. The family-violence evidence will not support the use of these concepts to mean the total, undifferentiated, and predictable tyranny of men and helplessness of women. Some of the family-violence victims were totally defeated, and they often became ill, crazy, or otherwise incompetent. But many were not, and did not stop strategizing and agitating to make a better existence for themselves and for their children. Many ended with greater happiness and autonomy than the men they were involved with. We need concepts of male supremacy that can explain the power that women have managed to exert, the more impressive because emanating from such disadvantaged positions; the compromises that men have often made, particularly in their personal lives, out of regard for individual women more than from any sense of injustice in their own privileges; and the extremely complex struggles, negotiations, and cooperation with which the sexes have faced each other and the social/cultural institutions that define gender relations. Without such flexible concepts, feminist theory is vulnerable to arguments that cite instances of women's power as evidence that sexism does not exist.

I find particularly ahistorical the use of the term "patriarchy" to mean a universal, unchanging, deterministic social structure which denies agency to women. I prefer to use the term, and have used it in this book, in a narrower sense, referring to a form of male dominance in which fathers control families and families are the units of social and economic power. This form prevailed among many of the traditional societies from which the book's subjects came, but was rapidly giving way to more modern forms of male supremacy in the United States.

One needs a generic conception of male dominance, but it will work only if it incorporates the chronic conflict, unpredictability, and ambivalent emotions that have characterized relations between the sexes. Historically, the outcomes of individual confrontations have not always been determined—although the collective victory of men has been—which explains why women never quit trying to do better for themselves. Some scholars read interpretations which attribute power to women as somehow diminishing the injustices done to them. On the contrary, it strikes me as an insult to the humanity of women to suggest that they could have been totally resigned to helplessness.

Although the outcomes of family violence are not predictable, nevertheless virtually all of it is conditioned in some way by sexual inequality. This does not mean that the women in these struggles were always or even usually "better"—kinder, gentler, more responsible—than the men. In fact, in this study I met extremely violent and cruel women, as well as women whose passivity was sometimes literally murderous toward their children. As much as I cheered on some of the women here, I also grew angry with them. Yet the abuse done by women as much as that done by men was also a product of the sex/gender order of society.

Furthermore, "patriarchy"—whether conceived in my specific historical sense or in the general sense as meaning sexism—is as importantly a system of parental domination over children as of men's over women. In the last century, feminists advocated women's and children's rights in tandem, and were responsible for a high proportion of all child-welfare reform. The second wave of feminism has had much less influence on child-welfare discussions, in part because many of the most active feminists were young, childless women, and even more because child-welfare work was by then professionalized and dominated by men. Until the 1920s, virtually all child-welfare reforms were gains for women as well—e.g., child-custody reform, public education, public-health projects; today there are competing interpretations about what children "need," and some conservatives argue that markers of women's increased autonomy such as employment, day-care centers, etc., may be damaging to children. Studying family violence suggests the relevance of feminist analysis to child-welfare policy.

The research for this book was so vast and tedious, and my writing of it so fragmented, that I was able to complete it only with support from many quarters. I benefited from grants and fellowships from the National Institute of Mental Health (Grant No. 5 RO1 MH 33264-03), the John

Simon Guggenheim Foundation, the American Council of Learned Societies, and the University of Wisconsin graduate school, for which I am extremely grateful. I appreciate the work of the University of Wisconsin Cartography Lab in preparing charts. The Bunting Institute of Radcliffe College gave me an office in the midst of energetic and challenging scholars, several of whom contributed more than they know to this book. Staff members of the Massachusetts Society for the Prevention of Cruelty to Children (MSPCC) and the Boston Children's Service Association (BCSA) offered me help and space, as did Richard Wolf of the Countway Medical Library, and Nicholas Olsberg, former Archivist of the Commonwealth of Massachusetts. Marvin Feuerberg and Milt Kotelchuck helped me get started. Material now in chapters 1 and 9 appeared in *Feminist Studies*, material from chapter 7 in *Social Problems*, from chapter 4 in *American Quarterly*, and from chapter 7 in *Journal of Marriage and the Family*; I thank those journals for their permission to re-use the material.

I have been influenced and helped by many people, the number growing as did the years it took me to complete this work. Many students and friends responded to my interest in family violence with critiques and insights now imbedded in this book. I think particularly of students in my courses on family violence, often themselves victims or abusers, and of my many passionate and irreverent women's history students at the Universities of Massachusetts and Wisconsin. Martha Coons, Anne Doyle Kenney, Jan Lambertz, Nancy McKerrow, and Paul O'Keefe worked with me on the research. Without Anne and Paul's commitment and patience, all would have been lost. Jan, to whom I am indebted for both research and interpretation, particularly about sexual abuse, has written the best work on this topic in English history. Wini Breines, with whom I coauthored a critical review of family-violence scholarship, influenced my thinking, as did many committed and compassionate scholars of contemporary family violence, too numerous to list. In the writing of this book and previous articles, several colleagues have offered valuable critical comments: Ellen Bassuk, Ros Baxandall, Caroline Bynum, Elizabeth Ewen, Stuart Ewen, Judith Herman, Jan Lambertz, Marilyn Chapin Massey, Nancy Miller, Eli Newberger, Eve Kosofsky Sedgewick, Christine Stansell, Pauline Terrelonge. University of Wisconsin students Cass Brady, Kathy Brown, Hannah Duggan, and Leslie Reagan offered valuable help with some final research details. Rosie Gordon

Hunter helped me tabulate some odds and ends of data, and Nancy Isenberg helped me proofread. Elizabeth Pleck took time out from her own book on the history of family violence to give me the benefit of her detailed critique. I owe a special debt to Nancy Cott, Susan Stanford Friedman, Judith Walzer Leavitt, Gerda Lerner, Susan Schechter, Barrie Thorne, and Ann Withorn, who found the time to read large sections and in some cases all of this manuscript and offered good advice and insights. Allen Hunter's critical thinking created a steady atmosphere of challenge and intellectual energy.

FOR ROSIE AND ALLEN

CONTENTS

TABLES AND CHARTS

HEROES OF
THEIR OWN LIVES

'Whether I shall turn out to be the hero of my own life, or whether that station will be held by anybody else, these pages must show.'
– Charles Dickens, *David Copperfield*

INTRODUCTION

In the past twenty-five years, family violence has appeared as a substantial social problem in the United States.[1] Starting with a wave of concern about child abuse in the 1960s, the concern widened to include wife-beating, incest (the sexual abuse of children in the family), and marital rape, as the women's liberation movement of the 1970s drew those crimes to public attention. The actual extent of family violence is controversial; estimates of child abuse vary, for example, from 50,000 to 1.5 million cases a year in the United States.[2] Whatever the real figure, the general awareness of the problem has increased substantially.

For most of these two and a half decades, I was not a family-violence scholar. My responses were probably typical: First, I wondered how anyone could be so bestial as to beat or mutilate their children (beating and mutilation were at first the dominant media representations of child

1

abuse); then, as I gathered how widespread the problem was, I wondered that so many could have so little self-control; then, as I began to meet former victims and perpetrators, I began to suspect that the boundary separating me from those experiences was by no means invulnerable. Finally, the issue provoked my historian's curiosity. I noticed that family violence had had virtually no history; that most who discussed it— experts, journalists, friends—assumed they were discussing a *new* problem. As my preliminary forays into libraries revealed that it was an old problem, I began to notice the distortions created in the public discussion by the lack of a history.

One example is the tendency of the media to cover only the most cruel cases, creating the impression that these were typical. I learned that, a century ago, the problem had also gained public attention through sensational cases, while the majority of cases were ambiguous, not life-threatening, more often crimes of neglect than of assault. Another example is that many diagnoses of the *causes* of family violence—e.g., the increasing permissiveness of recent family and sexual life—assume that the problem is unprecedented, which is not the case. By contrast, the ebb-and-flow pattern of concern about family violence over the last century suggests that its incidence has not changed as much as its visibility.

The changing visibility of family violence is, in my opinion, the leading indicator of the necessity of an historical approach to understanding it. Concern with family violence has been a weathervane identifying the prevailing winds of anxiety about family life in general. The periods of silence about family violence are as significant as the periods of concern. Both reveal the longing for peaceful family life, the strength of the cultural image of home life as a harmonious, loving, and supportive environment. One response to this longing has been a tendency to deny, even suppress, the evidence that families are not always like that. Denying the problem serves to punish the victims of family violence doubly by forcing them to hide their problems and to blame themselves. Even the aggressors in family violence suffer from denial, since isolation and the feeling that they are unique make it difficult to ask for the help they want.

About 110 years ago there arose for the first time a different response— an attempt to confront the facts of family violence and to stop or at least control it. The first social agencies devoted to family-violence problems arose in the 1870s, called Societies for the Prevention of Cruelty to Children. They originally focused only on child abuse, but were soon drawn into other forms of family violence as well. It is important to learn and evaluate this history for its contemporary value as well as its historical interest.

The central argument of this book is that family violence has been historically and politically constructed. I make this claim in a double sense. First, the very definition of what constitutes unacceptable domestic violence, and appropriate responses to it, developed and then varied according to political moods and the force of certain political movements. Second, violence among family members arises from family conflicts which are not only historically influenced but political in themselves, in the sense of that word as having to do with power relations. Family violence usually arises out of power struggles in which individuals are contesting real resources and benefits. These contests arise not only from personal aspirations but also from changing social norms and conditions.

The historical developments that influenced family violence—through the behavior of family members and the responses of social-control agencies—include, prominently, changes in the situation of women and children. Another major argument of this book, therefore, is that family violence cannot be understood outside the context of the overall politics of the family. Today's anxiety about family issues—divorce, sexual permissiveness, abortion, teenage pregnancy, single mothers, runaway or allegedly stolen children, gay rights—is not unprecedented. For at least 150 years there have been periods of fear that "the family"— meaning a popular image of what families were supposed to be like, by no means a correct recollection of any actual "traditional family"—was in decline; and these fears have tended to escalate in periods of social stress. Anxieties about family life, furthermore, have usually expressed socially conservative fears about the increasing power and autonomy of women and children, and the corresponding decline in male, sometimes rendered as fatherly, control of family members. For much of the history of the family-violence concern, moreover, these anxieties have been particularly projected onto lower-class families.[3] Thus an historical analysis of family violence must include a view of the changing power relations among classes, sexes, and generations.

Yet family-violence policy is mainly discussed today without an historical dimension, and with its political implications hidden. The result has been a depoliticization of family-violence scholarship, as if this were a social problem above politics, upon which "objective" scientific expertise could be brought to bear.[4] The questions raised by proposed remedies cannot be answered by "neutral" experts, but only by public decisions about the extent and limits of public responsibility.

A few examples may offer an introductory sense of what it means to call family violence a political problem. For over a century there has been a consensus that there must be some limits placed on the treatment family "heads" can mete out to their dependents. But setting and enforcing those limits encounters a fundamental tension between civil liberties and social control. In policing private behavior, one person's right may be established only by invading another person's privacy. Moreover, social control of family violence is made difficult by our dominant social norm that families ought to be economically independent. There is a consensus that children ought to have some minimal guarantees of health and welfare, no matter how poor their parents. Yet there is a consistent tendency to insist that social welfare be a temporary expedient, made uncomfortable, and its recipients stigmatized. These dilemmas must be confronted by political choices; they cannot be ironed out by expert rationalization.

The political nature of family violence is also revealed in the source of the campaign against it. For most of the 110 years of this history, it was the women's-rights movement that was most influential in confronting, publicizing, and demanding action against family violence. Concern with family violence usually grew when feminism was strong and ebbed when feminism was weak. Women's movements have consistently been concerned with violence not only against women but also against children. But this does not mean that anti-family-violence agencies, once established, represented feminist views about the problem. On the contrary, anti-feminism often dominated not only among those who would deny or ignore the problem but also among those who defined and treated it. In some periods the experts confronted wife-beating and sexual assault, male crimes, while in others they avoided or soft-pedaled these crimes and emphasized child neglect, which they made by definition a female crime. In some periods they identified class and in others gender inequalities as relevant, and in still others ignored connections between family violence and the larger social structure.

Political attitudes have also affected research "findings" about family violence. For example, in the last two decades, experts on the problem have tended to divide into two camps. A psychological interpretation explains the problem in terms of personality disorders and childhood experience. A sociological explanatory model attributes the problem primarily to social stress factors such as poverty, unemployment, drinking, and isolation.[5] In fact, these alternatives have been debated for a century, and the weight of opinion has shifted according to the dominant political mood. More conservative times bring psychological explanations to the foreground, while social explanations dominate when progressive attitudes and social reform movements are stronger. The debate is intense because it is not mainly about diagnoses but about their implications for policy. Social diagnoses imply social action and demand resources; psychological diagnoses may point to the need for psychotherapy but also justify criminal penalties and remove family violence from the range of problems called upon to justify welfare spending. When caseworkers lack the resources to help clients materially, they may focus on psychological problems—which are usually present— because at least something can be done about them. Those opposed to the commitment of resources on social spending are more likely to focus on individual psychological deviance as the problem. But both sides have often ignored the gender politics of family-violence issues, and the gender implications of policy recommendations, not only when women or girls were the victims of men, but also when women were the abusers.

Political attitudes have determined the very *meanings* of family violence. Family violence is not a fixed social illness which, like tuberculosis, can have its causal microorganism identified and then killed. Rather, its definitions have changed substantially since it first appeared as a social problem. Most of the discussion of family violence today assumes that what makes it problematic and requires social action is self-evident.[6] Yet what was considered spanking a century ago might be considered abusive today, and the standards for what constitutes child neglect have changed greatly.

To insist that family violence is a political issue is not to deny its material reality as a problem for individuals—a painful, often terrifying reality. If there were any doubt, the victims', and often aggressors', pleas for help would erase it. But to discuss the violence itself without attention to the conflicts that give rise to it is to avoid the roots of the problem.

It is equally important to look at the history of attempts to control family violence. These efforts illustrate many of the general problems of "social control," a phrase often used to describe processes by which deviant and, presumably, dangerous behavior is disciplined by the larger society. Agencies devoted to the problem of family violence are in many ways typical of the entire welfare state. They have faced great difficulties in maintaining a balance between social order and privacy, between protecting the rights of some individuals and preserving the autonomy of others, and they have often been the means of imposing dominant values on subordinate groups. As with other activities of the state, social control of family violence could hardly be expected to be administered fairly in a society of such great inequalities of power. Yet it is precisely those inequalities that create such desperate need for the intervention of a welfare state.

Thus the example of family violence also produces a more complex view of social control than has been customary among social theorists. One of the most striking findings of this study is how often the objects of social control themselves asked for intervention from child-protection agencies. Clients were troubled by their inability to raise children according to their own standards, or to escape domestic violence themselves, and were eager for outside help. Moreover, once becoming clients, they attempted aggressively to influence agency policy and the definitions of the problems themselves, sometimes successfully.

TYPES OF FAMILY VIOLENCE

Four major types of family violence predominated in the eighty years covered by this study. The original one was cruelty to children, a notion which evolved into the modern category: child abuse.[7] In 1880, as today, child-saving propaganda emphasized violent assault as the archetypical problem. In fact, child abuse is (and was) less common than child neglect, but it is more dramatic, less ambiguous, and—above all—it stimulates more outrage and financial generosity. Social workers in the nineteenth century, as those today, were aware that for effective fund-raising, they had to offer a distorted image of the nature of their work.

Child neglect soon became the most common form of family "violence" met by agencies. Its definition is of course extremely variable and relative to economic class, cultural standards, and family structure. What child-neglect cases have in common is that they must by definition project an inverse standard, a norm of proper child-raising.

Sexual abuse of children in the family—incest—figured prominently in family-violence case records. The "discovery" of child sexual abuse in the last decade has been only a rediscovery of a problem well known to social workers in the nineteenth century and the Progressive era.

Finally, wife-beating was also common in the case records. Logically, this should not have been the case, since the agencies studied here were exclusively devoted to child welfare. But women frequently and energetically attempted to force child-welfare agencies to defend their own interests as well as their children's. Included in their complaints were accusations of what we would today call marital rape, usually seen along with beatings as part of a generic male violence.[8]

These themes are addressed through a case study: how Boston-area social-work agencies approached family-violence problems, from 1880 to 1960. These dates cover the period since the "discovery" of family violence in the late 1870s, stopping just before the latest wave of alarm about child abuse.[9] Although the data in this book come exclusively from the Boston metropolitan area, which had certain demographic and social peculiarities, there is reason to consider the findings of this study typical of the urban United States. The largest environmental factors affecting family violence (e.g., poverty, unemployment, illness, alcoholism) were common to many areas. Moreover, the "discovery" of this social problem occurred simultaneously throughout the United States and in much of Europe, in the course of a single decade, suggesting similar patterns. The agencies whose records formed the source material for this study were local, but they were part of a national social-work profession—indeed, for most of this period the Boston groups were a leading influence in national family-violence policy.

THE CLIENTS

The protagonists of this story are the victims and assailants in family-violence cases: unusual heroes and heroines, to be sure, for they were almost always quite wretched, innocent and guilty alike. Nevertheless they were people with aspirations and complex emotions as well as ill luck and, often, self-destructive impulses.

These clients[10] of children's protective agencies were mainly poor immigrants of non-elite ethnic and racial backgrounds. These groups were the most numerous, not because they are the only ones involved in family violence, but because they were more likely to be "caught."[11]

Because I mean to describe these people as individuals rather than statistical generalizations, it will be useful here to offer a general profile of these clients. This profile cannot be construed to tell us anything about the characteristics that promote family violence, however, because this was not a controlled study. For example, the clients I studied were mostly poor and uneducated; but I have no way of knowing how many other poor and uneducated people did not have family-violence problems, or how many prosperous and educated people did. My guesses about the characteristics that contribute to family violence will rely on qualitative, not quantitative, evidence. But the reader will be able to know these people better, to understand their problems more readily, with a general description of the social and economic outlines of their lives.[12]

The clients' most pronounced characteristic was their poverty. Twenty-one percent were lacking basic necessities, such as food and fuel, and an additional 48 percent lived in constant insecurity as to whether they could maintain bare subsistence. Relatively more clients were extremely poor in the last century, confirming what is known about the disastrous living conditions in poor urban neighborhoods in the nineteenth century. While there was a decline in the poorest categories after 1910, the number of prosperous or even middle-class clients did not increase greatly.

The clients' poverty was reflected in how they supported themselves. Once federal welfare aid developed in the 1930s, 42 percent relied on it chronically and only one-quarter had never received welfare. The proportion of fathers who were main supporters of their families went down over time, not because women were increasingly employed, but because welfare contributed more. Very few of the client families contained regularly employed women. Employed women were probably less likely to need the help of, or to come to the attention of, child-protection agencies, because their families were better off and because they themselves had more independence and self-esteem. The extreme poverty of the clients was also indicated by the fact that for 40 percent of families, children were vital contributors to the family budget. After World War II, when child labor had become virtually negligible in the urban population, 31 percent of these clients still needed their children's wages to survive.

The clients were extremely transient. Forty-one percent had lived at their present address less than two years, and only 18 percent more than five years. The clients also appeared rather isolated, judging from the few social contacts they seemed to have. These characteristics do not necessarily distinguish family-violence clients, since poor people are often more isolated than the prosperous, but they illustrate one of the indirect ways in which poverty, through the lack of community rootedness it creates, reduced their social resources for coping with family conflict.

There is a common view that large households promote family violence, either directly or through the correlation of large families with poverty and overcrowding. On the contrary, neither the families nor the households of the clients were consistently larger than average, and in the first four decades of this study, they were a little smaller than Boston's average. This was probably because of the tendency to family disorganization associated with poverty and family violence: children tended to leave home earlier, marital separation and illegitimacy were frequent, and living arrangements with boarders were unstable.

The clients were mainly immigrants or children of immigrants. Until World War II, the foreign-born were overrepresented in proportion to their numbers in Boston's population, but not in proportion to their numbers among the poor. The leading foreign ethnic groups among the family-violence clients were the Irish, the Italians, and the Canadians. In later years, Afro-Americans and West Indian blacks became another large ethnic group in this study. No ethnic group was significantly overrepresented in any of the four major types of family violence (child abuse, child neglect, wife-beating, and sexual abuse). The proportion of foreign-born clients shifted from 70 percent in the first decades of this study to just under 20 percent at the end, a decline consistent with the slowing of immigration.

However, there were behavioral differences among ethnic groups which affected family-violence problems. Perhaps the most notorious of them was the heavy drinking of the Irish. Although there is no reason to share the caseworkers' (many of whom were abstainers) moralistic condemnations, the case records provide evidence that the Irish were heavier drinkers than any other nationality.[13] The Irish stood out even more in the amount of women's drinking.[14] With respect to family violence, Irish alcoholism contributed to unusually high rates of desertion, poverty, dependency, infant mortality, and fighting.[15] In the case records of this study, while the Irish were not disproportionately represented in cases of wife-beating, they did more often engage in mutual marital combat. But there is no reason to focus on liquor as the cause of this: the combativeness of Irish women may result from other factors in Irish and Irish-American history which accustomed Irish women to unusual independence.[16]

The Italians were the poorest of Boston's ethnic groups at the turn of the century.[17] Yet unlike the Irish, they were underrepresented in the city's almshouses.[18] This contradiction may be explained by the strong family cohesion among Italian-Americans, as evidenced, for example, in their low desertion rates.[19] Moreover, heavy drinking was rare among Italians.[20] There was less street brawling and marital fighting than among the Irish, yet plenty of wife-beating. The Italian-American families in these case records included many of the most patriarchal, in terms of fathers' control over wives, authority over sons, and sequestering of daughters. (These patterns were shared by other southern-European and Mediterranean immigrants, such as the Lebanese, Syrians, and Greeks, of whom there were many fewer in Boston.)

The Canadian immigrants were of French, Scotch, and English origin, and had no single ethnic identity. Many had lived long in Canada, particularly Nova Scotia, before coming to the United States; others, particularly French Canadians, had lived in northern New England before migrating to Boston. Thus many Boston clients of Canadian origin had relatives with farms in New England or Canada to whom they turned for help, a substantial advantage in coping with family stress which European immigrants did not have. According to studies of Massachusetts as a whole, the French Canadians resembled the Irish in their extreme poverty and concentration in unskilled jobs, but resembled more the Italians in their low rates of female employment; like all the rural immigrants, they had high rates of child labor.[21]

There were few Afro-Americans in the first decades of this study, and even by 1960 Boston had a much smaller black population than most other large eastern cities. Like all the other "ethnic" groups, they were overrepresented in family-violence case records in proportion to their numbers in the population, but not in proportion to their numbers among the poor. As with other ethnic groups, the increase of the black population came mainly from migration, and in many ways they shared with other immigrants the stresses of being alien.[22] Contrary to what contemporary expectations might suggest, blacks were not overrepresented in any characteristic relevant to family violence: not poverty, or single-mother families, or drinking.

Overall these ethnic cultural differences were of minimal importance in constructing family-violence problems in comparison to the general influence of being poor, migratory, or alien. The single ethnic patterns that can be identified as influential were Irish drinking-and-fighting behavior and Italian fathers' patriarchal control over family members. Even these fade in comparison to experiences that were common to all ethnic groups in this study. Yet that commonness was not perceived by the clients themselves. Ethnic stereotyping was practiced, of course, not only by agency workers but also among clients. They experienced themselves as ethnically unique and frequently attempted to interpret their behavior to caseworkers in terms of ethnic traditions. Among the clients themselves a kind of "pluralistic ignorance" is visible: Irish women, for example, were convinced that desertion was unique to their men; Italian women that wife-beating was an Italian problem. They were wrong in these analyses. Yet their frequent references to their cultural origins and traditions were attempts to assert to social workers something important about their identities, vital for caseworkers to understand if they were to help.

The "clients" in this study were as varied as any collection of several thousand people, perhaps more so, since many of them had recently come from separate foreign cultures. Yet they also had a great deal in common: their poverty, above all, and their experience of helplessness in the context of radical social and economic change, the more acute for those who had recently immigrated from agrarian societies into the metropolis of Boston. Most of them were inadequately housed; many of their children had serious medical problems; many of the men were frequently and sometimes chronically unemployed or underemployed. For the purposes of this study, what united them most was their common experience as "clients" of an agency of social control, devoted to protecting their children—from themselves. The very definition of their problems arose through their interactions with individual caseworkers and the developing child-welfare establishment.

THE CHILD PROTECTORS AND THEIR RECORDS

In tracking the history of family violence, I turned to a source relatively new to historians: case records of social work agencies devoted to child protection. Case records are rich in detail about daily life and personal relations. They are not, however, universally reliable, understandable, or easy to use. Since the nature of these records affects so much how I know what I assert in this book, it is important to discuss briefly here the nature of the records and their limitations.[23]

This study is based on the work of three Boston agencies, each exemplary of a certain type of child welfare agency, and each involved in family violence in a different way. The major source, and the dominant type of agency in this field, was the Massachusetts Society for the Prevention of Cruelty to Children (MSPCC, or the Society). Societies for the Prevention of Cruelty to Children (SPCCs), or child-protection agencies, as they were later called, arose throughout the United States and Europe in the 1870s; nearly every state in the United States had such an agency, and the Massachusetts SPCC was one of the most influential. The MSPCC investigated and prosecuted parents for child abuse and neglect and, in cooperation with other governmental and private agencies, arranged the placements of children ordered removed from their parents.

A second agency active in child-saving, the Boston Children's Service Association (BCSA), developed from alms-giving and asylum-providing groups.[24] While the BCSA always conceded to the MSPCC primary jurisdiction over protective work, the MSPCC in turn referred to the BCSA much of the arrangement and supervision of placements.[25]

A third major type of child-saving agency, which came into existence toward the end of the Progressive era, were clinics offering psychological diagnosis and treatment for disturbed or delinquent children. The example used in this study, one of the leading such clinics in the United

States, is the Judge Baker Guidance Center (JBGC), established in Boston in 1917. This clinic was the major place of referral by the courts and by other social work agencies, including the MSPCC and BCSA, when children were thought to need professional mental health services. A substantial proportion of JBGC clients had backgrounds of family violence, making its records a rich source of data for the second half of this period of study.

The keeping of case records was a basis for the professionalization of social work. In the nineteenth century, when the agencies studied here were charities, using volunteer and/or untrained labor, their record-keeping was skimpy and inconsistent. They used ledger books in which handwritten notes were entered about cases as they came in. If a "case" continued for more than one day, the worker might or might not remember to write on the bottom of the first entry, say, "cont'd volume IX p. 396." After five or six further entries, it was very easy to lose the trail. Since a worker had to pull down many heavy volumes to trace the history of a case, it seems reasonable to surmise that many did not bother to do this. The Progressive-era transformation of social work in the early twentieth century brought modern record-keeping: card files and a "loose-leaf" system, generally a folder and a case number for each case, so that new material could be added continually. Thus, from the point of view of the historian, the quality of records took a great advance around 1910, and that is reflected in this book in the disproportion of quotations from case histories after 1910.

Despite improvements, case records continued uneven in the information they contained. There were many reasons for this: sometimes the clients were so reluctant to cooperate at all that the workers did not want to struggle to get information beyond the absolutely necessary; sometimes the workers simply deemed some information irrelevant; sometimes the client interviewed did not know what the worker wanted; sometimes the workers were hurried. Case records varied also in length: from one paragraph to several hundred pages. All, however, consisted primarily of notes written by the caseworker(s), summarizing contacts with and information from or about clients. There were many interagency memoranda and, infrequently, notes from the clients themselves. With few exceptions, the case records represent the caseworkers' opinions, even when they were trying to represent the clients' point of view.

Thus agency workers, "child protectors," are also protagonists in this story, but only collectively. I have not attempted to individualize them here (indeed, I would have had no basis on which to do so, for *their* foibles and problems were not laid out in agency records). In that neglect, I am simplifying an already extremely complicated tale; I do not wish to distract attention too far from the central position of the clients. In avoiding distinctions among social workers, I am doing some of them an injustice; the limitations of the agencies as a whole did not pertain to each of their workers. But some might benefit from my generalizations, too, since some were even more limited in what they offered than the norm.

The bias, not to mention outright prejudice, of these caseworkers was often substantial. For the first twenty-five years of this study the workers were almost always male, while the clients were virtually all female. For the first fifty years of this study, the workers were almost always white, native-born Protestants, dealing with clients who were in the majority Catholic immigrants. Lack of adequate translators was a chronic problem. The most common result was the conclusion that clients were stupid or ignorant because of their inadequacy in answering questions or following instructions. Sometimes the caseworkers could not gather basic family information accurately because of their lack of language skills. Often case records were duplicated because, due to mistakes in spelling foreign names, workers did not find a previously existing record.

Social workers often disdained many aspects of the ethnic and religious cultures of their clients; for most of the period of this study, the child protectors were overwhelmingly native-born white Protestants, while the clients were immigrant or second-generation Catholics. Most caseworkers, reflecting the cultures in which they had been raised, assumed subnormal intelligence among their poorer clients. The agents' comments and expectations about immigrants in this early period were similar to views of black clients in the mid-twentieth century. The records abound with derogatory references, even when made with kind intent. One girl making an incest allegation against her father in 1910, and being accused of lying, was called "a romancer but not more so than the average foreign born child."[26] Black women were described as "primitive," "limited," "not nearly as talkative as many of her race, but apparently truthful," "fairly good for a colored woman."[27] White immigrants came in for similar abuse: e.g., "a typical low-grade Italian woman."[28] The characterizations of clients were also saturated with class arrogance. "A young girlish appearing woman with dark bobbed curly hair, ignorant, brassy, indifferent . . . coarse, had very poor standards. . . . Seemed to lack feeling, sympathy and understanding, decidedly hard."[29] Some social workers disdained their clients partly because they *were* clients: "typical Puerto Ricans who loved fun, little work and were dependent people," a caseworker wrote in 1960.[30]

After about 1920 these informal judgments were supposed to be replaced by scientific intelligence tests. It has been well documented that these tests were biased against immigrant, non-English-speaking, and poor people, and the case records provide direct evidence for that conclusion. In the Judge Baker records, the children's actual tests, in their own handwriting, are included, and one can imagine the experience of immigrant children in trying to answer them. Some 1930 examples: Make as many words as you can from the letters AEIRLP; Fill in the blanks: "The poor baby _____ as if it were _____ sick"; Answer: "Why did the Pilgrims come to this country?"[31] Moreover, the testing merely supplemented, but did not replace, arbitrary race and class labeling of clients. I compared the epithets used by MSPCC caseworkers, the least professionalized of the agencies in this study, to those used by Judge Baker professionally trained psychiatric social workers, for the same years (1910–17). The MSPCC records called clients shiftless, coarse, low type, uncouth, immoral, feebleminded, lazy, and worthless (or occasionally, positively, good or sober); Judge Baker workers characterized their clients as low-grade, of weak character, ignorant type, degenerate, of low mentality (or once, positively, as refined)—hardly a more scientific set of categories. Yet the caseworkers were often so in thrall to the objectivity of such testing that they credited it above the evidence of their own observation: "The psychological testing brought forth the fact very plainly that the child [Italian-born, fifteen years old] has a very distinct language handicap that is not evident when one is talking with her."[32]

Equally questionable was the use of testing to evaluate parents, almost always mothers. Test results might decide whether girls were placed in institutions; they might decide whether mothers could keep their children. For example:

. . . she graded at a median mental age of 7 3/12 years, which is 6 9/12 years below the average. As she could speak no English, test had to be given through an interpreter. . . . Although initial performance on Healy A was total failure, she showed good learning ability after demonstration. She did surprisingly well on problems of simple change from Stanford scale though she failed to count backwards from 20 to 1. . . . Her method on tests was a combination of chance, trial and error, and some elements of planning. . . . Although this woman . . . can neither read nor write Italian, speaks only a few words of English, is unable to spell her own name, does not know the year or the month, she does, however, know the date . . . that every child was born, is able to make change and manifests fairly good practical ability. She will probably be capable of caring for two or more of her children. Her responsibilities, however, should be carefully guarded and it should be kept constantly before her that the return of the children is to be the reward for the effort she makes to care for them. [This woman, deserted by her husband and left with four children, had come herself to a family service agency seeking help. She appears at greater length, under the name Mrs. Guarino, in chapter 4.][33]

In the face of such discriminatory attitudes and procedures, and of such power to disrupt clients' lives, it is to be expected that clients would not be frank with caseworkers. Even caseworkers trying to avoid arrogance and to help clients achieve their own goals met uncooperativeness and lack of understanding. From the clients' point of view, even well-meaning caseworkers could do a good deal of damage through mis-understandings and the structural inflexibilities of the system. What caseworkers saw as professional standards and procedures had entirely different meanings to clients. When the former asked personal questions, clients did not understand their relevance, considered them nosy, and did not trust the confidentiality of their responses. Most child-protection workers had no material aid to offer clients, but had to rely primarily on moral exhortation, counseling, or threats of punitive measures, even with clients who had themselves asked for help with violence problems. Clients interpreted this emphasis on talk instead of action as meaning that the caseworkers did not really want to help.[34] Clients so often had something to hide—who among us would agree to allow caseworkers free entry to their homes at any time? Boyfriends, liquor, boarders and guests, children not at school, luxuries that might provide evidence against needed relief, baby and child care that did not conform to expert recommendations, food that did not conform to American tastes—all these and many other infractions that clients might not even notice could convince a caseworker that the client was an unfit parent.

These mutually distrustful relationships were by no means the fault of individual caseworkers. Many caseworkers managed despite these limitations to offer sympathy and help to clients. These useful services were of many types: sometimes what clients wanted was exactly what agencies could provide, as in cases of prosecution of child abusers or wife-beaters; sometimes caseworkers provided referrals to other agencies that did have material aid to offer; sometimes the child protectors themselves provided encouragement, advice, confirmation of a client's own good judgment, or a brake on bad judgment; sometimes they offered informal support quite beyond the bounds of the professional minimum, ranging from small gifts to trips to the country to an ongoing, steady relationship.

The caseworker in her turn faced pressures that militated against scrupulously honest case records. These records were often the basis of the worker's evaluation by her superior and she needed, therefore, to note what she ought to have done, not what she did do. Furthermore, she needed to justify her actions by showing that they were appropriate to her clients—evidence that would mainly be taken from the record she prepared. She sometimes had to disguise both her inadequacies and her excellence; the case record could be allowed to show neither too little nor too much action for clients. I tried, where possible, to check caseworkers' characterizations against more reliable, objective data. Where caseworkers said that clients were mainly drunkards, I tried to look myself for clear evidence of alcohol abuse, for example. But since the evidence was usually presented or suppressed by the caseworker, these efforts were limited.

The interpretation of such case records involves the historian's creativity, even imagination—although not necessarily more so than with other sorts of historical sources. Their status as historical documents does not make them infallible; their truth must be gathered from among the varied and often conflicting stories they contain, and from the complex relationships that they expressed—between agency representatives, clients, and family members. In trying to grasp the will of the clients, I weighed what they did more heavily than what they said (i.e., what caseworkers said clients said). I tried to identify the actions taken by agency workers, not their promises and waverings.

I argued above that individual outcomes were not determined, that the collectively greater power of the social workers and the social order they represented could not predict any individual case. The interactions between client and worker which are central to my argument, central to the whole historical construction of family violence, can only be revealed in actual case histories. Throughout this book I have chosen to tell, as much as possible, whole stories rather than excerpts from stories, so that the peculiarities of every situation are inescapable, and so that my generalizations are seen for what they are: abstractions, not "typical cases." I also tell whole stories in order to maximize the readers' opportunity to "see" my interpretation and to argue with it, conscious that readers do not immediately have access to these confidential case records as they might to other forms of historical documents.

As we turn now to examine the historical construction and reconstruction of definitions of family violence, one such case history will serve as an example of the interaction of client and social worker. The "Amatos"[35] were clients of the MSPCC from 1910 to 1916. They had five young children from the current marriage and Mrs. Amato had three from a previous marriage, two of them still in Italy and one daughter in Boston. Mrs. Amato kept that daughter at home to do housework and look after the younger children while she earned money doing home piece-rate sewing. This got the family in trouble with a truant officer, and they were also accused, in court, of lying, saying that the father had deserted when he was in fact at home. Furthermore, once while left alone, probably in the charge of a sibling, one of the younger children fell out a window and had to be hospitalized, making the mother suspect of negligence.

Despite her awareness of these suspicions against her, Mrs. Amato went to many different agencies, starting with those of the Italian immigrant community and then reaching out to elite (Protestant) social work agencies, seeking help, reporting that her husband was a drunkard, a gambler, a non-supporter, and a wife-beater. The Massachusetts Society for the Prevention of Cruelty to Children agents at first doubted her claims because Mr. Amato impressed them as a "good and sober man," and blamed the neglect of the children on his wife's incompetence in managing the wages he gave her. The Society ultimately became convinced of her story because of her repeated appearance with severe bruises and the corroboration by the husband's father. Mr. Amato, Sr., was intimately involved in the family troubles, and took responsibility for attempting to control his son. Once, he came to the house and gave the son "a warning and a couple of slaps," after which the son improved for a while. Another time he extracted from his son a pledge not to beat his wife for two years.

Mrs. Amato did not trust this method of controlling her husband. She begged the MSPCC agent to help her get a divorce; then she withdrew this request; later she claimed that she had not dared take this step because his relatives threatened to beat her if she tried it. Finally Mrs. Amato's daughter (from her previous marriage) took action, coming independently to the MSPCC to bring an agent to the house to help her mother. As a result of this complaint Mr. Amato was convicted of assault once and sentenced to six months. During that time Mrs. Amato survived by "a little work" and help from "Italian friends," according to her caseworker. Her husband returned more violent than before: he went at her with an ax, beat the children so much on the head that their "eyes wabbled" [sic], and supported his family so poorly that the children went out begging. This case closed, like so many, without a resolution.

The Amatos, it must be remembered, exist only as they were interpreted for us by social workers in a particular historical period—the Progressive era. I want to press the Amatos into service to help illustrate the historicity and political construction of family violence, by imagining how social workers might have responded to the Amatos differently in different periods. A summary of these changes produces a rough periodization of the history of family violence:

1. The late nineteenth century, approximately 1875–1910, when family violence agencies were part of the general charity organization and moral reform movement, influenced by feminism.
2. The Progressive era and its aftermath, approximately 1910–1930, when family violence work was incorporated into professional social work and a reform program relying heavily on state regulation.
3. The Depression, when intrafamily violence was radically deemphasized in favor of amelioration of economic hardship.

4. The 1940s and 1950s, when psychiatric categories and intensely "pro-family" values dominated the social work approach to family problems.
5. The 1960s and 1970s, when feminist and youth movements began a critique of the family which forced open the doors of closets that hid family problems.

NINETEENTH-CENTURY CHILD-SAVING, 1875–1910

The nineteenth-century definition of the problem was cruelty to children, a concept subtly but importantly different from child abuse, which it later became. The former was a moralistic notion, directing attention to the cruel culprit, usually presumed to be an ignorant, "depraved, immigrant man," more than to the victim. This consciousness reflected the values of the social movements from which it grew. It shared the feminist emphasis on illegitimate male power, the moralism characteristic of the social purity (anti-drinking, anti-prostitution) campaigns, and the socially elite assumptions of both.

The anti-cruelty-to-children movement was particularly influenced by the temperance movement, and blamed drinking for virtually all family irregularities. The temperance orientation, too, contained a feminist interpretation: male cruelty was the constant subtext of anti-drinking propaganda. The image of maternal cruelty, less prevalent, also focused on alcoholism: a negligent mother, lying abed in a drunken stupor while her children cried for food.

The emphasis on drink, and the envisioning of cruelty to children as something that "they"—the immigrant poor—did, never "us"—the respectable classes—allowed even anti-feminist moral reformers to include wife-beating within their jurisdiction. They did not have to take the feminist message personally, so to speak. Similarly, child-protection agencies were able to prosecute many incest cases without offending anti-feminists. It was even recognized as an exclusively male crime, but was attributed to a male depravity that occurred only in the lower classes.

Had the Amato case appeared in 1890, the child-savers might have been quicker to see Mr. Amato as a brutal man, depraved, of inferior stock. The sympathy thus engendered for Mrs. Amato, however, would have been condescending and would have associated her problems primarily with alcohol rather than with her structural position in the family and city. They would not have helped her seek economic independence as a route to safety but would more likely have offered two choices: either reforming her husband through a combination of moralizing and punishment or institutionalizing her children to protect them from the husband.

THE PROGRESSIVE ERA AND ITS AFTERMATH, 1910–1930

Social work as a whole was becoming professionalized and "scientific" during the Progressive era, and a new group of middle-class "experts" replaced upper-class charity workers as those who set standards for family life. Environmentalist analyses led to an emphasis on child neglect (as opposed to abuse) as the major category of improper parenting. Neglect was, of course, the fundamental concern in the Amato case, which dated from this period. A decreased emphasis on alcohol opened the way for caseworkers to identify other sorts of stress—poverty, unemployment, illness—as contributors to child neglect. But understanding environmental stresses did not lessen the racism and class bias in family-violence diagnoses. The broader causal analysis revealed a deep dilemma in anti-family-violence work, vividly reflected in the Amato case: difficulty in distinguishing culpable parental negligence from the results of poverty.

The Progressive reformers, more than their nineteenth-century predecessors, believed that they were seeing an overall weakening of the family. One of their greatest fears was the apparent increase in single-mother families, a problem noticed in part because of the overrepresentation of single mothers in child-neglect cases. The agency workers' hostility to Mrs. Amato's desire for independence reflected a fear of establishing female-headed households.

Moreover, the Progressive era produced a cover-up of wife-beating as a form of family violence, which was evident in the reluctance to recognize Mrs. Amato's victimization. The old feminist diatribes against drunken, brutal men came to seem moralistic and unscientific. Instead, marital violence was portrayed as mutual, resulting from environmental stress, lack of education, or lack of mental hygiene. This was the diagnosis of Mrs. Amato's difficulties (and in response the agency undertook regular supervision of the family, attempting to "Americanize" them, to instruct Mrs. Amato in proper child care and housekeeping methods).

The cover-up also extended to that other highly gendered form of family violence, incest. In a pattern familiar to those who have followed the public alarm about sexual assault of children in the 1980s, in the decades 1910–1930 sexual assault by strangers was emphasized and incest—that is, sexual assault within the family—deemphasized. Sexual abuse of children was increasingly blamed on "dirty old men," who were considered sick or "perverted." Incest and sexual abuse were fit into a new category, sexual delinquency. In this new understanding, the victims, almost always girls, were labeled as sexually deviant and criminal, even when they had been raped or mistreated at young ages, and were often incarcerated in industrial schools. These developments were conditioned by the decline of feminism.

THE DEPRESSION

One of the major characteristics of Depression-era social work was a policy of defending the "conventional" nuclear family. This meant working against all centrifugal forces in the family, at the expense of asking women and children to suppress their own aspirations. The great advances in provision of general welfare necessitated by the massive unemployment of the 1930s have tended to obscure more conservative implications of social policy at that time. In treatment of conflict between the sexes, Depression-era family-violence agencies strengthened still further the Progressive-era tendency to deemphasize male violence as a significant family problem. A sympathy arose for the unemployed husband, the stress and role conflict that frequently engendered his violence; remarkably less sympathy was mustered for the situation of mothers doing double shifts—at work and at home—in attempts to hold their families together. Indeed, women were consistently held responsible for the treatment of children and the general mood of the family, as men were not. The treatments of preference for family violence were reconciliation and economic aid. The very meaning of family violence had shifted: it was seen as an epiphenomenon of extrafamilial events.

Indeed, violence altogether was deemphasized, and the SPCCs devoted themselves almost exclusively to child neglect, now conceived primarily in terms of economic neglect, such as malnutrition or inadequate medical care. But relief alone was no answer to family violence, since poverty alone does not cause family violence. After all, most poor children are neither abused nor neglected. A Depression-era agency might have offered Mrs. Amato relief, perhaps even in return for her agreement to work at reconciliation with her husband, and ignored her other aspirations, problems, and complaints.

WORLD WAR II AND THE 1950s

The defend-the-conventional-family policy in social work continued straight through the 1940s and 1950s. These decades represented the low point in public awareness of family-violence problems and in the status of child-protection work within the social-work profession. Family casework was, however, no longer reluctant to inquire into the roots of intrafamily conflict, but did so now in psychiatric categories. The goal of the new psychiatric therapy was individual maturity, and this was often measured by the patient's ability to adjust to a nuclear family life. The roots of most interpersonal problems were sought in individual "complexes," not in cultural or structural arrangements. The most notorious example of the psychiatric influence in family-violence work was in the blaming of wives for their abuse by husbands—again, a double standard in requirements of individual responsibility for their actions. The "nagging wife" of traditional patriarchal folklore was now transformed into a woman of complex mental ailments: failure to accept her own femininity and attempting to compete with her husband; frustration as a result of her own frigidity; a need to control resulting from her own sexual repression; masochism. These neuroses required diagnosis and treatment by professionals—friends were unlikely to be of help. Moreover, these neuroses indicated treatment not of the assailant but of the victim. Mrs. Amato, a battered wife, might have been urged to question how and why she provoked her husband, what were the angers she felt toward her second set of children, what was her part in her husband's failure to support.

Psychiatry in family-violence work also affected problems with children, and it is here that we see the most marked change from Depression-era social-work thought. Child-neglect cases were increasingly seen as products not of poverty but of neurotic rejection or negligence. Indeed, an entirely new category of cruelty to children was now developed: emotional neglect. Emotional neglect was a gendered form of child abuse—only mothers could be guilty of it. Emotional neglect as a category allowed the mystification of incest in a new way, the "discovery" of emotional incest, seductiveness between mother and child. I do not mean to deny the possibility that such seductiveness exists and might be bad for children. I am merely pointing to the irony of child-protection policies which avoided acknowledging the occurrence of actual sexual molestation of children but evinced interest rather in symbolic sexual behavior in the form of certain inappropriately intimate emotional relations indulged in by women.

THE 1960s AND 1970s

In order to avoid violating clients' privacy any more than necessary, I chose not to read any currently ongoing case records, which required ending this research in 1960. It will be helpful, nonetheless, to contrast this historical material with the contemporary context of family-violence discussion. Professional and public responses to family violence have undergone significant changes since 1960. One such change has been the increased medicalization of the issue. The first wave of anti-cruelty-to-children work had been a campaign of upper-class charity volunteers. In the Progressive era child-protection work became a branch of the new profession of social work—indeed, it helped to build that profession—and remained primarily a social-work concern to the end of this study. In the 1960s, by contrast, child abuse was seized upon by doctors, particularly pediatricians, its diagnosis and treatment medicalized, also as a means of building the prestige of the group.[36] If I were attempting similar research for the last two decades, I would turn not only to casework but also to medical records.

More importantly, the context of the rediscovery and redefinition of family violence in the last decades was the civil-rights, anti-war, student, and women's movements, all of them challenging family norms in different ways. Combined, these movements raised critical questions about the sanctity of family privacy, the privileged position of the male head of family, and the importance of family togetherness at all costs. The movements created an atmosphere in which child abuse, wife-beating, and incest could again be pulled out of the closet. Moreover, the critique of family violence was situated in an atmosphere of criticism of more accepted forms of violence as well—military, political, and cultural. In challenging the ideology of separate public and private spheres, the new social movements also challenged the power of professionals to define and then cure social problems. Their anti-authoritarian interpretive framework stimulated collective citizens' action on family violence. Self-help organizations of family-violence victims and assailants started competing with professionals for hegemony. Mrs. Amato might have gone to a battered women's shelter and discovered her commonality with many other women. She might have been encouraged by the shelter atmosphere, or that of other self-help projects such as Parents Anonymous, to identify her own goals and strategies for change. These projects render evident what was previously disguised—the role of victims, "clients," in defining the problem and the remedies.

This chronology is schematic, not only because the transitions between different periods were gradual and the boundaries blurred, but also because the histories of the four types of family violence with which this book is concerned were different. For that reason this book is organized only partly chronologically. Chapters 2 and 3 describe the development of the charity and then professional social-work response to family violence to approximately 1920; afterward the basic organization of the social response and the categories of diagnosis continued unchanged to 1960. Chapter 4 analyzes the central dilemma of anti-family-violence work—how to guarantee minimal conditions of good child-raising while rejecting public provision for families—through examining the problem of single-mother families, a critical and central problem for this entire history. The remaining four chapters then treat the four major categories of family violence: child neglect, child abuse, incest, and wife-beating.

Throughout the book my premise is that family violence is a problem inseparable from the family norms of a whole society or from the overall political conflicts in that society. It is a changing historical and cultural issue, not a biological or sociobiological universal. As a public issue, family violence has been a virtual lightning rod for different social and political perspectives. Born as a social problem in an era of a powerful women's rights movement, the 1870s, campaigns against child abuse and wife-beating have tended to lose momentum and support, even to disappear altogether, when feminist influence is in decline. In such periods family togetherness is often sought at the expense of individual rights and by ignoring intrafamily problems, rather than by exposing and attacking them. Alternatively, in periods without much feminist influence family-violence problems are redefined in ways less threatening to myths of the harmony of the normative family. In this book, then, there is no fixed definition of family violence. Tracing its history includes tracing its shifting definitions, and using them to illuminate not only the problems of deviant, violent, or uncaring individuals but also of ordinary, even exemplary families.

2

"THE CRUELTY": CHILD PROTECTION, 1880–1910

Child abuse was "discovered" in the 1870s. Surely many children had been ill-treated by parents previously, but child abuse had not been considered a social problem. Deviant behavior becomes a "social problem" when policymakers perceive it as threatening to social order, and generate the widespread conviction that organized social action is necessary to control it. In just such a manner the social problem of child abuse was constructed by reformers and charity workers. The evidence of that new social concern was the rapid worldwide establishment of Societies for the Prevention of Cruelty to Children: by the end of the decade there were thirty-four such societies in the United States and fifteen elsewhere.[1]

The modern history of family violence is not the story of changing responses to a constant problem, but, in large part, of redefinition of the problem itself. The nineteenth-century interpretation of child abuse, "cruelty to children," did not focus on *family* violence. The reformers who established the SPCCs did not conceive of family as the root of the problem, or as the logical jurisdictional boundary. In the twentieth century a cultural anxiety about the breakdown of the "traditional" family—specifically about gender and generational relations—influenced the child-protection movement, but nineteenth-century reformers were more affected by class, ethnic, and cultural anxieties. They were reacting above all against urbanism and the new immigration, which jointly created an urban underclass threatening to their whole vision of a good society.[2] They saw cruelty to children as a vice of inferior classes and cultures which needed correction and "raising up" to an "American" standard. Their emphasis on cruelty made children's mistreatment seem willful rather than structural, a view which in turn grew from their unexamined confidence that their own family patterns were better because they practiced self-control. One of the most poignant ironies of their project is that their clients turned around the meaning of their phrase and labeled their agency, the MSPCC, "the Cruelty." Poor children said to their immigrant parents, mothers-in-law said to mothers, feuding neighbors said to each other, "Don't cross me or I'll report you to the Cruelty."

In the late-nineteenth-century cities, child abuse appeared worse than before, and indeed it may well have been worse. Urban poverty was more stressful in many ways than rural poverty: housing was overcrowded and overpriced; homes and neighborhoods were filthy, without adequate facilities for disposing of wastes; the air and water were polluted; the food in the markets was often adulterated and rotten, and the urban poor could not grow their own; there were new dangers from fires, traffic, and other urban hazards; wage-earners were at the mercy of periodic unemployment and grinding hours and conditions. Immigration separated many newcomers from potentially supporting kinfolk, created neighborhoods that were not communities, left mothers more alone with children than they had been in the "old country." The anonymity of urban life promoted more theft, vandalism, and violence.

We can only speculate about how these stresses contributed to child abuse, since we have no way to determine its incidence in agrarian societies. We can, however, explain why child abuse was more visible and more disturbing in the late nineteenth century than it had been previously. On the one hand, the moral reformers who defined the social problem were influenced by a growing sensibility of tenderness toward children and revulsion against personal violence; on the other hand, the rough ways of the poor were more visible—in big cities people of different classes lived and worked in proximity and the poor, particularly children, lived much of their lives on the streets. Reformers considered child abuse not only a moral wrong but also a kind of pollution, poisoning the stock of future citizens and the daily order of civil society. Child protection was one of a range of campaigns to control social disorder.[3]

In the "gilded age," as the 1870s through 1890s are often called, in reference to the fortunes amassed by new industrial magnates, charity work took on a greater class consciousness—and class fear. In cities like Boston such fears were nearly inseparable from xenophobia as the working class became increasingly Catholic and foreign. A native-born Protestant elite was fearful of losing political and cultural control of their society to the immigrants, largely Catholic, streaming into the cities. The feared sources of social disorder now included not just disease, laziness, and depravity, but also organized resistance: labor unrest, even revolution, threatened, especially after the strike-ridden summer of 1877. As the threat to social order appeared to come not just from random deviant individuals but from entire social groups, so the response shifted from random individualized acts of charity, persuasion, and threat to organized collective action.

Helping children assumed a special resonance in part because of these new aspects of charity in industrial society. Because children were thought to be innocent (in contrast to previous Calvinist anxiety about children's capacity to be possessed by evil), they could easily be victimized. Because children were thought to be malleable (a view of children itself a product of "bourgeois" society, not characteristic of traditional peasant cultures), they could be molded into good citizens. The images of proper childhood that the child-savers sought to impose had class content, as we shall see, expressed in a sensibility about how children should behave in the present and toward what goals they should be directed. Protecting children from the wrongs of adults unified the charitable and the controlling impulses.

I do not wish, however, to offer here a functional argument, that child protection was seized upon because it fit some need outside its expressed purposes. The fit between child-saving and other social anxieties was an historical fact, not a causal explanation. Their concern about children was not merely a mask for intervention whose "real" purposes were other—such as labor discipline. The child protectors were primarily motivated to rescue children from cruelty. However, their own values and anxieties made that cruelty more visible and disturbing than it once had been.

A COMMUNITY DISRUPTED

While child protection was a national, even international movement, this study focuses on one city.[4] In most ways, Boston's experiences in the late nineteenth century were not fundamentally different from those of many United States cities: its geography and age may have made its poverty and the growing distance between rich and poor more vivid and more extreme, but basic conditions were similar throughout the United States. Still, Boston's peculiarities shaped not only its own child-protection organization—the Massachusetts Society for the Prevention of Cruelty to Children—but also the national movement, since the MSPCC was so influential.

Two major features of Boston's history affected the MSPCC: the relative strength, rootedness, and stability of its Protestant establishment, and the relatively early arrival of large groups of immigrants who were not Protestant or Anglo-Saxon. The Anglo-Saxon Bostonians, with two centuries of continuity in their social and political arrangements, had a sense of the order of their community that may have become visible to them only when it was so radically altered by the influx of immigrants.[5] In their attempts to "rescue" past order, their nostalgia mixed remembrance with fantasy. The old social order had always been riven by class struggle, commercial rivalry, and conflict between the sexes. Still, the large Irish immigration at the end of the 1840s produced a situation that appeared unprecedented to the old Protestant residents. Already by 1850 35 percent of the population and 45 percent of the labor force were foreign-born. The foreign-born proportion remained stable at about one-third of the population until immigration restriction

in 1929. But the proportion of the population that was culturally identified with these incoming nationalities grew higher: first- and second-
generation immigrants together made up 46 percent of the population
in 1850 and 74 percent by 1910.[6] At first this new population was
overwhelmingly Irish—75 percent of it in 1850. In 1905 the Irish still
dominated among the non-"Wasp" Boston residents, but by 1920 the
"new immigrant" groups—notably the Italians and Russian Jews—jointly
overwhelmed the Irish.

The physical expansion of the city allowed the foreign-born to enter
without integrating neighborhoods. Once a peninsula extending out
into the Bay of Boston, connected only by a thin strip of land (a cause-
way) to the southern mainland of Massachusetts, Boston was reshaped
by massive landfill projects in the first half of the nineteenth century.
It was a city of neighborhoods with distinct ethnic identities, but shifting
ones. By the end of the eighteenth century, the Anglo-Saxon wealthy
were already moving out of the North End, Boston's original main
settlement, toward Beacon Hill. By the 1840s, as the Irish immigration
increased, the North and West Ends were being deserted by the "respectable Protestants." The West End attracted the Irish, Jews, Italians,
Poles, and Ukrainians, in about that order, by 1900; but even among
these immigrants the neighborhood was informally subdivided into separated, unintegrated neighborhoods. The North End was shared by Jews
and Italians at this time. A small corridor of American blacks along the
western and northern slopes of Beacon Hill formed a veritable curtain
between the Hill residents and the new West End and North End.[7]

Despite such sharp delineation of neighborhoods, the influence of
the new population was great. The Irish were notoriously good at politics
(some said they practiced it as a competitive sport), and soon gained
substantial political power. Furthermore, the housing and environmental conditions in these new crowded slums produced fears of disease,
pollution, and violence even in prosperous neighborhoods. Many of
Boston's earlier residents believed that the immigrants had brought these
disasters with them to the new country. Indeed, the MSPCC, like many
of Boston's private charities, did not distinguish the problems of its clients
from the clients themselves. As in William Ryan's analysis of victim-
blaming, the immigrant poor often became the problem, rather than
people burdened by problems.

CHILD PROTECTION AND UPPER-CLASS REFORM

These experiences explain why an anti-child-abuse campaign arose, but not why it arose at that particular time. Some particular Boston events of the 1870s contributed: there was a smallpox epidemic in 1872; it was to be the last one, but no one knew that then. A general depression during this decade was worsened by a large downtown fire in 1872. This burned out the garment industry, then competing well with New York's, which in turn produced acute unemployment on top of that resulting from the general economic downturn. But to explain more decisively why "cruelty to children" became a social problem in the 1870s, not earlier or later, one must look at the conjuncture of long-term social changes with the status of political and reform currents at the time.

Child protection grew out of a more general child-saving charitable activity, dating from early in the century, devoted primarily to placing poor and abandoned children in asylums and in apprenticeships. Child-saving drew heavily on women's reform and philanthropic energy, and was influenced by feminist interpretations of social ills. For example, the Boston Children's Service Association (one of the three agencies studied here) originated in late-eighteenth-century women's activism. In 1800 a group of upper-class women established the Boston Female Asylum. Not proponents of women's rights, they were nevertheless developing a self-consciousness of themselves as women: "Females will sympathize especially with the sufferings of their own sex, when unprotected . . . Are there not many among the Children of prosperity, who wish to lay the foundation of an Institution, which at some future period, may prove an extensive blessing to thousands of Unfortunate Females?—To the benevolent Heart how delightful the Prospect!!"[8] Another similar group of women established the Boston Children's Friend Society in 1833, which was unique at the time in running coeducational shelters for children. These early child-saving efforts were characterized by what psychiatrist John Bowlby has called the "rescue fantasy."[9] The reformers saw themselves as gracious, privileged big sisters, not only of children but of adult women of the lower classes. Their sense of what they had to offer was deeply religious and evangelical; they considered Catholicism as hardly better than superstition. The rescue fantasy reflected not only their class condescension but also their search for an arena in which to feel powerful, and, as has often been the case with women, their religious conviction justified their stepping out of their domestic sphere.

Until the Civil War, despite growing tensions provoked by the increasing assertiveness of women's-rights advocates, there had remained a broad reform consensus that united temperance, moral purity, child-saving, and even popular health reform. In mid-century male reformers renewed and transformed the child-saving mission, mainly through Children's Aid Societies. Led by the aggressive Charles Loring Brace in New York, they sought so aggressively to "save" needy children that they were feared and criticized by the poor as child stealers. Meanwhile, in the 1860s most organized women's political activism was devoted to, and subordinated to, the Civil War effort. In the process, many women gained new organizational skills and self-confidence. By the 1870s women's-rights activists had established an autonomous women's-rights movement, under female leadership, and were pressing radical issues, such as woman suffrage, as well as those verging on the scandalous, such as divorce and "voluntary motherhood," an early conception of birth control. The antebellum reform consensus was broken.

More conservative women reformers, unwilling to join the autonomous woman-suffrage movement, nonetheless remained committed to female leadership in moral reform. They needed new projects. Since mid-century, female reformers had been important contributors to a growing sentiment against corporal punishment and for gentler disciplining of children. Child-raising manuals recommended that corporal punishment be used infrequently and only as a last resort; that deprivation of privileges, and only minor ones at that, be the favored form of punishment; and that explanation, reasoning, and prevention of mischief by distraction and humoring be substituted for punishment as much as possible.[10] The discourse was not dominated by pediatricians, as it later came to be,[11] but by lay women, influenced by feminism. Several suggested, for example, that unruly children were usually created by mothers who used excessive punishment.[12] Reformist writing also opposed physical punishment in schools and other institutions.[13] This softening of methods of child-raising was part of a middle-class romanticization of domesticity, idealizing the home as a place of harmony and cooperation. Feminists were among the most ardent purveyors of this ideal, emphasizing the parts that empowered women and dignified women's sphere.

The influence of this feminist vision was strengthened in Boston by the integration of upper-class charity and women's activism within the reform community, and then by the integration of another upper-class cause: campaigns against cruelty to animals, which had organized SPCAs several decades previously. Some SPCCs arose as additions to pre-existing SPCAs. (Many "humane" societies continue to connect the two functions today.) The legal basis for prosecuting animal abusers existed where there were no such means against child abusers, an irony appreciated by 1870s reformers, who used it as an argument for child protection. Historically, the two anti-cruelty campaigns reflected similar sensibilities: secularization and even Darwinian thought, which decreased the felt distance between humans and animals; the development of standards of refinement and "respectability," which brought with them rejections of overt displays of brutality, including blood sports; and the preference for gentle means of coercion.[14]

In Boston, SPCA men and child-saving women cooperated in forming a new organization, and the women retained substantial influence for several decades. By contrast, the New York SPCC was more exclusively created by the head of the SPCA, and as a result the two SPCCs went different ways; they even came to represent two alternative approaches to child protection. The New York group remained, much longer than the Massachusetts, dedicated to prosecution of parents while the Massachusetts emphasized charity and casework help to children and families.

Exemplifying the alliance between upper-class and feminist reform in Boston was Kate Gannett Wells, a key organizer of the MSPCC. Wells's great-grandfather was Ezra Stiles, one of the most famous presidents of Yale, and her minister father was a colleague of William Ellery Channing at a high-status Unitarian church (today Boston's famous Arlington Street Church). Born in 1838, from the early 1870s she provided the leading energy in the Massachusetts Moral Education Association and the National Association for the Advancement of Women. In 1884 she began to speak publicly against woman suffrage. Her class interests overwhelmed her concern for women's advancement and she feared that the "'wrong kind'" of women would vote.[15] A staunch defender of women's social activism, she continued a strain of thinking about women's role in public life—that women could play a useful role in projects that naturally extended their domestic skills and moral sensibilities, but should stay out of "politics." "Woman is naturally an organizer," she wrote. "Men can exist in a carpet-bag, but woman must have bureau drawers."[16] Yet, in defending women's participation on school boards, she also wrote:

> The success of a woman on a School Board depends chiefly upon how far she is willing at first to subordinate herself . . . When a woman proudly states that she has been treated by her masculine coworkers as [if] she were a man, her declaration is not [a] compliment to them and is a condemnation of herself.[17]

Wells's influence on the MSPCC was marked both in gender and in class terms.[18] She brought many colleagues from female reform activity into the MSPCC board of directors, and this network helped make the MSPCC the quintessential upper-class charity in Boston. She personally formed a "bridge between the world of society and the world of reform," as one Boston Brahmin put it.[19] Every president of the MSPCC through 1949 was a graduate of Harvard; every president through 1932 was a member of Boston's most exclusive men's club, the Somerset. The Society had twenty-six honorary vice-presidents,[20] all but one male, and equally upper class. Of the thirty-two active directors, however, eighteen were women—upper-class wives with the time, skills, and energy to do the society work. For the women directors, the MSPCC was simultaneously a social service project and a club with a group identity. (Sarah B. Otis, when she could no longer fulfill the directorial obligations, unilaterally appointed her daughter to fill out her term, assuming that her tenure was hereditary!)[21]

Women were tremendously important in financial support for charities such as the MSPCC. A study of fund-raising for Boston's charities, done in the early twentieth century, showed that women were responsible for more than half the contributions. While we have no equivalent data for the nineteenth century, the available evidence suggests the same pattern prevailed then. Individual women contributed 36 percent of the funds raised, in contrast to individual men's 37 percent, a remarkable proportion considering how much more money men had than women.

Moreover, women solicited most of the contributions from both men and women. Then, too, the child-helping agencies, more than any other charities, raised a high proportion of money from events such as fairs, teas, and bazaars, organized by women, providing the major source of indirect contributions.[22] As late as 1960 society women arranged teas, dances, and showings of their gardens and houses for the MSPCC.

In the MSPCC's first few decades, upper-class women not only raised money but also participated actively in the work of the Society. They found placements for children, became guardians of children, investigated farm and boarding homes. Individual cases were discussed at directors' meetings, and on at least one occasion the directors overruled the General Agent and countermanded one of his actions. Twelve directors took monthly turns advising regularly on the handling of cases. Directors attended meetings of the legislature and its committees to propose and lobby for legislation. The "Home Committee," headed by Kate Gannett Wells, undertook twice-weekly inspections of the Society's own temporary detention home to see that cleaning and repairs were done. These women collected contributions in kind for the home: oranges and English breakfast tea from Mrs. Atkinson, a quilt from Mrs. Hewes, twenty garments from Mrs. Peirce, stockings from Mrs. O'Neil and Miss Tower, candy and apples from Miss Tower, a barrel of potatoes from Mr. Tower, mittens from Mrs. Atkinson, etc.[23]

The MSPCC's images of good and bad child-raising were deeply influenced by the sensibility of these upper-class women. In their fund-raising they sentimentalized the sufferings of children, and found a sure touch for evoking tears and money from their audiences. They produced "before and after" photographs in which neglected immigrant children (the women liked to call them "waifs") were pictured first as they had been found and then dressed in Victorian finery to show how they could be "saved."[24] The way they conducted the temporary home expressed their mission, too. Emphasizing cleanliness, fine dress, good food, order, and quiet, they self-righteously used it to expose by contrast the inadequacy of the children's parental homes.[25]

Although women were active in organizing and fund-raising for the MSPCC, its managers, staff, and public spokesmen were all men. The men, too, were generally upper-class and had roots in the reform tradition as well as anti-cruelty-to-animals work. The first General Agent of the MSPCC was John Dixwell, maverick son of an upper-class family.[26]

Frank Fay, who became the first stable MSPCC leader (1880–1903), had been state senator and mayor of Chelsea (a separately incorporated town in greater Boston). However, he was also involved with the kinds of moral reform and charitable activities in which women figured importantly, having been a leader of the Prisoners' Aid Association, founder of a girls' reform school, and member of the Civil War Sanitary Commission.

"COMPLAINANTS" AND COMPLAINTS

It is remarkable how quickly the Society became very busy. By the end of 1881, after three and a half years of work, it had handled 2,017 cases involving 3,660 children. Its agents had filled up 3,600 ledger pages and 3,000 pages of a letter book.[27] It is not surprising that there was so much cruelty to children, but that a new organization received such a heavy caseload in such a short time makes one ask, How did the MSPCC find the cases?

Its success was largely due to the zeal of its agents, as its workers were then called. In these early years MSPCC agents went out onto the streets seeking abuses to correct. They looked for children begging, children outside when they should have been in school or inside, children improperly dressed or excessively dirty, children peddling.[28] During two months of the summer of 1880, for example, 45.2 percent of new cases were initiated by agents themselves.[29] The agents saw themselves as a street police for children, supplementing the inadequate resources of the police and truant officers.[30] The first General Agent, Dixwell, became a virtual ambulance chaser. He scanned the Boston newspapers for items that suggested mistreatment of children. When he read in the *Boston Daily Globe* of a "waif" begging without socks or shoes, he set out to find him, and did—on Washington Street, selling pins while his mother watched from a hiding place. Dixwell arrested the boy, who was sentenced to a reform school for two years—for what offense is unstated.[31] When Dixwell read that a man had murdered his sister's husband, and that two children had been left in the care of friends, he hurried off to investigate.[32] (The outcome is not recorded. The reader

should become accustomed to incomplete stories, as so many of the
early case records stop abruptly.) When the *Boston Herald* reported that
a boy playing in the street had been injured in his eye by something
his companion had thrown, Dixwell wrote to the Superintendent of
Boston City Hospital to find out how badly he was injured, collecting
evidence to prosecute the parents for neglect.[33]

MSPCC agents also wrote letters to newspapers and influential individuals to call attention to their work. When Mrs. G. T. Flanders,
wife of a well-known Universalist minister, wrote the *Boston Herald* to
denounce the excessive punishment of her daughter in school, the
MSPCC offered her assistance.[34] Responding to a newspaper item about
the conviction of a wife-beater, Dixwell congratulated the prosecutor
for his "prompt and energetic action."[35] Such tactics expanded the pool
of those who referred cases to the MSPCC.

Soon the majority of MSPCC cases came from non-staff, known as
complainants. Increasingly they were family members, who initiated
34 percent of complaints in 1880 and 61 percent by 1890.[36] Many
referrals began to come from Boston's notables, often involving poor
people in their own purview, such as servants. Other agencies and
authorities—Overseers of the Poor, truant officers, police officers, other
Boston charity agencies, the Associated Charities, teachers and school
headmasters, agencies in other towns seeking to trace people or to hand
over responsibility for roving clients—also began to make regular referrals to the MSPCC.

Not all complaints turned into "cases." Informants sometimes gave
wrong addresses; or agents, unfamiliar with densely populated working-
class neighborhoods and unaided by the residents, could not find the
people in question. Boston's poor in this period were extremely transient,
as we have seen. Furthermore, agents often found no evidence of wrongdoing despite a complaint. Hostile neighbors and relatives often turned
in false accusations. In 1880 56 percent of complaints were dismissed
by the agency for lack of evidence; in 1890 65 percent, and the pro-
portation was at least that high every year thereafter, sometimes reaching
almost 3:1. Some complaints were withdrawn by complainants. This
was particularly common when family members were the initiators,
because they were acting out of anger, which then subsided, or because
they began to see dangers to themselves if the MSPCC became involved.

For example, in one 1890 case, a woman complained that her husband had "wasted" $900 left to her by her former husband, and when she remonstrated with him, he struck and threatened her and refused her the rent money. But a few days later, when the MSPCC wrote to the man, she hid the letter from him and turned away an agent trying to see him.[37] Such ambivalence was most frequent in wife-beating cases, but also evident in many others. One fifteen-year-old girl complained of her father's abuse and asked the MSPCC to appoint a guardian for her, suggesting a particular person. That person first agreed, then declined, to accept guardianship, whereupon the girl withdrew her complaint.[38] Neighbors were often also ambivalent. They frequently made anonymous complaints, or asked the Society to disguise their identity. In the crowded, intimate neighborhoods of the poor, people were afraid of the disapproval of their peers for having tattled, and would not agree to testify in court, to talk with Society agents, or, sometimes, even to repeat their stories a few days later.

At first, neither the agents nor their clients had a clear sense of the MSPCC's jurisdiction. This was only natural: the agency was *sui generis*, and it was defining cruelty to children in its daily actions. For example, when a four-year-old boy was injured by a carriage in a hit-and-run accident (a common cause of child death in this period), the MSPCC agent prosecuted the driver.[39] Furthermore, the public, their thinking not as yet bureaucratically organized by a "welfare state" into differentiated expectations of different social agencies, thought, generically, that they could get help of all kinds from any charity. They came to the MSPCC asking for financial aid, babysitting, adoptions, divorces, as well as reporting on parents for cruelty. The MSPCC took on not only cases that would today be considered child abuse but also other social problems that its leaders saw as cruelty to children.

One such problem was the *padrone* system, a form of indentured labor. Beginning in the 1860s, children from Italian families, particularly in the poor southern provinces, were recruited for labor in the United States in return for payments to their parents. In exchange, the *padrone* kept the children's earnings, thus gaining incentive for severe exploitation of the children. As historian Robert Bremner has pointed out, "From the standpoint of [poor] parents . . . the boys and girls would be better provided for than under their own roofs; there would be fewer mouths to feed at home, and a little money coming in each month from across the sea."[40] In fact, the *padrone* system had counterparts among many nationalities, including the Irish and later the Chinese, but these reformers believed it to be uniquely Italian.

The *padrones* usually sent the children out as street musicians, sometimes with organ-grinders. The children were often overworked and undernourished, sometimes beaten and terrified. The *padrones* sometimes "sold" the children to others. The objection to the street-music activity of children had complex meanings, however. As disguised begging, their activity offended respectable sensibilities, which preferred the poor to be out of sight. The SPCCs sponsored legislation limiting street trades, even for adults.[41] Moreover, they disapproved of the public presence of children generally. The Victorian conviction that children should be domestic and unseen, and the fear of "precocity" in children, were part of the characteristic anti-urban bias of so many reformers of the time.[42] These feelings mixed with racist fears of pollution, evident in Charles Loring Brace's description of the "little Italian organ-grinders" of New York:

> Here, in large tenement-houses, were packed hundreds of poor Italians, mostly [sic] engaged in carrying through the city and country "the everlasting hand-organ," or selling statuettes. In the same room I would find monkeys, children, men and women, with organs and plaster-casts, all huddled together; but the women contriving still, in the crowded rooms, to roll their dirty macaroni, and all talking excitedly; a bedlam of sounds, and a combination of odors from garlic, monkeys, and most dirty human persons. They were, without exception, the dirtiest population I had met with. The children I saw every day on the streets, following organs, blackening boots, selling flowers, sweeping walks, or carrying ponderous harps for old ruffians. So degraded was their type, and probably so mingled in North Italy with ancient Celtic blood, that their faces could hardly be distinguished from those of Irish poor children—an occasional liquid dark eye only betraying their nationality.[43]

In Boston the MSPCC took credit for wiping out the *padrone* system and the work of children with organ-grinders,[44] but this claim was self-serving and disregarded what Italians themselves were doing. The Italian legislature outlawed this form of indenture and an active Italian-American campaign helped stimulate, in 1874, a federal law against "Italian white child slavery" and several well-publicized convictions.[45]

Other child performers also provoked the MSPCC, but its response was less united, because its interests sometimes clashed with those of other powerful groups. The world of the theater threatened all the values of the child-savers: immorality, irreverence, immodesty, intemperance, and children's "precocity." Few issues symbolized so well the new sensibility of domesticity, of protecting, even insulating, children from the "real world." The theater was doubly threatening to girls, who particularly required supervision. "Precocious female children . . . discount their future existence by over-nervous excitement . . . by the exposure of person not only accustoming them gradually to a loss of all modesty, but which coupled with lavish gifts of jewelry, fine clothes, and luxuries beyond their station in life, inevitably lure and lead to a life of 'splendid sin.' "[46]

Massachusetts legislated against children's participation in public "exhibitions" in 1877 and again in 1880, but the MSPCC remained dissatisfied because loopholes remained.[47] It won better legislation in 1882, but enforcement proved to be much more difficult than anticipated. Many groups resented its interference on this issue—the child performers, the parents who got their earnings, the impresarios who profited from theater, and the audiences. Every year the Society promised that the evil had almost disappeared, yet every year there were more contested cases, and in 1893 Agent Fay admitted that "there is a difference of opinion in the community" regarding this question.[48]

Some child performers were so popular that the MSPCC directors were divided on how to proceed. The 1882 case of "Little Corinne" is a good example. The New York SPCC had sued to enforce the law, prohibiting performances by this popular child singer and actress, and won; then the mayor of New York used his powers to give her special dispensation to sing at matinees, but not evenings.[49] When she was to open in Boston, the MSPCC directors voted 18 to 11 against attempting to enforce the law. Kate Gannett Wells wrote, thinking tactically, "Whilst admitting that we are legally able to prosecute, we are not absolutely compelled to do all that the law recommends . . . we are still a feeble organization; we have too important & increasing work to do to injure our reputation with the public, or to lessen our chance of subscriptions . . ."[50]

The complaints against child performers and the *padrone* system were sometimes put in terms of child labor. However, there is reason to doubt the seriousness of this concern, given the Society's infrequent attempts to monitor child labor in other situations. A few complaints about such places as the Wakefield, Massachusetts, Rattan Works, and a Newton woolen mill were investigated.[51] At the agency's request, Harvard Professor E. S. Wood examined samples of paints used in manufacturing wallpaper where children were employed, and found them to contain arsenic.[52] The MSPCC lobbied for and took credit for improvements in the state's anti-child-labor legislation.[53] However, considering the class basis of support for the MSPCC, it is not surprising that its activity concerning child labor in industrial or large commercial establishments was minimal. Major campaigns about the overwork of children were always directed against the poor, not the rich. Agents worried about immigrant children overworked by "lazy" parents or greedy *padrones*. Here the child-savers came into conflict with immigrants' traditional expectations that children ought to work and to contribute to a family economy.

The MSPCC also took on the problems presented by children without parents—lost, orphaned, or abandoned. Only the last group fits into contemporary concepts of child abuse, but for the early MSPCC all these problems seemed parallel, putting children in need of care. Many orphans left alone were reported to the Society. "[Agent] Smyth . . . to see B . . . children. Father & mother dead some years. [thirteen-year-old boy] in bed—so called—to keep warm. He got up and when dressed looked like a 'scarecrow.' " This boy was responsible for three younger siblings, even though he had kinfolk nearby: uncles in Dorchester, Hingham, and South Boston.[54] In December 1896 two children, ages six and five, were found alone, their mother having died in January 1895, their father being in jail for drunkenness.[55] In 1894 a school headmaster reported that a ten-year-old boy was alone, his foster mother having been imprisoned for running an "idle and disorderly house."[56] Some orphans came in on their own, and some needed only very specific kinds of help, as a fourteen-year-old boy who asked the MSPCC in 1883 to become his guardian so he could enlist in the Navy, having been wandering on his own for years.[57] Other needs were more total, as the two-and-a-half-year-old child brought in from Somerville with "scrofula. Cannot talk or walk. Has large head. Small body. . . . No names of the family."[58]

Babies abandoned at hospitals, police stations, or other institutional places were usually sent directly to asylums. Older lost children, however, were often brought to the MSPCC. (The rise of child protection coincided with police rejection of their earlier nineteenth-century practice of providing overnight accommodations for "lost" children, a reform which may not have promoted parent-child reunions, since these agencies were often in the business of placing out children.) The numbers of lost children were substantial—in Boston averaging five per thousand population in 1874.[59] Some children may have been recorded "abandoned" without adequate searches for their parents. However, the MSPCC also received complaints of abandonment of a less ambiguous sort: from women hired to board infants or even older children for periods of time, who reported that the parents had absconded. Inversely, parents often came to the MSPCC to find boarding homes for their children—or even permanent homes, because of poverty or illegitimacy, for example.[60]

Boarding mothers figured ominously and ambiguously in the sensationalized issue of baby farming. Baby farming originally referred simply to the practice of taking in babies for board and/or wet-nursing. Originally, its poor reputation was due only to the poverty, misfortune, or character faults that led the mothers to seek to give up their babies. Then, in England in 1868, the *British Medical Journal* published allegations that baby farming was a system of commercial infanticide. Women who earned their living as baby farmers took babies for the express purpose of killing them, it was charged, usually allowing them to die through deliberate neglect (starvation, dehydration, or exposure); and those who answered the advertisements of baby farmers did so with the intention of finding a safe way to get rid of an unwanted infant. A campaign of investigation and reform followed in England.[61]

In the United States, baby farming was one of the newly discovered forms of cruelty to children that built the SPCCs. Observers apparently found it hard to believe that infanticide could have been deliberate, especially in the cases of older babies.[62] With investigation, the evidence of purposive infanticide grew. In New York City in 1873 a woman who had been given babies to board by the New York Charities and Corrections Commission was charged with "wholesale infanticide," allegedly working together with a neighboring undertaker who got rid of the bodies.[63] Soon baby farming became one of the main concerns of the New York and Boston SPCCs.[64] In Boston in 1890 the bodies of thirty dead infants were found within three quarters of a mile of a private "lying-in hospital and nursery." An MSPCC "female detective" stated that mothers were charged $25 to leave their babies.[65] Better regulation of baby-boarding homes in the cities apparently pushed baby farming into the countryside: as late as 1910 there were exposés of baby farms in New Hampshire that took scores of Boston infants.[66]

The benign and the murderous forms of this practice were closely related and grew from the same conditions. When parents could not support older children, they could be placed in indentures, where they worked for their keep; but babies could not work. In the nineteenth century, babies in infant asylums were as likely to die as those with baby farmers. Poor and desperate parents may have been confused, conflicted, or self-deluding about what they wanted, or about what they would get. Offered an opportunity to get rid of the responsibility for a baby through ambiguous arrangements, parents may have accepted the ambiguity—and paid for it—partly as a way to avoid confronting their real desires. The ambiguity frequently continued in the financial terms, with a month's board collected in advance (often a relatively large sum for the very poor, such as $15). Often fathers, not mothers, brought in illegitimate children.

The intentions of the baby farmers may also have been mixed. Some claimed they tried to nourish the babies but could not support them when parental payments ceased. Others probably used the payments for themselves. Many poor women supported their own families by caring for children, in an occupation partly an extension of wet-nursing. Their poverty combined with the helplessness or indifference of parents to leave the babies vulnerable to mistreatment. Some advertised publicly that they desired to "adopt" babies, then "got rid" of them either themselves or through farming them out to yet others.[67] In 1905 the New York SPCC prosecuted a child-care operator who allegedly subcontracted 700 babies out to other women. The accused, Mrs. Letizia Tombarina, took babies into her care for $10 per month and then farmed them out to other Italian women for $5 per month. Many of these children had been sent to her by established child-saving groups. She and her agents found the "subcontractors" by reading the death notices in the Italian papers; when a nursing infant had died, the mother would be approached and offered a baby to nurse.[68] Several baby farms functioned also as lying-in homes for unmarried women; their services included the confinement as well as taking the baby for "adoption placement" afterward. One such establishment was described as a prosperous and respectable-looking building.[69] In another, women paid substantial fees for these services: $5 a week for staying in the home, $10 for attendance during confinement.[70] Whatever the truth about the incidence of deliberate infanticide, the mortality rates among infants resulting from inadequate child-care arrangements remained high.

In these last cases the baby-farming service resembled that offered by abortionists, and the fees were similar. In fact, the public alarm about baby farming was contemporaneous with the press's discovery of abortion and the rise of a social-purity campaign against it. Several historians have noted that abortion seems to have increased after about 1840. Moreover, abortion had previously been considered primarily a crime of unmarried pregnant girls; in mid-century it was becoming a common form of birth control among married women.[71] It is possible that baby farming was similarly becoming a more widespread form of dealing with unwanted or unsupportable children, and one increasingly used by married parents.[72]

Child protectors saw another form of abuse in the widespread practice of insuring children. The practice originated as burial insurance, organized by working-class mutual-aid societies. Many child-savers considered insurance at best "an offensive symbol of the prevalent materialistic orientation toward childhood";[73] at worst as an incentive to murder.[74] But the child protectors were less unified on this issue than on others, and some SPCC spokesmen defended the insurance of children. In 1895 the MSPCC sought legislation prohibiting the practice, but failed. The agency's weakness in this campaign was not surprising, since, for once, its adversary was wealthy and powerful. After about 1875 the large insurance companies, Prudential, Metropolitan Life, and John Hancock, had begun selling insurance on children. They did door-to-door selling with great success: by 1902 three million children were insured.[75]

The child protectors' division on this issue indicated their confusion about what children were being insured for, and their disdain for working-class families. Prosperous reformers often disapproved of the poor's spending substantial sums on funerals and wakes, while to many people anything less than a generous funeral was a statement of disregard for the child who had died. A pauper burial "confounded tragedy with degradation."[76] At the same time children often produced regular income on which their families were dependent, and for this reason insuring children was no more cynical than insuring their fathers. It was of a piece with the practice, common at this time, of suing for damages in the "wrongful death" of a child, damages often awarded in exact replication of the child's expected earning power.[77]

THE MSPCC IN ACTION

In identifying the problems in need of correction, early child protectors saw the mistreatment of children through their own cultural lenses. Indeed, their sense of mission was more powerful because it came from a feeling of unquestioned superiority to the masses among whom child neglect and abuse were so widespread. This very sense of superiority made them more able to face the existence of problems—including, as we shall see below, sexual abuse of children and wife-beating—often considered unmentionable. They did not see themselves in the caricature of drunken, brutal parents they intended to reform.

Social workers' bias in their view of clients has been a consistent problem in child-protection work. In the nineteenth century, it was at its worst, because the social distance between clients and workers was greatest. The fact that agency workers commonly visited clients in their homes in this period only widened the distance, since the clients' home lives seemed repulsive to the child protectors, who saw only their filthy, ill-furnished apartments, their unkempt and odorous persons, their dirty verminous children, their shouting and profanity, their diets of bread and beer (or wine, as Italian clients became more frequent) and stew. The agents hated the garlic and olive-oil smells of Italian cooking, and considered this food unhealthy, overstimulating, aphrodisiac. Their languages were so different, even when the clients spoke English, that there was little opportunity for clients to make their individual personalities known to agency workers.

Such bias and social distance affected the diagnoses of the causes of cruelty to children. In the nineteenth century, two themes dominated child protectors' analyses: drunkenness and the cultural inferiority of the immigrants. Moreover, they believed the two to be connected, despite the fact that some immigrant groups, such as Italians, Portuguese, and Southeast Europeans, did not have patterns of high alcohol consumption.[78]

Until Prohibition the MSPCC consistently cited intemperance as the main causal factor in cruelty to children.[79] The majority of the agents were probably teetotalers, since that was the norm among respectable Wasps in Boston at this time. Furthermore, MSPCC leaders were among Boston's politically active "drys." In the 1880s the MSPCC supported a Citizens' Law and Order League pressing for the tighter enforcement of these acts.[80] Heavy drinking did in fact create great misery among Boston's poor, causing illness, greater impoverishment, violence, and depression, but the child protectors were unable to distinguish it from moderate drinking. The presence of any alcoholic drinks or bottles, including wine and beer, in the homes of their clients was evidence of alcoholic depravity, and any woman who touched spirits was considered *ipso facto* unfit.

MSPCC agents also traced child mistreatment to vices inherent among inferior nationalities and cultures, a problem usually called "depravity." Their conviction that "Americans" were superior, as evidenced in their more humane treatment of children, was explicit: for example, "mother will never bring up her children according to American standards," a caseworker wrote of a recalcitrant client, or, in a more hopeful mood: "Worker [caseworker] pointed out that there were standards here [in the United States] she would be expected to meet and that we were interested in helping her in this."[81] In the nineteenth century depravity was more often seen among men, in part because it was not distinguished from drunkenness. It also reflected feminist emphases on male brutality and irresponsibility, which in turn were saturated with racist caricatures of immigrant (that is, non-Wasp) men.

The clients, no doubt, had their own stereotypes, perhaps equally inaccurate, about the Wasp charity workers they met. But this was not a situation of social distance created by misunderstanding. The main dynamic here was not difference but domination. The child protectors were men of privilege and confidence, prosperity and status, and they had not only political power in their community and country but power over the lives of their clients. The latter were poor, separated from supportive communities, members of minority ethnic and religious groups. Not only were they usually not citizens, but they were often illiterate and ignorant of even those rights that they might have claimed. Moreover, much was at stake for them, little for the agents: the clients could lose their children and end up in jail.

If the early child protectors were insensitive to the power relations in their work, if they saw their clients as helpless and grateful, that very ignorance left them a clear emotional path on which to follow their kind and helping impulses. They responded like the amateurs they were—personally. In many cases, agents, or equally often their wives, paid from their own pockets to help children, or intervened personally in family problems. In the winter of 1879, one reads, Mrs. Dixwell gave breakfast and warm clothes to a boy, and Mrs. Otis (an MSPCC director) gave him warm mittens.[82] In 1883 a fifteen-year-old boy was placed informally with an MSPCC agent's uncle who had an estate in Waltham.[83] Or, later that year, Agent "A. J. Smyth at the request of [a father] took his son from the grandparents . . . and carried him to the fa[ther] . . ."[84]

Society workers, influenced both by the traditions of "friendly visiting" and by the need to investigate cruelty allegations, spent a great deal of time on the streets and calling upon families in their homes. Agents were detectives, looking for absconded fathers, finding runaway or lost children, verifying addresses, checking marriage, death, birth, and divorce records. In their detecting, MSPCC agents acted far more like police than like friendly visitors. Like police, they were not always law-abiding. As an *Annual Report* put it, delicately, "It is true we have taken risks on the margin of legal liability which seemed needful to rescue the child . . . but without cost to the society."[85] Agents visited homes late at night or early in the morning—at times calculated to find wrongdoing. Unable to gain entry, they climbed in windows.[86] They searched without warrants. Their case notes frequently revealed that they made their judgments first and looked for evidence later.

Agents relied very largely on warnings and threats in their efforts to help mistreated children, believing that the specter of action would be enough to reform parents. Even among our random sample—which includes only cases in which cruelty was confirmed by the agency—no action was taken in many cases: 47 percent in 1880, down to 32 percent by 1893.[87]

Somewhere between action and inaction was "advice and referral." This was used increasingly as the MSPCC delineated its jurisdiction and refused to accept certain cases. For example, many came to the Society for relief (i.e., financial aid), which it never provided. Nevertheless, clients were often clever to do so. Sometimes an agent's referring a client elsewhere resulted in a run-around,[88] but at other times an MSPCC referral was practically as good as cash. Thus a father came in with eight young children, asking for vaccinations for the children, rent money, and employment. When he went on to the Overseers of the Poor, the Provident Association, and the Industrial Aid Society, he came with an MSPCC recommendation.[89] Similarly, the MSPCC had the power to get children released from other institutions. In one case a widow was able to persuade the MSPCC that her child had been mistakenly taken. She earned her living doing garment-finishing work and like all home workers had to travel to and from jobbers to pick up and deliver bundles, and to look for jobs. While thus temporarily absent she had taken sick and gone to a friend's house to recuperate, she claimed. When she returned, she found that her children had been taken to the Chardon Street Home, a shelter run by the Overseers of the Poor. The MSPCC agent gave her a letter to get her children back.[90] The MSPCC's influence over other agencies was thus an important aspect of its power and function.

The MSPCC also assumed substantial authority to arrange adoptions, trusteeships, child support, custody, and guardianship agreements; it became, in modern terms, both an arbitration and a mediation agency.[91] One man came in seeking to challenge his wife's custody of a child they had adopted four years earlier—from the MSPCC! (Such informal adoptions were still common.) Now he had learned that his wife's previous husband was still living, and suspected that she had been seeing him; he wanted to leave his wife, but to make sure he retained the child.[92] Many men came to get help in finding wives and children who had left them.[93] Mrs. Sarah E. Dawes, the president of the Nickerson Home (a private nonsectarian Roxbury home for children), called about a fourteen-year-old girl who had lived there eleven years. Her mother, about to be released from prison, had declared her intention of coming to get her daughter, but Dawes sought to prevent this and asked MSPCC help. The agent advised her on how to seek guardianship.[94] Here, for example, is an agreement developed by an MSPCC agent in 1889 between a quarreling husband and wife:

> Whereas Francis M. . . . and Mary M. . . . do not live harmoniously together and the said Mary has determined to live separate and apart from the said Francis . . . therefore I the said Francis . . . for the purpose of furnishing support for my said wife and our child . . . do promise to pay to Edwin R. Smyth [MSPCC agent] . . . Ten Dollars each and every week. . . . I also agree with the said Smyth not to interfere with or disturb my said wife and also agree that she may have the care custody and control of [daughter]. . . . And the said Edwin R. Smyth hereby accepts the office of trustee . . . and agrees to pay over to the said Mary . . . the sums . . . from the said Francis.[95]

The MSPCC also negotiated private placing-out agreements, sending children, for example, to the Shakers.[96] An excerpt from one private placing-out agreement illustrates the form of parents' sacrifice of their rights:

> For and in consideration of expenses incurred, or to be incurred, by Mass. Socy P C to C in behalf of my child eleven years of age, and to enable said Society to procure for said child a suitable home . . . I hereby delegate to said Society my authority over said child; and I . . . give up said child to said Society unreservedly . . . or such other disposal as may seem to said Socy best for its welfare, agreeing that I will neither seek to discover its home, attempt its removal therefrom nor in any way molest the family in which it may be placed, or other parties interested.[97]

When the Society decided upon legal action against child abusers, it had relatively few options: It could prosecute a child abuser for assault and battery, drunkenness, or rape; alternatively, it could have the children adjudged neglected and committed to a city-run institution. Among the MSPCC's earliest actions was lobbying for increased legal powers. Legislation of 1882 gave the MSPCC two important new powers: (1) a probate court judge could appoint the Society as guardian for any neglected, ill-treated, or abandoned child under fourteen, for a period of

EARLY CHILDHOOD PROTECTION

A girl performer, by definition an abused child to the 19th-century child protectors. Undated. *(Courtesy of MSPCC, Boston.)*

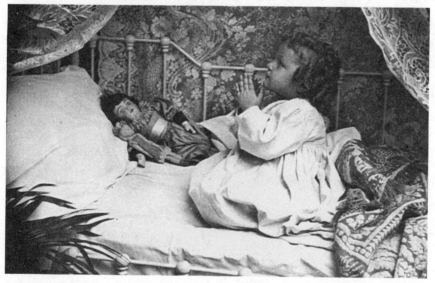

By contrast, this was the MSPCC's image of a healthy childhood. *(Courtesy of MSPCC, Boston.)*

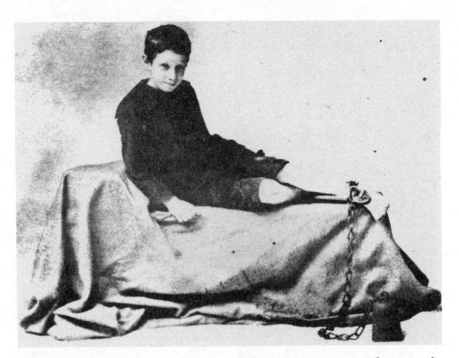

The MSPCC posed boys in chains and in bonds, reconstructing cases of sensational child abuse, for publicity and money-raising purposes. Undated. *(Courtesy of MSPCC, Boston.)*

The MSPCC used "before-and-after" pictures like these to demonstrate its effectiveness and the need for its services. Approximately 1900.
(Courtesy of MSPCC, Boston.)

Staff of the MSPCC, 1883. *(Courtesy of MSPCC, Boston.)*

time during which the MSPCC could retain or assign custody; and (2) any judge could give the MSPCC immediate thirty-day custody of abandoned or deserted children under five. With these powers the MSPCC could remove children immediately to its own temporary home, without the delays of trials; it could place children for long periods in other homes or in foster or even adoptive homes. These powers, of course, depended upon the Society's influence in court. But judges usually accepted the agency's advice. While the MSPCC did lose criminal assault cases at times, in the legally noncriminal cases of neglect, it was virtually a judge's private advisor. "Judge Burbank," wrote Dixwell, "true to his promise made to Gen Agent [i.e., Dixwell] has invariably passed prompt sentence on children cases where possible to do so."[98]

The MSPCC also obtained legislation against particular behaviors which it deemed cruel to children. Against baby farming an act of 1882 required that local boards of health register all boarding homes, and that the Overseers of the Poor register any illegitimate child given out to board.[99] Against child performers, the MSPCC won the removal of all exceptions to the ban on children in "public exhibitions," and a prohibition on the admission of children under thirteen to shows.[100] Exhibiting deformed children in circuses was specifically prohibited.[101] The sale or gift of tobacco to minors was prohibited,[102] as was the sale of firearms.[103] A whole series of acts regulated peddling by minors.[104] Tougher laws were passed against sexual abuse, including raising the age of consent to fourteen.[105] Truancy laws, too, were toughened.[106]

Another of the Society's weapons against child abuse was publicity. The agency sent out frequent press releases about its cases, its legal victories, or merely dramatizing the horrors of the problems it confronted. One purpose was, of course, to raise money. A Fair for Abused Children in 1880 held in Boston Horticultural Hall raised $15,000 net, for example.[107] Another was deterrence. Cases for prosecution were chosen carefully, and judges concurred. In 1913 Theodore Lothrop, later to become head of the MSPCC, cited Judge Ludden's "desire that the case should be followed up vigorously owing to the relative prominence of the [M] family in the Italian community of the town, believing that the example of this case would be widely felt."[108] The Society's punitive spirit can be seen in its commitment to scaring parents into better behavior: "If we rescue from a tenement house a child who has been neglected or abused, every family in that house and neighborhood are warned . . ."[109] "The fear of justice has gone abroad . . ."[110] "The knowledge that an organization exists whose purpose is to prevent and punish, keeps the terrors of the law before the parent, and thousands of blows are averted which would otherwise have fallen upon the defenceless victims. . . . The children, we trust, imbibe the spirit of a better way, and, in their turn, will practise it when they have families of their own."[111] The last statement anticipates the view common today that family violence is passed from generation to generation: parents repeat behaviors they learned as children. Notwithstanding its antiviolent aims, the MSPCC's rhetoric was in itself rather violent. Its agents spoke of punishing bad parents, instilling fear and terror of the law; they emphasized brutality and blows, even though apathy and neglect were the more common problems. That the Boston poor referred to the Society as "the Cruelty" did not seem regrettable to its agents.

LAW ENFORCEMENT OR CHARITY?

The MSPCC belonged both to the upper-class charity community and to the world of law enforcement, and experienced no contradiction between these two identities.[112] The Massachusetts agency, unlike its New York analogue, never took public funds or had its agents deputized, but it must nevertheless be considered part of the state regulatory apparatus.[113] (As late as 1960, a study of MSPCC former clients showed that most of them thought it a governmental agency.)[114] In its first two decades the MSPCC was a key force behind the increased state regulation of children's activities and parents' child-raising. Though they opposed governmental welfare programs two decades later, in the 1880s MSPCC leaders believed they had only to gain from state intervention— partly because they assumed they could direct that intervention. Even more important was their day-to-day assumption of authority over the definition of appropriate treatment of children and punishment of violators. As the New York SPCC put it, and the Massachusetts group agreed,

There were plenty of laws existing . . . but unfortunately no one had heretofore been held responsible for their enforcement. The Po-

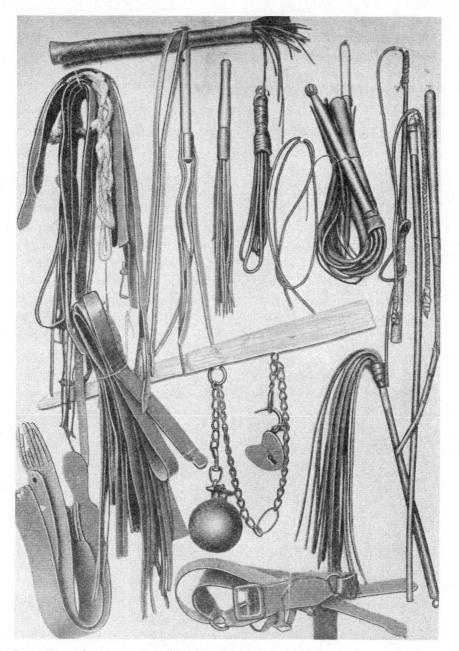

Instruments of torture, collected by the MSPCC for an illustration in one of its reports. *(Courtesy of MSPCC, Boston.)*

lice . . . were engaged in the prosecution . . . of offenses of a graver legal character and . . . could not be expected to discover and prosecute those who claimed the right to ill-treat the children over whom they had an apparent legal control. The Society proposed to enforce legally, but energetically, the existing laws . . .[115]

Moreover, MSPCC leaders believed that they themselves were entitled to some leeway in respecting the law:

> . . . we have every motive to keep strictly within the limits of positive law . . . but we must not be diverted from the performance of our duty by outside influences, by newspaper criticism or by fear of public opinion. . . . If "indiscreet zeal," which is made such a bugbear, occasionally leads us into mistakes, the public will condone the error . . . much more readily than they would approve the opposite fault of timidity or lukewarmness in cases of well ascertained cruelty . . . It therefore does not become a society organized for our purposes . . . to err often on the side of self-protection . . ."[116]

The first MSPCC head, Dixwell, issued edicts that represented the literal assumption of state authority. For example:

MASSACHUSETTS SOCIETY
FOR THE
PREVENTION OF CRUELTY TO CHILDREN

The parents and guardians of children within the Commonwealth of Massachusetts are hereby requested to have at least one article of clothing upon their children plainly marked with the child's FULL NAME AND RESIDENCE, so as to assist the local police and M.S.P.C.C. officers in returning children to their homes when lost or stolen.

Boston, July 1, 1879   John Dixwell, M.D., General Agent
                            No. 6 Pemberton Square[117]

Dixwell's crude style was too blunt for the establishment, and it was modified by later MSPCC directors. But their confidence in their own rectitude did not waver.

MSPCC agents gathered information from the police, asked police officers to bring cases to them, conscripted police officers as supervisors in cases where mistreaters of children had been warned but not punished, and took referrals from the police. Boston MSPCC agents did not themselves make arrests; rather, if they thought an arrest likely, they stopped first at the local police station to bring an officer with them. Once on the scene, the police deferred to the MSPCC agent as the expert on domestic law, and followed his directions.

Otherwise, MSPCC agents acted like police in countless small ways. They called people to their office with letters that sounded like legal summonses, and their recipients usually complied. They threatened families with arrest or with taking custody of children. They regularly interviewed neighbors and relatives, attempting to entrap them into damaging statements about those under investigation. They searched homes, confiscated unacceptable objects, such as liquor bottles, and ejected "unwholesome" visitors.

CHILD PROTECTION AND THE EROSION OF PATRIARCHY

This confidence was the more extraordinary because of the SPCCs' new jurisdictional claims. Previously, child-savers such as the Children's Aid Societies directed their efforts at "dependent" children—meaning those reliant on the public or community for support. Children became dependent through orphanage, desertion, the impoverishment of their parents, or by running away (becoming "little wanderers," in the language of the time). While the earlier child-savers probably did "steal" some children from poor parents, they did not publicly claim the right to do so. Following the activist lead of the SPCAs, the SPCCs proclaimed their intention to intervene in existing, not necessarily "dependent," families.

In claiming this right to intervene into intact families, child protection was challenging patriarchal relations. A pause to consider the definition of patriarchy is necessary here. In the 1970s a new definition of that term came into use, first proposed by Kate Millett but quickly adopted by the United States feminist movement: patriarchy became a synonym for male supremacy, for "sexism." I use the term in its earlier, historical, and more specific sense, referring to a family form in which fathers had control over all other family members—children, women, and servants. This concept of a patriarchal family is an abstraction, postulating common features among family forms that differed widely across geography and time. If there was a common material base supporting this family norm, it was an economic system in which the family was the unit of production. Most of the MSPCC's early clients came from peasant societies in which this kind of family economy prevailed. In these families, fathers maintained control not only over property and tools but also, above all, over the services and labor power of family members. That historical patriarchy defined a set of parent-child relations as much as it did relations between the sexes, for children rarely had opportunities for economic independence except by inheriting the family property, trade, or craft. While women were subordinated, mothers too benefited in some ways from patriarchal parent-child relations: their authority over daughters and young sons was an important value when women lacked other kinds of authority and independence, and in old age they gained respect, help, and consideration from younger kinfolk.

The SPCCs' claim to speak on behalf of children's rights, and to intervene in parental treatment of children, was an attack on patriarchal power. At the same time, the new sensibility about children's rights and the concern about child abuse were signs that patriarchal family expectations and realities had already been weakening, particularly in the United States. Father-child relations had changed more than husband-wife relations. Children had, for example, gained the power to arrange their own betrothals and marriages, to obtain wage work independent of their fathers' occupations, although of course children's options remained limited by class and cultural privileges or the lack of them, inherited from fathers. By contrast a wage labor system and long-distance mobility often left women, on balance, more dependent on husbands for sustenance and less able to rely on kinfolk and neighbors to defend their interests against husbands.

Early child-protection work did not, of course, envision a general liberation of children from parental control. On the contrary, the SPCCs aimed as much to reinforce a failing parental/paternal authority as to limit it. Indeed, SPCC spokesmen viewed excessive violence against children as a symptom of *inadequate* parental authority. If assaults on children were provoked by children's insubordination, this showed that parental weakness, children's disobedience, and child abuse were mutually reinforcing. Furthermore, by the turn of the century, the SPCCs discovered that the majority of their cases concerned neglect, not assault, and neglect to them exemplified especially vividly the problems created by inadequate parental supervision and authority.

In sum, the SPCCs sought to reconstruct the family along lines that altered the old patriarchy, already economically unviable, and to replace it with a modern version of male supremacy. This new system included state (later, professional) regulation limiting parental rights and prescribing new standards for proper child-raising. Children were to be disciplined with patience and indulgence. Fathers, now as wage laborers rather than as slaves, artisans, peasants, or entrepreneurs, were to have single-handed responsibility for economic support of their families but little direct participation in domestic life. Women and children were not to contribute to the family economy, at least not monetarily. Children instead were to spend full time in learning—cognitive lessons from professional teachers, psychological and moral lessons from the full-time attention of a mother. Children's respect for parents was to be inculcated moralistically and psychologically, because it no longer rested on an economic dependence lasting beyond childhood. The family as a whole became an object of ideology, no longer just a given. In the next century the concept of "family violence" gained resonance because it seemed to represent a contradiction, a violation of a space and a set of relations that were to be inherently peaceful.[118]

Feminism was important in this renovation of male supremacy, and an important stream of its influence flowed through child-saving work in general and child protection in particular. In this era, after all, women's political claim to respect was largely based on an ideology that nearly sacralized motherhood. In taking that approach, first-wave feminism thereby helped to maintain women's dependence and men's power, if only temporarily.[119] Child protection offers a capsule example of that complex, perhaps even contradictory, influence of feminism because child protection so closely integrated gender as well as class, religious, and ethnic goals. It never represented the interests of a single, homogeneous dominant group. Rather, the anti-patriarchalism of the child-protection agencies was the unstable product of several conflicting interests. Of these we have examined two overlapping groups: upper-class Protestant Bostonians hoping to subordinate the new immigrant poor, and conservative feminist reformers hoping to impose their vision of a domesticity based on respect for women and children. Next we must look at how a third group influenced the definition of the family-violence problem: professional social workers, whom we will meet in the next chapter.

3

THE PROGRESSIVE-ERA TRANSFORMATION OF CHILD PROTECTION, 1900–1920

A stenographer hired at the MSPCC in 1908, and remaining until 1947, left a vivid memoir of the appearance of that agency when she first arrived.

> We started at the top in the Children's Home where Miss Wilson a typical key-ring-bunch matron, with dyed hair and a compelling voice conducted us on a tour of the Home. . . . the children arose and sing-songed the Lord's prayer which they followed with a rendition of the National Anthem, as their eyes rolled about in restless fashion and their hands were tightly folded. One sprightly little girl wanted to be hospitable

but was advised by the Matron not to be a clatter-mouth. . . . Coming down to the next floor below we found a segregated group of older girls, so-called "moral delinquents." They . . . were kept apart lest they contaminate those who were said to be, as the Matron said, the "more wholesome type."

. . . we had seven special agents to cover the entire state. They were Benjamin Loring, a Civil War veteran . . . Accustomed as he had been to fight the battles of the Civil War while in it, and re-fight them verbally after it in the halls of the Grand Army of the Republic, he believed in action. Packing his telescope bag, he would go to the western part of the state to clean up situations reported there. . . . He would recount as follows. . . . "I put the fear of God into them. I took the children, where I thought it best, to the court, and the judge had a special sitting, and I brought them right back to Boston with me. I spread them out . . ." Mr. William R. Critcherson had joined the staff coming from the Boston Police Department. Through the passage of years his word became to be relied upon to the extent that some judges took it as evidence without following certain recognized court procedures . . . he brought many a wayward apprentice around to see the light of better days . . . James S. Carter, the remaining special agent, had been a newspaper reporter. To him all cases appeared like "hot stuff" and he just itched to give them great publicity which of course was forbidden. All of these seven special agents carried police badges on the reverse of their coat lapel. . . . If the occasion demanded they exposed that badge to clients and then they report "all was clear sailing."[1]

In 1908, the MSPCC was not very different than it had been several decades previously. The rigid treatment of children was the same, as was the agency's orientation to law enforcement. The agents had no special experience with family problems and lacked critical perspective on their authority and power over the poor.

In the next two decades, this agency, and child-protection work in general, underwent major transformations. The principles and practices developed during this "Progressive" period remained the basic system of regulation of child-raising in place today.[2] Child protection became integrated into the developing social-work profession, specifically into the new field called child welfare, changing both who the workers were and their conception of the problem. Child-protection work became professionalized and secularized, ending the influence of religiously motivated charity volunteers. While the organization's official agents had always been men, the female Christian volunteers had had considerable influence; now the workers became mainly female, although authority and leadership remained in the hands of men. The very definition of their cause changed fundamentally. While they did not desert the title "cruelty to children," the child protectors now saw the problem as family violence. Within this rubric they emphasized child neglect rather than child abuse; and they made out the characteristic villain no longer as a drunken immigrant father but rather as an incompetent, insensitive, and possibly untrained mother in need of professional guidance. They adopted environmentalist rather than moralistic explanations for family violence; they preached a preventive rather than punitive set of solutions.

These transformations were not only fundamental but lasting. In most respects, though certainly not all, the perspective and structures that child-protection work developed by 1920 remain today. The field is still dominated by secular, professional, private agencies using a casework method, although it is often psychiatric as well. The personnel are overwhelmingly female, and the management overwhelmingly male. Environmentalism and prevention remain key slogans for basic policy orientation. Neglect remains the characteristic problem, and mothers are held primarily responsible. Thus, while tracing the history of child-protection work to the present would divert us too long from our focus on the violent families themselves, a discussion of the Progressive era transformation of this work is essential because it was so enduring. We will look, in turn, at the professionalization of the child-protection agency and its workers, and at their substantive redefinition of the problems they defined as relevant.

PROFESSIONALIZATION

The professionalization of social work had its roots in the late-nineteenth-century "charity organization" movement. "Charity organization" emerged, in England in the 1860s and in the United States in the 1870s, out of a self-critique by charity workers who denounced the wasteful "sentimentality" of indiscriminate giving. They planned a new "scientific charity" with the eradication of poverty, rather than its temporary amelioration, as their goal. Although they did not anticipate professionalization of charity work, the women volunteers who began the movement were using the idea that social helping should become "scientific" to upgrade their own status. Contesting the demeaning Victorian stereotype of "ladies bountiful" meddling among the poor to while away their leisure, they wanted to transform their charity into skilled labor (like other reformers who tried to reinterpret women's domestic occupations—housewifery and child-raising—as skilled labor). In Boston a group of women charity leaders, particularly Annie Adams Fields, began the Cooperative Society of Visitors in 1875 with the goal of investigating every application for help and providing workrooms and jobs rather than money or goods. This effort gave rise to Associated Charities (AC), Boston's charity organization agency, in 1879.[3] Both the MSPCC and the Children's Aid Society (predecessor of BCSA) were active in the AC.[4]

The most important concept in the charity organization vocabulary was *pauperism*. Poverty was lack of resources; pauperism was permanent, hereditary poverty caused by the loss of will, work ethic, thrift, responsibility, and honesty. Emphasizing the old distinction between the deserving and the undeserving poor, the scientific charity workers believed that alms-giving was counter-productive, because it could weaken independence and the sense of responsibility to provide for oneself and one's family.

The "scientific" approach to clients' needs later became "casework," the first methodology of the new professional social work. Casework began with the collection of the most complete information possible about any individual or family, with the aim of long-term independence, not merely immediate survival, and the conviction that each case required an individual approach. For child-protection agencies, the merits of the casework approach were readily apparent, for looking at each act of child abuse or each desertion as a separate crime had been evidently futile and wasteful, and child-protection workers had quickly learned to look at long-term family patterns. Although the casework method allowed reform-minded social workers to identify environmental causes of clients' problems, and to seek public remedies,[5] in the 1880s the dominant motivation among its organizers was to prevent the undeserving from receiving relief. To put it in modern language, the charity organization societies (COSs) wanted to stop welfare chiselers.[6] To this end COS organizers created a central registry of aid recipients. Agencies were asked to report the names of all those applying to them, and to check the file before offering help. This system worked to prevent duplication of effort, contradictory policies, and clients' cheating.

The charity organization movement also contributed to professionalization through the establishment of the National Conference of Charities and Corrections in 1874 (becoming the National Association of Social Work in 1917). By 1921 it had 4,000 professional members. Agencies squeezed out volunteer workers, except from the most powerless of tasks, and formed staffs of paid and, gradually, trained professionals. In 1898 there were no professional social work schools, and by 1928 there were forty in the United States and Canada. By 1924 virtually all major cities had "community chests" organizing and centralizing fund-raising.[7] In the 1880s, child-protection work had been central in the COS movement, but in the 1890s the SPCCs temporarily fell behind the leading edge of social work activity. Particularly noticeable was their lack of connection with settlement house and social reform activity.[8]

The MSPCC grew very little before the turn of the century; for example, it had the same number of agents from its origins until 1907 (five or six). After its rapid take-off in the 1880s, the Society felt its legislative influence decline, complained that it was inadequately appreciated by the public, and experienced limitations on its activities due to inadequate funds.[9]

In Boston these doldrums were ended with the arrival from the New York Charity Organization Society of Carl C. Carstens, a national child-welfare leader, to head the MSPCC in 1907.[10] Carstens was to lead the MSPCC back into national leadership in child welfare.

Carstens's appointment represented the rejection of the simultaneously punitive and charitable approach to family violence which had prevailed hitherto, in favor of a new "scientific" emphasis sloganeered as "prevention." MSPCC president Grafton Cushing was already using the new phrase "social work" in announcing the change in leadership: The policy of "prosecution of offenders ... and taking of children from immoral or unhealthy surroundings ... [meant that] there is no 'social' work done."[11] The MSPCC's adoption of the casework approach led to a national split among child-protection agencies, between "restriction-ists" and "liberals." The former, tied to their origins in prevention-of-cruelty-to-animals work, belonged to the American Humane Association, which promoted a narrow reading of their jurisdiction—enforcement of the law. The "liberals," who were soon to recognize Carstens and the MSPCC as their leader, joined the professional child welfare movement.[12]

Carstens became a national lobbyist, publicist, and professional spokesman for the children's cause. His speeches defined child protection work throughout the country. The MSPCC had always had substantial influence in the state legislature, drafting the basic child-protection statutes; now that influence spread to related issues. In 1914 the Society was able to dictate how the newly established mothers' aid pensions should be administered.[13] The General Agent issued public statements on the size of the appropriation for the Wrentham State School for the feebleminded, the need for more school visitors, the organization of the juvenile courts, the need for a domestic relations court, community responsibility for building more playgrounds. MSPCC president Cushing became chairman of the Massachusetts State Child Labor Committee[14] (which met in MSPCC offices) and joined the Massachusetts Child Welfare Committee.[15] Carstens was instrumental in the establishment of the Children's Welfare League of Roxbury, drawing together representatives from various children's agencies working in that poor, predominantly Irish community to agitate for better services: it had committees on housing, recreation, education and employment (offering job placement through the schools), eugenics and child hygiene (offering "home economics" and child-care lessons).

Carstens ran the MSPCC until 1920. He began with a budget of $25,000 and a staff of five (male) agents; he ended with a $150,000 budget and a staff of thirty-nine, the majority women. Seeking to change the bad reputation of many child-saving groups which had literally snatched children from parents, placed them out, and—literally—lost them, Carstens began by insisting on systematic record-keeping.[16] New information-collecting forms were standardized, supervision regularized and intensified, and more of the agency's work was professionalized.

Caseworkers were "trained experts" by the end of the 1920s, the MSPCC claimed,[17] although they had mainly on-the-job training rather than social work degrees.[18] The MSPCC training plan dating from the late 1920s required "one hour's informal talk" with the supervisor on the general scope of work, an explanation of the "Office Machinery," reading "selected case records illustrating good case work," writing daily reports for the first two weeks on the job, and the approval of a supervisor for any court complaints during the first two years, for example. Three books were required to be read by all agents within three months of the time of employment, and they were the then classics of the new casework: Mary Richmond's *Social Diagnosis*, Joanna Colcord's *Broken Homes*, and Ada Sheffield's *Case Records*.[19]

Carstens continued and even expanded the use of volunteers, but trained them to conform to the Society's "standards" and subordinated them systematically to professional supervision. The professional agents became specialized—for example, in sexual assault, in medical neglect. Carstens handled few actual cases himself and concentrated mainly on supervision, public relations, and leadership in the profession, through research, lecturing, and writing. More controversially, he reduced the jurisdiction and power of the directors and their committees. For example, annual reports and fund-raising appeals were now done by the staff; legal work was no longer done by "advisory counsel" but by a salaried staff lawyer. Accounts were moved to the central office and the budget was prepared by the staff.

Carstens's administrative reforms had both class and gender implications. The whole process of professionalizing social work might be described as a middle-class *coup* against upper-class control, disempowering the upper-class, amateur volunteers who had run charity enterprises in the nineteenth century. Many of the MSPCC's directors and vice-presidents had contributed much personal attention in its first decades. When social work was a profession, male volunteers were limited to money-raising.

The implications of professionalization for women were more complex. Originally the MSPCC had provided not only an affiliation but engrossing work for many upper-class women. They had a place because of the dual identity of the MSPCC as law-enforcement agency and charity, each aspect with its gender connotations. The former work was legal, tough, masculine; the latter needed a tender, familial, feminine hand. By the Progressive period, the COS women found themselves defeated by their own strategy: the movement they themselves had created now expelled them, as the charity field became professionalized. "Scientific" charity wanted no sentimental, muddle-headed ladies dispensing alms, but tough-minded men engaged in long-range vision and strategies.

Professionalization of social work brought in other women: usually single, middle-class women who not only had professional aspirations but needed to earn their living. But despite the growing numbers of women agents, policy control became more male under Carstens, because the upper-class women volunteers (who constituted the majority of the directors and several committees) lost power to the male-directed professional staff. Women volunteers continued to run the temporary home, but it was an increasingly marginal aspect of the Society's work (replaced by foster care and longer-term institutionalization). Carstens's authority was supreme, and he was much adored by his female workers. " 'To have walked in the shadow of his friendship was like a benediction,' " wrote Mary Irene Atkinson. [20] This adoration was at least in part a response to Carstens's willingness to entrust substantial responsibility to women, not only in his MSPCC work but in his research and his later role as head of the Child Welfare League of America. The social work field in the early twentieth century was attracting many dynamic, capable, intense women, proportionately more of them reaching positions of authority, in the 1910s and 1920s than in later decades. Their influence on local and national child welfare policy is incontestable. [21]

What difference the presence of so many women caseworkers made is harder to appraise. The first women in these positions were diffident and insecure, as reflected, for example, in their dress:

As to the fashion of clothing which was adopted by our women agents, the whole initial procedure was interesting. As we all wore high buttoned or laced boots with black cotton stockings, there was none of the so-called giddy footwear to disturb the client on whom the agent must make a very stern and overpowering impression. To give austerity to the costume, a professional-appearing and large leather bag similar to a nurse's bag was carried all day by the women. High necked shirtwaists, a black bow in the hair at the nape of the neck, a black hat and a navy blue tailored suit was the accepted costume. To make the women appear more like policemen, a bolt of navy blue broadcloth was purchased from the Police Department and the suits were tailored from this . . .[22]

Certainly these early women agents had not rejected the male style of self-presentation to clients.

As women agents gained in confidence through their numbers, they tried less to disguise their femininity, not only in dress but also in behavior. Women caseworkers drew closer than male workers to the predominantly female agency clients. They continued to some degree the nineteenth-century tradition of making personal gifts to and doing personal services for clients. One worker loaned an adolescent a typewriter and gave her private typing lessons; another arranged for piano lessons and weekly picked up the child and took him to his teacher.[23] Despite Carstens's emphasis on training, in the Boston MSPCC office there was still no sharp boundary between clerical and caseworker women. At times the former handled complaints. Stratification among women increased, however, as professional distinctions grew, and the sense of a women's community in child-saving work diminished after the 1920s.

Women's power in the Society was increased by its expansion beyond Boston into other parts of Massachusetts. The MSPCC began opening branch offices in 1908; by 1928 it had twenty-seven districts and branches, forty-one by 1943.[24] In these regions women had often taken the organizing initiative, and it was harder to find men to do the work. In comparison to Boston, several smaller branches had more progressive orientations, challenging the more conservative attitudes of local residents. The Hampshire branch lobbied against child labor in the mills and the housework that girls were expected to do, urged medical aid for the poor, criticized xenophobia during World War I, demanded better enforcement of compulsory education, and complained that crimes against women were not being punished severely enough. The Fall River branch declared low mill wages responsible for child neglect.[25] Was this militant social consciousness related to female leadership? Without a comparative study of various SPCC offices it would be hard to know, but certainly the branches afforded women greater opportunity for autonomous decision making.

Women caseworkers gradually claimed sex abuse cases as their area of specialization. Nineteenth-century propriety had dictated that only men should come near these potentially polluting victims, and Carstens at first continued the practice of asking women, including stenographers, to leave the room when sex cases were being discussed.[26] He first assigned women to work in the "home making area," that is, advising allegedly incompetent mothers how to keep house and raise children better, but then community pressure led the MSPCC to appoint women to the sex cases.[27] Soon Katherine D. O'Rourke was promoted to direct "girl protective work." However, the feminization of that work did not create feminist policies toward girl sex victims, as we will see below. Women child-protection workers were not usually feminists at this time; feminists interested in social work were more drawn to settlement and other more militant social welfare campaigns.

The professionalization of social work similarly affected the BCSA, the second agency providing data for this survey. Moreover, the third agency, the Judge Baker Guidance Center (JBGC), a psychotherapeutic clinic founded in 1917, was professional in its origins. The Judge Baker clinic arose in response to an increasing consciousness of juvenile delinquency as a social problem. The first major reform directed at delinquency was the establishment of juvenile courts; the experts involved in these courts created a demand for the scientific psychological evaluation of delinquents, a field in which Boston became a leader. A successful juvenile court had been created in Boston in 1906, and in 1917 a diagnostic and treatment clinic was attached to it, named after its first judge, Harvey Humphrey Baker (1869–1915). Although Baker himself had direct ties to the child-saving movement,[28] the clinic was not a product of the old-style charity establishment, but rather of the new scientific psychology, its emphasis on diagnostic data collection and analysis rather than casework. Its founder and director, William Healy, exemplifed the new "scientific as opposed to merely affectional" approach to delinquency.[29] Healy intended: "To attempt *understanding of success or failure* through analysis of the causes which lie beneath is the practical scientific procedure . . ."[30] The JBGC was the most high-status, professionally, of the three agencies, as psychiatric social work was to become the elite area of social work. Its clinical staff contained the fewest women, was the most highly supervised and coordinated through regular case conferences, and the most restricted in the services it provided: primarily psychological testing and diagnoses for other agencies, less frequently ongoing psychotherapy.[31]

By the end of World War I, the child-saving establishment in Boston had changed substantially. It was more unified as a result of interagency communication and division of labor. Most agencies were staffed primarily by professionals, and shared professional assumptions about the importance of expertise and the necessity to have only trained personnel handle child welfare problems. In rhetoric all agencies agreed on the limited value of prosecution, and if their actual treatment of cases did not hold back from recourse to the courts, the rhetoric did serve to offer yet another justification for their own informal power in families. Judge Baker clinicians led the way in presenting their conclusions as expert, scientific evaluations upon which judges should base their decisions. MSPCC caseworkers already had a tradition of making recommendations to court officers; now they too sought a more "scientific" basis for these recommendations.

THE REINTERPRETATION OF CRUELTY TO CHILDREN

The transformed child protectors in turn transformed the definition of the problem they were addressing. Four closely related new approaches grew in this period: an emphasis on neglect as opposed to abuse, environmentalist explanations, a sense that the major problem was familial, and a preference for professional guidance rather than criminal prosecution as a remedy. Under Carstens's leadership in particular, child-protection work expressed in microcosm the values of Progressivism: a combination of reformist with profoundly controlling impulses.

The conception of cruelty to children with which the MSPCC began was mainly a vision of vicious and extreme mistreatment of children. The cruelty they saw was shocking, stark, and offensive to a standard they perceived as universal. Today that "cruelty" is usually categorized as child *abuse*, and is distinguished from child *neglect*, the failure of caretakers to meet certain minimal standards of child care, which comprises by far the largest share of the caseload of children's protective agencies. Carstens pioneered in the recognition of neglect, in the rhetoric of environmentalism and alarm about erosion of the family, and in the sloganeering of "prevention." Prevention became a euphemism for a social work rather than a judicial approach, a method that gave greater leeway and autonomous power to social workers and relied less on prosecution or court orders.

It would be wrong, however, to imagine that these changes arose from actual changes in the mistreatment of children. For example, there were a majority of neglect cases even in the Society's earliest records, although they were not identified as such. Consider the following list of new cases, the first fifteen from a randomly chosen monthly list, that of January 1881:[32]

1. Orphan. Abused by dissipated aunt. Sent to Marcella Street Home.
2. Poor, need looking after. Case given to . . . Sub. Agent.
3. Neglect, cause dissipation. Made papers for guardianship.
4. Drunken father—Mother wished to rescue children. 3 of them sent to Alms House to be transferred to Marcella Street.
5. Father was soldier—Mother asks aid. Gave her a letter to Associated Charities.
6. Inquiry as to disposition of an infant. Referred to Mass. Infant Asylum.
7. Acrobat. Performing at the "Howard." Interviewed Proprietor & Parents.
8. Boy ran away from home. Wrote to parents, boy would be likely to visit, no information.
9. Cruel whipping of oldest girl. Investigated. Mother promised not to whip again.
10. Lame. One of its feet turned under. Will take it to Dr. Cabot, on his return.
11. Neglected and whip'd by father, who is dissipated. Mother sober and industrious. House and children cleanly.
12. Father dissipated. Mother sick & destitute. Took case to Dr. Wheelwright, State House.
13. Father and mother separated—former having custody—alleged to be growing up under bad influences. [illegible]

14. Alleged cruelty by mother . . . is willing to place child. Gave Mother letter to Children's Friend Society.
15. Abuse by stepmother. Advised sister to find some one to become Guardian.

Only five of these cases, one third, mentioned actual whipping, cruelty, or abuse. A decade later, the preponderance of neglect cases was even greater:

1. Boy 17 disobedient and untruthful. Advised Navy or arrest as stubborn child.
2. Mother left baby 4 mos and disappeared. Gave letter to Chardon St. to take child.
3. Father does not support. Seen and cautioned.
4. Father has spells of insanity and takes child 2½ away. Advised mother to take guardianship.
5. Father away. Mother dead. Gave advice as to care of children.
6. Wife complained. Man does not support. He claims he has a bad arm and cannot work. Both intemperate.
7. Father colored. Mother white. Man not supporting. $50 rent due. Party will report further. Referred to Overseers of the Poor.
8. Stepfather blind. Two older children will provide for mother if husband can be provided for.
9. Father intemperate. Mother dead. Four older children live away from home. Younger ones not regular at school.
10. Illegitimacy. Mother and J . . . M . . . are living together. The judge discharged . . . [illegible]
11. Girl 10 kept from school by stepmother. Seen and warned.
12. Marriage forced. Parents live apart, child sick. Grandmother is caring for it.
13. Father dead. Mother intemperate. Boy 11 don't know much about her. Has been with an aunt.
14. Mother dead. Party wish to adopt girl. I made the papers.
15. Boy 10 was made to lead a dangerous bull. In correspondence.

In these 1891 cases, again all from one month, there was no assault, nor any images of the kind of cruelty that awakened the passions of child-saving and dominated MSPCC publicity. These might be vignettes of ordinary daily life among the very poor.[33]

Their new sensitivity to neglect in the early twentieth century made MSPCC agents believe that their caseload had actually changed, but they were wrong. Rather a different generation of agents was viewing their cases with new assumptions regarding the nature of child development and societal problems. For example, "Children may soon recover from a whipping, while their suffering from the various deprivations is continued for years."[34] Systemic family problems such as desertion and non-support, rather than cruelty, were seen as causal. The state was responsible for improving individual family upbringing. "The city that does not provide adequate playgrounds or wholesome recreations and amusements . . . airy, sunny and sanitary dwellings, that does not enforce its laws dealing with school attendance and child labor . . . will be constantly creating the supply which will make the stream of neglect conditions perpetual."[35] Behind these new assumptions were the complex attitudes usually characterized as Progressive: in this case, particularly the view that crime and violence were caused by the social environment, by structural problems of the society; and that state action could compensate for and correct negative environmental features.

Like many reformers of the Progressive era, child protectors adopted the rhetoric of "prevention." "This is an age of prevention," an MSPCC annual report informed its readers. "In medicine, sanitation and the conservation of natural resources, the theories of prevention are rapidly gaining precedence over the theories of cure."[36] A medical model was adopted: child neglect was "a preventable social disease."[37] However, "prevention" did not have many implications for practice. There was no marked decline in the MSPCC's reliance on prosecution in the Progressive era. Some mothers and children were sent for vacations in the country—actually to farms where they were expected to work,[38] but very few preventive policies were attempted. Preventive emphases created only slight changes in diagnoses, and did not dilute the certainty of superiority with which child-protecting agents approached their clients.[39]

The new conception of neglect was diagnosed in terms of *family* pathology. Although this pathology might be seen to be rooted in poverty, racial, or ethnic inferiority, and the degradation of urban life, the Progressive-era child protectors were mainly drawn to the opposite causal conclusion: that family weakness was at the root of larger social problems. Ameliorative proposals were always aimed at reforming families, not society. In this context, prevention meant protecting children from harm by disciplining parents. As a result, child-protection policy did not significantly move away from its law-enforcement emphasis. The substantive emphasis on family was paralleled by the casework record-keeping system. The family became the definition of the "case"—and notes on dealings with different siblings, even with different generations, were incorporated into the same case records. (By contrast, the pre-casework recording system, notations in ledger books, gave each incident or allegation of child mistreatment a separate case number.)

The diagnosis of cruelty to children as a result of family pathology was characteristic of a widespread Progressive-era alarm. Alarms about the "decline of the family" have been periodic in U.S. history since the 1840s, and they have been mainly backlashes against the increasing autonomy of women and children. The child protectors particularly blamed "individualistic tendencies" in family life, by which they meant particularly divorce and increasing numbers of non-family households and recreations.[40] The nineteenth-century feminist influence, which had offered a more positive interpretation of this "individualism," was now missing. Caseworkers condemned choices—and even necessities—that took women out of their homes. MSPCC rhetoric toward juvenile delinquency, an increasing concern in Carstens's regime, blamed mothers for inadequate supervision and family togetherness (and fathers for inadequate discipline), an analysis distinctly contrasting with, say, Jane Addams's of the breakdown of community as a result of industrial patterns of labor, housing, and social relations.

Mother-blaming was particularly prominent in this analysis of the evils of family change, and it too was a product of the new environmentalism. When child *abuse* had been emphasized, and individual vice blamed, men were the spotlighted culprits. When neglect was emphasized, and social conditions blamed, women were responsible, because they were in charge of children's care. Even in two-parent families, mothers were blamed if children were found malnourished, ill-clothed, dirty, unsupervised, or exposed to immorality. "Much work comes to us because of ignorance of the home virtues and especially because of the lack of training of the mothers . . ."[41]

Their solution to family decline was to rehabilitate families in their traditional organization and pattern, not to reform them. MSPCC pronouncements called for more discipline of children. Both nineteenth-century and Progressive child protectors wanted more gentleness and more discipline toward children, but the emphasis had shifted. The campaign against corporal punishment was no longer evident, and lack of parental control was now the major theme. ". . . with the kindlier treatment which children receive from their parents . . . there seems also to have grown up a failure to provide a substitute for that rigid discipline of former times, and the parental neglect in this particular frequently allows the child to remain an undisciplined, self-willed individual."[42] Despite the environmental analysis, child protectors continued to feature moralistic appeals to will power, as if individual determination could hold off the centrifugal forces of modern urban life. They echoed Progressive laments for the dissolution of the community controls which had effectively regulated child-raising, it was believed, in simpler, traditional, rural societies.[43]

The child-savers opposed cultural as well as familial modernism. Indeed, they were suspicious of urban life altogether and their imagery of good environments for children was rural. Despite evidence accumulated by the MSPCC's own branch offices that rural neighborhoods contained as much child mistreatment as city ones,[44] a hostility to urban child-raising conditions still pervaded, and workers continued to promote country placements for foster care. Child protectors not only continued their opposition to children's involvement in the theater or dance halls, but also to children's exposure to such entertainments. They particularly suspected movies of encouraging low morals and anti-authoritarian attitudes among children.[45]

Even in rhetoric, whenever the Progressive child protectors got specific, the limitations of their reform vision showed. Carstens's 1921 proposal for a "square deal" for each child was quite different from Franklin Roosevelt's "deal," which it prefigured as a slogan:

1. Children must be protected from physical brutalities. . . .
2. Children must be protected from early exhausting and degrading labor. . . .
3. Children should receive suitable physical care at the hands of their parents and guardians. . . .
4. Children, and particularly girls, need a vigorous agency in every community for their protection from early sex irregularities. . . .

5. Children should also be protected from immoral associations . . .
6. . . . a man should support . . . his children . . .
7. The child born out of wedlock needs an active agency in every community to safeguard his reasonable rights. . . .
8. Crippled children and others suffering from physical or mental defects must be given . . . training . . .
9. Children should be protected from constant contact with habitual gamblers, drug users and criminals.

Only two of these points (#2 and #8) might be construed as supporting an environmentalist, social welfare program for child welfare. This was a program for private parental responsibility and for community enforcement where parents failed. It emphasized protection of children from parental cruelty and immorality rather than social deprivation. It was a program the execution of which still required more law enforcement than reform.

The continuing individual rather than social, and moralistic rather than environmental, approach to family violence showed in the use of hereditarian explanations. This use of hereditarian thought was by no means unique nor was it then in any tension with the newfound environmentalism. Eugenics was prevalent in all reform thought from the late nineteenth century through the 1930s, based on pre-Mendelian genetics and assuming the inheritability of acquired characterological traits. The distinction, common by the mid-twentieth century, between environmental and biological causes of maladjustment was not current in the thinking of these nineteenth-century child-savers; as a result their identification of neglect as a widespread social problem did not require a shift in their causal analysis.[46] It remained possible for them to continue to blame the problem on hereditary "depravity," a tendency toward badness inhering in an individual, because they believed that such a trait could be carried in the blood of families, "types," and whole racial groups.

Thus the distinction between child abuse and neglect was not at first analogized to a distinction between social and personal problems, nor between environmental and intrapsychic causes. The focus on child neglect did not reduce victim-blaming. Parents, mainly mothers, who had not been accused of any active cruelty were nevertheless labeled "bad women," dissolute, dissipated, profane, lazy. The implication of poverty, unemployment, alcoholism, and ill health in neglect cases did not lead the child protectors in this period to question the innate (in modern terms: biological) inferiority of Italians, Irish, and other non-Wasp immigrants. One major transcription of that perception of inferiority was the widespread discovery, after about 1910, of feeble-mindedness among the MSPCC's client population, neglected children and neglectful parents alike.[47] Moreover, the eugenic emphasis coexisted with the call for prevention. For example, in 1915 the MSPCC organized other agencies into the League for Preventive Work, which pressed for institutionalization of the feeble-minded and prohibition of marriage among them.[48]

In some ways, nineteenth-century child welfare had been more reformist, more ready to break with the past, than that of the Progressive era. Coming to power in association with the influence of the women's-rights movement and campaigns against corporal punishment, the nineteenth-century child-savers were arrayed against patriarchy, even if they did not grasp all the implications of their demands. The Progressives, by comparison, were in a panic about the erosion of "traditional" values.

This transformation away from nineteenth-century reformism was strengthened by the development of casework. This new social work technique, focusing on helping particular people with particular and urgent problems, discouraged a community-organizing or social-reform approach such as the settlements attempted. While settlement workers looked askance at what they considered the futile efforts of child-savers, the latter believed that the content of their task required different methods. Their casework was predicated on a scientistic view that professional expertise could supply nonpolitical solutions, remedies that transcended political conflict. "Our central office is a laboratory where experiments are being constantly made under careful supervision, and our deductions being tested again and again in their practical operation. . . . In our laboratory we diagnose the causes of family disasters, and we study the remedy through years, perhaps, of experimentation. If the law is insufficient, we help to have the law modified,"[49] an MSPCC annual report said.

Carstens envisioned strengthening family authority by providing expert supervision. He thus took a positive view of state responsibility in child welfare, in contrast to the older charity-establishment commitment to protecting private agencies' jurisdiction. Like most Progressives, Carstens was unabashedly statist. He urged that the state take over child-protection work and the private societies turn to education.[50] In this line of thought he was developing to its logical conclusion the notion of children's "rights" that had underlain, however unarticulated, the entire child-saving movement from its inception: for how could such "rights" be meaningful without a custodian of them, and who but the state could claim such a legal and moral role. ". . . some day, as a result of an educated public sentiment, the community will take over the work that this Society is doing, at least, the grosser forms of neglect. This is a proper governmental function . . . The state owes a duty of protection to children that it does not owe to adults."[51]

In thus willing themselves to be pushed aside by government, MSPCC leaders were neither offering to disappear nor expressing humility. Rather, they longed for more power than their private, para-governmental status could allow. They believed that state control could give them more enforcement powers. And they probably doubted that state responsibility would deprive them of control, since their experience had taught them that their leadership, already influential in legislatures and courts, might be equally powerful in bureaucracies. Moreover, they wanted to expand their leadership: they wanted to define in positive terms the standards for right family life, not to limit themselves to the more modest and constricting task of defining deviations from it.

THE DEVELOPMENT OF SCIENTIFIC STANDARDS

In 1914 the MSPCC began a statistical annual ranking of "elements and factors" in their cases. These included:

Physical neglect
Moral neglect
Intemperance
Non-support
Delinquency
Separation of parents

Illegitimacy
Medical neglect
Semi-orphanage
Desertion
Physical cruelty
Feeble-mindedness
Belated marriage
Violation of chastity
Insanity
Divorce
Exposing children to immoral influence
Other forms of improper guardianship

The categories were non-parallel—some identified problems and others identified causes—and ambiguous. For example, six of them, or one-third, referred to "moral offenses" which might not be considered improper today. Nevertheless, the very fact that the Society felt it necessary to articulate such a list represented a new awareness among child-savers that cruelty to children was not necessarily self-evident or homogeneous. The resulting categorization exemplified what the MSPCC considered its newly scientific approach to child protection.

Simultaneous with this attempt to specify bad influences on children, MSPCC leader Carstens set out positive "home standards," virtues without which the family group was "but an empty husk of what it was intended to be." These were: self-support, without which the other virtues would not grow; decency and morality; training and education, including religious life and schooling; and discipline. Kindness, or the absence of cruelty, was not mentioned, although Carstens wrote that the Society was "unalterably opposed to such an interpretation of discipline as makes it synonymous with brutal corporal punishment."[52] The standards referred to protracted patterns of child-raising, not drunken episodes. Sobriety was not mentioned. The virtuous family was being defined here in systemic and positive terms, not merely as the absence of vice.

This emphasis on neglect as distinct from abuse allowed the child protectors to expand their jurisdiction. Beyond policing wrongful treatment of children, they were moving toward prescribing the correct treatment of children and supervising their recommendations. Such a prescription had two faces: it could trample on those with different child-raising ideas; yet simultaneously it was a step toward the adoption of minimum standards of living for children as a social goal.

In arguing for the latter, however, child protectors (and indeed, all child welfare workers) met a stubborn practical and philosophical problem: how to force parents to provide that standard of living when they simply had not the resources (economic, physical, cultural) to do so, or when they did not agree to the standard. The child protectors' definitions of neglect skirted the problem of distinguishing between willful mistreatment of children and poverty or cultural difference. For example, in the "elements and factors," they consistently ranked non-support very high—second, third, or fourth in importance; but they did not analyze the reasons for the non-support—the responsible father might have been ill, injured, unemployed, and/or angry and refusing to help. Recognizing the impossibility of "self-support" in many cases, the definition of that "home standard" picked its way delicately through the complexities of who was required to support. "A widow with a number of dependent children may with safety to herself and her children look to others for part or all of her family's support, but where there is an able-bodied man or there are grown sons and daughters who refuse to carry their responsibility . . . and the mother and dependent children are required to look outside of the family for the satisfaction of their wants, the other virtues will not grow."[53] Behind these difficulties in formulating even an ideal program of child protection lay the conviction that families ought to be economically private and independent; that families needing public support were deviant and ought to remain uncomfortable, lest they be seduced into dependency. Yet the child protectors were also convinced that the best environment for children was in private homes with parents. These contradictions in defining minimum standards for children were most visible when the only parent, or the only "good" parent, was a mother, as we shall see in the next chapter.

After the 1920s, child protection rapidly lost its influential place in the child-welfare establishment. Carstens's departure, which left the MSPCC without comparable leadership, cannot be the reason, because the tendency was national. The Depression reduced the MSPCC's financial base, but it similarly affected virtually all private child-welfare organizations. The relative decline in social work attention to family violence had deeper causes, which will be described in the following chapters. A leading cause must, however, be at least identified here: the decline of feminism. Since the mid-nineteenth century, it was the women's-rights movement that had opened the family to scrutiny of its inner power relations. Now the decline of feminist influence weakened the impulse to challenge family relations. Other progressive social movements of this period, such as union organizing and socialism, implicitly accepted women's subordination or, at best, resisted opening the topic for discussion. They treated men's familial dominance as a benign and even healthy counterweight to capitalist exploitation and effectively shut the door on the oppressions and violence which occur in family privacy. Without a feminist or other radical inquiry into the bases of domination, including "personal" varieties, even the most progressive analyses traced virtually all social ills to class inequalities, and the proposed solutions to child welfare problems were strictly economistic, calling for a bigger welfare state without questioning existing power relations.

Carstens's expectation that the government would take over the major enforcement role was wrong. Indeed, the welfare state altogether failed to grow as broad and strong as the Progressive social workers had expected and wanted it to. Child protection became a weak specialty within a relatively weak child-welfare establishment. The Depression and World War II produced a substantial increase in state programs for children and the poor. But then agencies such as the SPCCs, too specialized in their focus on child abuse and neglect to diversify into other child-welfare fields, were relatively isolated from larger social policy debates. In their continued focus on intrafamily strife they appeared conservative, avoiding what were then defined as the key issues of injustice. And indeed their analyses and policies did not successfully integrate personal violence with larger-scale cultural, social, or economic injustice, despite the high proportions of neglect correlated with deprivation and despite the rise of several new areas of concern equally rooted in social problems.

The decline in relative influence and dynamism in child protection from about 1920 to 1960 (the end of this study) probably contributed to the continuity of its premises. The fundamental conception of the problem and approach to solving it did not alter much until the sensational rediscovery of the more violent forms of child abuse in the early

1960s. In the following chapters, we will see the effect that this relative inattention had on the definition and identification of particular types of family violence. But first we must turn our attention to another aspect of the originating concern with family violence—its relation to changes in family life and family structure among those who were to become the clients.

4

SINGLE MOTHERS AND
THE CONTRADICTIONS OF
CHILD-PROTECTION POLICY

Defining the mistreatment of children always involves defining acceptable child-raising. Progressive-era child protectors, while gesturing to a concept of cruelty to children incorporating environmental neglect, were actually most influenced by a cultural alarm about family life. They feared "individualism," inadequate parental authority, and the erosion of domesticity, and believed that they were defending "traditional" family values. In fact, they were attempting to impose a modern version of the family, associated with urban, industrial society. They broadened the definition of cruelty to children in one way, including all sorts of passive neglect, and narrowed it in another way, focusing exclusively on abuse within the family and ignoring nonfamilial sources of child abuse such as child labor. They were using child protection not only "negatively," to patrol against transgressors, but also positively, to promote the kind of family structure and relationships they valued. Their demands were often beyond the reach of poor parents, even when parents shared the implicit values. Agency attempts to impose their standards sometimes worsened the problems of poor parents and children by punishing them without compensatory help. This does not mean that poor children would necessarily have been better off without SPCCs—many poor people welcomed their help—but that their contribution mixed help and oppression.

Nowhere was the tension between social work standards and values, and clients' needs and possibilities, greater than in the case of single-mother families. Single mothers were the most wretched group of clients. This was partly because they were the poorest, but also because they were in a double bind, as they struggled to meet the contradictory expectations of raising and providing for children in a society organized on the premise of male breadwinning and female domesticity. Moreover, single-mother cases put even the most sympathetic caseworkers in a double bind, as they tried to meet the contradictory expectations of helping victims and reinforcing "proper" families.

This chapter focuses on single mothers and the problems they raised for child protection, offering a case study within the case study. It concentrates on the Progressive period, approximately 1890 to 1920, because the social problem of female-headed households was defined at that time. By looking at the double binds single motherhood created both for clients and for social workers, we will be able to explore the deepest contradictions of anti-family-violence policy. Furthermore, the single-mother focus provides a bridge between the preceding section of this book, which has told the story from the perspective of the agencies, and the perspective of the family-violence victims and participants which follows. The behavior of these single mothers also demonstrates another major theme: that the clients were not merely passive recipients of help, advice, or punishment, not merely manipulated, but also manipulators, active in attempting to get help according to their own values and goals.

SINGLE MOTHERS BECOME A SOCIAL PROBLEM

During the Progressive period single mothers were consistently over-represented in family-violence cases. This was, first, for all the reasons that the poor were overrepresented: the crowdedness of housing conditions in poor urban neighborhoods, which meant less privacy; the anomie and transience of the population, which made it less likely that friends and neighbors might mediate conflicts or pacify assailants; the separation from kin, created by migration and immigration, depriving people not only of support and affection but also of the authority of those who might have intervened against family violence. Second, single mothers had their own unique stresses. No group of child-protection-agency clients was so bereft of kinship and community support as single mothers. For no other group was the contradiction between the norm of private child-raising and public guarantees of children's "rights" so difficult to negotiate. In no other group of the working class were the changes in family and interpersonal relationships caused by the transition to industrial society so great. Third, single mothers were over-represented in part *by definition*. Their very life-style was suspect. Single motherhood and child neglect were mutually and simultaneously constructed as social problems, and many of the defining indices of child neglect, such as lack of supervision, were essential to the survival of female-headed households. [1]

Single mothers' interactions with social workers were in some ways emblematic of those of all the poor, for they experienced the greatest difficulty in conforming to the new family standards being imposed. They could not conform to norms of domesticity, since they by necessity worked outside the home, or tried to; or their domesticity was suspect because they were paupers, dependent on charity or the state. Failing domesticity, they by definition failed at proper femininity and mothering. Their children might thus fail to respect them as mothers should be respected, which in the eyes of many middle-class experts involved an adoration and tenderness earned through delicacy and self-sacrificing devotion to children. Not only single mothers but all poor or employed mothers thus failed their children of both sexes: they did not provide proper role models for girls, and neglected training in domestic arts;

they deprived boys of true fathers, either by living without them or by demoting them from their entitled place as breadwinners and family heads.[2]

The norms these single mothers violated have been called bourgeois. That is a misnomer if it is taken to mean that the bourgeois class set the terms, for in the United States in the mid-nineteenth century they were being adopted by working- and middle-class people as well. Calling them bourgeois is correct if we understand that term to characterize the entire culture of a society based on wage labor, urban life, and individual rights.

Still, these standards were not easy for the immigrant poor to achieve, even had they unambiguously aspired to do so. The fathers in these families rarely earned "family wages"—that is, enough to support a wife and children on one (male) wage. And many of these poor families did *not* aspire to this new model of family life. On the contrary, they were acculturated to a family economy in which all worked and all contributed. They considered it inappropriate for children to be at leisure while adults labored. They doubted the value of educating their children, since there was no evidence that education benefited them.

Both the inability to live up to these standards, and the reluctance to accept them, were more common among single mothers than in two-parent families. In agrarian societies, single motherhood was also commonplace, as among widows, for example, but it was less visible as a social problem. Single mothers were often absorbed into relatives' family economies, if not their households, particularly if they had young children. In an economy based on farming or crafts, single mothers and their children could more easily earn a living in the same way that men did, often "inheriting" land or a craft from a husband or father. Immigration, urbanization, and wage labor made these survival strategies unavailable. Breadwinning usually took place away from home, making it more difficult for one person to earn and raise children; and jobs were scarce for women in the first place. The crowded living conditions and unstretchable budgets of the urban working class made it harder for poor relatives to take in their unfortunate sisters or daughters. City life meant that friends and relatives who could help might live many long blocks away, and immigration often separated single mothers from relatives.

In addition to material difficulties, single mothers met negative attitudes. Lacking support from kinfolk, they often sought to establish themselves as heads of households. But this put them in conflict with family and gender proprieties. Where single mothers did not meet disapproval, they met oblivion, a social denial that they existed; or they were treated as more exceptional than they actually were. The belief that men should provide for women, and that women should be taken care of by men, became so powerful that it was assumed to describe reality.

In fact, at the turn of the century, approximately 20 percent of Boston's families were female-headed.[3] There is no way to be certain that this figure represented an increase (because of limited data from earlier years), but it seems likely that it did, because new urban conditions both created more single mothers and forced more of them onto their own. Whatever the pattern of actual incidence of single motherhood, concern about it as a social problem arose sharply in this period; today's concern about female-headed households is a second wave of awareness of this social problem.

Child protectors contributed to the discovery of single motherhood as a social problem in two ways. They found and reported that single mothers were overrepresented in cases of children's mistreatment, particularly neglect. They sometimes increased the hardships of single mothers, and their anxieties, by refusing to support their independence and recommending instead the removal of their children more often than they did in two-parent cases. Describing what they observed, caseworkers concluded that parenting and breadwinning by one person alone frequently led to child neglect. Prescribing from what they believed, experts argued that single mothers were morally bad, bad for children, bad for society. The experts did not distinguish their appraisals of the difficulties of single parenting from their moralistic judgments about its undesirability or the attributes of the women who found themselves in such situations. Their logic then became circular, as their moralistic views worked against helping single mothers to be better parents.

In 1917 Cora Simpson, a twenty-five-year-old mother of girls aged three and one and a half, came to the office of the MSPCC seeking help. She was penniless, she said, because her husband had deserted her. Her case record read, in part:

Mother . . . is in great need as she has no . . . income. She has previously received temporary aid from A.C. [Associated Charities] . . . She had the father in ct. for non-support in March 1916. . . . Rosemary [age 1½] is rickety as recorded by a Doctor. . . . The chn. were about half-starved during the winter; the mother was about ready to give the chn. up but she reconsidered this when Mrs. W. offered to take her into her home to board but the expense was too great. . . . Mrs. W. felt the family would have to go. Mrs. S. . . . former landlady, reported that the chn. were really destitute when with her.

The MSPCC did not help her get any direct aid but concentrated instead on ordering her husband to pay $17.50 every two weeks. This was not forthcoming and, in September 1918, Mrs. Simpson returned with a new problem: a third baby, illegitimate.

Mother is weaning baby and thinks she might go to work and start a home for herself and chn. with aged colored woman to care for chn. during day. . . . Miss B. [the Associated Charities worker] seemed to think that mother was an immoral woman . . . does not feel like reestablishing family will try to get relatives in NY to help or may place two of chn. . . . mother go to service with the third.

This history did not end happily. No relatives would agree to board the children for free, and no agency would provide aid either for a boarding home or directly to Mrs. Simpson. In May 1919 Cora Simpson was earning $15 a week as a seamstress and was paying over half of that to two different women for the board of her girls, keeping the baby with her in the tailor shop where she worked. In July of that year she was evicted, accused by her landlord of earning "by illeg. means." She left her three children with friends and disappeared. Her children became wards of the state and were placed in an orphanage.[4]

A few years later another mother on her own, with a somewhat more complicated story, also asked for help. Letizia Guarino, Italian-born, mother of three and pregnant with a fourth, came to the Boston Family Welfare Society saying she had been deserted. Since she did not speak English well, caseworkers thought they had misunderstood when they could find no record of her husband; but they soon discovered that she had given a false name for him, nor had she been legally married at all. Her story was by no means unique among immigrants of her generation: she had been brought to the United States in 1914 by the Central Italian Bank Steamship Agency for an arranged marriage, but the ceremony turned out to be a fraud, and the "marriage license" to be Guarino's naturalization papers, for he was already married to a woman in Italy. Now his legal wife of twenty-two years had arrived and he had deserted—with the cooperation of the second Mrs. Guarino, who repeatedly lied to the social workers. The FWS worker was "unable to learn where mother secures enough money to buy food for self and chrn." Entering her North End home, the agency worker found it unsuitable for children. Mrs. Guarino's two rooms, without toilet, were

> . . . filthy. . . . Windows dirty, curtains dirty, floor and everything else in room dirty. . . . A fountain syringe was hanging on the wall and a vessel which was in unsanitary condition was sitting on the floor . . . no heat [this was February]; chrn clad in only one garment each . . . buckets of ashes, various odds and ends of food and rags littered floors of both kitchen and bedroom.

The landlady and various neighbors went into the house several times a day to check on the children (ages six, four, and three) who were left alone from 7 a.m. until after 5 while their mother worked. Mrs. Guarino claimed that she paid a babysitter $3 a week to care for the children, not knowing that her landlady had given a different story; she refused to tell where she worked. She also refused to go to the hospital for her confinement, preferring to be "attended by some woman who has looked after her when the other chn were born."

Concerned about child neglect, the FWS worker turned the case over to the MSPCC. Mrs. Guarino refused to help agency workers find her husband so that he could be forced to support her, so the MSPCC sent her to the Overseers of the Poor, Boston's municipal relief authorities; they refused to help her since she had had three illegitimate children and was therefore immoral and undeserving. The forelady at Mrs. Guarino's place of work, the Blackstone Tailor Co., helped them trace Mr. Guarino. Mrs. Guarino then admitted she had always been in contact with him, that he was paying what he could, but it was not enough (he was a pick-and-shovel laborer); she had been feeling weaker as she approached confinement and doubted how much longer she could continue her job, so had sought agency help. The MSPCC forced her to make a legal complaint against her husband, which created bitter conflict between Mr. and Mrs. Guarino, between Mrs. Guarino and the "first wife," between agencies, even between the children of Mr. Guarino's two women.[5]

Cora Simpson and Letizia Guarino were different in background, in resources, and in their survival strategies. Nevertheless, in the broad outlines of agency policy, both women had the same basic problem: they had no supporting husbands. As a result, both were neglectful mothers. Both wanted the same thing: financial aid. Whether or not they would have cared for their children adequately with this aid, they could not do so without it. In this respect they were typical of the scores of single mothers studied in this survey of case records, and it will be useful to learn more about exactly who they were.

WHO WERE THE SINGLE MOTHERS?

"Single mother" is a recent concept, and in some respects it is inferior as a category to the more specific, earlier labels: widow; deserted wife; unmarried mother; divorcée. These labels called attention to the mothers' histories, to the circumstances that brought them to single motherhood and influenced their subsequent behavior. But these labels were moralistic: the widows and deserted wives claimed sympathy; the unmarried and divorced mothers, condemnation. The labels continued a tradition of distinguishing the deserving from the undeserving poor, and in the hands of the child-savers they operated to determine how the behavior of the women would be evaluated morally and what sorts of help might be offered.

Specifically, who were these child-neglecting single mothers? The charts on page 90 suggest something about how the meaning of this term has changed.[6]

The proportion of never-married women was small, but it increased over time and may have been increasing in the nineteenth century. Young women's increasing separation from their parents made them

1. SINGLE MOTHERS IN CHILD-NEGLECT CASES, BEFORE AND AFTER 1934

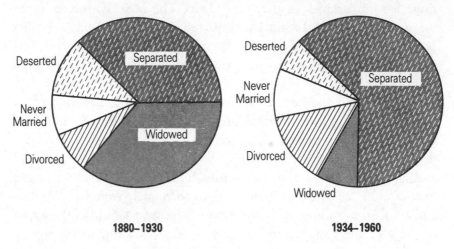

1880–1930   1934–1960

more vulnerable to sexual exploitation and less able, when pregnant, to enforce marriage on their lovers.

The most dramatic change was in the decline of the proportion of widows. Widows were not only more numerous, proportionately, in the earlier period, but they were also younger and more often had young children, because illness and industrial accidents killed relatively more young men than they do today. The proportion of never-married and divorced women changed much less (although it has increased radically since 1960).

The primary significance of divorce for these women was that it allowed legal remarriage. Many separated women reconstituted marriage-like relations and claimed to be married when visited by social workers. (However, the child-saving agencies always traced marriage registrations, a boon to researchers if hardly to clients.) Their children, nevertheless, were illegitimate. The low divorce rate explains why the majority of illegitimate children in these agency records were born to *married* women. Indeed, the category "illegitimate" tells nothing about whether the children actually had supporting or potentially supporting fathers.

The distinction between separated and deserted women was fuzzy.[7] Desertion, particularly in the earlier period, referred both to a behavior and to an interpretation of it; both to different forms of marital separation and to different experiences of it. Women's economic dependence, both their actual helplessness and their sense of helplessness when left without husbands, made some wives call themselves deserted when a modern observer might describe them as separated. After the 1940s, the case notes show the increasing substitution of the word "left," as in a woman "left by her husband," for "deserted," a change that reflected a decreasing moralism about these separations. However, in the earlier period, more separations were actually created by men's unilateral actions than is the case today. There were several reasons for this. Women's very economic dependence made it harder for them freely to agree to marital separations, and thus forced men who wanted to leave marriages to do so unilaterally. Many Americans, particularly immigrants, were separated from community and kinship networks that enforced marital commitments. Industrial wage-labor conditions as well as the space and mobility of the United States made running away from a wife easier. The same conditions also created a double bind for many poor men: unaccustomed to cyclical, structural unemployment, they often experienced it as personal failure and became depressed; at the same time, they were equally unaccustomed to the contradictory expectation that they were to be the sole support of their families, the only breadwinner, no longer part of a family that worked and earned together. Many men ran from these obligations.

Just as it was hard to distinguish between separation and desertion, there was also a permeable boundary between deserters and non-supporting husbands. Many separated couples in these case records colluded in presenting their story as one of desertion in the hopes of winning aid for the wife; many husbands dropped in and out of their families, appearing occasionally by the week, the month, or even the year.[8] Other husbands lived with their families but did not support them adequately. As a result of these definitional complexities, the boundaries between female- and male-headed families were not fixed. Many women labeled single by the agency were in *de facto* common-law marriages;[9] and other women, considered married, ran their households and supported their children alone. Furthermore, these conditions were shifting and many mothers were only temporarily single.

Single fathers appealed occasionally to family-violence agencies, but there were too few cases to allow a full comparison. There were seventeen single fathers, or 3.3 percent of cases, almost all between 1880 and 1910; there was not one single-father case after 1934. This distribution may well be inversely related to single mothers' situation: in the earlier period, single mothers were so desperately poor that fathers had to keep children lest they be abandoned, while after 1934 better conditions for single mothers meant they less often lost their children. In the earlier period also, remarriage, which enabled men to gain a woman's services in child-raising, was difficult for the poor to obtain.[10]

SINGLE MOTHERS AS CHILD NEGLECTERS

Single mothers headed one-quarter of all the households in this study.[11] This is slightly higher than the proportion of all Boston families headed by women—about one-fifth. But in neglect cases, single mothers were overrepresented at almost double their rate in family-violence cases generally.[12] This overrepresentation can be seen vividly by comparing the rate of single mothers in child abuse and child neglect.[13] Viewed from another perspective, of the single mothers known to family-violence agencies, 83 to 84 percent were in child-neglect cases.[14]

Part of the explanation for this overrepresentation lies in agency labeling policy. Caseworkers were more likely to believe the worst of single mothers, and to be quicker to apply pejorative labels to them than to other adult clients. In the nineteenth and early twentieth century, social workers were likely to believe the worst of working-class men, quick to label them depraved or degenerate. By contrast, women benefited from assumptions of good intentions, moral purity, and blameless victimization, if one can benefit from such condescension. Women, however, could lose this high evaluation at any sign of failing. Women were, for example, more than twice as likely as men to be labeled immoral by agency workers.[15] Yet men more often conducted extramarital sexual affairs. Single mothers were even more likely to be called immoral than other women. Naturally, single mothers were more likely than married women to have nonmarital sexual relationships, but, as noted above, many of these relationships were de facto marriages. Across-the-board application of standards of propriety came down harder on single mothers. In a similar pattern, women were somewhat less likely than men to be labeled intemperate,[16] but women were less likely to drink heavily. Sin-

2. SINGLE MOTHERS IN CHILD-ABUSE AND NEGLECT CASES, BY YEAR

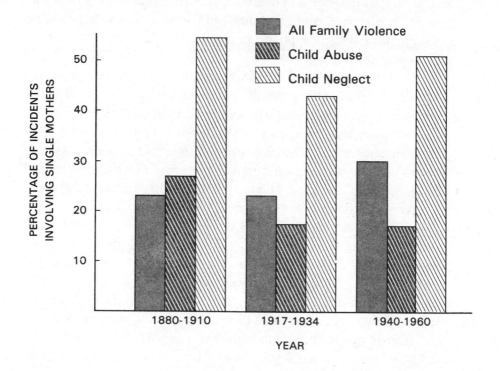

gle mothers were even more often called intemperate than other women, without evidence that they actually indulged in heavier drinking.

Furthermore, the weight of these labels was heavier for mothers than for fathers, for single mothers than for other mothers. Sexual immorality or intemperance in a mother was in itself grounds for child-neglect charges; not so in a father. When a mother had adulterous relations with a boarder, she was immoral; when a father did so with a house-keeper, *she* was the menace to the household morality.[17] In two-parent neglect cases, the mother was more likely to be considered the culpable parent. This pattern was particularly strong in "moral neglect" cases.[18] For example, even though mothers were less likely to be considered intemperate than fathers, they were more likely to be charged with child neglect due to intemperance. Of those charged with child neglect due to immorality, more than three-quarters were mothers.[19] This double standard was justified by the agencies' conviction that mothers had the greater moral influence on children. From the point of view of single mothers, however, it meant that they had to take on the responsibilities of men, with neither the privileges of men nor the leeway granted to male peccadillos.

The best measurement of the MSPCC's attitudes toward single mothers was in its actions. For example, police were more often involved in complaints against single mothers than two-parent families.[20] The most important index was the agency's most drastic action—removing children from their parents. In cases of equal severity, as defined by the agencies, children were removed from 75 percent of single-mother homes and 54 percent of two-parent homes, up to 1930.[21] Furthermore, children were even more likely to be taken against the wishes of a single mother than of two parents. In 18 percent of all cases, parents asked for the removal of children from their household, usually seeking temporary placements during illness, until a job could be found, in order to get a rest, or until the children were old enough for school or work. Despite their hardships, single mothers were less likely to want the removal of their children: only 15 percent of child-removal requests came from single mothers, although they comprised 28 percent of all cases.[22] By contrast, where a male-headed family was neglectful, neglect charges were less likely to be brought. Rather, the agency's strategy was more often to get the father arrested, e.g., for drunkenness or non-support, with a short or suspended sentence, or alternatively to issue warnings; both strategies were intended to pressure the parents into providing better care for their children.[23]

Children without fathers also appeared[24] more likely to be "stolen" (as the clients saw it) without due process. In 1893 a boy was arrested for street fighting in front of the shoe factory where he worked. Within a half hour, he was convicted of being a "common railer and brawler," and given an indeterminate sentence; his mother learned nothing of this until he was imprisoned, but got him freed on a pardon, with the support of her priest and the chairman of her board of selectmen. (The trial magistrate admitted that he had not informed the boy of his rights.)[25]

Only one variable other than single motherhood was a better predictor of child removal: poverty. But this was just another aspect of the same phenomenon, for single mothers were poorer than other parents. From 1880 to 1920, 44 percent of single mothers were in economic deprivation as compared to 26 percent of two-parent families.[26] Only 10 percent of single-mother families reached the economic level defined as competence, as compared to 31 percent of two-parent families. Of course, most of the MSPCC's clients were poor. The Society was sensitive to allegations that it kidnapped poor people's children, and its stated policy was that it never removed children from their homes for poverty alone. But poverty was never alone. The characteristic signs of child neglect in this period—dirty clothing, soiled linen, lice and worms, crowded sleeping conditions, lack of attention and supervision, untreated infections and running sores, rickets and other malformations, truancy, malnutrition, overwork—were often the direct results of poverty.

The problems of single mothers in child neglect cases defy any clear distinction between agency bias and objective reality. The "bias" of social workers against single mothers might, for example, be described as prediction based on past experience. Furthermore, neither the social workers nor contemporary researchers studying the case records could easily distinguish children's deprivations caused by poverty from those caused by parental indifference or hostility: because parental indifference and hostility were among the most common products of poverty, and because parents' depression was implicated both as cause and effect of poverty. Further, the social workers' very standards of what constituted deprivation, and the entire notion of children's rights to a certain standard of treatment, were "biased," the product of specific class and cultural experience.

PARENTING AND EARNING ALONE

Single mothers won a major victory in the United States in the nineteenth century: the establishment of legal preference for mothers in child custody cases. However, the preference remained an abstraction for most single mothers, since to keep their children they had to be able to feed and care for them. Women won custody rights just as children lost their earning power and became an economic burden.[27] Until approximately 1910, there was no public or private program of aid to single mothers; at best, women in that situation could beg small and irregular donations from private "provident associations" or public relief officials.

Between 1910 and the late 1930s, when federal Aid to Dependent Children went into effect, a small proportion of "deserving" white single mothers could get "pensions" in varying but usually mean amounts from state programs. Many single mothers lost their children to institutions because they could not support them.[28]

Surprisingly few of the mothers in these case records were able to live in other family households. From 1880 to 1930, only 22 percent shared a household with other relatives, and in some of these situations the others were additional dependents on the single mother. After 1930, 37.5 percent did so. (Contrary to the view that non-nuclear households were a traditional and declining form, they were least common in the earliest years of this study, because the urban poor were so poor, so transient, and lived in such cramped apartments.) But an average of 69 percent of single mothers were dependent on their own earnings for their and their children's survival. They were thus the group most damaged by the general difficulties for women in earning a living and caring for children.

First, jobs were scarce and wages low. Boston was not a mill town hungry for women's and children's labor power. There was some light-industry factory work—candy-making, for example—and sweated garment work. (Clerical work had not yet expanded and was still primarily male.) The most common occupation was, of course, domestic service. But for all these jobs young unmarried women were preferred. The scarcity of employment, moreover, depressed female wages for jobs other than domestic service even lower than in more industrial cities.[29]

A second problem facing working mothers was the lack of child care. Day nurseries were rare. It is not surprising that inadequate supervision of children was cited in 18 percent of MSPCC cases overall but in 43 percent of single-mother cases. Lack of child care resources was the reason that mothers, unlike childless women, preferred home work to outside jobs. They took in boarders, or washing, and did babysitting for others. Limiting the availability and the income of such work was the fact that the poor could afford very little for these services, while the rich preferred to have them done in their own homes. Thus few women successfully earned a living in this way. Better pay could be gotten from manufacturing piece work, usually hand sewing or hand assembly in the garment or millinery industries, but the working conditions were worse. Piece rates were low and women worked twelve, fourteen and sixteen hours a day, neglected housekeeping and child-care, and put young children to work with them in order to make a living wage. At that, few women managed on this basis. A 1913 study, averaging nine cities including Boston, showed that only 28 percent of widows lived on home work. In comparison to work outside the home, home work produced lower earnings, longer hours, more stress, and more damage to health.[30]

Other kinds of home work led to "immorality." Taking in boarders was frowned upon by the MSPCC and most agencies as a source of immoral influences,[31] although boarders' payments were vital to a large proportion of households. In Boston the boarding clientele was predominantly male, and many mothers in the MSPCC cases did indeed appear to be having sexual relationships with boarders—such allegations were made against 41 percent of single mothers—which offense automatically made them "unfit" mothers.[32] These "star boarders," as landladies' lovers were called, also figured importantly in MSPCC cases as abusers of children, another danger facing the mothers. Single mothers with abusive lovers or boarders faced a dilemma similar to that of wives with abusive husbands: their desire to keep their children and need for help in supporting them made them less able to protect themselves and their children from molestation or abuse.

Some of the most lucrative home work was illegal—notably prostitution and bootlegging, both common among single mothers; even before Prohibition many women manufactured and sold home brew. Both were virtually automatic grounds for child neglect charges. In several MSPCC cases women turned parts of their flats into informal bars or speakeasies.[33] In other cases already crowded families gave up space to small-scale commercial uses in return for help with the rent.[34]

In seeking outside jobs, the presence of relatives or friends to care for children was crucial to success. A deserted wife or a widow might manage if her parents or a sister would take her and her family in, and others might even manage to maintain their own household with babysitting help. But such solutions were usually unstable. Many mothers resented the indignity of becoming a dependent again, subject to another head of household; babysitters, even relatives, were themselves often unreliable and neglectful.

Most domestic servants were required to live in, and at best, in some cases, might be allowed to bring a nursing baby. Older children would have to be placed elsewhere. Employers sometimes "helped" their maids by applying to a charity for placement of older babies.[35] In these cases the mother's choice was to sign away her child or to lose her job. For such reasons mothers seized the opportunity to do non-resident house cleaning, or "day work," as it was called. One common form of day work was laundry. Several MSPCC cases offered the irony of filthy children in unwashed bedding whose mothers washed, bleached, and ironed for others. Day housecleaning work gradually increased in this period, not in private homes, but in office buildings. This "day work," was usually night work. (In a 1913 study, 48 percent of widows worked at night.)[36] Since arranging child care then was even harder than in the day, many children were left unattended, unless the mother also had boarders, lodgers, or relatives in her home. The MSPCC cases contain numerous examples of mothers trying to hide the fact that they worked nights so as not to have to answer questions about what they did with the children. Night cleaning furthermore deprived mothers of sleep and often meant that they worked around the clock.

In these circumstances mothers often leaned on their children to bring in income. This expectation continued traditional family economy patterns for many clients, but in their new urban situation, child labor was defined as neglect. Its frequency, nevertheless, was evidenced by the important role of the truant officer in referrals to the MSPCC. Other neglected children did illegal peddling or stealing (as for example from the coal scuttles of rich houses or railroad yards); these children's mothers were often even more "neglectful" than the authorities imagined, not only failing to prevent such mischief, but encouraging it.

In trying to provide adequate parenting, single mothers were often caught in a series of double binds. Their very attempts to nurture children could produce neglect. Doing home work led to overworking children, depriving them of attention and supervision, and overcrowding the apartment, with the likelihood of failing to provide adequately despite these hardships. Going out to work might require leaving children alone and vulnerable, or placing them with unloving and irresponsible baby-sitters. Looking for a male breadwinner might lead to immoral relations. Trying to protect children from the abuse of others might deprive the family of a breadwinner. Agency policies made it risky for single mothers

SINGLE MOTHERS

A single mother and her children, dressed for earning by playing in the streets, probably 1880s. As with many other pictures used by the MSPCC, this was probably posed and photographed in a studio. *(Courtesy of MSPCC, Boston.)*

The six children of a widow, allegedly a drunkard, found occupying one bed in a filthy and unheated house, the youngest with its foot frozen, February 14, 1905. The children, ages 2 through 11, are posed in a studio, or possibly at the MSPCC Temporary Home, cleaned and dressed up according to the tastes of the MSPCC matrons. *(Courtesy of MSPCC, Boston.)*

A mother with her bruised baby. This photo may have been taken in her own home. Undated. *(Courtesy of MSPCC, Boston.)*

A single mother and her children, 1910, studio portrait. Not all single mothers were wretched. *(Courtesy of MSPCC, Boston.)*

to be honest, and they attempted to conceal their jobs, their babysitters, their lovers, their pregnancies, even their illnesses for fear of losing their children.[37]

CHILD PROTECTORS CONSTRUCT A FAMILY POLICY

The notion of single mothering that had influenced court decisions for maternal custody assumed prosperous women who could devote full time to mothering because they were supported by others. Despite the fact that their clientele was not in that economic position, child protectors' attitudes toward single mothering made the same assumptions. Indeed, the whole nineteenth-century view, shared by feminists and anti-feminists, that mothering, as distinct from fathering, was essential for children's nurture, was a class attitude.[38] In this view, mothering appeared not as work but as "natural," a secondary-sex characteristic. If it was not done well, according to the standards of the child protectors, that inadequacy was not a sign of obstacles, resistance, or inadequate resources, but of character flaw. Progressive environmentalist rhetoric failed to weaken the intensely moralistic condemnation of bad mothering.

These were the underlying attitudes governing the construction of a child welfare policy toward single mothers in the Progressive era. This policy was debated throughout the profession, but agreement was achieved on how to deal with four main problems connected with single mothers—desertion, illegitimacy, women's employment, and mothers' pensions. On each issue the influence of family-violence workers was significant. In confronting each issue, social workers aimed to censor immorality, to protect children, and to encourage the construction of proper families. Many aspects of these policies have been criticized as oppressive forms of social control; in relation to women, they have been viewed as steps in the replacement of the old family patriarchy by a new state patriarchy.[39] This critique is at best too simple. In practice, the policies represented compromises with the needs and demands of assertive and recalcitrant clients. Moreover, the caseworkers often experienced contradictions in their own goals and methods, and this was particularly the case when female-headed households were an option.

Desertion was perceived as an escalating and urgent social problem by the turn of the century and had been incorporated into the MSPCC program as *ipso facto* a major form of cruelty to children.[40] That desertion became a social problem was equally a result of deserted wives' vociferous complaints and requests for help, as indicated by their use of desertion bureaus and child welfare agencies.

The child protectors worried about desertion not only from the perspective of children's deprivations but also as a violation of the proper roles of men and women. Desertion was a result of a father's weak and cowardly evasion of masculine responsibility.[41] Therefore, aid to wives and children of deserters had to meet the criterion that it did not further undermine the father's role as breadwinner, his duty to support, and his authority over his family. The Society's moralistic and punitive attitude toward deserters often required accepting, as a consequence, that the deserter's wife might have to suffer also. As Mary Richmond, influential social-work spokesperson, argued, "It is absurd to go into a home and do for it what the legal and recognized head . . . has deliberately shirked . . . and then to suppose . . . that you have not interfered between man and wife."[42] Clearly, she was arguing against the demands of deserted wives and mothers for relief. Even when blaming men unilaterally for their cowardly desertion, social workers resisted wives' requests for support: the most anti-male rhetoric, such as that of Ada Eliot, who considered the problem to result from men's "brute-like" nature, accompanied arguments *against* aid to homes without men.[43]

Whatever the wishes of single mothers, agencies attempted to force deserters to pay. In pursuing this policy, agencies expanded their control over their clients. For example, although the MSPCC had declined to accept jurisdiction for arranging relief, it took responsibility for obtaining court orders requiring deserted or non-supporting fathers to make support payments. Then, adding yet a new responsibility, the MSPCC arranged for fathers to turn over payments to the Society, which it then doled out to the mother, supervising her expenditures in the process.[44] The MSPCC became a virtual collection agency as its staff billed and dunned and tried to extradite deserters. It was influential in lobbying for legislation to increase the criminal penalties for non-support and desertion.[45] Since many deserters had not disappeared but were merely non-supporters, agency policies sometimes increased an irresponsible husband's control over his family. For example, one estranged husband would make his payment to the MSPCC, then force his wife to return the money to him so that he could circulate it back through the agency for his next payment.[46] Numerous estranged husbands offered to support if their wives would let them return to the household, although their wives had been requesting MSPCC aid precisely to free themselves of abusive husbands.[47]

Since the definition of desertion was elusive, and some deserted wives colluded with their husbands, hid their whereabouts, and/or let them return to the household periodically,[48] it was difficult to distinguish desertion, non-support, and unemployment. Agency workers often did their casework meticulously, examining the whole individual picture for evidence of motives, possibility of reform, and resources. Nevertheless, the overall effect of MSPCC policy was to punish all families without wage-earning men indiscriminately. Thus in a 1920 case a one-legged father, periodically unemployed, had broken his wooden leg and lost his job again. The social worker knew this but did not call on the family because "it is her intention to try and develop initiative in the family."[49] In a 1912 neglect case, children had been out begging and the agency threatened to remove them if they did not stop; the mother wanted to leave her good-for-nothing husband if there was a way she could do so without losing her children; but the agency recommended against aid to the family because it would encourage the father's laziness.[50] Agencies often urged wives to prosecute husbands for non-support. Their success would bring a jail sentence, thus punishing the culprit and, it was argued, setting a deterrent example; but it also deprived the family of support. Some mothers lost their children because a jail sentence intended to reform the family took the father away.[51] Furthermore, prosecutions required wives to testify against their husbands, a procedure which could weaken the chances for future reconciliation, and which many wives refused to do out of fear and/or ambivalence.[52]

Another occasion demonstrating distrust of female-headed families, and conflicts between clients and social workers, was illegitimacy. In the wisdom of the profession in the early twentieth century, if the illegitimate mother kept her child, she ran a risk of failing to provide good mothering because of her immorality. But if she were helped to get rid of her child, was not her immoral behavior being rewarded? Still, to force an unwilling girl to keep her child was not necessarily in the best interests of the child, and the child-savers believed that children ought not to be punished for the circumstances of their conception. Furthermore, most charity workers, even if they believed in punishment for sexual immorality, also perceived the unwed mother as herself a child in need of help and wanted to give girls-gone-wrong a chance to reclaim an honorable life.[53]

Starting in the 1890s, the MSPCC and other progressive agencies came to believe that, even without marriage, mother and child ought to be kept together.[54] This belief represented a victory for the sentimental cult of motherhood; charity workers believed that the experience of childbirth and the opportunity to be with the infant would create love and a sense of responsibility in the mother, and that this maternalism could in itself help to reform wayward girls.[55] Tolerance for keeping mother and child together also represented the influence of the illegitimate mothers' own demands, and sometimes a capitulation to immigrant patterns of extended family child-raising. Many illegitimate mothers came to the MSPCC and the BCSA asking for relief, for temporary placements with their babies, mostly as domestics, or for temporary placement for their babies while they established their own homes.

Agency responses were divided and confused. The sentimental outlook rested on a view of these mothers as girls, and in the MSPCC cases they were rarely that: most were previously married women, and many were currently living in marriage-like relations. Thus the traditional first course of action—to arrange a marriage—was inappropriate; even if the mothers were girls, they would not usually have been at the agency had a marriage been possible.[56] Agency and client were likely to agree on the desirability of mobilizing relatives to take in mother and child, but these arrangements were not common, because the illegitimate mother had other children or because the relatives had poor and crowded households. A 1920 Boston survey showed that only 20 percent of illegitimate mothers aided by agencies were able to live with their parents, and of those only half did so with their child.[57] Another study showed that mother and child usually lived with her parents for a short time only.[58] Extended-family solutions no longer resolved the long-range problems of single motherhood.

Placements in service positions were also temporary, limited to the child's infancy. Even when the mother had initially agreed to this strategy, her acquiescence frequently evaporated as she experienced the lack of personal freedom characteristic of live-in domestic service.[59]

Even when resident in other households, single mothers often needed and wanted to earn. Their major obstacles to doing so were structural: lack of jobs with decent wages and lack of day care for children. But these obstacles were heightened by social workers, who were critical of women's employment and of the nonmaternal child care it usually required. Many child welfare workers believed there was no point in keeping mother and children together if someone else had to take care of the children. In practice MSPCC policy was all or nothing: agents arranged placements in institutions or foster homes, but opposed day nurseries or babysitters. (Day nurseries were extremely uncommon in any case: there were six recorded by the census in the whole United States in 1880, 166 in 1904, and those that existed were distrusted by working mothers.)[60] Several MSPCC workers simply ordered women to stay home and look after their children, and women sometimes tried to hide their employment from agency visitors.[61]

Even social workers who wanted single mothers to become self-supporting expected women to remain economically dependent when living with husbands. Whenever a husband was in the home, no matter how poor, disabled, or irresponsible, charity workers were hostile to wives taking employment. One MSPCC record read:

> Mother . . . desiring to obtain elderly woman to come into her home and care for the chn as mo has to go out and do day work; sometimes earns as much as $18 a week. Fa has not had a steady position for quite a period of time, but is doing the best he can, and mo has no fault to find. . . . [I] made it quite evident to mo that the desirable thing was for her to stay at home and care for the chn and have fa obtain a steady position.[62]

The opposition to mothers' employment was so ideological and dogmatic it was often very costly to mothers and children. In 1943 one mother, separated from an abusive husband, survived with the makeshift child-care arrangements typical of many "neglectful" single mothers: she worked at a café from 4 p.m. to 3 a.m., a babysitter stayed with her three children until 11 p.m., then they were left alone until she returned from work. The MSPCC worker did not offer to help her find babysitting help or another job, but reminded her that " 'Mo's place is at home.' "

The woman's only solution was to board the children for a year, in the hopes of finding better work and money to do what the caseworker called "reestablish a home." (The implication was that a working mother's house was not a home.)[63]

Social workers believed that economic contributions from wives would weaken a man's sense of his reponsibility. Women who were wage earners before marriage tended to be "unfit for married life: [a woman] from the very fact of being economically independent may be led to assert her independence in ways which will in themselves be provocative of household friction."[64] Joanna Colcord, a casework expert, wrote in 1919: "Many a non-supporter got his first impulse in that direction when his wife became a wage-earner in some domestic crisis." Her advice to the wives of non-supporting husbands: " 'If your husband comes home crying, and says he can't find any work, sit down . . . and cry until he does.' "[65]

By the early twentieth century, many reformers had grasped what the single mothers themselves knew: that some form of public aid was necessary if the children of the poor were to be kept alive and at a minimal standard of health. The first such programs, called mothers' or widows' pensions, were state-funded welfare provisions for single mothers. There was substantial opposition to mothers' pensions from the social-work establishment, particularly from child-protection agencies, although the arguments against them tended to disguise their gender and family implications. The social-work establishment debated the merits of public vs. private responsibility for charity, and "outdoor" vs. "indoor relief" (the traditional British terms for giving aid to people in their own homes vs. institutionalization), as deterrents to pauperism.[66] (By contrast, gender issues were explicit in contemporaneous arguments about protective legislation.)

A closer look at the debate, and at the practice of agencies like the MSPCC, reveals that anxiety about gender relations was important in the opposition to mothers' pensions. C. C. Carstens, general agent of the MSPCC and at this time the most influential man in the United States child-saving movement, was an opponent, and family-centered concerns were primary for him: his purpose was to abolish the class of single mothers, not establish it. "The enthusiast in favor of widows' pensions . . . is likely to hold lightly the ties of kinship."[67] This statement only makes sense if Carstens's implicit definition of kinship, one shared by many opponents, was marriage, since the very goal of mothers' pensions was to preserve filial ties. When Mary Wilcox Glenn argued that the pensions would "lessen the family's sense of responsibility for its own," by "family" she meant fathers.[68] Similarly ideological was Edward Devine's definition of "family" when he argued, "The breaking up of a family by an outside agency is justified only when it is merely the outward expression of a destruction which has already taken place . . . separation of husband and wife . . ."[69] Only a definition of family which made it essentially a married couple could produce his conclusion, that mothers' pensions were "an insidious attack upon the family, inimical to the welfare of children . . ."[70] Devine excluded not only single-mother households, but also extended kin networks, from his definition of family.

Mothers' pensions caught on widely and quickly, despite substantial social-work opposition, not only because they made sense for children, but also because agency clients were stubbornly demanding them. Thirty-four percent of single-mother cases were brought to the MSPCC by the mothers themselves asking for help. Their most common requests were for "separation and maintenance" orders, legal recognition as heads of family, child support payments from fathers, or public relief.

These requests reveal something crucial about the single-mother "problem:" most of the women did not want husbands. This is not to say that they had sought out single motherhood; most of them had been married. Rather, they often appeared embittered and exhausted from the efforts of holding together a two-parent family and now preferred living alone with their children. Knowing the MSPCC's influence in the courts, they tried to get the agency's support for their independence. Some mothers used subterfuge. One woman in 1880 asked the Society for $12 to go with her three children to their maternal aunt in Cape Breton; this was just the kind of solution the agency approved and the worker gave her the money. She left, but instead went to another relative in Cohasset, where she temporarily left her children; three months later she returned to the MSPCC, having set up her own household, asking support for her children. The agent suggested she take her husband to court for non-support but she refused: he was abusive and she did not want him to be able to find her. She badgered the agency for help again and again and ultimately won the MSPCC's recognition and support of her household.[71] The caseworkers often felt used, since the mothers could not confess their real desires in this regard. "Agt. felt that she definitely does use this agency as a means of getting a separation . . . with the hopes that we would help her to get another apartment."[72]

Theoretically women were free to leave their husbands, but the common denominator among virtually all female agency clients was the struggle to keep their children. As reported above, single mothers were even less likely than other parents to ask for the placing out of their children. Mothers whom the child-savers viewed as indifferent to, even hateful toward, their children would exhibit unheard-of rage, tenacity, wiliness, and force in the face of threats to remove those children. In Somerville in 1917, the police found seven children, ages one through nine, nearly naked, in a house without heat, crying for food, with a crippled mother and her sister, who supported them all by working out as a domestic. When the police took the children, the mother struck at them, threw dishes, smashed chairs, then seized a razor and threatened suicide.[73] Distinctions between responsible and irresponsible mothers did not necessarily corrrespond to degree of attachment. Also in 1917, a widowed mother of six, living "in sin" with a man and a woman friend, lost her children to the Home for Destitute Catholic Children. She went to court repeatedly attempting to get her children back, until her death in 1923; when the children were placed out, she became a resourceful private detective trying to find their location. Yet this mother was also an alcoholic who continued to have illegitimate children (one in 1917, one in 1918, one in 1921) that she could not support. In 1919 she won the return of one child, but lost him again in 1920.[74] The point, it should be obvious by now, is not that social workers persecuted innocent mothers. The social workers were often right in their suspicion of mothers' incompetence. The point is that even incompetent mothers wanted to be with their children.

As a way of summarizing the origin and impact of these contradictory policies on child-saving practice, let us return to the story of Mrs. Guarino. She had her own agenda. Choosing not to fight to keep her "husband," she wanted help in supporting her children, estimating, no doubt correctly, that he would never be able to support two families. Why were the agencies not willing to help on her terms? Their objections to her goals were not personal—there were at this time no accusations against her virtue—but social; the objections were not about her past but about her future. By definition, the social workers saw no possibility of stable family life for her without a husband. The MSPCC placed out her children until their father hired an Italian attorney and won them back for her. (Note that in this case the three Guarino parents appeared able to agree, making this potentially an easier case to handle than many others in which ex-spouses were embittered and angry. Unfortunately, the MSPCC's hostility to these irregular relations among the parents was exacerbated when Mrs. Guarino became pregnant again in 1926, apparently by her ex-"husband," who could not give her up.)

Granted, Mrs. Guarino's form of single motherhood was complicated; social workers disliked bigamy, out-of-wedlock relationships, and the Guarinos' subterfuge in dealing with them. Yet "blameless" single mothers did not necessarily fare better. Discrimination against single mothers resulted simultaneously from observation of their actual difficulties, from ideological anxieties about pauperization, from fear of destabilizing the proper sexual division—and from the single mothers' own goals and demands. Bias against single mothers was a result not of malevolence but of fear and concern for children. Nevertheless, the result was a contradiction: child-saving agencies were not always doing that which would best secure the welfare of neglected children. For example, despite insistence on the vital importance of mothering, child-savers frequently recommended the institutionalization of children rather than granting aid to their mothers. In 1900 the majority of children in institutions were only "half-orphans."[75] Between 1880 and 1920, 74 percent of the neglected children of single mothers were taken from those mothers by the MSPCC. Even assuming that a substantial proportion of these mothers would have remained permanently incompetent parents, many others were affected primarily by remediable problems such as poverty and overwork. Furthermore, mothers would have had to be extremely abusive to have done worse by their children than the usual institutions.[76]

At the same time, the rise of the child-protective movement, in bringing out these contradictions, stimulated reform. Despite their intentions, child-savers had created agencies to which single mothers came pleading their desires and arguing their own proposals. One result of that pressure, both from the steady, stubborn, manipulative clients and from desperate, hysterical clients, both from "good" mothers and from "bad," was the rapid change of social-work opinion to favor mothers' pensions by 1920. In this way the SPCCs, despite their ideological and culturally specific notions of good parenting, may in the long run have been beneficial even to parents of whom they disapproved.

SINGLE MOTHERS IN RECENT DECADES

In the last few decades it has finally become clear to many that single motherhood is not a "deviant" phenomenon. To study it is not to study a minority group with a special problem. Today in the United States single motherhood is more like a majority event. Fifty percent of children born in the late 1970s and early 1980s will live in single-mother households, and not just briefly: these households endure an average of five to six years for divorced mothers, eight to twelve years for never-married mothers. Fifty percent of women today will divorce, and although the remarriage rates are high, 50 percent of second marriages will again end in divorce.[77]

This study has cast some doubt on the widespread assumption that single motherhood is a recent phenomenon. But the experience of being a single mother, and its meanings, have changed. Paradoxically, in some ways the turn-of-the-century assumption that single motherhood was always a misfortune and never a choice made that condition easier. There was pity for the widow and the deserted wife, and a sense of dignity attached to a mother struggling alone with children which has diminished since the mid-twentieth century. On the other hand, single motherhood was by definition on the edge of immorality in the nineteenth century, and preserving respectability in that situation required angelic behavior and luck.

Most changed about single motherhood in the last half century is its increasing occurrence today among middle-class, prosperous women, mainly because of divorce. Poverty in single-parent households was greater and more universal in the nineteenth and early twentieth centuries. It is difficult to measure this in terms of dollars, because we lack the data for the earlier years, but one good index is the abandonment of children. (Abandonment was distinct from "desertion," a term often applied to any mother who moved away from her children, even if she left them with their father or, more typically, their grandparents.) The abandonment confronted by child-saving agencies usually took the form of parents' placing their children in boarding homes and then absconding. When the boarding fees had been unpaid for a length of time, boarding-home operators would contact the police or charitable agencies for help. There was a sharp decline in abandonment in the second half of this study. Another indicator of improving conditions is that more single mothers got help from relatives in the second half of this period, despite the declining sense of financial responsibility among extended family members. Before 1934, 37.5 percent of single mothers got such support, 61.5 percent later—evidence that the relatives were living better themselves and had a bit extra to share.[78]

Mothers' aid programs were vital to these improving conditions. Publically funded support for single mothers was arguably more effective against family violence, child neglect, and wife-beating above all, than any other policy. These programs—both state mothers' pensions begun between 1910 and 1920 and the federally funded Aid to Dependent Children, part of the Social Security Act of 1935—have been discriminatory and humiliating, and kept recipients at grinding levels of poverty. Moreover, ADC continued the assumption that mothers should not be employed and functioned to weaken women's bargaining position in the labor force. Nevertheless, ADC represented a governmental commitment to supporting children with their mothers, and thus encouraged in mothers a sense of entitlement. They helped women avoid the Hobson's choice of either supporting or keeping their children. ADC was also consequential for married as well as single mothers. By creating the possibility that women could *leave* marriages, it offered them more power *within* marriage to demand respectful treatment—to refuse to accept abuse of themselves or their children.

Nevertheless, ADC did not reduce the proportion of single mothers in family-violence cases. The absolute improvements for single mothers were not relative ones, and over the century "male-headed" households gained more than "female-headed" ones. There were desperate single mothers in the recent as in the older cases. The incidence of alcoholism declined, but suicide attempts increased. For example, in 1934, faced with a mortgage foreclosure on her house, her eldest son having reported her for child neglect to their priest, a single mother took poison, and was barely saved after a two-week hospitalization.[79] The more recent cases contained a higher proportion of women hospitalized for mental illness, probably not because more of them were deranged but rather because medical solutions to such mental problems were more available.

As economic conditions improved, new difficulties developed. These case records suggest that the support offered by extended family networks has been consistently overrated, at least among the poor. For single mothers, conflicts with kinfolk were common, although their patterns changed over time. For example, single mothers in the first half of this study frequently complained about their parents-in-law. In-laws in turn complained to child-saving agencies about their sons' ex-wives, and sometimes tried to get custody of the children.[80] In one case a mother with two former husbands had both sets of parents-in-law making accusations against her.[81] In several cases women had been living in the same dwellings with their in-laws while married; once separated or widowed, they lacked any mediator between themselves and hostile parents-in-law. By contrast, in-law problems seemed to diminish later in the twentieth century. Marital separations were more common, and there was less condemnation of separated women. Moreover, those single mothers who gained in economic and emotional independence became thereby less vulnerable to in-laws' opinions and interventions. On the other hand, modern single mothers experienced more difficulties with their own parents. After 1930 single mothers relied on relatives more often for support and a place to live, but minded it more. Mothers frequently moved in and out of their parents' houses, trying independence and not being able to afford it, trying to live with their parents and not being able to stand that.[82] Several mothers felt dominated by their mothers.[83] Others experienced hostility from and to their mothers.[84] Moreover, evidence of mutual support between siblings is almost completely lacking after World War II. As the nuclear family norm came to define not only the household but also the limits of child care and financial responsibility, "horizontal" (sibling) obligations were shed before "vertical" (filial) ones. The remaining vertical obligations were not mutual: parents took responsibility for children as children did not do for their parents.

"Blended families," as they are being called today, did not decline in number. Women continued to have children by several fathers and to couple with men who already had children. (The presence of so few single fathers in the recent decades is matched by the presence in the case records of many remarriages, producing stepmothers to take on the child-raising work.) These new complex households did not always smooth child-raising tasks. Illegitimate children often created difficulties between their' mothers and new stepfathers, sometimes because they symbolized guilt for their mothers.[85] Stepchildren were similarly the objects of marital tension.[86] Several researchers have argued that stepchildren are more vulnerable to physical and sexual abuse, an issue to be taken up in chapters 6 and 7. Here I am interested in the role of stepchildren in child neglect by single mothers. The child-raising burdens of the single mother were often increased, rather than helped, by her marriage or remarriage. Illegitimate children or stepchildren were more likely to be experienced by husbands as competitors for their wives' attention; women were more likely to sacrifice the interests of illegitimate children, or children from previous marriages, in order to protect a badly needed new relationship. For every case of a "wicked stepmother," abusing her husband's children,[87] there was a case of a rejecting natural mother, apparently choosing husband over children.[88] Mothers' neglect of their own daughters was often implicated in incest cases (see chapter 7). One such case, in 1940, involved a former single mother, now in a couple with three young children of their own and the wife's thirteen-year-old girl; she was illegitimate, and the mother was so ashamed of that fact that she hid it from everyone, including daughter and husband, and kept a framed picture of an alleged father in the living room. The daughter felt herself made into a Cinderella by her own mother: kept from school to do housework, unloved and never complimented, and, above all, unprotected against her stepfather's sexual advances.[89]

Another indicator of the continuing difficulties of single mothers was that they had to rely on their older children more than did mothers in two-parent families. Conflicts between parents and agency workers about the tasks children should do and about compulsory schooling had been common in the early years of child-saving, as we have seen. In the later years, single mothers were more likely to violate norms about child labor. In 1940 an immigrant mother was working in a tavern at night and keeping her twelve-year-old daughter out of school to care for a two-year-old boy so the mother could sleep.[90] Another mother got wartime factory work, but also at night, and used her teenage daughter the same way.[91] A mother with daytime work needed her seven-year-old to care for two younger children after their nursery school.[92] Yet another relied on her teenage girls to help her run rooming houses.[93] These cases provide clues to many less visible hardships for single mothers, such as the difficulty of even temporary absences from their children.

At the same time single mothers continued to face contradictory expectations and policies about women's employment. Not working outside the home meant, for most single mothers: poverty, the hassles and humiliation of collecting aid, deprivation of adult company and time away from home, and social condemnation as "welfare" recipients. But working meant: tedious, low-paid jobs, inadequate and unreliable child care, the exhaustion of the "double day," and condemnation as a neglectful mother. An unusual mother who had a job she enjoyed and child care support from relatives was told by her caseworker that she must be suffering a great deal of guilt.[94] In the same year, a caseworker from the same agency gave the opposite diagnosis to a woman factory worker: severely nervous, fearful that she was going crazy, the mother slept poorly and had nightmares that she would hurt herself on the machines at work, but needed the money for her independence from her withdrawn and abusive husband. Yet the caseworker would not concur that the job was the cause of her stress, or help her in finding another source of support.[95] The vulnerability of single mothers to such contradictory and double-binding attitudes about employment was created by the contradictions of the realities they faced, since they were expected both to raise and to provide for children.

The emergence of child neglect in such cases is not hard to understand. In 1950 a Lithuanian immigrant mother worked full-time at nights in order to be home during the days, doing all the housework, averaging three to four hours of sleep a night. She was reportedly affectionate toward her children, aged twelve and four, but they were dirty and untidy, engaging in stealing and doing poorly in school. She received counseling at Judge Baker, but a year later her now five-year-old girl was "roaming the streets, dirty, unkempt, neglected . . . a constant source of breeding germs and contagious diseases, lighting fires, breaking bottles." In 1952 the MSPCC became involved, paying a few home visits and urging the mother to be stricter with her girls, especially in relation to the reported promiscuity of the older. But in late 1952, when the case closed, the basic facts were the same: the mother was still working all night, trying to earn enough to buy a house.[96]

The intersection of single motherhood and child neglect is revealing about both, showing how standards of and supports for adequate parenting have been based on two-parent nuclear families with men as the primary breadwinners. There has been a continuing tendency within both family scholarship and social welfare policy to treat single motherhood as aberrant, rather than common and "normal." Similarly, child neglect has been conceived as a product of parental pathology, rather than as in good measure a structural aspect of women's powerlessness and poverty. Moreover, many of the problems of combining breadwinning with child-raising are experienced also by married working mothers, who now constitute at least 60 percent of all mothers. Welfare provisions, child care, and women's wages are still inadequate to provide good child-raising conditions. Single mothers have become merely the extreme case for all mothers.

Whatever the number of single mothers, their treatment, and the way the single-mother "problem" is construed, affect conditions of mothering and marriage for all women. A lack of social support for single mothers makes marriage coercive. If mothers must be supported by men to be good mothers, then it would appear that good mothering is dependent on women being dependent; yet child protectors know that women's dependency on men is likely to promote family violence. Lack of ability to support themselves and their children holds many women in abusive relationships; and this low confidence and lack of resources for independence in turn stem from a social organization which encourages women's dependence on men. Moreover, the requirement that mothers keep or find a man on whom to depend was palpably impossible in many cases, as child welfare workers frequently observed, because fathers frequently rejected responsibility for wives and children. The whole social organization of child-raising—that men must support women who must take care of children—is predicated on often unobtainable conditions.

These dilemmas remain at the core of child-saving work. There has been progress in the last century, and many women and children have more options. Nevertheless, the essential dilemmas have not been solved:

how to protect children's rights, given the social consensus that families ought to be economically autonomous; how to help single people in parenting and breadwinning alone, given the norm that public aid, "dependency," ought to be discouraged; how to punish social deviance without simultaneously punishing "innocent" children. The problems of single motherhood go to the heart of the definitional problem in family violence, the problem of setting standards: how to protect children without imposing the standards of one social group upon another. Above all, the situation of single mothers shows that these standards for proper child-raising—and thereby the definitions of deviance—include not only economic, ethnic, religious, and "class" norms but also gendered assumptions about how families should be organized.

I do not imply that neglect is inevitable in single-mother households. Most single mothers are not bad parents, but the problems and/or bad luck of those that are have been exacerbated by the injuries of class, race, and sex subordination. One of the results of the simultaneous alarm about single motherhood and child neglect in the Progressive period was the intensification of mother-blaming in child protection. Standards for good parenting need to be reconsidered in awareness that gender relationships in families are changing, and that the traditional sexual division of labor in child-raising is no longer typical, nor is it the necessarily best arrangement.

Scholars and policy makers have assumed that stable families are and must be economically independent, and that families needing "outside help" to support children could not be stable in the long run. The tenaciously high incidence of female-headed families for over a century, and the severe material problems that faced responsible and energetic as well as irresponsible and depressed single mothers, suggest the need to question whether economic independence should be the highest goal or even the desirable norm for good child-raising.

The intersection of single motherhood and child neglect shows that policy toward child mistreatment cannot be separated from a gender analysis of how child-raising is done. There has been a tendency in the recent decades of family-violence scholarship to assume that marital violence requires a gender analysis while mistreatment of children does not. That is not the case. By a gender analysis of child mistreatment, I do not meant simply measuring, say, the differential culpability of mothers and fathers, or the differential mistreatment of girls and boys.

I am referring to fundamental social norms for family life, the cultural images of mothering and fathering, and the ways in which social policy—from income tax regulations to educational funding—influences the sexual division of labor in family life. Many cases of maternal child neglect and abuse are conditioned not only by the difficulties of parenting with inadequate financial and social support but also by the common consequences of sexism for women—low self-esteem, limited aspirations, lack of assertiveness. In parallel, many cases of paternal child abuse are conditioned by highly masculine expectations of children's behavior and family life. We will see these gendered influences as the next chapters examine four major forms of family violence—child neglect, child abuse, incest, and wife-beating.

5

"SO MUCH FOR THE CHILDREN NOW, SO LITTLE BEFORE": CHILD NEGLECT AND PARENTAL RESPONSIBILITY

Agt stated that [girl] wd have to go to church Sun mornings and also to Sun sch and that the rest of the fam wd have to go also; that the house wd have to be cleaned up as agt was very much displeased w conditions she found . . . reprimanded [girl] severly for swearing in agt's presence. Stated that if she heard [girl] use such language again, she wd not hesitate to remove her.[1]

As a friend of the poor I want to ask you if you want to call at . . . and see if their is something you can do a poor woman with 2 children that has a common drunkard for a husband that don't work one fourth of the time he makes licquor keeps drunk just as long as it will last his wife and children are hungry the third of the time he is a big man and able he has been doing this for 2 or 3 years he can't keep a job for getting

drunk. Would you drive him out to work and stop making licquor I
wish you would show this to the Probation officer the police has been
there a lot and do no good. His wife has $25. a month.[2]

The most important change in the history of child protection work was
the "discovery" of child neglect in the Progressive era. By emphasizing
the more prevalent source of children's suffering, the focus on neglect
called attention to the inseparability of standards of parenting from the
overall health and welfare of the citizenry. The child protectors' confrontation with neglect introduced them to a fundamental contradiction
in the treatment of family-violence problems. As one parent put it, there
was "so much for the children now"—after they had been declared
neglected and removed from their homes—"so little before." Stingily
guarding every penny spent on social services, leaders became outraged
and punitive when confronted with the evidence of children's sufferings.
Committed to the notion of family economic independence, policy was
constructed on the assumption that social support to families should be
temporary and uncomfortable for clients. This assumption underlay not
only child protective but all welfare policy. Child-protection work played
a key role in exposing this contradiction, and in so doing contributed
to the establishment of basic welfare programs.

But the positive results of the neglect emphasis were limited. Most
of those concerned with family violence continued to work within this
contradiction, accepting the limitations on their ability to help created
by meager funding of social services and the stigmatizing of those who
needed help, and did not campaign for better social services. Furthermore, the emphasis on neglect also intensified gender and class inequalities. It increased the woman-blaming that has been inherent in
much child-protection work. Accompanied by a de-emphasis on violence, including a virtual cover-up of wife-beating between 1920 and
the 1960s, and by a continued attribution of exclusive child-raising
responsibility to women, the neglect emphasis separated women's and
children's interests from each other and from a critique of male dominance in the family. Moreover, the emphasis on neglect strengthened
discrimination against the poor both in the diagnosis and in the response
to family-violence problems.

Neither the deleterious nor the beneficial effects were the inherent
results of the concept of child neglect. Like all family-violence cate-

gories, this one has been consistently politically manipulated, its definitions and causal analyses affected by larger social movements and political currents. Had it developed in a time of a strong grassroots women's movement, child neglect might have been used to promote more democratic results both for women and for the poor. By tracing the more disappointing developments, this chapter may also offer some hints about better interpretations of child neglect for the future.

DEFINING NEGLECT

Child neglect was the most common type of family "violence" throughout the period of this study.[3] The emphasis on neglect which began during the Progressive era corresponded to a fundamental change in the overall social significance of family violence: cruelty to children was redefined as mainly a family problem, neglect its most common form.

Neglect was not only the largest but also the vaguest category of family "violence." For that reason, before proceeding to a narrative of historical changes in the conception of child neglect, this chapter offers first a discussion of the basic categories of neglect. Although these were established during the Progressive period, and changed little in succeeding years, the notion of neglect itself was like an empty vessel, a container for residual anxieties about child-raising which did not fit any of the more precise definitions of family problems. Many different social anxieties—about changing gender relations, sexual mores, and economic security, for example—were poured into the pool of child-neglect concerns and influenced their definitions. These anxieties were in turn influenced by some specific historical events, such as wars and the Depression. Above all, the concept of child neglect became an expression of fears about changes in family life wrought by women's entrance into the labor force and parental loss of influence over their children.

That child neglect was vaguely defined and difficult to remedy does not mean that its existence as a social problem is dubious. It is true that neglect was hard to distinguish from poverty, and many poor parents who did their best for their children were wrongly classified as negligent.

Nevertheless, child neglect was not identical with poverty. Despite the biases of social workers and their norms of proper family life, most neglect cases were not characterized by disagreements between agency workers and clients about what standards were desirable. In many cases the clients were judged as neglectful by their own peers, by neighbors and relatives, even by nuclear family members. The majority of neglect cases were those of "multi-problem families," to use a modern expression, in which poverty was compounded with other, not strictly economic, difficulties. Consider these examples, from the same neighborhood forty years apart:

1917, Roxbury. An Irish-American nuclear family. On a January night at 8 p.m. two children were found in an icy-cold house, "half-starved," their father out, their mother unconscious from drink. Ages seven and six, the children were first described as tiny six- and four-year-olds, so undernourished were they. Both parents worked, their father as a casual laborer for a Roxbury slumlord (who owned their tenement), earning $6–7 a week, described as a "worthless" man dressed "as though he came out of an ash heap." Their mother also "worked out," doing washing for another $6 per week, and the children were left alone all day. Both parents were heavy drinkers, she apparently the worst; indeed, at first she seemed mentally dull to the MSPCC agent, but this was later ascribed to the effects of alcohol and to being "just a low type mentally." These parents' indifference to their children would seem to be indicated by the fact that they made no attempt to reclaim their children after they were removed. Indeed, many factors implicate parental depression in this case. For example, two of the four rooms in their tenement were let to a fruit-and-vegetable peddler, who kept his produce there, and although those rooms were stuffed with food, there was no evidence that the parents used it to feed their children. Considering that the woman's job was to clean clothes, it is notable that her husband was so terribly dressed (and perhaps symptomatic of her hostility to him). (Although since she did her washing out of the home, she could not combine care of her family's clothing with it, and the house had no fuel to heat water for washing, nor washing implements.) In the summer of 1916 a baby had died, the third child lost by this couple, and the mother was apparently very affected and neighbors reported that she began acting *"queer" since then; particularly, she attacked her husband, throwing knives and forks at him and lighting fires while he was sleeping. The parents claimed that all their relatives were dead, a claim as likely as not to have been false, considering that clients usually did not wish to give such information to investigators. The claim nevertheless probably reflected accurately their sense of isolation from responsible and helping connections.*[4]

1956, Roxbury. A nuclear family with children fifteen, eleven, eight and one. The father had worked in a foundry and a pickle factory but was currently, and frequently, unemployed, and in and out of jail on short sentences for drunkenness. The mother, who had had her husband arrested several times because of his abusiveness when drunk, usually survived on welfare—$24 a week. Sometimes when he was in jail they lived with a maternal aunt. The MSPCC had been monitoring this mother since 1950, and brought neglect charges against her twice. Agents criticized her for keeping the house dirty, not getting rid of lice, not providing dental care, not providing treatment for the oldest girl, who had cerebral palsy. About the last accusation the mother offered her own story: the agents considered this daughter feeble-minded as well, and wanted to institutionalize her, but the mother had once allowed her to be placed temporarily in the Fernald School and witnessed disgusting conditions there: "She said that the women were running around exposing themselves and doing things which she didn't think the child should be observing . . . no physiotherapy had been done and the ch. had not been allowed out of the building since she went there." However, the mother had not been reliable about getting her daughter to outpatient physiotherapy sessions either. In 1956 she was reported again by a neighbor, who says the children were left alone and not fed properly and that the mother drank and had men in the house.[5]

In both cases the child neglect was caused by several factors—by parental conflicts, by alcoholism and resultant ill health, by poverty and depression, by women's double responsibility of breadwinning and child-raising; possibly by isolation, low self-esteem, and mental illness.

PHYSICAL NEGLECT

Despite the complexity of contributing factors, neglect cases generally fell into two large categories—physical and moral. Under the rubric "physical neglect," several large subcategories commonly reoccurred, such as lack of supervision, dirtiness, lack of proper food and clothing, medical neglect. The concept "moral neglect" included many forms of deviance, not only from norms of sexual and marital practice, but also with regard to other household arrangements not necessarily directly connected to sex, such as liquor and drug consumption, sleeping arrangements, children's participation in adult conversation and activity. If our society experienced a growing moral relativism, and has learned some respect for alternative life-styles, this loosening was hardly reflected in these child-protection cases. Case records from 1960 contained the same moralistic condemnations of parents' and children's lack of propriety that were found in 1880.

All types of neglect cases were strongly correlated with poverty, more so than any other type of family-violence cases, but this was particularly true of physical neglect. In general the standards for physical neglect encapsulated class expectations about standards of living. Many of these standards were not only inaccessible to, but unimaginable by, most turn-of-the-century agency clients.

Child-protection agencies tried to distinguish neglect from poverty, but it was not easy. At the 1933 White House Conference an MSPCC-headed committee produced this definition: "When, through the culpable neglect of their parents, children are suffering from hunger, insufficient clothing, improper housing and sleeping conditions, or living in the midst of filth and squalor . . ."[6] But in practice, caseworkers were not successful at determining parental culpability. The stresses of poverty can indeed produce neglectful or abusive parenting—but only when they interact with intrapsychic and interpersonal stresses. Moreover, poverty was also implicated in the origins of these "personal" problems, such as illness, alcoholism, anger, and isolation. The greatest contribution of poverty to child neglect lies not in direct deprivation of children's physical well-being, although these deprivations were often painful to contemplate, but in the demoralization, failure of self-esteem, and defeatism that hardship induced in many parents. And what was to be done for children whose parents were doing their best? Even where parents were struggling hard for their own and their children's well-being, poverty itself might create such suffering for children that action was needed, and that action was often only possible through having a child adjudicated as neglected, a procedure that brought with it considerable stigma and punishment to parents. Consider this case of a black father, widowed, who was supporting three sons, ages two, four, and five, during the Depression. Mr. Stone, as we will call him, was reported by neighbors because the children were unsupervised, running in the streets, inadequately fed and clothed, and injured themselves frequently. Stone was receiving aid from the OPW but claimed that his $12 a week was inadequate and that his incompetent caseworker did not pay him even that regularly. His weekly budget included:

Insurance	$ .75
Rent	3.50
Child care	3.00
Gas, oil, coal	2.00
Ice	.60
Total	9.85

This left less than $3 a week for food, which was not enough. The MSPCC pressured him to get rid of his housekeeper, reported by neighbors to be unreliable and a drinking woman. Stone responded angrily to this offer of criticism without aid. Nevertheless, he complied and hired another, younger woman. When the agent went to interview her in his home, a "middle-aged white man came in with a package and left." The agent then "emptied out contents, a pair of silk stockings, women's shoes, 2 cigarettes and a bottle of alcohol. [This was during Prohibition.] Mrs. _____ denied that they were meant for her and did not think cigarettes contained dope." Mr. Stone was, the agent reported with disapproval, angry not at the woman but at the agent. The father continued to find different housekeepers in response to agency complaints; in between, the children continued to be on the streets from morning till night, aided but also reported on by neighbors.[7] The specific neglect allegations in this case record concerned inadequate food, inadequate child care, and a father's hostile responses to agency workers.

THE LOOK OF NEGLECT

Children outside their home. Undated. *(Courtesy of MSPCC, Boston.)*

This large immigrant family is photographed at home, dressed in their best. Heads have been shaved to fight lice. Not all poverty meant disorder. Undated. *(Courtesy of BCSA.)*

Children and their teenage mother or, more likely, sister, at work in the kitchen. Undated. *(Courtesy of BCSA.)*

Neglected children on the streets,
1905. *(Courtesy of MSPCC, Boston.)*

Interior, early 1930s. This kind of filth and disorder was often an outward emblem of depression and child neglect. *(Courtesy of MSPCC, Boston.)*

Although posed as a proper family, they were not, because the parents were unmarried and the children, therefore, illegitimate. A case of moral neglect, about 1915. *(Courtesy of MSPCC, Boston.)*

Medical neglect, about 1920: rickets. *(Courtesy of MSPCC, Boston.)*

It is hard to know how much of alleged parental inadequacy was due to social workers' misperception of his options, how much to his hostility to professional intervention, how much to irresponsibility.

In most neglect cases an element of parental hostility to or rejection of the child was evident. But in many such cases the parental hostility, negligence, or depression were themselves the results of poverty. Consider, for example, this woman's complex of problems:

> Mrs. Liss [grandmother and custodian of the children] goes out to work and earns what she can but she now is 59 yrs. old and in poor health and is not able to earn enough money . . . They live in one room . . . As the children wet the bed and Mrs. L. smokes the air is very foul. There is not enough bed clothes . . . and Mrs. L. is not wise in the way she spends her money, for instance she paid $12 for a toy automobile for [boy] and then could not buy him a coat so that he could go to school. She is more fond of [boy] than she is of [girl] and favors him in various ways. Even now [the children's] mother applies to Mrs. Lindstrom for money when she needs it as Mrs L. never brought her up to do any work and the result is that Mrs. L. is growing old and has nothing laid by for her future . . . She has no clothes for herself and spends her Sundays washing and ironing for the children . . . she is not strong enough to care for them and is too lax in her discipline.[8]

In a 1916 case a twenty-two-year-old mother was reported to the MSPCC by a neighbor for leaving her two children, ages three and eighteen months, alone nights until 2 a.m. or later while she went out with men. Yet just before this report the mother herself had gone to the Boston Children's Aid Society asking for a boarding home for herself and her children.[9] Not grandmother Liss's or Mr. Stone's or this young mother's alleged neglectfulness meant they were unconcerned about their children.

In other neglect cases the parent's history suggested deep emotional incapacity to care for a child. In 1930 a woman adopted a child (through an advertisement in the newspaper) in order to "save her marriage": she thought a child in the home might prevent her husband from leaving. As a teenager, this woman had been through a "marriage" that later turned out to be phony, gave birth to a crippled child, who died young, and spent two years in a women's reformatory on an idle and disorderly charge. Arriving in Boston at age twenty-four, working as a prostitute, she met a taxi driver, fifty years old, who took her in and, after living with her for thirteen weeks, married her. He became her pimp, abused her, and then refused to support her. He claimed he married her only as an act of charity, supported her as well as he could afford, and that she procured the baby without his consent. The MSPCC learned of this case when neighbors led them to a one-year-old baby alone in the middle of the night, in a South Boston apartment without heat, on the floor, with few clothes, its legs blue. [10]

Lack of supervision, a type of physical neglect, was a category strongly affected by the cultural and class biases of the child-savers. For example, 1933 MSPCC guidelines decreed that any child in charge of siblings should be over twelve, certainly not the prevalent standard among the poor. [11] Child protectors were disturbed not only by children left alone but also by those spending their time in the streets. Crowded, uncomfortable, and, in the summer, stifling hot apartments literally squeezed children onto the streets just as the middle classes were consolidating a norm of domesticity, a romanticization of "home" (as distinct from house), which required that respectable children as well as women stay inside. [12] In rural and even small-town environments, children of all classes played outside, and all but the most upper-class contributed work to the family economy—farm work, errands, child care, for example. City children's street activity was in part devoted to the same purpose: their families' need for money. Children on the streets in early neglect cases—" 'These gatherers of things lost on earth . . . These makers of something out of nothing' "[13] —were often peddlers of newspapers, fish, or manufactured goods, or of stolen goods or collected odds and ends; they performed services for money such as shoeshines; they picked from rubbish bins or stole or begged. Their parents usually approved of their work, which was an urban translation of a pre-industrial assumption that all family members worked. Attempts at regulation of street labor were inefficient. For example, despite a statute requiring licensing of newspaper boys, an MSPCC study during one sixty-day period in 1901 found three hundred out of four hundred such boys selling illegally. [14] The police could not catch the swift and well-organized children.

But the cities presented new kinds of dangers, and the reformers had some cause for concern about inadequate supervision. Children were frequently injured or even killed by falling from roofs or the windows of high buildings, run over by streetcars or cars, electrocuted by trolley wires, burned by lamps, poisoned by illuminating gas, assaulted, robbed, and raped. In 1910 the Boston School Board reported over 1,800 children's accidents in that year alone.[15] But the child-savers also reacted to the way poor city children looked (dirty, unruly, ragged) and acted (saucy, manipulative, aggressive), and to their grown-up responsibilities.[16]

Blind to the conditions of their own economy, child-savers tended to misinterpret the situation of the street children, considering them *ipso facto* unloved and neglected. Since mothers were, in fact and in ideology, primarily responsible for these children, it was but a short leap from the presence of the children on the streets to the conclusion that their mothers were incompetent at best, depraved in many cases.[17] When parents sued for compensation for the accidental injury or death of their children, defendants often argued mothers' negligence as a defense.[18] So strong was the ideology of domesticity among the child-savers that they interpreted the gregariousness of the urban poor to mean that these people had no *homes*: " 'Homes—in the better sense—they never know.' "[19]

At the turn of the century the reformers' concern was mainly with street *boys*.[20] Girls' labor on the streets was more likely to be caring for younger siblings, and perhaps because this was consistent with "proper" female behavior, it was less obnoxious to the child-savers. Instead, they worried about the girls' young charges, deprived of real mothers and dependent on "little mothers," as these big sisters were called.[21] Girls' street activities became of concern when they appeared sexual.

Not only was factory child labor generally ignored, but so too was industrial home work, widespread in many Boston families, children working with their mothers at sewing or assembling millinery. The MSPCC focused on children's labor in the streets and truancy.[22] Nine percent of cases in this study listed children's overwork as one of the problems, and children were kept from attending school in 5 percent. A closer look at the child-savers' reasoning shows that the amount of labor was not in itself the source of their concern. There was, for example, a double standard concerning rural and urban labor, the former considered healthful in almost any quantity—indeed, boys were placed with rural families where they were, to modern eyes, exploited as unpaid farm hands. This was a class standard: child labor was considered healthy if it was prescribed for the children's sake and not needed by parents.[23]

In the definition of overwork we see the anti-patriarchal assumptions behind the standards of child neglect. The crime was for children to contribute to parents. The standard for overwork as a form of neglect involved domesticity, compulsory education, and fathers' obligation to support their families single-handedly. As the political campaign against child labor grew, the child-protection agencies adopted its rhetoric: by 1921 the MSPCC used the label "exploitation" to describe this form of neglect. But the exploiters were parents or other individual guardians, not wage-paying employers. Despite the dependence of many poor families on children's economic contributions, parents' cupidity and indifference were commonly cited as the root of the problem.[24]

The reasons for this use of children by parents are not hard to find. In almost every case the work required of the children was essential to the family economy. A Polish-American family in 1917 had nine children: the father worked in a coal yard, the mother at housework, the oldest daughter at thirteen was in service, and daughters twelve and ten were responsible for the management of the entire household and the care of the younger children.[25] In 1910 a Syrian-born mother whose husband had just died tried to earn a living by continuing his peddling; she therefore insisted that her thirteen-year-old girl stay home from school to mind the house and two younger children.[26] At home parents relied more on girls' than on boys' labor. In the infrequent cases when boys were required to do domestic labor, it was usually outdoors, often at farmwork, even in urban settings, as in the case of a German-born father whose wife did the drudgery for numerous boarders (while the family of nine lived in two rooms) and who required his children to work long hours in a large vegetable garden.[27] Boys were more likely to be sent out to work for wages, a duty enforced by requiring them to pay board.[28]

The majority of these clients were recent immigrants from rural economies in which children's labor contributions were standard. The expectation that children would work should not, however, be seen as a vestige of a previous social organization, quickly eroding away as it lost its utility. It was supported, in fact, by the new urban economy. It has often been argued in the abstract that while children in rural economies were resources, creating value for parents, urban children were a drain on the family's budget. This shift occurred only over a long historical period, however. In the short run, the conditions of the new urban poor escalated the need for children's labor, as wages were so low, work so erratic, and single-parent families so common that families could not survive only on adults' labor. Parents who overworked their children were not lazy—most often they were mothers already exhausted and fearful for the family's survival. Compulsory education was an economic blow to many families; the truant officer was the enemy of parents, not of children, at least until the 1930s. While social reformers were concerned about child neglect, their poor clients were often more concerned about parent neglect.

Furthermore, the expectation that children should work for their families was imbedded at the deepest psychological levels, in the *definition* of parenthood in traditional societies. Fathers', and secondarily mothers', control over children's labor was the fundamental basis of patriarchal power and family unity. For the prosperous, this control had one set of meanings, with parental control over property and marriage looming large; in poor families, the control was directed more exclusively at labor. Without a cycle in which children ended up taking care of parents, parenthood had no authority and no rewards. It not only seemed wrong that able children should be idle at school while tired parents drudged; this arrangement also deprived parents, particularly mothers, of the evidence of love and respect that made their lives bearable. The abuse with which parents sometimes responded to "lazy" children, as we will see in the next chapter, is understandable only when conceived as developing out of threats to parents' dignity.

MEDICAL NEGLECT

Medical neglect was another aspect of physical neglect defined on the basis of class-specific expectations and standards of living. In 1910 Judge Harvey Baker, defining what constituted a neglected child under Massachusetts statutes, led with medical examples: lack of treatment for ophthalmia neonatorum or for bowed shinbones.[29] By the 1920s the

MSPCC and the BCSA considered "want of needed medical or surgical treatment" as one of their major reasons for intervention, usually ranking ninth in importance.[30] The untreated health problems found by MSPCC visitors included infected sores of various kinds, lice and many kinds of vermin, malnutrition and the prevalent rickets, eye and ear infections, ringworm, tuberculosis, scabies, impetigo and other rashes, not to mention the frequent acute infections—colds, influenza, measles, chicken pox, mumps. Parents were sometimes unaware of their child's illness, frequently ignorant of germ or contagion theories, and at other times unaware of the availability of treatment. But perhaps equally often the caseworker might assume this ignorance, or the parent might plead ignorance, when the reasons for neglect were complex.

Consider one 1917 story. A family was reported as uncooperative by the social service department of Boston Children's Hospital: an unmarried couple with two "illegitimate" children, aged two and six months. The older girl was in a convalescent home with "acute" rickets, her spine so affected that she was being kept recumbent on a "Whitman frame" in an attempt to prevent permanent, serious deformity. The hospital had reported the case out of concern to keep the younger child from a similar affliction. In November the older girl was sent home and the mother refused to continue her treatment, since she reported the child seemed well and was able to stand a little on her feet. A closer questioning by the MSPCC agent revealed that this was not a case simply of ignorance or negligence: the mother believed that her daughter had not received proper care in the convalescent home, that she contracted a very bad cold because she had been released without warm clothing, wrapped only in a blanket.[31]

Fear of hospitals was a widespread, even a majority, phenomenon in the nineteenth century, and it continued among the poor well into the twentieth. The fear was based not only on superstition but also on experience of infectious diseases and filthy conditions in hospitals. Since most medical care available to the poor, especially that which a social agency could procure for them, was dispensed in hospital clinics, this fear represented an obstacle to treatment. More serious problems usually required removing children to institutions, and this produced a doubled resistance; parents did not want to give up their children and feared not being able to get them back; they suspected the institutions themselves of cruel and negligent treatment.[32] Sometimes parental hostility to medical treatment stemmed from, or had advanced to, suspicion of all representatives of regular modern medicine. In 1930, another family was referred by Children's Hospital, which wanted the MSPCC's co-operation in forcing a four-month-old boy into treatment for weight loss and feeding problems. A diagnosis of pyloric stenosis had been made,[33] and surgery advised, but the mother refused to allow it. Fragments in the case record offer some hints about her attitudes: She had once been told by the New England Hospital for Women and Children that she would never have children if she did not submit to an [unspecified] operation, but she refused and became a mother of four. She had another child who, she said, weighed only two pounds at birth but grew up normally. Some of her claims were dubious, but some of her skepticism was borne out by this case itself: she resisted the surgery on her baby boy so long that the earlier diagnosis was rejected by the Children's Hospital staff—"it couldn't have been stenosis or the child would now be dead. It is a pyloric spasm. Child should have been operated on then. Would not operate now"—the case record quoted. Instead, med-icine was prescribed, but the description of its side effects determined the mother not to administer that either, until the MSPCC worker literally took her with the baby to the hospital and directly supervised its treatment.[34]

Overt refusals of medical treatment for children diminished after 1930;[35] yet medical neglect continued in different forms. Perhaps the most common was parents' and of course it was always presumed to be mothers'—unreliability about keeping medical appointments, and "obliviousness" to pathological conditions which middle-class standards would consider as requiring attention. This modern medical neglect usually coexisted with other forms of neglect, suggesting that the in-difference to medical problems was merely an aspect of a more gen-eralized indifference to dominant standards of child-raising. In 1960 a Boston City Hospital social service worker referred to the MSPCC a two-month-old boy, brought in with maggots in his rectum, weighing less than at birth. The baby was hospitalized for two months, and discharged in good health when his mother, aged twenty-one and preg-nant with her third child, promised that she would reform and bring the baby for regular checkups. But she almost never came, citing dif-ficulties in getting child care for her older child. Visits to her home revealed no change in the situation until the baby was sent to live with his maternal grandmother in 1962 (who had allegedly neglected her daughter, the child's mother). This medical neglect appears to have arisen not out of cultural conflict but from parental depression, lassitude, and hostility induced by poverty and hopelessness. The father had a long criminal record, was mainly unemployed, and deserted in 1963, when his wife was pregnant with her fifth child. She had all the earmarks of depression. Although her person and apartment were neat and clean, MSPCC visits to the home frequently found her lying down; her pattern of not keeping appointments was general, not only with doctors but with social and legal workers equally. Her refusal to keep appointments might have been a way of bringing people to her, bringing her help; the removal of her children in 1965 may have been what she wanted. Or she may have been so depressed and lacking in energy that she could not manage the arrangements and travel about the city that medical care of her children required.[36] Whatever the specific explanations, her case was emblematic in that her medical neglect was not so much a specific denial as a general aspect of her withdrawal of parenting.

MORAL NEGLECT

Child-protection workers had always labeled some parents immoral, but moral *neglect* became a diagnostic category only in the 1890s. For the three decades following, it was considered the worst form of neglect, in the 1920s constituting 24 percent of the total agency caseload.[37] Although the contemporary reader may find this the vaguest and least definable of criteria, child-protection agencies did not share these doubts, and believed they could specify moral neglect objectively.

As types of moral neglect the 1933 MSPCC guidelines cited (1) children with "bad habits whose parents are indifferent"; (2) parental "drunkenness, debauchery, immorality, vice, or crime"; (3) parental separation, where children live with the least desirable of the parents; (4) boy victims of sex offenses; (5) girls in violation of chastity cases.[38] These categories require some decoding. The concerns were mainly sexual; stealing, cheating, drinking, and wife-beating were not usually classified as moral infractions, although taking drugs was. "Bad habits" meant masturbation, sex play, or promiscuity. The circularity of the second item, the assumption that parental deviance automatically produced child neglect, indicated how self-evident the child protectors considered their concepts. The concern with a child living with the least desirable parent suggests the breadth of jurisdiction claimed by the agency. The double standard of the last two categories was to continue throughout this history: boys were morally neglected if they were sex-assault victims, but girls were thus labeled if they engaged in any sexually improper activity, even without the commission of a crime. Not only were these standards subjective, but they were not usually practiced. Rather, MSPCC records and reports characterized parental inadequacies in vague moralisms: "weakness of character," "vice," "children get no training in honesty and sobriety," "low moral standards," "mentally and morally lax."[39]

The most common form of moral neglect, which fit into category 2 above, appeared to be out-of-wedlock relations, an extremely widespread phenomenon, particularly among men and women separated but not divorced from legal spouses. Lack of legal marriage *in itself* was considered neglectful by agency workers throughout this study, even in the 1950s and 1960s.[40] Clients did so much lying about these relationships that estimates of frequency are not reliable. In attempting to disguise their living relationships, clients often made their sexual arrangements appear more casual than they were: instead of presenting themselves as living with a man, women were often discovered to be sleeping with a "boarder." (The slang phrase we met before, "star boarder," illustrates the prevalence of this phenomenon.) A common consequence of parental "immorality," and another form of "immorality" in itself, was illegitimate children. Just as the parental fault might be nothing worse than common-law marriage, so these "illegitimate" children often lived in nuclear families with both their natural parents.

Occasionally immorality appeared alone in the neglect accusation. More often, however, it was accompanied by other infractions, since it was more likely to be discovered in cases where poverty or other forms of neglect called social-work attention to the children. The coincidence of moral with physical neglect due to patterns of agency discovery reinforced, of course, the agents' own moralism. An example is the case of Anola Green, a black mother of three who migrated from Washington, D.C., in 1920. Part of a steadily increasing black migration northward after World War I, her reasons for moving are of a (female) kind often neglected in the histories of labor migrations: she was fleeing an abusive husband. Leaving her oldest son, sixteen, with her brother in Washington, she took eight- and twelve-year-old daughters to Roxbury, where she earned a living scrubbing offices and doing washing for private families. She came to Boston with her lover; both were still legally married to others, but they lived together in a three-room tenement which was "fairly well furnished . . . the chn. are attending sch. and are properly clothed; have enough to eat." Her *only* infraction was living with her lover. Her brother-in-law, angry at Anola's sister for leaving him, retaliated by turning Anola in (presumably blaming her for taking her sister's side). She was arrested for lewd and lascivious conduct, her children seized and placed in the MSPCC temporary home, where the older one "was quite independent and saucy. Raised some trouble . . ." As to the effects of the immorality on the children, "medical examination proved that [older girl] had not been tampered with, but [younger] was a masturbater [sic]." Mrs. Green fought for her children, at one point a friend of hers actually stealing them from the court as they were about to be sent back to their father in Washington. Her court-appointed lawyer, almost as hostile to her as the prosecutor, was able to help her keep them only by getting her sent back to Washington with the condition that she would never see her lover again. The MSPCC agent wrote ahead to the Washington Board of Children's Guardians, which was to supervise her: "I sincerely hope that Mrs. Green has been taught her lesson."[41]

Victimized not only by her own abusive husband but also by her sister's, perhaps by her race and her poverty, certainly by moralistic caseworker, police, and judge, Mrs. Green nevertheless came out better than some women caught in similar situations. Typically, she chose her children over her lover; less typically, she was successful in keeping her children, although she was likely to be steadily under the surveillance of an agency afterward. Her relative success at fending off jail and loss of her children may have been related to the fact that immorality was the only accusation against her: every evidence suggests that she was a collected and responsible person.

Many other poor and vulnerable mothers caught in immoral situations fared worse. Teresa Caroli, twenty-nine, the third wife of an Italian man of forty-seven, had four children, ages two through seven. She ran away from his beatings, and became involved with another, younger man. At first she left the children with her mother, but the latter, trying to save money to return to Italy, complained that she couldn't afford it. Not sure how she could earn a living herself, Mrs. Caroli became "discouraged and worried" and attempted suicide in 1920. She did not die but stayed away four to six weeks, during which time her husband complained to Associated Charities that she had deserted. The night she returned he beat her black and blue, she said; but the MSPCC agent examined her, reported finding no bruises but only a small scratch, decided she was an unfit, immoral mother, and brought her to court for lewd and lascivious conduct.

This case record continued to 1931 and so we know the unhappy outcome. Convicted, Mrs. Caroli was given three months' probation. A neglect complaint was also brought and the children taken to the Home for Destitute Catholic Children. A repetitive pattern began: the children placed out, returned, and placed out again; Mrs. Caroli bringing assault charges against her husband and then becoming reconciled with him; he beating her and/or bringing charges against her for immorality, usually with men whom he himself invited to his house to play cards. In 1931 the children were all placed out, the father was not contributing to their support and was ill with gonorrhea (making it noteworthy that *he* was never charged with immorality).[42]

This case was more typical than Anola Green's in that it concerned a "multi-problem" family, beset by wife-beating, desertion, irregular employment, gambling, fighting and obscenity in the house, allegations of the father's membership in the Black Hand, illness, and severe depression. Mrs. Caroli seemed unable, for whatever reasons, to get away from her husband. To the contemporary reader, her extramarital affair does not appear the major aspect of her neglectfulness, as it was treated by court and MSPCC. Their exclusive focus on immorality had destructive consequences for the children.

Immorality charges were almost never directed against men, and they functioned to double-bind mothers—blaming them for child neglect yet preventing them from finding ways of becoming stronger and better parents. Furthermore, the focus on immorality as the major evil influence on children made it harder for client mothers to associate good parenting with greater independence and self-respect for themselves; instead, the immorality emphasis encouraged them to remain in marriages or in secretive relationships that may in fact have interfered with good parenting.

The problem with parental immorality was, allegedly, that it was passed on to children. The child-savers slid from a hereditary theory of depravity, including sexual depravity, into a socialization theory of how children learned "clean living," without a substantial change in their diagnostic and treatment policy. Their fundamental assumptions were continuous. Marriage was important because it represented literally and symbolically the responsible adult organization of sexual activity. The capacity of a legal marriage to transform sexuality from an unacceptable into an acceptable activity, to turn an immoral into an upstanding relationship, is visible in its most fetishized form in these records. There were cases in which neglect and/or abuse were so severe that children's health and safety were in question, yet the workers' primary concern was to coerce the parents into marriage.

However, even legal marriage did not make parents' sexual relationships clean. It was also important that children should not actually see sexual activity, or clues as to its presence. A major social-work concern about the poor-client population was sleeping arrangements. Very few MSPCC client families provided separate bedrooms for all individual children, many children shared rooms with their parents, and a substantial minority shared beds with parents. Makeshift arrangements, such as curtains strung up between beds, suggested that the poor too longed for privacy, but these efforts did not reassure social workers that clients shared their high standards for the "protection" of children. Failure to insulate children from intimations of adult sexuality was even worse, of course, if the sexual partners were unmarried. The out-of-wedlock relationship was thus worse if it was unhidden, if there was no pretense that the man was a boarder or an uncle. Even more seriously, mothers were sometimes accused of promiscuity and prostitution. These categories cannot of course be taken at face value. The presence of any male visitors could lead to an allegation of promiscuity, especially if they were drinking or if a husband was not in the house. We know from other analyses that nineteenth-century reformers exaggerated the number of prostitutes and stretched the definition of that occupation so as to include a great deal of casual sexual activity, sometimes even all nonmarital sexual activity.[43]

The fear of children's exposure to adult sexuality was related to the nineteenth-century fear of precocity in children, which was in turn related to the age-segregated patterns of industrial society. Reversing a rural preference which rewarded children for their early assumption of adult responsibility, the child-saving movement had grown out of a preference for lengthening childhood "innocence" and delaying the acquisition of adult "sophistication." (The anxiety about children's participation in theater described in chapter 1 was a product of this attitude.) The word "sophisticated" applied to children was pejorative and referred to sexual or related knowledge, such as the ways of the streets. Ordinary sexual knowledge obtained prematurely was viewed as damaging, and the result would be a morally damaged child.

The precise damages caused by parents' immoral behavior were not usually specified, nor was there any burden of proof on child welfare workers; it was not necessary to *prove* damage to children before labeling the parents neglectful. The child-saving perspective on immorality was largely predictive rather than descriptive. The immorality of parents was expected to produce an immoral child. Key to this logic was the view that children had to learn sexual misbehavior, that they did not by themselves turn to "self-abuse" or dirty games.

The entire perspective on parental immorality was gendered. Parents' low "standards" were thought more dangerous for girls than for boys, and, indeed, male sex delinquents never appeared in the child protection case records.[44] Since it was almost exclusively mothers who could become immoral, their presumed greater closeness to and influence over daughters put the girls in greater danger. Indeed, it was dangerous for a daughter to love an immoral mother:

> Born out of wedlock, her first ten years spent with an immoral mother who lived in a wretched tenement in a poor district . . . the background of thirteen-year-old Jane who came to us from one of our courts as a delinquent child. . . . Jane proved to be untruthful, restless, never happy. She had great affection for her mother and was determined to be with her although she knew the kind of life she was living. Several times she ran away to her, and to the vicious old neighborhood which she seemed

to love. We have every reason to believe that she was not involved in immoral conduct when truanting from our foster homes. . . . We believe the chief factors in our failure were the bad home background, strong affection for a mother she knew to be immoral . . .[45]

Similarly gendered was the concern in these records about masturbation. There were several cases in which girls' masturbation was considered as the evidence of immoral upbringing, but none about boys' until the 1950s. This absence is in striking contrast to the previous alarm about boys' masturbation, in the mid-nineteenth century.[46] In the Progressive era, "expert" opinion on masturbation went through a double transformation: the sickening effects of "self-abuse" were transferred from the physical to the emotional sphere; and it was girls' indulgence which was feared.[47] This is consistent with the general attitude that lower-class girls constituted a moral problem and a danger to others. Male sexual misbehavior, by contrast, was seen primarily as a danger to the individual himself, due to the bodily weakening it would cause.

These basic categories of child neglect remained constant, but their content and relative priority shifted several times during this period, mirroring waves of public concern about family life—the undoing of family stability, women's more public economic and social roles, and sexual permissiveness. These concerns were in turn affected by larger political, social, and economic events, including two world wars, the Great Depression of the 1930s, and political realignments such as the New Deal liberal consensus and the McCarthy conservatism of the 1950s. The rest of this chapter will describe these various historical influences on the definitions of child neglect.

WAR, DELINQUENCY, PROHIBITION: 1917–1930

Until the Depression, although some Progressive-style efforts to improve children's environment continued, through health and recreational campaigns, for example, the child protectors defined neglect mainly as a sign of family moral inadequacy and attempted to restore parental control. These emphases were supported by the war and its effects, especially noticeable in a naval-base city like Boston; a concern with juvenile delinquency and the correlation child-savers believed it to have with inadequate parenting; and the Prohibition "experiment," strongly supported by most child-savers.

World War I escalated child-welfare activism. Just as conscription had revealed the ill health and ill education of masses of teenage boys and young men, so the war effort called attention to the need for healthy children.[48] The child-protection organizations joined the general child-welfare establishment in denouncing child labor. Children were described, as they were to be again in World War II, as a national resource in need of "conservation." "Society as a whole, represented by the State, realizes that to ensure its own future economic and social welfare, it must secure to its children equal opportunities for health, happiness, sound education and character."[49] In their public pronouncements, the child-savers shifted their emphasis to national social welfare issues and de-emphasized intrafamily violence.

The war hastened the feminization of child-protection work. Male agents away in the armed forces were replaced by women, a change the MSPCC considered an unfortunate and temporary expedient in 1918. But the two-to-one female/male proportion of MSPCC agents created by the war then became permanent.[50] The use of female agents was further encouraged by the increase in sexual offenses involving sailors and underage girls, and the accompanying fear of venereal disease.[51] The War Department called on the MSPCC to assist in protecting "the personnel of the nation's soldiers and sailors from evil sex practices with vicious young women and to protect the foolish and innocent girl from contact with the depraved."[52] The moralism and woman-blaming of this interpretation expressed, of course, the fact that the War Department was concerned more with the spread of venereal disease than with child abuse. In fact, teenage girl delinquents (of whom more in chapter 7) had for many years been found frequenting the Charlestown Navy base, Revere Beach, the Boston Common, looking for sailors, a good time, escape from home, and perhaps a bit of money. The wartime addition of thousands of young sailors increased the incidence and the awareness of the problem, and changed its definition. The wartime sexual scandals continued patterns that the MSPCC had recognized for at least a decade, but somehow when the boys or men involved were sailors it seemed worse. Uniforms raised the status of these working-class boys, turning them into victims needing protection from "vicious young women." Furthermore, the war also had a considerable cultural effect in eroding standards of propriety and weakening parental authority, and thereby also producing a demand for greater control.

In the publicity about these immoralities, two different interpretations competed—a child-protection view that saw sexual abuse of children and a military one that saw girls seducing and ruining sailors. Integrating those interpretations was the new but rapidly spreading concept of delinquency. Consider *how* the MSPCC narrated these 1918 cases:

> Two girls of 13 and 14 who were "picking up" sailors at Revere Beach last fall belonged to a father and mother who had made shipwreck of their home. The father drank and lived apart most of the time from his family. The mother kept a lodging house in a poor part of Boston and was probably immoral. The older girl was found to be diseased, and the younger was still chaste. The home offered no protection. The other was committed by the court to the Industrial School for Girls. An aunt of good reputation came forward to train the younger, who was placed on probation.

> A second year high school girl of 16 whose mother was very sick with heart disease and whose father was brutal to all his children, found no interest or attraction in her home. Instead she frequented Boston Common and acted there in a very demonstrative way with sailors. She acknowledged being immoral. The father was found to be irascible and cruel rather than co-operative and helpful. An older daughter who was at home had an illegitimate child. The influences that surrounded this girl were not favorable for her protection or correction. She needed a new home where she could have kind and firm treatment. So far the father has not consented to our plan, but we hope still to carry it through.[53]

This perspective was not less moralistic than the nineteenth-century views, but now the girls were both blamed and excused. They were active wrongdoers, but their misbehavior was a product of abuse and neglect.[54]

Parental responsibility for children's misbehavior was at the heart of the meaning of delinquency for child-savers. To them, delinquency was not just criminality in the young; it became in itself a form of child neglect, or more precisely, the *prima facie* evidence of the existence of neglect.[55] Since girls' delinquency was usually sexual,[56] it was evidence of moral neglect. Boys' delinquency, defined as an increasing problem in the decades to come, was more often violent or thieving, and it was interpreted as a product of a slightly different type of neglect, failure of supervision and discipline.

Many of the client parents had a different understanding of child development. They experienced their children as fundamentally autonomous, bad or good by chance or predetermination. As with so many of the categories of child abuse, in the use of the delinquency category the child-savers were imposing new norms of responsibility upon parents.

The involvement of child-protection agencies such as the MSPCC in delinquency grew out of their earlier concern with children's street life, with a new emphasis on the dangers of peer pressure. Children went wrong because of the influence of other, already bad, children. Social investigators discovered gangs.[57] Reformers among them, criticizing the repressive approach of older child-savers, looked for environmental causes and remedies.[58] The child-protection agencies, by contrast, looked more to parental fault.

Delinquency became one of the major themes in child protection. MSPCC reports cited divorce, domestic discord, parents' failure to offer discipline and spiritual guidance, and lack of religious ideals as the sources of juvenile delinquency. These familial inadequacies were vaguely but ominously connected to permissive patterns in the popular culture, such as unchaperoned forms of recreation. For example, Pauline Bachelder of the MSPCC denounced dance halls, automobiles, and restaurants as sources of the ruin of girls with "unsheltering homes and unsympathetic mothers."[59] Citing "the menace of low grade motion pictures," Carstens argued that films presented "the abnormal in family life, and unfaithfulness to family ideals and the breaking of the marriage tie . . ."[60] Ironically, even as the agency lobbied for more and more expert influence in the courts and in informal child-welfare decisions, it complained that parents were sloughing off their responsibilities for training and guidance onto "the church, the school and the public authorities."[61]

The MSPCC used this concern to expand its jurisdiction and to increase the concern of other agencies with child protection, as any case of delinquency became *ipso facto* a case of neglect. "Domestic discord and family disruption spell child neglect and delinquency. The remedy lies in a better understanding and respect for the sanctity of marriage and the duties and responsibilities of parenthood."[62] The delinquency concern increased inter-agency dealings. The child protectors used the new juvenile clinics, of which the Judge Baker Guidance Center was a preeminent example, for psychological evaluations of clients. The MSPCC increasingly turned to the Children's Aid Association and other predecessors of the BCSA for placements and supervision of children. In turn, other agencies accepted the notion of parental neglect as a source of delinquency. For example, consider this analysis offered by Children's Aid:

> Virginia, a 15-year-old girl who was constantly nagged by a stepmother with four stepchildren besides a brood of her own. On a certain Sunday when one of the mother's own children broke a dish, the stepmother vented her displeasure on Virginia, who ran away to escape her abuse. At Revere Beach she fell in with a soldier with whom she spent the rest of the day . . . We got the stepmother, an ignorant, careless woman, to take a greater interest in her husband's children, among them Mary, a girl older than Virginia, who had also run away from home because of the terrible atmosphere and who, when we found her, had been taken to a hospital, suffering from the after effects of attempted abortion. . . . We have also prevented the younger girls from following in the steps of Mary and Virginia.[63]

Boys' delinquency, too, was associated with family problems: "Dan had started suddenly in a career of crime . . . when from the taunts of children in the neighborhood he learned that he was not really the child of the people he had come to know as his own."[64]

For the client families, the delinquency emphasis had mixed results. It helped legitimate mother-blaming and prejudice against "deviant" and culturally different family patterns. But it also sometimes led to the uncovering of serious child abuse, because of the ways in which children "act out" as a means of attracting attention. Girls became sexually delinquent, boys stole and fought, and children of both sexes ran away;

investigations then revealed their mistreatment by parents.[65] A South Boston Irish boy of thirteen ran away fifteen times, sometimes staying out as long as a week, despite great privation and cold. The case record, from the years 1918–20, raised no question as to why he was running away. But a Judge Baker therapist, to whom the boy was referred, discovered that he had experienced extreme abuse by his father.[66] In Boston's West End in 1920 an eleven-year-old Jewish boy, son of immigrants, had become a major behavior problem—fighting, breaking windows—although his four siblings were well behaved. Investigation revealed that the boy was the butt of serious abuse by his father, who had identified him as bad from his earliest years.[67] In another 1920 case, five siblings, all delinquent, led agents to a stepmother who beat the children with pokers.[68] Many girls' delinquency cases led to the uncovering of incest.[69]

The campaign for Prohibition was as important as delinquency in influencing child protection in the 1920s. The child protectors were enthusiastic about that reform, viewing intemperance as the leading cause of the mistreatment of children.[70] Indeed, child-savers had been active in campaigns against liquor and "housebreakers" (the temperance slogan for saloons) for decades, and with significant local success.[71] Thus the MSPCC and like-minded reformers rhapsodized about the beneficial effects of Prohibition.[72]

There was a high correlation of family violence with intemperance, but Prohibition did not remedy the problem. Leaving family violence aside for the moment, we know that drinking rates in the United States had been declining since the 1830s. (By the turn of the century, average per capita consumption of alcohol in spirits was 22 percent, in beer 54 percent, of what it had been in 1830.[73] Moreover, the temporary decline wrought by Prohibition was short-lived. Patterns of family violence paralleled these changes exactly. As the graph on page 142 shows, the rate of drunkenness in family violence cases was declining before Prohibition, took a sudden dip at the beginning of Prohibition, then began to climb again while Prohibition was still in effect (as illegal bootlegging and saloon-keeping became organized).[74] The figures cannot be interpreted to prove a decline in drinking since we cannot know if we are seeing changes in clients' behavior or in caseworkers' sensibility. It is questionable whether drinking behavior could have altered so quickly after National Prohibition began on July 1, 1919, since Massachusetts enacted state prohibition enforcement procedures only at the end of 1924. The drop may have reflected caseworkers' expectation that clients would be drinking less. Furthermore, the Prohibition experience shook the child protectors' belief that temperance was a solution to family violence. Already in 1921 the MSPCC, despite its satisfaction with the immediate decline in drunkenness, reported increases in moral neglect, non-support, delinquency, and illegitimacy.[75] Throughout Prohibition the MSPCC reported surprise at the steady increase in its volume of work.[76]

The almost universal judgment has been against Prohibition, not only because it did not "work," but also because its origins and its operation were discriminatory, particularly against the immigrants who dominated the poor sections of the large Eastern cities.[77] Prohibition campaigners, including the child protectors, blamed immigrants for the problem and used temperance rhetoric to organize and promote nativist prejudice. Not only was the temperance movement ridden with class and ethnic inequality, but so were drinking patterns themselves. Early in the nineteenth century drinking and drunkenness had been more evenly distributed across classes: even meetings of the Protestant clergy had often been drunken affairs.[78] Temperance began as a middle-class movement, and by the 1850s a wide class chasm in drinking habits had opened, as a substantial portion of the middle class had renounced hard liquor and the working class used it more intensively than ever.[79] Heavy drinking was an Irish tradition, but it was also a symptom of and a remedy for stress, worry, hopelessness, tiredness, illness, depression, hunger, and a host of other aspects of the experience of the immigrants and the urban poor.

Temperance has been reevaluated recently partly because of the rediscovery by historians of its feminist agenda.[80] Previously, the usual image of women's role in temperance featured Carrie Nation smashing saloon windows, and supported the view of women temperance activists as hysterical, prudish, and elitist. Women's hostility to drinking did contain repressive and anti-immigrant attitudes, as did that of male temperance leaders, but also an analysis of drinking as an activity supporting male privilege and producing destructive consequences for women and children. They emphasized its contribution to violence against women and children, the baneful influence of the saloon as a preserve

3. DRUNKENNESS IN FAMILY-VIOLENCE CASES, BY YEAR

PERCENTAGE OF CASES IN WHICH
ASSAILANTS WERE ALLEGED DRUNK

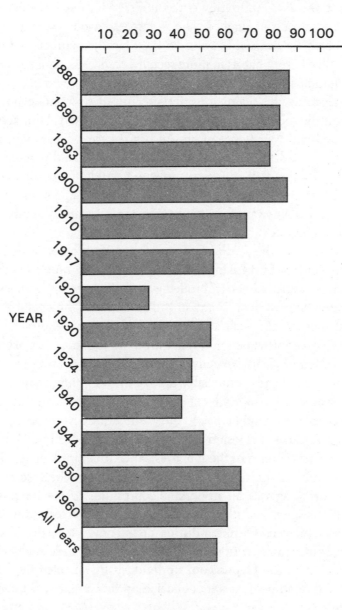

of male irresponsibility, the removal of men from participation in family life, and men's expenditure on liquor of money needed for family food, heat, and rent.

The child protectors' pro-temperance views shared the feminist as well as the nativist sensibility about temperance. The neglect cases might even shake one's anti-Prohibition convictions, so terrible is the evidence of the destructiveness of alcohol. The widespread addiction to it created misery not only for its users but also for their family members and other intimates. Like heroin habits in more recent decades, alcohol consumed disproportionate shares of tiny family budgets. It caused pain, illness, and premature death, again not only affecting the alcoholic but also depriving family members of companionship and support. Drunkenness also escalated family violence. Physical-neglect cases were often associated with heavy drinking, which deepened poverty and parental listlessness; the filthiest flats, the most unkempt children were frequently those with alcoholic parents. Alcoholism contributed to poor supervision of children. Drinking was also a major factor in intrafamily conflict and emotional disruption.[81]

Not surprisingly, the feminist supporters of Prohibition overlooked the problems caused by drinking women. Fathers were more often drunk than mothers, yet mothers embroiled with child-saving agencies apparently drank a great deal, if any of the caseworkers' observations can be trusted. The male-female difference in drinking was substantial in child abuse and adult violence cases, with male-to-female drunkenness ratios of 50:35 and 72:50 respectively. In child-neglect cases, in which a mother was considered responsible almost by definition, male-female difference was smaller (overall 71.5 percent of fathers in neglect cases and 63.6 percent of mothers). Of course the attitudes of the agencies as well as the uneven division of child-raising responsibilities led to overrepresenting mothers in these figures, since their drinking was more likely to be noticed and disapproved of. Nevertheless, the case records reveal that drinking was an important contributor to the depression, apathy, unreliability, and ill health that so often characterized mothers of neglected children. Drinking during pregnancy, especially in combination with the malnutrition and chronic ill health of so many of the urban poor before the Depression, no doubt badly affected the health of infants, although no data were collected on this problem. Moreover, in comparison to contemporary estimates of the sex ratio in drinking—historical estimates are not available—the women in these family-violence cases drank far more heavily than average women.[82] Women drank differently from men: they drank at home, not in saloons, and thus drank more often in isolation. Boston's immigrant tenements were noted for their home manufacture and sale of liquor, predating Prohibition (as a result of scarce licenses and high fees for licenses), and women handled most of the manufacture and sale.[83]

Consider, for example, the 1935 case of English-Canadian immigrants with two sons, five and eight. Mr. Scott, as we will call him, appeared a stable working-class man: a machinist, president of his union local, member of the Odd Fellows and the Masonic Order. After five years of marriage Mrs. Scott began to drink heavily and to deteriorate rapidly: she was evicted for hosting loud and late drinking parties and arrested for receiving stolen goods. The children were loitering on the streets and accused of stealing, and the agency worker, upon entering the home, encountered an extremely neglectful scene. The children slept on a dirty mattress with dirty blankets, their clothing black with dirt; there were dirty dishes, a bad smell, no food, little furniture, and 150 empty liquor bottles.[84]

In this case, as in so many others, the drinking was as much a symptom of poverty and stress as a cause. For example, in the nineteenth century liquor was often the only pure drink available, although Boston had better water earlier than other large cities; even in the twentieth century advertisements emphasized the purity of beer. Moreover, beer was cheaper than, for example, milk.[85] It is difficult to isolate and measure the impact of alcohol specifically, as few heavy-drinking parents could be shown to have had more promising situations before they began drinking.

And while feminist and anti-family-violence perspectives stimulate a more positive appraisal of the Prohibition impulse, they do not vindicate its effects. The child-savers' expectations of Prohibition were unrealistic, not only because they put too much faith in legal regulation, and surely not because they exaggerated the evils of alcohol. They lacked, however, self-critical consciousness about the cultural and class significance of temperance and its relation to the cultural and class differences between themselves and their clients. The child-savers' endorsement of Prohibition, their unsympathetic attitude toward alcohol, and their inability to distinguish moderate from addicted drinking increased their alienation from many (though not all) of their clients, and in the long run did nothing to alleviate the contribution of drunkenness to violence.

THE DEPRESSION AND WORLD WAR II:
ECONOMIC STRESS AND FAMILY LIFE, 1930–1945

Beginning this research, I set out to examine the impact of stressful times—wars and economic recessions—on domestic violence. I found several surprises. There was no evidence of an overall escalation of family violence during these periods. Certain types of family violence stood out in particular periods—moral neglect during World War I, as we have seen, and physical neglect during the Depression—but these shifts reflected the sensibility of caseworkers as much as family behaviors. Most surprising were the continuities between periods in which I had expected to find different patterns, the Depression and World War II. Under closer scrutiny, these continuities turn out to be relevant not only to family violence but to general patterns of family and social-work adaptation to national, shared stress.

Child protectors responded to the Depression and war, from 1930 to 1945, with an emphasis on physical neglect as opposed to other forms of family violence. Neglect had been, as we have seen, the main form of family violence since the Progressive era. The rhetoric of child protection, in part for fund-raising purposes, had remained focused on violent assaults, and the major forms of neglect remained moral. By contrast, in the Depression and war periods, both in case records and in public pronouncements, the characteristic victim suffered from physical deprivation.

Contemporary studies leave little doubt that economic depression worsens family violence problems, but they do not single out neglect as distinguished from other forms of family violence. Poverty in itself, declining standards of living in particular, and the stresses of unemployment lead to anger and self-blaming. These stresses detonate aggression as well as apathy and depression. But experts of the 1930s emphasized only neglect.[86]

The MSPCC reported an 8.4 percent increase in caseload in 1931, and

16.4 percent in 1932, even as its income fell off severely.[87] This increase was mainly in neglect cases. The MSPCC insisted that unemployment produced "irritability and domestic discord" over and above the effects of poverty itself. A variously expressed distinction—between poverty (read: chronic) and unemployment (read: acute), between poverty itself and the demoralizing effects of poverty—became particularly important during the Depression because the agency was having to defend itself against renewed accusations that it stole the children of the poor: "Our help was asked for these children not because they were in trouble through family misfortune, such as sickness, unemployment or death, but because they were the innocent victims of brutality and crime, of vicious and degrading surroundings, or of parental abuse and neglect."[88] Several petitions called upon the state legislature to investigate malfeasance by the MSPCC. Early in 1934 the Massachusetts House Committee on Public Welfare held hearings on a bill calling for an investigation; it was defeated, but not before a great deal of public hostility to the Society was expressed.[89] Judges were more critical than previously:

> Judge A. asked . . . about signed consent [of parents surrendering care and custody to the MSPCC] . . . He then talked for an hour vehemently about the malicious practice of taking liberty away from children, deceiving parents, using high-handed methods with poor uneducated people, even instructing Atty W. to call at MSPCC office to . . . ask how frequently we used the signed consent, ask to see them, and then report back to him. He told the parents . . . that the organization could be sued civilly for depriving the children of their liberty and gave the children permission to go to their homes . . .[90]

Poor people had always been more likely than others to lose their children to MSPCC action. But the Depression increased both the number of physically neglected children and the child protectors' sensitivity to that problem, which in turn increased public awareness of poor children being declared neglected. Boston's agencies believed that they were seeing a decrease in assault cases—but this was more likely an artifact of the greater visibility of neglect. There were more underweight, seriously malnourished, and physically defective children, and more medical intervention was found necessary.[91] There were cases of wandering, hobo children.[92]

4. THE CONTRIBUTION OF ECONOMIC STRESS
TO FAMILY VIOLENCE, BY YEAR

YEAR	PERCENTAGE OF ASSAILANTS AFFECTED BY:		
	Unemployment	*Poverty*	*Illness*
1880	58.3	40.9	NA
1890	28.6	60.5	NA
1893	17	41.9	30.6
1900	34.4	42.9	11
1910	34.1	59.6	16.4
1917	16.6	50.3	14.9
1920	20.6	40.2	9.6
1930	41.1	54.5	22.3
1934	35.2	59.6	21.9
1940	42.1	69.2	28.4
1944	13.3	35.8	16
1950	19.4	45.8	32.7
1960	23.6	72.2	10.8
Overall	28.3	53.1	20.3

5. THE CONTRIBUTION OF ECONOMIC STRESS
TO CHILD NEGLECT, BY YEAR

YEAR	PERCENTAGE OF ASSAILANTS AFFECTED BY:		
	Unemployment	*Poverty*	*Illness*
1880	100	46.2	NA
1890	50	70.4	100
1893	33.3	67.6	27.3
1900	40.5	47.7	18.4
1910	42.1	74.6	29.3
1917	24.2	59.1	11.8
1920	42.9	65.7	20.7
1930	51.6	67.7	38.9
1934	31.7	77.4	41.1
1940	54.7	84.1	35.7
1944	9.8	30.2	23.8
1950	23.5	51.9	48.9
1960	25	82.4	14.3
Overall	35.2	65.2	30

Attempts to measure precisely the contribution of economic stress to family violence results in similar ambiguities: are we measuring increases in violence or in its discovery? For the whole period of this study, poverty was considered (by the caseworkers, the clients, and/or the historians studying the cases) a major contributing factor in 53 percent of all cases and 65 percent of all neglect cases.[93] The correlation of poverty with family violence in general and neglect in particular was at its lowest in 1944 (when poverty correlated with 30 percent of neglect cases), a peak year of prosperity and employment in Boston due to war industries. It was high during the Depression, when poverty correlated with 77 percent of neglect cases. But this correlation was also high in 1910 (75 percent of neglect cases) and 1960 (82 percent). These erratic figures remind us that what is being measured is as much the sensibility of caseworkers as the conditions of clients. For example, while poverty was certainly more prevalent in 1934 than in 1920, there is no reason to think that it would have been more influential on family behavior. But in the 1930s the entire population, including social workers, was conscious of the stresses of poverty and quick to blame it for other problems.

The implication of unemployment as a contributing factor in family-violence cases may have been more reliable because more specific. It was represented only half as much as poverty—in 28 percent of all family violence and 35 percent of neglect cases. Lows in the influence of unemployment for 1917 and 1944 (24 percent and 10 percent, respectively) corresponded to two wartime highs in employment in Boston, while the drop in 1934 (down to 32 percent from 52 percent in 1930) reflected New Deal employment projects.

With caution, several generalizations may safely be drawn from these figures. One, poverty was the leading contributor to all forms of family violence and especially to child neglect. Moreover, the poverty/neglect correlations are so high that these figures support the concerns that poverty was confused with child neglect, and that poverty caused the discovery of child neglect. Two, the higher rates of poverty than unemployment as contributing factors in these cases suggest that economic stress contributes more to family violence when it is chronic than when it is acute. The devastating effect of chronic poverty lies in the fact that it so frequently produces *many* forms of stress. For example, poverty, unemployment, and illness often accompany each other, along with alcoholism, isolation, depression, and marital conflict; and each is a worse experience because of the presence of the other problems.

Child neglect in particular was frequently accompanied by problems often considered individual and psychological rather than social, such as hostility, mistrust, and miscommunication between parents. One family hard hit by the Depression had had several separations starting in 1929. The father had lost a barber shop he had owned. In 1934 he constantly lied: mystifying his family about whether he worked, promising to leave money for food and bills and then not doing so, promising to come home but going to his parents for meals when his wife and children had no food.[94] Lack of money, like a diagnostic stain, flowed directly to the weak points in a relationship and exposed them. Even in the case of single mothers, most vulnerable to the pressures of poverty, the Depression did not function as a unique, acute cause of child neglect. A Portuguese-American mother struggled to maintain three children while she worked at a tavern at night. Her children had lice and impetigo, were sent home from school because of inadequate clothing, and were unsupervised. But this woman was also contending with an abusive estranged husband who now sought her out to threaten her and who spitefully reported on her at every opportunity to the MSPCC.[95] Family violence, including child neglect, is always personal; the influence of "external" pressures, such as poverty or sexism, is felt through the content of particular relationships.

The multiple causes of family violence suggest the need for skepticism in distinguishing one fundamental form of stress from other, supplementary, ones; and for caution in diagnoses and remedies focusing on one problem alone. Yet this was just the direction child-protection agencies took: under the impact of the Depression, they began to concentrate on meeting material needs. They viewed themselves increasingly as part of the general field of child welfare, and, like most social workers, were drawn into political alignment with welfare Democrats, supporting New Deal relief programs.[96]

This alignment has generally been seen as exclusively positive for child welfare. The perspective of child protection, however, yields a somewhat more mixed view of these developments. In criticizing the exclusive focus on economic need among anti-family-violence agencies, I am not criticizing the increased public responsibility for economic welfare, except insofar as it was not enough. I am making a much more specific criticism, of the implicit view that family violence is a problem of poor people. Relief may have been the single most helpful thing a worker could provide, but it was not the only sort of help needed, and it had some unfortunate effects. Child protectors' power of referral to relief-giving agencies increased the caseworkers' power, since the way a client was described by a referring agency could determine how much she or he would get. One widower, for example, hired housekeepers to care for his three children. The MSPCC objected to these arrangements on moral grounds, and to the fact that he had insured his children, and therefore recommended to the OPW against increasing his welfare payments.[97] Memos between agencies conducted a kind of triage among clients. For example:

> Soc[iety] has spent a great deal of time and money on this family Feel they have made no headway [Parents] are low grade and very little can be done with them They are receiving city aid practically all the time . . . Feels it is a waste of time to continue supervising this family . . .[98]

Sometimes, in a reversal of influence, relief agencies feared the judgments of the child-protection workers, and clients were caught between. In one 1940 case a single-mother family had lived in desperate poverty, without a stove, the children without shoes or stockings. The OPW, which had this family on its caseload since 1938,

> hesitated . . . because the ct.[court] might feel that the OPW was partly to blame for the lack of chn's meals because OPW did not notice the lack of the stove and did not get a stove for the fam. Felt that regardless of whether or no mo[ther] had ever had a stove she would have neglected the chn. and would do so in the future.[99]

Moreover, Depression attitudes changed the very definitions of neglect. The child-welfare establishment extended its view of children's rights to include entitlement to a standard of living independent of what their parents could provide. This new principle, emanating from a democratic, equality-of-opportunity perspective, ironically deepened the potentially discriminatory effect of efforts against family violence. While it led to increased emphasis on material aid, it also meant that the children of the poor were by definition neglected, that family "pathology" was a problem of the poor.[100]

The definition of this deprivation denied the inequalities of gender. The dominant causal analysis of neglect implicated poverty and an inegalitarian class structure, and ignored other, equally structural causes such as sexual inequality and women's exclusive responsibility for parenting. As neglect became the general framework for the understanding of all children's mistreatment, mother-blaming became still further established. Neglect became *by definition* a female form of child mistreatment. Neglect diagnoses usually accepted as a given the absence of paternal responsibility for children, beyond the obligation of economic support. Child welfare workers did not notice evidence that many problems of child-raising stemmed from sexual inequality. Their definitions of deprivation ignored gender, within households and within the economy.

In promoting a view of child neglect as an epiphenomenon of poverty, caseworkers also contributed to a well-warranted skepticism about their own objectivity and ability to help. If child mistreatment is simply a result of poverty, why not abolish casework and instead guarantee full employment and adequate relief? There is some merit in this suggestion. As an illustration of the limitations of that approach, however, consider what would have been the dominant understanding of what "full employment" has meant: jobs for men, not for women. Or consider the implications that relief has had—loss of autonomy, submission to humiliating supervision, a reputation of parasitism. The failure to question the normative (yet, even in 1930, not necessarily typical) sexual division of labor—male breadwinning and full-time female domesticity—left untouched many other sources of stress that are implicated in family violence.

The exclusive concentration on poverty as a cause of family violence made the Second World War period seem entirely different to many child welfare workers. Maintaining a more complex view of the sources of family stress reveals, instead, important similarities between the two periods. Just like unemployment, militarization and increased women's employment brought structural pressures on many families finding the conventional sexual division of labor uncomfortable or economically impossible. Both were national, shared crises in which women were called upon to play new economic roles under heavy pressure, but with no supporting encouragement to rethink their identities, aspirations, or relationships. Women supporting their families were nevertheless expected to carry on alone all the conventional women's labors, including deference to male family "heads." These contradictory demands were reflected, as we will see, in the advice of child protectors. In both periods many men were more dependent on women, losing the material base for their dominance—due to unemployment or absence—and panicky in response. Child protectors urged women clients to shore up these men's confidence, ignoring how empty such reassurance was bound to be.

Clinicians saw connections between new stresses and intrafamily relationships, but the lessons they drew continued to insist on the integrity of the family unit as the highest goal and the responsibility of the wife for maintaining it. This vignette was used as an example of a *typical* Depression family problem in an MSPCC staff conference: "The wife is likely to blame her husband and resort to fault-finding and scolding. It is difficult for her to give up former standards of living. The husband then is facing two situations,—his inability to find work and his strained relationship to his wife and children."[101] If one can ignore temporarily the use of the "nagging wife" stereotype to exculpate a husband, the vignette accurately renders the interaction between external stress— unemployment and a hopeless economic outlook—and intimate relationships. But the analysis remains gendered in a most unequal way: agency workers considered the stresses of the Depression as mitigating circumstances of (his) violence as they did not in the case of (her) neglect. They considered her behavior as provocation to his violence, but not his behavior as provocation to her neglect.

The double bind of mothers tightens considerably in an economic depression: on the one hand, mothers' earning capacity is the weakest of any group in the society, but on the other hand, they continue to bear virtually the entire material and psychological responsibility for the welfare of their children. In measuring the effects of unemployment, social workers assumed women's domestic role as inevitable and natural, and thus their sacrifices and difficulties went unnoticed. They frequently faced problems they could not solve. The Depression decreased the old charity tradition of blaming housewives' budgetary inefficiency for their families' inability to live on their incomes. But a general cultural blaming of mothers, and the mothers' self-blaming, continued.

Husbands were often active participants in this blaming.[102] Reporting wives for child neglect was so common a practice, since the beginning of the child-protection agencies, as to be practically a tradition in itself. In a sense this "tattling" was but introducing a new weapon into marital struggles. That shortage of money escalates marital disputes about how money is spent should surprise no one. One father in 1940 blamed his family problems on his wife's desire for luxuries, which turned out to mean furniture.[103] Other relatives, frequently in-laws, also accused mothers of unwise budgeting or poor housekeeping.

Sometimes these accusations against mothers were true. A 1934 mother of six living children (three had died), staying with her mother-in-law, was accused by the latter of being a "slack housekeeper." The neighbors, furthermore, had stopped donating old clothes to the family because the mother would not take care of them. The children attended school only irregularly and were filthy. The father was regularly employed by the city street department, but his wages had been cut from $28.80 to $20 a week. This mother was ill and in pain, obese and diabetic; later it was revealed that the oldest daughter had been forced into an incestuous relationship with her father.[104] The mother-in-law's complaints may have been justified. The point is not that women were always falsely accused of poor housekeeping (though sometimes they were), but that their apathy was often symptomatic of deeper problems.

The widespread employment of women during World War II did not fundamentally alter the norms of women's domesticity and exclusive responsibility for children. The popularity of working women during the war was temporary and superficial; the "Rosies" were charming precisely because they represented a titillating, transient turnabout in femininity and, moreover, a *sacrifice* made for the patriotic emergency. (In fact, the evidence suggests that the women who actually got the industrial, unionized war-production jobs did not consider the experience a sacrifice but, overwhelmingly, an opportunity which they hated giving up.) Nearly everyone expected that they would leave their jobs to returning men when the war ended. Similarly, the existence of many non-nuclear-family households during the war was integrated as a brave and extraordinary adaptation to hardship, not as the beginning of new forms of living.

From their origins, child protection agencies had been so hostile to mothers' employment that they virtually considered it child neglect by definition. While married women's employment had been steadily increasing throughout the whole period of this study, its increase during the war was more rapid, and the perception of its increase was exaggerated beyond that.[105] In the past, agency objections to women working had been *a priori*, applied even when women had no alternative or when their employment seemed to have little bearing on the family violence. For example, in 1920 an Italian immigrant father owned and operated a shoe repair shop and the mother worked intermittently at piecework machine sewing for the garment industry. The family was reported by a teacher when one of their five children arrived at school with welts on his face. The father admitted that his wife was "a little hasty" in punishment at times. The MSPCC responded by trying to get her to quit working. Yet there was no evidence to suggest that her staying home would have helped.[106]

During World War II patriotism created a temporarily positive image of the working woman. But at the same time, objections to women's employment gained new arguments concerning child neglect and delinquency. This contradictory mood among child welfare workers produced a great deal of waffling in public statements. The MSPCC reported increases in child neglect among working mothers but insisted that it was "inevitable" and "unintentional," that "relatively few working mothers have willfully neglected their children."[107] The consensus that working mothers were the cause of juvenile delinquency, so dominant in the 1950s, was conditioned by this interpretation of the World War II experience.[108] Even at the peak of the war effort, the U.S. Children's Bureau branded children of employed mothers as the group most "vulnerable" to delinquency.[109] The Society reported a doubling of the incidence of delinquency among the children of working mothers in one year, and then tried to stanch what it called "hysterical publicity" about juvenile delinquency by showing that, despite recent increases, it was still below its 1931 level.[110] There can be no doubt that there was severe inadequacy in child care facilities for working mothers, but the child protectors were not active in campaigning for day-care centers. Just as in the Progressive era anxiety about female-headed households had prevented the offering of help which might have improved their conditions, so now anxiety about working women produced a victim-blaming response. Women war workers were praised for their "sacrifices" but were not offered a great deal of help in child care or housework, and the double bind in which they found themselves was then displayed as evidence that mothers' employment was bad for children. In 1942 an MSPCC survey found that lack of child care and abuse by improper caretakers were increasing. However, this survey counted new cases involving working mothers without a controlling comparison to cases with non-employed mothers or to prewar cases.[111]

There was a decided contrast between the MSPCC and the Judge Baker attitude toward working mothers and delinquency. The Judge Baker social workers and psychologists had less ambivalence in their absolute condemnation of women's employment, seeming to absorb none of the rosy approval of women war workers. Even in 1944, at the height of the war effort, a Judge Baker psychotherapist blamed a mother's employment for her fourteen-year-old son's truancy and ill temper.[112] A mother working at an Army base is described as having a "gay old time."[113] There were two reasons for this difference. First, the psychiatric orientation at Judge Baker focused its workers particularly on fears of women's rejection of femininity. Second, the difference also reflected the class of the clients. MSPCC clients were overwhelmingly poor and contained high proportions of single mothers. The agency was well aware that employment was often a necessity for its clients, and that their failure to provide adequate child care was a function not just of employment in itself but of class:

> Although S.P.C.C. cases may not be regarded as a barometer of general child care provisions for children of working mothers, certain difficulties that do arise when mothers in the lower income and social brackets seek employment are revealed. And, conceivably, it will be these women who increasingly will be going into industry as employer specifications for women workers are revised downward because of the decreasing labor supply.[114]

Furthermore, MSPCC workers were aware of the greater "temptations," as they would have described them, threatening to lure poor girls into sin, with or without working mothers or jobs.[115]

In fact, at no child-protection agency did the case records show evidence of an increase in neglect related to women's employment. Nor did later studies find any such evidence.[116] It is possible that despite the hardships resulting from women's employment, the gains in budget, mood, and self-esteem among working mothers compensated for any negative effects children might have experienced from the long hours of women doing a double day's work.

The MSPCC was also concerned with the contribution of child labor to delinquency. Boston work permits to children increased radically: 383 had been issued to fourteen- and fifteen-year-olds in 1940, and in 1944 there were 85,000.[117] The MSPCC's worry about the centrifugal impact of wartime labor on the family was expressed, in keeping with its moralistic past, in terms of the decline in "moral fiber" resulting from increased prosperity. The agency worried about how these children would be persuaded to return to school when the war was over: "lured from school to war work by high wages, and, without the training and discipline of good home life, without . . . church, without a sense of their duties as citizens . . . bent on exciting pleasures . . ."[118] A concern with discipline and moral standards, rather than education, underlay the child labor protests. "We are getting a more difficult type of children, especially the teenage girls," reported the matron of the Temporary Home. "They are more sophisticated . . . their idea of a good time is being allowed to stay out all hours of the night, entertaining men in uniform, and being allowed to do exactly as they please . . ."[119]

There was parallel concern about mothers' morality:

Deprived for so long, excesses by way of unwise spending are quite natural,—not only for home and personal needs . . . but recreation and harmful indulgences, such as drinking parties, both in road-houses and in homes. Many mothers have taken jobs, leaving young children without adequate care or supervision. With newly acquired economic independence many mothers have left their husbands and children to escape marital tensions, and the drudgery of home and family duties . . . In general, these situations are not due to viciousness, and are easily corrected by friendly advice and persuasion.[120]

Women's infidelity in the absence of husbands—and the presence of sailors—produced many condemnations. Mothers were frequently accused of "promiscuity" because they had lovers, even if they were regular boyfriends.[121] Some angry husbands questioned the paternity of children and reported their wives.[122] "Great care should be taken in determining the legitimacy or illegitimacy of children of married women whose husbands are away in service," the MSPCC instructed its workers.[123] In this context it becomes clear that the child-protection agency's concern during the war was not so much an *a priori* objection to women's employment as a confused uneasiness with a permissive society and what it meant for the traditional family.

Throughout the twin crises—Depression and war—the emphasis on poverty and its relief tended to hide intrafamily conflicts, oppression, and violence. The crisis sensibility promoted a view of family unity as essential to survival and of intrafamily tensions as ephemeral products of economic hardship. Popular culture romanticized family together-ness, and many caseworkers operated as if naming and discussing family conflict, let alone violence, was encouraging it. The attitude that one should work to "strengthen" families often meant urging individuals to ignore grievances.

Recently scholars have noted that family violence, including both child abuse and wife-beating, escalated as a result of Depression stresses;[124] but at the time, the emphasis continued on neglect, not abuse. Not only was intrafamily aggression losing visibility within the protective agencies' own caseload, being replaced by the emphasis on material neglect, but family violence as a social problem ceased to compel pop-ular attention.[125] After a severe drop in income during the Depression, the MSPCC did not regain its successful money-raising status during World War II or the 1950s.

This resuppression of concern with child abuse and wife-beating was doubly problematic for women. Not only was the violence against them hidden, but the greatest concern was with the form of family violence for which they were considered exclusively responsible: child neglect.

THE FEMININE MYSTIQUE AND EMOTIONAL NEGLECT: THE 1950s

The hostility to women's work expressed so intensely by Judge Baker clinicians was part of a reassertion of conventional feminine domesticity that has been called the "feminine mystique." It fit both the dominant American Freudian school of psychology and the general social conservatism that emerged after World War II, which included attacks on all forms of radicalism. Because of its psychiatric orientation, the Judge Baker clinic was the earliest and the most extreme in its attempts to enforce this women's domesticity and subordination through the categories of psychic health and pathology, but the prevalent gender conservatism was evident, beginning a bit later, at all three agencies in this study. The child protectors enforced their strictures about women's proper behavior through an escalated woman-blaming. This was particularly vivid in cases of wife-beating and incest, which will be discussed in the relevant chapters below. It was also present in neglect cases.

For example, a twelve-year-old girl, one of nine children, was referred to Judge Baker as a delinquent, accused of shoplifting and other larceny. Her father was "brutal," according to the record, and beat the children badly when angry. The MSPCC record focused on the "moral" problem: the first six children were born in an out-of-wedlock relationship (indeed, the record always refers to the "illegimate father") and the next three by, allegedly, three different men. The Judge Baker therapists, by contrast, diagnosed the girl's difficulty in terms of maternal neglect, stemming from an inadequate ability to form relationships with women due to her mother's inadequacy—although, it bears emphasizing, neither agency's record contains any specific allegations of poor parenting against the mother.[126]

Psychiatric social workers were particularly concerned with "gender confusion," notably girls' failure to accept their femininity, as evidence of maternal inadequacy. For example, a sixteen-year-old girl steals from her father and stepmother, overeats, lies, and is "unruly." She is described as "not very feminine looking" because she is overweight, wears masculine-looking clothes, and has a tomboyish manner. Her therapist concludes that the girl's fear of men makes her in reality passive but she resolves this in her fantasy life by assuming the dominant position and assigning to the male a weak, feminine role. "As far as the F [father] is concerned . . . an underlying rape fantasy at the very bottom but just above that is an attempt to be like the father instead of submitting to him . . ." The stepmother is criticized for working full-time in a factory and going out with her girlfriends from the factory.[127] Another neglected child, a twelve-year-old girl with an "inferiority complex" who does not do well at school, alarms the Judge Baker therapists because she wears cowboy clothes. The mother had been first an incest and then a wife-beating victim; now she was considering marriage with a man she has known for two years but hesitated because she was fearful of sex. The psychiatrist noted with approval that the mother "forced her to use girls' clothes last time she came in. I do think it is a positive reaching out; she can do it when she is made to do it." Another psychiatrist thinks "this patient has, in a sense, had a chronic depression since her F has left." In fact, she had been separated from her father since she was four, and he did not leave—rather her mother left him after enduring his alcoholism and abuse for eight years.[128]

The case notes of the MSPCC's child-protection workers did not contain such comments, because their training did not encourage collecting specific information along these lines. Psychiatric language was just being introduced into the MSPCC's analyses in the mid-1950s.[129] Yet caseworkers' concern with the looks of clients—commenting frequently on women's grooming and clothing—revealed the existence of such judgments. A study of neglecting parents, done by the MSPCC for the American Humane Association, measured clients' self-images along three indices: accepts sex identity, accepts identity as spouse, accepts identity as parent.[130] Such criteria left little room for clients'—mothers'—expressions of frustration and discontent with conventional sex roles.

All the agencies in this period shared a hostility to separation and divorce, and a policy of urging preservation of marriage at almost all costs. In one 1950 case a delinquent eleven-year-old boy lived with a single mother and two older siblings. His father had been committed to the state hospital for alcoholism and violence in 1939, when the boy was three months old. In 1942 the mother joined the Army, flourished, and remained in until 1946, earning the rank of captain and the training for her current job as a physical therapist. She loved her work, a fact which her Judge Baker therapist saw only as a problem. She was never divorced.[131] In 1949, out of the blue, so to speak, the father sent Christmas presents for the children (thinking they were much younger than they were) and asked to return to the family, reporting that he had joined Alcoholics Anonymous. The mother had no interest in this, but the

Judge Baker therapist argued that she was ambivalent: "Throughout this discussion it is quite obvious that mother was talking herself into the fact that it would be foolish to take father back." On the grounds that the boy needed a man to identify with, the therapist condemned her disinterest in her estranged husband. Furthermore, her relationship with her father, who had supported her in leaving her husband, was interpreted in negative terms, as her failure to be able to break from her parents.[132]

As the last story indicates, not only did social workers tend to support marriage, even at great cost, but they also endorsed nuclear family separateness and looked suspiciously on active extended-family networks. This bias was shared by social caseworkers and psychiatric social workers. It was simultaneously a class bias, reflecting the patterns of urban, educated strata accustomed to the erosion of kinship ties as a result of mobility and property accumulation; and a professional bias, hostile to those who would interfere with their relations to clients. It meant failure to recognize the importance of a vital resource for the poor and troubled: supportive friends and networks.

Although we of course have no control for comparison, many child-neglecting mothers seemed to lack such support.[133] A deserted mother moved with her daughter every few months between 1950 and 1960 as a result of hostilities with neighbors and landlords; the mother was so lonely she kept her daughter out of school in order to have company.[134] Sometimes the isolation of women was a result of patrilocality. Another 1950 mother was single much of the time because her husband, an itinerant juggler, was usually on the road. She and her four children lived in Everett (a suburb), next door to his parents and three sisters, who complained to the husband and the MSPCC about her mistreatment of the children. Upon investigation, however, the caseworker discovered that the husband did not support the family; that he was abusive; that she had not a single friend or acquaintance in Everett, having given up her own work as an "acrobatic dancer" (perhaps a euphemism for something disreputable); that she was dependent on money sent by her mother in upstate New York to support the children.[135]

Indeed, in some cases the social workers worsened the clients' isolation. In another 1950 case we meet a black family who had migrated from Georgia during the war. Soon afterward the father began to drink and became abusive to both mother and children; she took him to court repeatedly and finally won a legal separation. Living alone with her four children, she developed a relationship with a landlady, who often looked after the children. In fact, the mother said the landlady was "almost like a mother to her." The MSPCC helped by arranging for her to collect ADC but also decided her quarters were too small and found her a larger apartment elsewhere; here her situation deteriorated and she was accused by her new landlady of neglecting the children, leaving them ill fed, dirty, and unsupervised.[136] Whatever this mother's weaknesses, and they may have been considerable, her move to a larger apartment, away from her motherly friend, did not help.

One new diagnostic category emerged from the feminine mystique—"emotional neglect." At root it was a gradual development from concern with delinquency beginning in the 1920s, and a replacement of the old "moral neglect" category by a term more psychological and scientific.[137] Although the category reflected the dominance of psychiatric social work within the child-welfare field, in fact it was too crude and undifferentiated to be used by psychiatric social workers themselves, who sought to pinpoint specific parental failings, such as ambivalence, overprotectiveness, overrestrictiveness, or rejection.[138] But by 1950 emotional neglect became a standard diagnosis used by child-protection agencies, and in 1960 it was codified as one of the indications for protective services in the Child Welfare League's official standards.[139]

Like moral neglect, emotional neglect is primarily a description of an inadequate mother-child relationship; the diagnosis included fathers only secondarily, or if there was no mother. Certainly the concept did not acknowledge the part that non-parents might play in bringing up a child. Indeed, emotional neglect tended to converge with bonding and attachment theory, quintessentially a product of nuclear-family child-raising.[140] For example, in the nineteenth century a mother's attempt to place out her children was often encouraged and even applauded as evidence of an appropriate and rational commitment to the child's good. By the mid-twentieth century a mother making such a request would almost certainly be viewed as unloving, unmotherly, forfeiting her future credibility as a mother.[141]

The notion of emotional neglect substantially influenced social-work diagnostics. A diagnostic questionnaire for neglect, the "Childhood Level of Living Scale," developed for the Child Welfare League, allotted 36 percent of the score to "emotional/cognitive" care. The standards used for measuring parental adequacy were highly culturally specific. For example, if "Mother expresses feeling that child should cooperate without reward," she got a point against her, as she did if she complained that her work was harder than the father's, or did not punish the child for using profanity. Other items included "A prayer is said before some meals"; "Mother expresses pride in daughter's femininity or son's masculinity"; "Mother expresses feeling that her job is the housework"; "Mother mentions that child, if son, prefers to be with father; if daughter, prefers to be with mother."[142] The standards also reflected class expectations; for example, "Mother plans meals with courses that go together"; "Child is taught to swim or mother believes child should be taught to swim"; "There is an operating electric sweeper"; "Clothing usually appears to be hand-me-downs"; "There are leaky faucets"; "Planned overnight vacation trip has been taken by family"; "Child has been taken fishing"; "Mother mentions that she makes effort to get child to eat food not preferred because they [sic] are important to child's nutrition." This questionnaire was still being recommended as an evaluative device in 1981.[143]

The father's behavior was not interrogated, although in a few items a collective parenting is implied, e.g., "Parents guard language in front of children"; or "Family has taken child downtown." The view that mothers were uniquely responsible for child-raising, always implicit, now became explicit. The neglectful parent became the neurotic or even pathological mother. By correlating scores on the Childhood Level of Living Scale with measures of parents' attributes, its author determined that the "mother's degree of maturity" played the predominant role in predicting quality of parenting.[144] He also developed a "Maternal Characteristics Scale" to measure five "prevalent types of neglectful mothers": the "Apathetic-Futile," the "Impulse-Ridden," the "Mentally Retarded," the "Mother in a Reactive Depression," and the psychotic.[145]

This mother-blaming, it might be argued, merely described the reality that women do most child-raising work. As an MSPCC leader wrote in 1965, using the language of sociological role theory, "The very word *mother* identifies a particular social role, and a certain pattern of behavior is expected from the individual occupying that role. The word *mother* normally calls to mind a woman who loves, feeds, and protects her children, and if she does not meet her role expectations, she is thought of as a 'bad mother.' "[146] But women's mothering was not merely being described as a reality, it was being prescribed, insisted upon. And this norm of full-time devotion to children was itself at times a contributing cause of neglect itself, a factor in causing the "apathy-futility syndrome" so prevalent among neglectful mothers.

This psychologizing of child neglect also resulted in treatment that de-emphasized material aid in favor of therapy to the "damaged parents," focused on the transference relation between caseworker and client. The neglectful mother is really a child and needs mothering herself. The value of material aid was merely to provide "tangible evidence that the mother substitute, the caseworker, actually cares for her." "She derives great value from a constructive relationship with a person in a position of authority."[147]

In identifying the *evidence* of neglect, moreover, the traditional difficulty in distinguishing it from poverty continued. Some of the questions relating to physical neglect from the 1981 Childhood Level of Living Scale seem as ignorant of the hardships of poverty as they might have been in 1900: "Mother has evidenced lack of awareness of child's possible dental needs. . . . Mother sometimes leaves child to insufficiently older sibling. . . . House is dilapidated. . . . Windows have been cracked or broken over a month without repair. . . . Mattresses are in obviously poor condition. . . ."[148]

Fortunately, many caseworkers demonstrated more humility about their own standards than the Childhood Level of Living Scale in determining neglect. Social workers' common sense and sympathy, not diagnostic science, permitted such help to clients as was offered.

The social workers' capacities for insight and empathetic response were, of course, activated by the clients' own struggles to be understood and helped. Nowhere was this relationship more evident than in child neglect cases, for mothers themselves were the predominant complainants, defining by their own standards both their own inadequacies and the help they wanted—which was mainly economic aid. Unfortunately, by the time they got to the agencies, their desperation had often gone too far. One case summary prepared in 1960 contains many of the

strands that form the complex knot that is child neglect: the condescension (in this case, racism) of the caseworker who nevertheless shows
some insight into the client's point of view, and certainly grasps that
her agency's offerings and child-raising standards were useless for this
client. Now twenty-eight, married at sixteen, a black migrant from
Georgia, where she had worked picking cotton, married to an extremely
abusive man, the client sought help but got only disapproval:

> Mother is a limited person who has not been able to adequately care
> for her [6] children. She blamed this on father, stating that there were
> so many fights and so little money she never had a chance to really
> make a home. She had a somewhat removed manner in talk about her
> children and it is therefore difficult to accurately ascertain how she feels
> about them. She expressed no concern about their whereabouts, but her
> whole personality became warmer when she talked about them. How-
> ever, she did not indicate either shame or anxiety over the fact that she
> did not know where [her 10-year-old son] was during the day and evening
> or where he had dinner. One gets the feeling of a limited person who
> has had so much fear that she is trying not to feel any emotion very
> deeply now. When I asked her how she viewed the future she replied,
> "Where I'm sitting, there ain't no future."[149]

CHILD NEGLECT AND FAMILY NORMS

Child neglect is a concept onto which have been projected a wide variety
of anxiety-causing social issues: delinquency, venereal disease, sexual
permissiveness, women's employment, for examples. As the organization of child-raising has changed, with fewer adults working in their
homes and more reliance on institutions to care for children, charges
of widespread child neglect have reflected, and possibly increased, alarm
about these social changes. Child neglect discussion has particularly
vividly revealed anxieties about women's "desertion" of domesticity.
Moreover, child neglect is politically as well as emotionally laden with
meaning, manipulated in the interest of particular social policies. Both

public and professional standards for neglect have been swayed by the political climate.[150]

Nevertheless, a critique of political shifts in the definition of child neglect will not make neglect disappear as a social problem. As these family-violence cases show, there are children's sufferings which are, at the particular historical moment, not inevitable; which are caused by parental failure to maintain the minimum standards of the society; and which are perceived by most citizens to require intervention.

Examining these interventions reveals the irrationality of a social system in which parents cannot get help until *after* their children have suffered. Few things made the clients angrier. "Mo asked why so much cd be done for her chrn now & so little done for them previous to her breakdown."[151] Relief authorities commonly said to the MSPCC, as one Overseers of the Poor agent did, "if the Society wished to make a neglect complaint . . . he could assist by giving enough aid so that she could stay home for a little while."[152] This system is founded on the premise that families should not require public help except in emergencies. This expectation, in turn, assumes full employment and family wages for men and full-time domesticity for women—both of which are often unattainable or undesirable by the people involved. In other words, the assumption of family independence contains a politics of gender and family, as well as of class. The very concept of child neglect, as we have seen, arose from the establishment of this norm of male breadwinning and female domesticity. In fact, this pattern is not "traditional," as is often claimed today, but was new when child protection originated. Indeed, child protection was part of the efforts to enforce this arrangement.

This norm was never unchallenged. It was implicitly challenged by the majority of working-class people, and many of other classes, who did not conform but nevertheless defended their family lives. At several times during the period of this study, it was challenged ideologically, notably by feminists concerned with the subordination and dependence that this family norm often meant for women. It was also challenged by a democratic reform vision of equal opportunity, on the grounds that it was unfair for children to be deprived because of their parents' lack of resources. Still, the "independent" family—the male-breadwinner/ female-housekeeper family—remains as a norm despite the fact that so few live this way, and that disjunction between ideal and reality also creates stress in child-raising. When social welfare policy adopts that norm as a goal, the result is often the denial of help to those who need it most, or until their need is too great. In the actual neglect cases, we have seen how often class and sexual inequalities were themselves implicated as causes of child neglect, as well as in defining it in the first place.

6

"ONLY TO BRING MY CHILDREN UP GOOD": CHILD ABUSE AND SOCIAL CHANGE

1900. A sixteen-year-old Polish girl complained to the MSPCC about mistreatment by her parents, who had sold [sic] her in marriage to their boarder for $15. She was accustomed to being severely beaten by them, but when they and the boarder, her new husband, jointly whipped her, she ran away to a friend. Her husband had her arrested as idle and disorderly; the judge dismissed the case and she applied for a divorce.[1]

1917. A black family, two parents and five children, immigrants to Boston from South Carolina, came to the attention of the Judge Baker Guidance Center because a sixteen-year-old daughter was caught shoplifting. Mrs. Todd held the same domestic service job for sixteen years. Mr. Todd was a carpenter but often worked as a gardener or at other unskilled labor. A hardworking, "sober" man, he had built their house *himself, in a "good district" of single-family houses; the social worker described it as clean and well furnished, and it even had a piano. The girl client, the social worker reported, had musical talent, and left school to do housework in order to earn money for music lessons.*

Mrs. Todd was fond and respectful toward her husband, hesitant to criticize him; nevertheless, she gave a mixed evaluation of him to the social worker, describing him as a "very strict man, too strict." She also believed he had dangerous tendencies, but she did not mean his violence; rather, she referred to his inordinate, in her opinion, love of money. Beyond this she would not specify, but she feared that her daughter would "inherit" these tendencies. Mr. Todd whipped his daughter much too hard, his wife believed, and lacked patience with her. The girl had run away several times and had had some "nervous breakdowns," according to her mother. Mr. Todd was clearly incensed by her shoplifting, and beat her severely for it. But he did not see, as his wife did, the ways in which his own values contributed to her desire to steal. Mrs. Todd explained that her daughter "is very fond of nice clothes. M [mother] is continually telling her not to try and dress beyond her means. White girls in school seem very fond of [client] and she wants to dress as well as they do. F. encourages this, which M. feels to be a great mistake." The girl's shoplifting continued, undeterred either by her father's beatings or by the clinic's short-term intervention. In early 1924 she was sentenced to a women's reformatory on a larceny charge; in late 1925, paroled to her sister, she again entered domestic service, but began stealing again, this time more ambitiously—fur coats and jewelry—at the command of her lover, who was a fence.[2]

1930. In Chinatown, a relatively prosperous Chinese small businessman—he owned a grocery store, two tenements, and part interest in a restaurant—had been severely beating and overworking his daughter for years. She had been running away since age eight and probably before. Now at age fourteen she had run away again and was sleeping in the streets. Neighbors told the investigators that they had thought she was a slave brought from China. Also in the household were an adopted brother a year older, the girl's stepmother, and that woman's children, daughter-in-law, and granddaughter. The girl herself explained that she was beaten only when she was naughty, accepting her parents' definition of her obligations. When the MSPCC tried to get this girl placed out,

*her stepmother at first objected that she needed the girl to care for the
other children. When it became evident that this reason did not carry
sufficient weight with the MSPCC, the parents sent to China for a
husband for the girl, and, while they were waiting for the bridegroom,
sent her to cousins in New York to keep her from the clutches of the
agency.* [3]

These three stories are "typical" of the child abuse cases in this study. [4]
Complex and ambiguous, they show how child abuse is influenced by
a variety of factors—individual and psychological, collective and cultural—and by specific historical conditions, as some of the questions
they raise may illustrate. Was the Polish girl's "sale" into marriage a
continuation, adapation, or deformation of a Polish peasant norm, a
"bride-price"? (The information in this case is but a few handwritten
lines in a ledger book.) Who was the boarder? Possibly someone already
"engaged" to the girl through a parent-made arrangement? For what
infraction was she beaten? Apparently she accepted her parents' beatings;
what was it about the collusion in punishment between parents and
"husband" that was intolerable to her? The questions suggest the historically and culturally variable meanings of fundamental familial concepts, such as marriage, engagement, husband, parent. Lacking
information, the researcher spins out explanatory hypotheses. The girl
has been influenced by different marital and gender arrangements in
the United States: she already had a girl friend to run to; she seemed
unwilling to accept her parents' authority over her marriage; she seized
on divorce as an option despite her Catholicism. Her husband too
displayed a reaction common to immigrants: a surprising quickness to
turn to the courts, that is, the state, to enforce familial patriarchal rights.

The Todd family's conflicts embodied many of the pressures of social
change. Mr. Todd displayed a concern on the one hand for economic
success, usually associated with a modern, mobile, individualist outlook,
and on the other for traditional patriarchal discipline within his family.
His ambition combined family-centered commitments with individual
personal drive. Mrs. Todd blamed her daughter's desire for social climb-
ing through clothes on her husband's lack of business honesty. She was
simultaneously more "modern" in her preference for softer discipline
and more traditional in her hostility to individual ambition. The daughter, like many immigrant youth, attempted to adapt to her father's

contradictory demands for upward mobility and family loyalty, and to the standards of her schoolmates, although her adaptation was unsuccessful.

The Chinatown story is told in two different vocabularies: in the categories of the Chinese, undoubtedly misrepresented, and in those of the social work profession. The mixture provides us with little certainty. "Slave girl," "adopted brother," "daughter-in-law," "bridegroom"—the meanings of these representations of kinship for the various parties to this case cannot be certain. What, even, is the definition of "daughter" regarding the main client? (In the old China, slaves and adopted girls were categories on a continuum.[5])

Did the father believe he was treating this girl worse than an ideal daughter? That she was badly behaved? Were the neighbors making an accusation of wrongdoing when they called her a slave? If so, would they have done differently themselves or were they trying to get an enemy in trouble?

Attempts to answer questions like these reveal that child abuse emerges out of historically changing conditions of child-raising. Child abuse is not usually a product of unilateral brutality but of familial power struggles, shaped by extrafamilial social factors and historical change. The previous chapter, on neglect, emphasized changing social work definitions of the problem; the focus on child abuse in this chapter will help us to see the historical construction of parent-child relations themselves.

THE CHANGING AND THE CONSTANT

Even more than with other sorts of family violence, child abuse may appear outside of history. The rediscovery of child abuse in the 1960s revealed the same tenacious problem, evoked a similar naïve public alarm, and posed parallel obstacles to solutions, as it did in the 1870s. The stubborn constancy of violence against children has tended to support ahistorical conceptions of the problem, blaming, for example, inadequate parental bonding with non-biological children.[6] It seems more likely that the tenacity and constancy of child abuse stem from the continuity of patterns of family and child-raising.[7] That human beings have a "biological" capability of violence tells us little, since all our biological capacities are culturally controlled. Similarly, psychological diagnoses are sometimes advanced as if they were outside of history. As psychologist David Ingleby put it, "The political order is usually seen as a source of extraneous variance which must be partialled out of the data to make them truly 'psychological.' "[8] Putting child abuse in an historical context does not deny the presence of mental pathology, but it insists that such conditions are part of socially constructed culture.

To characterize child abuse as an expression of power struggle does not blame children or justify their mistreatment. In avoiding a victim-blaming stance, and in rejecting a view of children as bad or mean, some recent scholarship has gone over into the opposite exaggeration, conceiving children in child-abuse cases as mere objects, incapable of initiative. Children are active, purposeful participants in relations with caretakers. Even a baby's crying, instinctive though it is, can be an infant's entry into a contest with its caretaker to win something. To acknowledge this activity of children in creating abuse is not to blame them or to lessen in any degree the absolute and singular responsibility of parents. Moreover, some children are born difficult. Colicky infants can make parenting an ordeal. Some toddlers are relaxed and pliable while others flit from trouble to trouble, power struggle to power struggle. Sick and disabled children require more patience and nonjudgmental acceptance than many parents (who have had a fine time with "normal" children) can give.[9]

Certain patterns of child abuse have been remarkably constant, and it will be worth summarizing a few as a frame for what is historically changing. For example, most family-violence experts believe in a "cycle of violence," the intergenerational repetition of violence making those abused as children more likely to abuse their children. Since the mid-1970s, this "cycle" theory has been questioned and the evidence for it found lacking.[10] In this study, 31 percent of client families had agency records of family violence from previous generations, succeeding generations, or related families of the same generation. But many factors made it more likely for families once in an agency caseload to be picked up again, or even to seek out agency help again, so that the evidence tells us nothing about the causality of the violence itself.

A subjective version of this "cycle of violence" theory is more defensible: that many abusers feel themselves to have been victims. They experience themselves as powerless, their wishes disrespected by their children, a feeling which may accurately reflect their actual social and economic status. A form of role reversal is also common among child abusers, in which adult-sized motives are attributed to the victims and their misbehavior is interpreted as deliberate humiliation of the parent.[11] In this study, too, expressions of powerlessness on the part of assailants, and their repeated descriptions of themselves as victims, were widespread. Parental complaints in these historical records also confirmed another contemporary finding: that child abusing parents characteristically expect more from their children than is customary, in terms of physical, cognitive, and emotional maturity.[12]

Contemporary studies are unanimous in finding that "stress" factors, such as poverty, unemployment, and economic recession, contribute greatly to abuse, as do drunkenness and alcoholism. In this study, virtually, all the families were "stressed" by poverty, urban squalor, migration, and disruption. Drunkenness was a widespread problem. However, the client families may not have lived with worse stress than many others in Boston who were not child abusers, or were not caught at it. Moreover, the measurable stresses were less correlated with child abuse than with child neglect or even adult violence, as illustrated on the next page.[13]

Past and present, parents of both sexes are approximately equally represented as child abusers: my data showed mothers as "assailants" in 46 percent of cases, fathers in 54 percent. These figures mean that fathers were *much* more likely to abuse children in proportion to how much time they spend in child care,[14] a finding that helps explain the strong influence of unemployment on male-perpetrator child abuse.

The role of women as child abusers is important because child abuse is the *only* form of family violence in which women's assaults are common. Studying child abuse thus affords an unusual opportunity to examine women's anger and violence. Unfortunately, feminist influence in anti-family-violence work has not historically supported such an examination, because of an ideological emphasis on women's peaceableness and a rejection of victim-blaming that have pervaded much feminist thought.[15] Many female child abusers are also themselves victims, and assuming that many other women victims were unreported, we might expect the actual overlap to be great. Nevertheless, most wifebeating victims did not beat their children. We cannot explain women's

6. FORMS OF STRESS AND FAMILY VIOLENCE

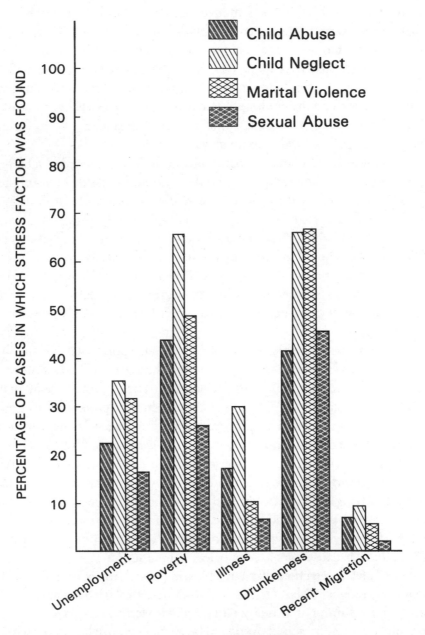

violence against children with an analogy to referred pain or deflected anger. Women's violence in these historical cases exceeded expectations, qualitatively as well quantitatively.

The child-abusing women were no milder than the men.[16] A 1944 divorced businesswoman beat her seven- and five-year-old children so severely they were bruised and marked. Pressured by the MSPCC to modify her disciplinary style, she turned to imaginative punishments "in kind"—making her son eat all the sugar in the bowl when he stole a few lumps, forcing him to sleep without covers in the attic.[17] Fathers punched their children, beat them with hammers and tools, threw them, attacked them with knives and axes, and threatened to shoot them; mothers scratched and burned their children, pulled their hair out, locked them in cold and damp rooms, starved them. Girls abused their siblings, girl friends beat up girl friends, daughters struck their mothers. Neighboring women and relatives conducted feuds, cursing each other, throwing things, destroying property, hitting and kicking.[18] There may have been a gender difference in the forms of violence used, men often being stronger and more comfortable with weapons, but the differences were not consistent, and to characterize women as less violent toward children would be mistaken.

Some women's violence was intensified, possibly even provoked, by intervening social agencies. The threat of losing one's children was an extremely anxiety-provoking stress in an already stressful life. In many cases, agents did not tell the accused parent who the informant was, and this policy of protecting complainants' anonymity provoked clients' distrust of friends, neighbors, and relatives. Furthermore, the immediate impact of agency intervention was embarrassment and humiliation before neighbors and relatives.[19] Motherhood was often the major source of dignity in women's lives and labeling a woman inadequate in that work was a stunning blow. Yet, although violent women felt badly about hurting those they loved, they did not necessarily condemn violence against children; they more often condemned other women's failure to discipline children.

The gender of child-abuse victims is also important. One contemporary study found that among infants, more girls are abused and neglected; beginning at age two, more boys; and after age twelve, more girls again.[20] The gender breakdown of victims in this study was similar.[21] There were substantially more female *victims* in this study (1,002 girls and 744 boys), because teenagers were overrepresented.[22] However, the gender breakdown of the *clients* was different. The distinction between a client and a victim is an important clue to attitudes about family violence: a client is someone about whose victimization a complaint was made, and in whose name social-work action was begun and a case record opened. Despite the overrepresentation of girls among victims, there were almost as many male clients as female (702 girls and 628 boys),[23] probably because abuse of male children was considered a more serious affair, making outside intervention more likely.

The historical evidence demonstrates that child abuse is not new, but it cannot tell us anything about its incidence over time, because it is without controls. We know the number of child abuse cases handled by different agencies, but not the incidence of undiscovered child abuse. We can trace the changing proportions of various types of abuse in agency caseloads,[24] but we cannot know the reason because these changes often reflected shifts in the agency's sensibility, and decisions about which cases to accept. Since the agencies' caseloads were limited, accepting more of one type of case reduced the numbers of other types. For example, the MSPCC claimed just a few years after its establishment that it had reduced the number of assaults against children.[25] In the early 1890s the Society lost its certainty about this claim and feared rather that it had merely forced brutality against children into hiding.[26] By the second decade of the twentieth century MSPCC observers regained confidence that "instances of brutal corporal punishment [were] now rare," and alleged that permissiveness had become the problem, "a failure to provide a substitute for that rigid discipline of former times, [allowing] . . . the child to remain an undisciplined, self-willed individual," thus offering the clue as to why it saw less child abuse.[27] In the 1930s child-welfare experts again believed that child abuse was on its way to extinction.[28] More likely, the proportion of child-abuse cases went down *because* the proportion of child-neglect and sexual-abuse cases went up. (This agency optimism was also influenced by the "pro-family" mood of the interwar period, discussed in the previous chapter. Neither social work, nor family sociology, nor family law texts of the 1930s discussed child abuse.)[29]

Child-protection agencies may have been on stronger ground in their belief that the most violent assaults against children had been reduced by the 1920s. There was, for example, a reduction in the rate of police

involvement, from 53 percent of cases before 1893, to 41 percent between 1900 and 1917, to 33 percent after 1920.[30] Moreover, weapons
appeared decreasingly in case records.[31]

There is no quantitative evidence of any changes in the incidence of
child abuse over the past century, but there is some qualitative evidence
that it has declined.[32] Changing standards of child-raising have reduced
the amount of physical punishment considered acceptable. Today's abuse
includes much that was yesterday's punishment.

PUNISHMENT

Child abuse is unique among forms of family violence because it is so
often connected to or confused with punishment. Everyone condemns
child abuse, but most Americans practice and advocate some form of
physical punishment.[33] Most abusive parents feel angry with their children, and many intend their violence as punishment. (Most children
experience it that way too.) In some cases parents lose control and exceed
their own intentions; in some cases what seems to parents legitimate
and needed punishment is branded as abuse by others.

Differing standards of punishment are correlated with social class,
but only if class is understood not as a static category with fixed cultural
patterns and without individual difference. Rather, class differences in
child-raising reflected aspects of familial experience in rapidly changing
social and economic conditions.

Twentieth-century social psychologists have generally concluded that
working-class parents use more physical punishment than middle-class
parents.[34] This observation has had political implications, as in sociologist Seymour Martin Lipset's argument that these "authoritarian" family patterns are partly responsible for a greater authoritarianism in the
working class in general.[35] By contrast, critical views of middle-class child-
raising have emphasized its psychological manipulation and appeals
to guilt, its greater rigidity in frustrating impulses (as in toilet training
and table manners), and blamed these for personalities turning aggression upon the self. One 1940s study comparing child-raising among Polish working-class and Wasp middle-class people found that the former
were quick to "apply the fist and whip rather indiscriminately," while

the latter relied on withdrawal of love as a threat; the working-class children, it concluded, grew up less neurotic than the middle-class.[36]

Not only are the data regarding class differences in child-raising difficult to interpret, but their relevance to family violence needs to be carefully specified, for false connections are sometimes made. Contemporary surveys correlate child abuse with habitual physical punishment, but these surveys are not properly controlled because there are so many variables determining what child-abuse cases get counted. This historical study showed that 94 percent of abusers regularly used physical punishment, matching contemporary findings that 84 to 97 percent of parents today do so.[37] There is danger of circular logic, too, since many family-violence activists believe that physical punishment is child abuse.[38] Whatever one's personal predilections regarding physical punishment, equating it with abuse is problematic. The equation entirely leaves out the problems of emotional coldness and rejection as forms of discipline. Moreover, the lines connecting punishment to abuse have not been traced. For example, the correlation between physical punishment and abusive violence, in the present or in the next generation, might be explained by the greater poverty and other stress in the sample population. Above all, "punishment" has been treated as a solitary and random practice, its different contexts and cultural meanings ignored. Punishment, moreover, has been studied without reference to the nature of the victims' infractions, conceptualized as a unilateral act, not a response in a relationship.

Child-raising can be harder or easier depending on class privilege, on personal networks of support, and on historical context. These factors influence not only the handling of problems, but also the experience and definition of the child itself. Infants are more often defined as "difficult" where mothers have no respite, or where others in the household are disturbed by the fussing and call it frequently to the caretaker's attention. Parents, particularly mothers, are vulnerable to the judgments of others: children appear as their "product," and a misbehaving, dirty, or unappealing child as a condemnation of the mother. An accepting community may encourage an indulgent attitude toward children's misbehavior, while a judgmental neighbor, teacher, or boyfriend may lead a mother to decide her child needs harsher discipline. When babysitters or nannies do most of the child care, even the worst brats can appear angels to their parents.

VICTIMS OF CHILD ABUSE

This and the following portrait of client groups were taken by the MSPCC to illustrate the need for its work. (*Courtesy of MSPCC, Boston.*)

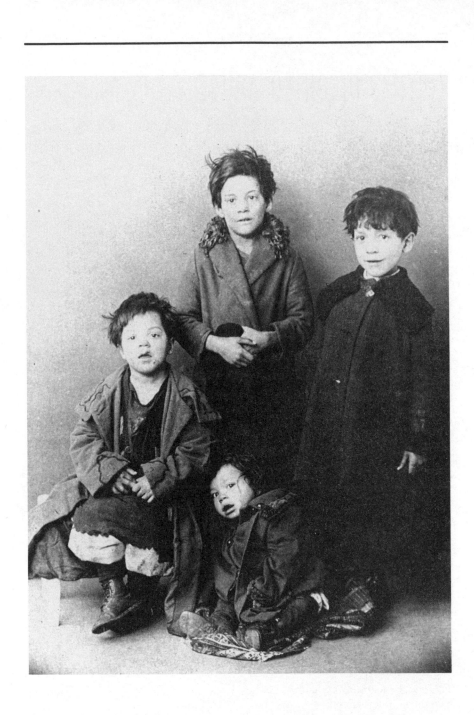

If the poor used more physical punishment than the prosperous, when caught and reprimanded by the representatives of those classes—the child-savers—the poor tried hard to explain why they did so. Their very concern with their children and their limited ability to protect them created a pressure to punish. First, their children faced considerable dangers in their everyday life and needed to learn protective behavior early on if they were to survive. The streets and alleys of the Boston poor were filled with violence, theft, "white slavers," and unsympathetic police, while their flats were often so uncomfortable that children were drawn to the streets. Overburdened mothers lacked time and energy for supervision. Poverty, malnutrition, illness, and depression made children and adults cranky and aggressive. Poor and particularly immigrant parents conceived of the city as riddled with traps for their children, and their children's misbehavior threatened to expose them to those traps. The discipline they sought to instill in their children was not an abstract stylistic preference, or a dangling cultural vestige, but a mode of ensuring their survival. Second, they may have lacked the resources to command their children without physical force. Indeed, they had an unusually low reservoir of parental power. Fathers no longer had farms, craft shops, dowries, advantageous marriages, and social status to pass on to their children; mothers did not offer their daughters advantageous connections and training in social graces.

That corporal punishment seemed a deeply rooted and reinforced pattern among the poor does not mean that there was unanimity among them about how to treat children, or that child abuse was simply an artifact of class difference. Referring back to the stories at the beginning of this chapter, for examples, in neither the Chinese nor the Afro-American family were the problems constructed by cultural disagreement between Wasp social workers and minority clients. Both cases have charges of abuse from within the clients' ethnic and class group. To say that child abuse is affected by history is not to say that it is "all relative."

Furthermore, there were disagreements about discipline within families, and these conflicts escalated tensions. Mothers often tried to protect children from fathers' violence, thus incurring violence themselves. Often, too, mothers considered fathers too lenient and resented fathers' avoidance of their share of the disciplinary work.[39] One Italian-American immigrant mother in 1950 worried about her husband's severe punishment of their twelve-year-old son for petty theft and "answering back," and the Judge Baker therapists supported her preference for milder discipline. Yet at other times she feared that she was overindulgent, and when her husband was not home, she called upon her brother to punish the boy. This particularly infuriated the boy, who, no doubt influenced by more nuclear-family American standards, questioned his uncle's "right" to intervene.[40]

These intraclass and even intrafamily disagreements about punishment were overshadowed by the politicization of issues concerning the treatment of children, first in the campaign against corporal punishment, and then in the anti-cruelty-to-children movement. These mobilizations set a largely middle-class, feminist sentiment for gentleness with children against poor people's patterns of physical punishment. Furthermore, the reform impulse moved even further away from corporal punishment in the last century. Child protectors of the 1880s accepted relatively harsh beatings as appropriate and drew the line at the use of weapons, while child protectors of today look askance at spanking and draw the line at anything described as beating.

Has this change in the dominant professional-class sentiment been accompanied by a parallel shift in working-class patterns? The answer is uncertain. The majority of Americans who use physical punishment today is overwhelming, and is not declining. Murray Straus reports that more young (under thirty) than old (over fifty) people support spanking.[41] But there is evidence for considerable change in punishment levels. Ordinary "punishment" was significantly more violent a century ago. Moreover, in this study the proportion of child abuse that arose from punishment declined over time: through 1917, 70.6 percent; from 1944 and after, 44 percent of child abuse cases began as punishment,[42] a finding which confirms that equating punishment with abuse is inaccurate.

In this study, changing appraisals of appropriate punishment were particularly evident among *children*, who were often the initiators in getting social work attention. Noticing children's activity in defining child abuse (and thereby setting limits on punishment), as well as in provoking it, is vital to historicizing this problem. Children often complained to agencies about their parents, particularly on behalf of their younger siblings. Not even punishment was an event in which children were passive, but was often a contested issue about which children could alter their parents' behavior.

CHILDREN'S LABOR

Disagreements about discipline often emerged from conflicts about children's work obligations. These conflicts were the most frequent origin of child abuse before World War II. In the agrarian societies from which most migrants to Boston came, production was a joint family occupation. Children were expected to work—to help their parents and sometimes to take sole responsibility for aspects of the family economy, such as tending farm animals, preparation of materials for handicraft production, looking after younger children, cooking. Industrial production and urban living made such assignment of responsibilities to children less appropriate. Labor was individual and the father was usually not head of a family enterprise but a wage worker; men in this situation could no longer benefit directly from the labor of their children but had to rely on getting the fruits of that labor, money. Thus traditional parental control over their children's labor was turned into parents' demands that children hand over wages.

These conflicts were more frequent and more bitter between mother and daughter than between other parent-child combinations. Mothers more often remained, in a sense, heads of a family productive unit— doing housework and sometimes industrial home work. More than fathers, therefore, mothers of the poor demanded that their daughters share responsibility for domestic work. Overworking girls and punishing them for not working enough were characteristic maternal forms of abuse. The intensity of these conflicts came from the fact that the children's obstinacy not only challenged parental authority but also deprived mothers of help they badly needed. Compulsory education seemed a more egregious violation of girls' traditional role than of boys'. For example, in 1925 a Norwegian-born stepmother, beaten by her husband, worked as a private nurse all day and expected the house to be immaculate upon her return. She would rub her hand over the floors and walls to check for any dust and, if she found any, would scold and abuse her sixteen-year-old stepdaughter, at times scratching her in rage and once stabbing her with a carving knife.[43] In 1920 a French Canadian stepmother ran a twenty-six-room boardinghouse in the West End, not only helping to support her Boston family but also paying the board of two children in Montreal. She required three children ages eleven to fifteen to maintain the boardinghouse rooms and beat them because she alleged they were lazy and stole from the lodgers.[44] An Italian immigrant mother in east Boston ran a small variety store beneath her family's five-room apartment; the family had been very poor during the Depression, but in 1940 her husband and seventeen-year-old son got jobs in the Bethlehem shipyard; the house, threatened with foreclosure in 1936, now was in their hands if income could be kept up. Driven to keep the store open long hours, she forced her fifteen-year-old daughter to do all the housework and the janitorial work in the store, run errands, including heavy carrying of stocks for the store, and stay in the store at every free moment; the mother and daughter fought about whether the girl could stay in high school. The result of all this conflict was that the girl was badly beaten by her mother and by her older brother, at her mother's instigation.[45]

Many of the mother-daughter relationships in these case records were characterized not only by conflict but also by mutual support and friendship. Immigrant girls were usually close to their mothers and often shared their mothers' views about family obligations; mothers looked forward to receiving not only help but also devotion and friendship from grown daughters. Thus it was not surprising that when mother-daughter conflicts about work obligations occurred, the daughters were often deeply ambivalent. In a Russian immigrant family in 1930, a widowed mother of three kept a boardinghouse and worried about meeting her mortgage payments. The oldest, a girl of fifteen, was an ambitious, straight-A student in the ninth grade when her mother took her out of school and placed her as a live-in domestic in Mattapan. The girl "remembers the regret she felt when she left sch., but that now the step is taken, she is relieved and pleased. She says herself that she hardly understands her change of attitude. . . . 'Perhaps it is the peasant coming out in me.' . . . Has focused ambitions now on younger sis who shd become teacher."[46] This girl not only epitomized the inner ambivalence created by the family norms of the new world, but she understood them exactly as a conflict between her peasant past and her "modern" ambition.

When the father was the abuser in these overwork-and-punishment cases, he was likely to be an independent, not a waged, worker, perhaps a farmer or a small businessman, or a widower—in either case a person in need of his children's work.[47] There were, of course, variations. One 1917 father worked alone as a boilermaker but forced his children to work a vegetable garden at their home.[48] In another 1917 case, an Irish widower father working as a night watchman expected his oldest daughter to give him more of her wages than she thought appropriate. At one point, she complained, he demanded $10, even though her weekly wages were only $4.50 and she was expected to buy all her own clothing and lunches. His patriarchalism can also be seen in the family's eating patterns: he insisted on meat and other good things for himself but allowed his five children mostly bread, oatmeal, and tea.[49]

In most cases reaching agency attention, the child's overwork was considered improper even by members of the family and/or neighborhood. Occasionally, however, a generational power struggle arose out of conflicting expectations of what children owed their parents. Some children's refusal to work seemed inappropriate to most adults in their community; such refusals resulted from the differential rate at which immigrants adjusted to the new economic relations among kinfolk produced by urban industrial forms of labor. This kind of disagreement often involved children's contribution of their wages, as opposed to domestic labor; and conflicts about wages occurred more frequently with sons than with daughters. Among the immigrant working class in turn-of-the-century cities, girls gave more of their wages, and gave more consistently, to their parents than did boys.[50] Sons were more willing to challenge patriarchy directly in order to keep their wages. In 1910, an Irish youth of nineteen argued that he should have no obligation to support his "father's children," i.e., the boy's siblings. His father was a habitual non-supporter, to be sure, but in the context the boy's refusal was a denial of help to his mother, sisters, and brothers.[51] An Italian mother in 1920 was outraged at having to work in a candy factory while her fifteen-year-old son "loafed."[52] By the end of World War II it was the children who were winning such battles. In 1944 another Italian mother threatened to put out her fourteen-year-old son unless he paid board; in other words, unless he got a job. The boy complained to the school authorities, who agreed that he was too frail to have to work.[53] An Italian-American boy of twelve conformed to the family demand that he work—selling boxes, doing deliveries—but then refused to turn over the money despite severe beatings.[54]

The struggle over children's work obligations sometimes reflected misunderstandings about the nature of an economic system new to so many of its victims. Unemployment, a frequent irritant in husband-wife relations, also entered parent-child conflicts. For example, in the North End in 1930 another Italian household fought about a daughter's unemployment: she claimed that she kept getting laid off from factory jobs and then could not find a job at all—hardly surprising in this Depression year; but her parents claimed she lost the jobs due to laziness and punished her for it.[55]

In nineteenth-century Boston concern about exploitation of children produced state legislation regulating factory work and street peddling. These occupations were most likely to be boys'; girls' labor in Boston was less likely to be wage work, in contrast to the pattern of the nearby textile-industry towns, and more likely to be domestic. This work, no matter how oppressive, was less visible and no doubt less reprehensible to the reformers, who did not challenge the "naturalness" of girls "helping their mothers" at housework. Ironically, this form of abuse of girls may have been further masked by the fact that many girl household drudges were often the victims of sexual abuse as well, an abuse with which the MSPCC was familiar. The agency's understanding of the connection between girls' enforced and exploitive domesticity and their sexual victimization did not prompt criticism of girls' housework, however. The only recognition of girls' *particular* vulnerability to labor exploitation came in the form of campaigns aimed, ironically, at reinforcing their domesticity, as when the MSPCC, in its campaign for licensing of child peddlers, won the prohibition of any peddling by girls at all.[56] Oddly, the MSPCC had never generalized from the fact that such a large proportion of its abuse cases developed from conflicts about children's labor,[57] and by the twentieth century it had dropped the issue of child labor from its propaganda efforts altogether.

MISBEHAVIOR

After World War II, the more commonly cited provocation for child abuse was misbehavior, rather than children's recalcitrance about family obligations. Of course there were parents angered by their children's disobedience in the earlier records too, but these infractions were more often serious misdeeds or defiance that created material costs for parents. Several factors were probably responsible for this historical change. One was the decline of parents' demands for children's work. Another was the rise of new standards for children's age-appropriate and socially "well-adapted" behavior, appearing among working-class parents later than among the middle class. Concomitant with these new standards was an intensifying norm which held parents, particularly mothers, responsible for their children's good behavior, a responsibility which often imposed upon parents a great sense of failure and stimulated anger toward children who may not have directly "wronged" their parents. Yet another pressure upon both parents and children was that the latter spent more time inside their homes than had been typical before, say, 1920, as children's independence and street life declined.

Some examples may clarify this point. In the first half of this study, children were often beaten for crimes resulting in arrest, such as stealing. In these cases it was often unclear whether the crime or the getting caught was being punished.[58] Running away and bed-wetting also appeared prominently as the provocative behavior in the early child-abuse cases. In the later period, parent-child power struggles often arose in response merely to normal childish behavior. In one 1960 case, a father beat his children aged six, four, and one and a half if they cried, and the mother's response was to try desperately to keep them quiet; when she divorced this man, who also abused her, she began to hit the children to force them to stop crying.[59] In a 1944 case a father responded to his two-year-old's tearing a book by making him sit for two hours to complete tearing it into pieces, switching his fingers whenever he stopped tearing. When a toddler soiled his clothes playing football, his mother made him go on a family trip sitting on the floor of the car.[60] Children's sauciness was frequently cited by parents as a source of frustration, and it is difficult to know whether children actually were increasing their insolence, due to more age-egalitarian social standards, or whether parents were more threatened by this challenge to their status, because of their general low status as poor people and often foreigners.[61] Another common provocation was children's lying or stealing from their parents. Such infractions suggest that children were caught in conflicting standards, wishing to join a peer group's activities but constrained by their parents. In any case, parents appeared to be less successful in regulating their children's behavior.

Both mothers and fathers responded strongly to children's misbehavior. Nevertheless, here too there were gender differences. Bed-wetting, for example, provoked mothers' rage.[62] Mothers often beat children furiously for wetting their beds, even at very young ages. One French-Canadian girl was punished by having her face rubbed in saturated sheets.[63] One foster mother forced a four-year-old to sit naked for a half hour on the floor in a cold apartment for wetting.[64]

Leaving aside the question whether the bed-wetting was perhaps a *result* of abuse, it certainly contributed to mothers' misery. Few client children before the 1940s had their own beds, and others suffered and complained from the discomfort of wet and smelly bedding. Washing linen, always a substantial addition to a mother's domestic workload, was an even heavier task under the circumstances in which most of these clients lived: certainly no washing machines or dryers, probably no hot water or outside space in which to hang wet clothes, and often no water at all in the apartment. Laundering meant fetching water in buckets, often up stairs, and washing in large pots on the stove. Beyond the burden of work, some mothers were affected by child-raising standards which expected early toilet training and considered violations to be bad manners, laziness, or even defiance, requiring firm punishment.

Children's stealing, like bed-wetting, was both a symptom and a provocation of abuse, but one more often punished by fathers. It was also a crime more often committed by sons. The Judge Baker Guidance Center, its clientele mainly composed of juvenile delinquents, urged parents not to beat their children as punishment for getting in trouble with police, but with little success, no doubt partly because its therapists never saw fathers, only mothers. A Polish couple, both employed in a rubber factory in Watertown in 1934, had an eight-year-old son already active at petty theft; his father punished him by tying him to a chair and whipping him with a strap. (The more he was punished, the more he stole, it seemed, and his activities sent him to reform school in

1941.)[65] In either case it appears that the usual division of labor between parents made fathers feel particularly responsible for these kinds of infractions, or perhaps for boys, who most frequently committed them. Since thievery by children was usually associated with spending time on the streets, refusing to stay at home, and general insubordination, the conflicts emerging from stealing took the form of intense father-son struggles.

A similar double meaning attached to children's running away: they were often fleeing from abuse but got abused as a result. "Bunking out," as staying away from home was called fifty years ago, was common in the poor neighborhoods, and children frequently bunked out in doorways when the weather was temperate, at friends' and even relatives' houses in all weather. Even more perhaps than with stealing, this infraction stimulated parental anxiety about children's welfare. (In incest cases, running away frightened fathers, because it meant daughters' escape from their control, including the possibility of their reporting their fathers' immorality.) Among children younger than about ten, boys were more likely to be disobedient to commands to stay inside or near home. At older ages the range of mobility allowed to boys was greater, while parents worried intensely about girls outside the household. Parents of both sexes worried about children's running away, but even here there was a gender breakdown. Mothers continued in this urban setting the pre-industrial pattern of greater responsibility for younger children; fathers' concern increased as the children reached adolescence.

ADOLESCENCE

Adolescence engendered a high level of child abuse. I suspect that conflicts between parents and adolescents were particularly intense among the immigrants and migrants who so predominated among agency clients. The new consciousness of adolescence as a separate, transitional, and difficult age was not just an academic theory but reflected the problems of child-raising in an era of rapid social change. Immigrants experienced adolescence in particularly concentrated form, for they had so recently experienced the loss of a family economy, in which children worked with, learned from, and were dependent on their parents. Many of their family conflicts were caused by parental rage at loss of economic power over children, and children's quickness to exploit that parental weakening. The new economy, based on individual wage labor and increasingly requiring formal education, meant that traditional patterns of socialization did not necessarily fit children for the world they would face as adults.[66]

Historian Joseph Kett has argued that the identification of adolescence as a problematic stage was a figment of the class and cultural biases of the child-savers: what the "latter saw as evidence of lower-class depravity was actually an autonomous lower-class tradition . . ."[67] This argument contains a well-founded skepticism about elite misperception of lower-class life, but it lacks curiosity about lower-class experience itself, or respect for that class's ability to report its own experience. This is another example of the inadequacy of "social control" critiques.

Child-protection cases suggest that parents and children experienced adolescence as a problem even before the experts did. G. Stanley Hall, usually considered the inventor, so to speak, of adolescence, did not emphasize those years until the Progressive era; the image of adolescents as hostile and uncontrollable became widespread only in the 1920s.[68] Decades earlier, the immigrant poor were experiencing intense conflicts between parents and adolescents.[69] Weakened family and community networks meant that adolescents relied on peer approval and companionship, and often came to disdain their parents, while parents could not trust these peers to protect children and orient them toward secure futures.[70]

Teenage girls' independent social life, with the overtones of immorality that unchaperoned activity had for many Old World people, drove some fathers virtually to frenzy. A southern Italian father, in the North End in 1920, could not work out a peaceful *modus vivendi* with his sixteen-year-old daughter. She was the only child living with the Vitellos, as I have called this couple; other children were in Italy, as the family, after migrating to Boston thirteen years previously, had returned there several times. Mr. Vitello had not been able to find steady employment, but worked casually as a watchman and plasterer; he had many relatives in the Boston area, all of them more successful economically than he; Mrs. Vitello had been the main supporter of the family for years. It is possible that Mr. Vitello's economic failure galled him and made him need even more strongly to assert his power over his daughter. Lucia, as I will call her, liked to go to dances and to dress up; the social workers believed she only associated with other girls and doubted that she was "immoral." Nevertheless, her parents were furious at her most of the time. Mrs. Vitello tried to accompany her every time she went out; Mr. Vitello made Lucia walk in front or in back of him, never by his side, and whistled at her to give her orders. When he caught her once walking down the street arm-in-arm with a man she knew through his cousins (remember that walking arm-in-arm was common among Italian-Americans and carried no sexual implications in itself), he became abusive on the street, beat her, drew a knife, and said he would kill her when she came home.[71]

Conflicts about children's labor, such as those previously discussed, were also related to adolescence. Just as children grew old enough to be of substantial help to their parents, compulsory education, the abolition of child labor, and new norms of leisure for children deprived parents of the means of getting that help. Urban commercial culture supported children's defiance of their parents' demands. A fourteen-year-old girl from Boston's secluded North End

> . . . feels much discriminated against and very unkindly treated [the Judge Baker therapist summarized]. Frightfully restricted . . . Has no recreations or pleasures. Has gregarious desires. So far as can be ascertained standards are not particularly poor. her M. doesn't let her go out at all . . . never let [her] go to movies or go out with the girls . . . admits getting into trouble at sch. Says it is bec. she laughs and talks with the other girls. It is the only fun she has. Her M. thinks it is wicked to laugh. . . . Says very definitely that she wants to leave home.[72]

Nor did parents always see an advantage in compulsory education. Hope for children's upward occupational mobility was rare among parents in these case records, and their skepticism about opportunity through education was well founded for people of this class, the poorest in Boston.

Fear of the streets and hostility to education were especially pronounced when the adolescents were girls. Poor parents' appreciation of children's use of the streets for petty earning—through begging, peddling, scavenging, and pilfering—was overwhelmed by anxieties about girls' vulnerability to sexual attack. Parents did not see why high school was an appropriate or necessary preparation for marriage, or why it should be preferred to domestic work within the family. Street dangers represented a separate kind of threat for girls. Boys ran the risk of arrest if they were delinquent; girls ran the risk of permanently ruining their chances of marriage and community standing, even if they were not themselves delinquent but merely victimized by assault or by reputation.

Parental violence against adolescents of both sexes was often intense, but more so with girls, perhaps because the fears were greater and perhaps, too, because boys' ability to strike back had a restraining influence. One Irish father, a fireman in Roxbury in 1910, beat his teenage son and daughter both, but the girl was so viciously assaulted that the case drew special attention within the MSPCC. Once when supper was late he beat her with a heavy knotted rope. He beat her with a three-foot-long rattan because she had gone to dances without the permission or knowledge of parents. Then the parish priest told her father [sic] that she had had "immoral relations" with a "Technology student" [MIT student, no doubt], and he beat her so badly the principal of her school personally came to the MSPCC office to bring an agent to see her.[73] This girl may have been a sex delinquent, but even for those who remained chaste, the temptations of teenage recreational activities must have been great, especially in comparison to a home life that consisted largely of hard work.[74]

Adding to these temptations, and to family conflicts, was the growth of teenage purchasing and a consumer economy which made children crave commodities. The Todd daughter as early as 1917 was shoplifting to fill these cravings, and being beaten for it. Judge Baker cases included many examples of girls' thievery; the therapists' response tightened the double bind on these poor girls by emphasizing the importance of fashionable appearance and dress for self-esteem.[75]

In trying to control their adolescent children, parents sometimes prosecuted them under the stubborn-child law. Dating from 1646, the Massachusetts incorrigibility laws had prescribed the death penalty for stubborn or rebellious sons over sixteen years of age. The death penalty was repealed in 1681, but the basic legal form—the criminal prosecution of children whose parents could not control them—remained in effect in Massachusetts until 1973. By the nineteenth century, however, the stubborn-child law was a catch-all, a tool dull and misshapen by many interpretations and precedents. Originating in a Puritan cultural outlook, as one modern student of juvenile law put it, the law assumed that "parents are godly and children wicked; when those propositions are reversed, as nineteenth and twentieth century reformers tended to believe, the laws lose part of their rationale."[76]

Enforcing upon children the duty of obedience was an odd tactic for reformers bent upon exposing parental vice, punishing children an odd solution for those who believed parents were responsible for children's misdeeds. But the difficulty of collecting enough evidence for a neglect verdict meant that social workers often found it convenient to use stubborn-child prosecutions to arrange the placement of a child away from its home.

Parents, fathers in particular, used stubborn-child prosecutions as retaliation against children who left home or made public accusations against their fathers.[77] When Lucia Vitello's father threatened her, she went to the police and stayed at an institutional home until her mother succeeded in getting her to return; in response Mr. Vitello brought a stubborn-child charge.[78] It was common for fathers accused of incest to levy stubborn-child charges against their accuser in attempts to undermine the girls' credibility.[79] Another father made a complaint against his daughter in an attempt to take her away from his estranged wife.[80]

Fathers used stubborn-child prosecutions more often than mothers. Commonly these legal actions were the extension of a power struggle raging in the home, a refusal to give in when the father's own resources were insufficient to control the child. A widower father brought stubborn-child charges against his thirteen-year-old son for running away from school and bunking out.[81] Another father took his daughter to court in 1930 for her refusal to work.[82] One father literally tied up his thirteen-year-old daughter after she had run away and when that did not prove a stable solution, filed a legal complaint against her.[83]

Mothers were less likely to turn to courts to discipline their children, for several reasons. First, women more often wanted to keep their children with them no matter how great the difficulty. Second, mothers seemed to have less faith in coercion altogether as a means of discipline. Third, mothers were more able to accept the loss of control over a child, having had lesser expectations of this kind of power in the first place. When mothers did use stubborn-child prosecutions, they did so at the recommendation of social workers, and social workers may have been quicker to suggest it to mothers because of skepticism about mothers' ability to discipline difficult children. A typical case of mother-initiated stubborn-child actions might be that of a 1940 black woman struggling with her fifteen-year-old daughter. The girl had been hanging out in the streets, because she was escaping her father's drunken violence, or so the mother claimed. The mother had been trying to separate from her abusive husband for five years. (Her nine children were a significant part of her difficulty in finding a way to independence.) The mother believed that a stubborn-child complaint was her only means of getting the girl "straightened out." She hoped for a temporary foster-home placement to protect the girl from her father, and perhaps also to reduce overall family tension.[84]

The use of legal complaints between parents and children went both ways, of course, in cycles of attack and retaliation in which it was often impossible to know who was most to blame. Adolescent children, daughters as well as sons, frequently reported their parents to agencies, and it was not always clear that the children were exclusively victims.[85] Economic and emotional dependence limited the children's daring in this regard, of course, but as they reached adolescence, such actions became more conceivable and, perhaps, their provocations to do so became greater. Naturally, children complained to an agency more often when family members had already had dealings with it.[86]

Adolescents often tattled on their mothers—never fathers—for sexual irregularities. These actions were provoked by more protracted resentments—feelings of deprivation, jealousy, and/or desertion; and they also came about because children were simply doing that which would get results. When a twelve-year-old boy in 1929 complained of his mother's immorality, "which he was forced to see," he added that she also abused him directly, had burned and cut him; but his previous complaints of abuse had been ignored.[87] Other children taking similar action found themselves wielding a devastating power over their parents, suggesting a search for revenge. In 1920 a twenty-two-year-old illegitimate son reported his single mother, impoverished, neglectful, and with a long history of victimization herself, for immorality. His revenge was successful, and in the process he disrupted the lives of his siblings as well: distraught, the woman fled, taking her nine-year-old youngest and deserting her fourteen-year-old.[88] At other times, the power children experienced was short-lived, and might backfire. When a teenage girl brought charges against her mother in 1935, the woman was convicted of adultery and moral neglect and sent to prison. But the father, who had been separated from his family, then reestablished a home with the mother's sister as housekeeper (the record provides no evidence as to whether she was also the man's lover), and the girl then accused this housekeeper—her aunt—of abusing her.[89]

It is striking that children did not "tell" on their mothers for other crimes, such as bootlegging, prostitution, stealing. "Immorality" charges were the most certain to capture the attention of social agencies. These relationships may also have been the most disturbing to children, because they provoked jealousy, perhaps even more intensely fifty to one hundred years ago than today. Single mothers, for example, became more dependent more quickly on male lovers than such women might today, because of women's weak economic position and lack of resources for raising children and earning simultaneously. This meant that the children encountered not "boyfriends" but substitute fathers, living in their homes, sharing not only their mothers' beds but probably the children's own bedrooms.

The use of stubborn-child prosecutions as retaliation suggests how often children appeared to their parents as the aggressors in these conflicts. There were no cases of children assaulting parents without having been beaten themselves, but there were several cases of mutual combat. Moreover, adolescent children were often stronger and more aggressive than their parents, particularly mothers.[90] Nor were these violent children all boys, although only boys were likely to challenge fathers. Combat between women and girls was ordinary among the clients of this study, as was fighting between adult women, particularly among drinking women. The girl who turned her mother in for adultery later began attacking her aunt physically. (When boys fought with their mothers, the violence is best understood as a form of wife-beating, for these teenagers had usually been accustomed to their father's violence against their mother.)

PREJUDICE

Family violence is influenced by social prejudices such as racism and interethnic hostility. We have seen how such biases in relations between social workers and clients affected the very definitions of family violence; now we must address the influence of prejudice on child abuse among family members themselves. Consider the 1934 case of a white woman, married to an abusive black man, who sought blood tests to determine if their five children were colored or not. It is not clear what logic lay behind this request, and the Judge Baker record labeled her "increasingly neurotic" and of "inferior mentality."[91] Perhaps; but from the point of view of the child abuse a vital aspect of the problem was that she felt her anger for her husband in racial terms. (She may have feared that if her children had "black blood" they would be violent like him.)

Many family conflicts in these records were experienced and expressed in terms of cultural differences, especially in mixed marriages. Because such differences often became the idiom of conflict, it is impossible to say whether such "mixed" relationships actually exacerbated tension. The definition of a mixed marriage changed substantially over the last century: once Protestant-Catholic and interethnic relationships were nearly as "mixed" and as disapproved as white-black ones became later. For example, conflicts over the religious identification of children were frequent and sharp.[92] Even allowing for changes in definition, it is difficult to separate the effects of mixed marriages from other tensions. In 10.5 percent of the client families in these records, religious or ethnic differences were named (by social workers and/or by the clients them-selves) as leading causes of intrafamily conflict. Conflict with in-laws ranked highest at 24 percent, and conflict over a family member's drink-ing habits next, at 18 percent. However, there was considerable overlap among these types of conflict. In-laws were often the leading disapprovers of mixed marriages, for example, and drinking patterns markedly differed among, say, the Irish and the Italians.

Race, religious, or other prejudices could not be separated from per-sonal angers. Consider the case of an eight-year-old Cambridge boy of a "mixed" marriage between an Irish father and a Portuguese mother, referred to the Judge Baker clinic in 1944 by teachers who could not handle his misbehavior. Contrary to their expectation that he was never disciplined at home, he was brutally punished and abused: his mother "licked" him daily, and his father singled him out for worse, even sadistic, treatment. The boy's two younger sisters were favored. In de-scribing his own anger at his son, the father referred to how dark-skinned the boy was, resembling his mother, whom the man had been "forced" to marry. The mother reported that her husband abhorred physical contact with the boy. The father had an exaggerated terror of the boy's anger: from the moment the first girl child was born, the father feared that the boy would hurt her and would not allow him in the room with her. At the same time, the mother feared that he would grow up ef-feminate, because of "homosexual trends" in her husband's family. This racism and homophobia do not alone explain the boy's torment. Both mother and father had been abused children. The father when a teenager had turned the tables on his brutal stepfather, beating him up; but he did not appear ever to "turn the tables" on his mother, who opposed his marriage and predicted his children would "turn out badly." At age thirty-seven, he still described his mother as "making him" do things. The boy's mother had been obese and isolated since childhood; obsessive about cleanliness, she was extremely anxious about housework, ac-cording to a caseworker. A high-school graduate, unlike her husband, she had once had a job as a legal secretary—a relatively high-status job for a woman—but had given it up at marriage. She had left her abusive husband when the boy was eight months old, walking from Dorchester to Cambridge with the baby to her mother's house; but the latter would not let her stay: she had made her bed and had to lie in it.[93] It is hard to know how to weigh separately the role of grandparents, of personal unhappiness and low self-esteem, of sexual fears; or how to distinguish racism and homophobia as driving forces from their operation as lan-guages in which other hostilities and fears are expressed. But even if the prejudices provided only the language, they nevertheless affected deeply the experience of the abuse and deepened alienation within the family.

More commonly, racism entered parent-child relations through con-flicts over relations outside the family. Parents worried not only about their children's peers and potential spouses, but even about more casual contacts. In 1944 a fourteen-year-old Italian boy, whose mother beat and bit him, and attacked him with a knife, began hiding out with a black neighbor. This woman fed him, let him spend long hours at her house, and in the summer she and her husband took him cranberry picking in Cape Cod. This relationship worsened his relations with his own family. The boy's father, angry because his son would not get a regular job, feared that these people would "teach [him] to be shiftless. . . . He does not feel it is favorable for boy to be living with Portuguese [sic] and colored . . . their ways are different, they work only crop harvesting and loaf other times."[94] The racial difference no doubt escalated the Italian parents' feeling of rejection by their son.

Homophobia also affected family relations, not only between husbands and wives, as might be expected, but also between parents and children, particularly boys.[95] Some boys had homosexual experiences, which provoked parental anger and panic; others merely did not seem "manly" enough. Descriptions of children's activities among the immigrant poor suggest that homosexual play among boys was common, which in turn suggests that the parents' responses were caused less by what actually went on and more by the parents' anxieties and the meanings they attributed to homosexual identification. A thirteen-year-old Irish boy in 1920, who wept constantly, had run away fifteen times, staying out sometimes as long as a week despite privation and bitter cold. His father was physically abusive and taunted him with derogatory terms about his reputed effeminacy, considering him polluted and uncleansable from a previous homosexual experience with an older man, even though it had probably been a rape.[96]

Prejudices such as these are commonly at the root of street and mass violence; they have not been identified as salient in domestic violence. These social fears and hatreds grew from old traditions and were then reshaped by the particular mixture of different immigrant groups that Boston received, their adjacent separateness, economic and political competition, their efforts to re-create communities. Homophobia was at the same time being reshaped by changing gender roles—by the inability of the poor to achieve many traditional marks of masculinity, such as economic independence and control over other family members, and by women's agitation against patriarchal controls. These were the very same forces that were reshaping family life.

WANTED AND UNWANTED CHILDREN

Another kind of "prejudice" contributing to child abuse was hostility toward a particular child. The child victim was usually identified by the whole family as "bad," an identification so imbedded in family dynamics that its origin might be unknowable. Sometimes the child was in fact more badly behaved than the siblings. One fourteen-year-old boy exposed himself to his sisters and "handled the genitals" of his three-year-old sister.[97] A twelve-year-old beat a calf with a strap, a cow with a shovel, threw stones at birds.[98] An eleven-year-old, with three very well-behaved siblings, was violent and obscene, throwing stones at people from rooftops, breaking windows deliberately, beating up younger neighborhood children. The Judge Baker diagnosticians could not explain this behavior, considering as causes his premature birth, early overindulgence by his parents, coffee and tea consumption.[99]

In other cases the victimized child might be so young he or she could hardly be badly behaved, merely difficult or unattractive. In a 1960 case a two-month-old baby boy was hospitalized for severe neglect, with maggots infesting his body; he weighed less than he had at birth. This child, second born of a mother who had five children by 1964 (one a year), continued to be singled out for abuse and neglect: at thirty-two months he was diagnosed by Boston City Hospital as "failure to thrive, battered child, welt on left thigh, hand print on pelvic area, and bruises and marks across the back," while the other children were adequately parented.[100] One mother was reported to have said about her small boy: "She didn't know why she disliked him but she did and couldn't help it."[101]

In cases like these, it may not be helpful to ask which came first, the abuse or the child's difficultness. Abuse was a result of the *interaction* between a child's temperament and family members' personalities and predispositions. A 1930 Boston mother, only twenty years old, had a son of two and a half, a son of one and a half, and a daughter several months old, and strongly disliked the middle child. His birth had left her ill for a year. She believed the boy to be feebleminded, but when examined for mental retardation, he was diagnosed instead as malnourished. When the hospital social worker brought him home, his mother said that she did not like "half nuts" and was indignant at his return. Still unable to walk or talk at age three, the boy was picked on by his siblings, including his stronger younger sister, and whipped by his mother whenever the children quarreled."[102]

Capricious as it may seem, the scapegoating of individual children was, like all other manifestations of child abuse and neglect, affected by historical changes in parenthood and children's behavior. In the above case, feeblemindedness may have been merely a category through which a depressed and overburdened mother expressed her rejection of one child; but it may also be that this vague concept of hereditary mental defectiveness, so widespread at that time, affected her experience of her child. For another example, one abused boy was the child of ambitious, disciplined Eastern European Jews who valued above all good school-work, reliability, and obedience in their children. The boys' three siblings lived up to parental expectations, while he was unruly and a poor student. A union tailor, the father prided himself on bringing up his kids right, with high moral standards: "I'll dig dirt—anything—only to bring my children up good," he said. The parents' rigidity and intolerance for undisciplined behavior was connected to their religious/cultural values and to their struggles to win prosperity in this country.[103]

As some children seem to be rejected by their parents, so in recent decades there has developed the notion that some could be unwanted even before birth. The possibility of unwanted children assumes, of course, the existence of birth control and a "planned parenthood" sensibility. For most of the period of this study, most women assumed that children came as a part of the nature of heterosexual relationships. This does not mean that they did not try to limit their reproduction—mainly by avoiding sex or with abortion—or that they did not complain and grieve at repeated conceptions. But the idea that some particular children were wanted before birth, others unwanted, would have been unfamiliar.

There was no evidence that children "unwanted" before their birth, by any definition, were more vulnerable to abuse (or to neglect). For example, large family size was not in itself an important contributor to child abuse, nor were child-abusing families larger than those with other forms of family violence.[104] In only 14.6 percent of child abuse, and 18.5 percent of neglect cases was there any evidence, or judgment by caseworkers, that unusually large families or closely spaced children had contributed to family violence. These proportions did not change over time despite the fact that caseworkers adopted steadily smaller norms of appropriate family size.

Changing reproductive behaviors affected child abuse patterns more through their impact on women's self-esteem and aspirations. The contraceptive era gave women consciousness of choice and decision—and, therefore, ambivalence. Resulting conflicts and guilt affected all their family relationships. One neglectful mother, separated from her husband but still sleeping with him, expressed such conflict in 1960: On the one hand, she said, she didn't want to be pregnant; she had had two children, three stillbirths and a miscarriage two weeks previously; but "she likes to be pregnant because everyone else has a baby and her chn. ask her if everyone else is pregnant she should be pregnant, too."[105] Until at least the end of the Depression, women in this study who felt overburdened by children were likely to try to withdraw from sexual relations altogether. This solution led some, as we have seen, to seek economic independence as heads of households, and led others into intense sexual conflicts with their men. By the 1930s, the agency workers often informed clients about contraception, and some received the possibility eagerly. One Judge Baker worker recorded: "Believe in Cath relig, except for doctrine on birth control. . . . Mother believes that only sin is using medicine or other means of abortion. . . . Talked w/ priest, he wdnt consent but they began practicing w/drawl."[106] There was marital tension about reproduction, both from male hostility—e.g.: "Whenever he sees her dressed up he says 'it's time for you to have another baby . . .' "[107]—and from women's own ambivalence about birth control and motherhood.

But there was no evidence that the women clients' failure to adopt "planned parenthood" as their goal contributed to child abuse. Among these poor and troubled families, women's conflicts about reproduction were most often emotional longings *for* children, even if they thought it impractical. They had few other activities that could compete with motherhood for their attention. Before World War II not one woman in the case records had work that she cared about other than mothering; these women saw the only purpose of their wage labor as supporting children. After the Depression, there were a few women eager for some sort of vocational achievement, more often in small businesses than in professions. Some mothers expressed ambivalence about motherhood, but on the whole these attitudes were foreign to the poor women of this study.

"Unwanted children" in the first six decades of this study was more likely to mean stepchildren. Some contemporary studies have found that stepparents were more likely to be abusive than biological parents. Although this finding has been challenged by other studies, the issue seemed worth exploration with the historical data here.[108]

Defining stepparenting requires care, for it does not necessarily involve divorce and remarriage. Contrary to a popular impression, marriages were not more long-lasting a century ago than today, particularly not among the poor; they were less likely to end with divorce and more likely to end with separation or death. Stepparents came into these children's lives most often, particularly among the poor Catholics who populated these records, through out-of-wedlock relationships. Social workers often could not tell whether a mother's boyfriend or a father's girlfriend was assuming parental responsibility for children. Indeed, contemporary studies have been sloppy about their definitions too, and one suspects that there are many unreported "informal" stepparents who figure importantly in children's lives.

This study used the broadest possible definition of stepparents—including spouses in second marriages, foster parents, and parents' lovers—and still did not find them overrepresented in child abuse cases (although they were in cases of sexual abuse, as we shall see in chapter 7). Stepparents were responsible for 13 percent, natural parents for 87 percent, of child abuse in this study. Given the high rate of single-mother households (and therefore, often, of mothers' lovers functioning as stepparents) among this poor sample population, stepparents were not overrepresented.

Stepparenting did not produce more child abuse, but its different stresses produced different family conflicts. In a period without aid to single parents, economic motives were relatively more important in remarriage than they are today, but these were different for men and women: men sought housekeepers and child-raisers, women sought breadwinners. Stepmothers often suddenly incurred heavy new burdens of work. Moreover, stepmothering might not produce the rewards that mothering did—for example, the loyalty and help of grown children. These factors help explain why the historical data show the equal representation of stepfathers and stepmothers as child abusers, in contrast to contemporary studies which show an overrepresentation of stepfathers—one in three male abusers are stepfathers, only one in twenty-two stepmothers.[109]

Stepparents of fifty years ago did not expect a fusing of the two families;

the goal, common today, of treating stepchildren (or stepparents) identically with one's "own" was alien in the nineteenth century. These expectations were influenced by dominant practices of fostering (then called placing out) or even adopting children in order to get their labor, creating relationships based on contractual labor obligations. Actual rejection of children was, however, more common among stepfathers, who might refuse to support the children of a new wife. Mothers often placed out their children for this reason.[110]

The child protectors harbored strong suspicion of stepparents' cruelty. It focused particularly on mothers, despite the evidence that stepfathers were equally often abusers.[111] A Cinderella theme flourished—that is, stories about women's favoritism toward their natural daughters and arbitrary cruelty toward stepdaughters. In 1918 a Norwegian immigrant housekeeper married her employer, inheriting his two daughters and two sons. The oldest girl was turned into a Cinderella: she was expected to do all the housework and child care while the stepmother "worked out" (i.e., away from home). All the stepchildren were beaten and deprived, while her natural daughter was better fed and clothed.[112] In 1940 a Jewish widower, father of one girl, married a Spanish-American Catholic woman with two children; then they had a child together. His daughter, then about twelve, was allegedly turned into a drudge, given no time to play, "slapped and banged around the house [until] her head ached all day from stepmo. banging her against bureau." Above all, the girl complained that her stepmother did not love her.[113] The point here is not that there were no wicked stepmothers, but that the anxiety about their cruelty exceeded the actual problem.

How are we to interpret the intensity of emotions constructing the prevalent Cinderella plot? Judith Herman, a psychiatric expert on incest, has suggested that the whole Cinderella story is about incest, about the dangers to a daughter who lacks the protection of a mother.[114] It is also possible that step-maternal abuse expresses jealousy of the girl's relationship with her father. In fact, many of these cases of stepmother abuse did contain father-daughter incest. Moreover, the focus on stepmothers reinforced the father's freedom from responsibility for his children. The passivity of fathers in allowing their own children to be disfavored (as in Hansel and Gretel and similar fairy tales, where the father allows the stepmother to plot the death of his children) is certainly as irresponsible as that of mothers in incest cases, though rarely noticed.

The fathers' failures do not remove the stepmothers' responsibility for their abusiveness, but suggest the need for a cultural and historical analysis of "Cinderella" which includes the perspective of the stepmother (and, possibly, the stepsisters) and the father.

Child abuse has been a continuous social problem for over a century, but its definition, circumstances, and patterns reflect the specific organization of child-raising in a particular place at a particular time. Child abuse arises most often from real power struggles, family members quarreling, raging, over their opposed interests. Theories that do not analyze these opposed interests, relying instead on biological givens such as "human nature" or statically conceived pathologies, cannot explain child abuse. An historical and political perspective on child abuse need not minimize the influence of mental disorders. Theories of child abuse or other family violence that cite only "stress" provide no explanation either: after all, most people who suffer from great stress, have difficult children, live in poor neighborhoods, and/or believe in spanking do not abuse their children.

Rather, we must look for explanations to the interaction between psychological and social determinants. It bears repeating that the distinction between social and psychological is not the same as that between change and continuity. On the contrary, mental life is as historically created as society. Similarly, to focus on biology or "evolution" is not to identify timeless as opposed to historical factors. There has never been a purely "biological" human, unadulterated by culture.

Both adequate and improper child-raising are defined within particular cultures of child-raising, and in our society, at least, this culture has changed considerably in the last century. At ages when children in the past were running households, working at agriculture, or placed out as servants far from their parents, many children today cannot be allowed to cross streets, stay alone, or feed themselves. At the same time, today's children absorb a culture that no longer insists on respect for their elders but defers to youth in many ways, and thus confronts them with contradictory expectations. Their parents also encounter contradictory expectations. Fathers' self-respect often requires them to exert an authority over their children, which children's actual situation undermines. The expectation that women will be almost exclusively responsible for children has weakened hardly at all, while many other demands on women, particularly employment and the responsibility to earn wages for their families, have made mothering harder. To the degree child-raising remains a gendered activity, not one shared equally by men and women, its failures as well as its successes are affected by the sexual division of labor. The relevance of this division will become even more clear in the next chapters about two highly gendered forms of family violence, incest and wife-beating.

7

"BE CAREFUL ABOUT FATHER": INCEST, GIRLS' RESISTANCE, AND THE CONSTRUCTION OF FEMININITY

One of the most striking things about incest, that most extraordinary and heinous of transgressions, is its capacity to be ordinary. In myth, incest occurs among tragic figures of heroic proportions. In the family-violence case records it is a behavior of very ordinary people. While incest is above all a violation of family expectations, incest participants made sense of their behavior precisely in terms of their family positions. Men referred to their paternal rights, girls to their filial duty. No less importantly, they rationalized their behavior, both as aggressors and as victims, in terms of that most ordinary of their characteristics, their gender. Men spoke of men's sexual "needs" and their prerogative to "have" women. Girls interpreted both their resistance and/or acquiescence in terms of femininity and girlhood.

It should be evident by now that part of the purpose of this book is to reveal the ordinary in all family violence, to show how it develops from normal conflicts which are "put" into our lives not only by human foibles but also by the everyday structures of society. Incest, however, is never just an exaggeration of the acceptable, as child abuse may be an exaggeration of punishment. Incest is not ordinary and its participants know that too. Their contradictory experience, of being both ordinary and deviant, illustrates some of the contradictions of familial and gender expectations, particularly for girls. In the modern version of the sexual double standard, a good girl has been above all sexually pure: a virgin until marriage, innocent of sexual thoughts and experience. But she has also been expected to be obedient to and under the protection of parents and men. Father-daughter incest creates confusion and double binds for girls because of their attempts to meet *both* these standards of virtue. Both girls who resisted and girls who acquiesced did so in the cause of their virtue. The difficulties of these incest victims are reminders of a normal girlish uneasiness about virtue, about achieving a feminine balance between modesty and submission, chastity and obedience. I do not wish to overstate the universality of these problems of girlhood, or the connection in male sexuality between taking charge and raping. The painful stories that follow are not the norm. Still, if we see ourselves in the vignettes of incest, that is because it is like seeing normal patterns of parental and male domination reflected in a distorting mirror.

In 1934 school officials complained to the MSPCC of a large family of children in very bad condition—filthy, with ragged clothes. Since the investigation revealed that there was neither drinking nor immorality in the family, no neglect complaint was filed! The father's steady employment disqualified the family for welfare, although the OPW paid some of the medical expenses for the diabetic, severely obese mother. School authorities kept complaining, and child protectors taking no action, until 1939, when the oldest daughter, now twenty, accused her father of incest with her from the ages of ten to fifteen.

Mo was sick and "could not have anything to do with fa" and he was going out with other women and mo did not like this and so fa began having relations with her She told mo about this but mo did nothing . . . Bro also knows about it Does not know whether other chn in the house do or not Fa used to call her into his room and force her to have relations with him If she did not have relations he would be very abusive to her . . . He used to use safes . . . Bro blames her for not being able to fight off fa . . . Mo blames her too . . . she thought that when people loved you they weren't supposed to hurt you and couldn't understand why fa would do this to her She was his own dau and that he should have gone out and done it to someone else Thinks she should have had more courage and fought back . . . Then again would stop and talk about fa hitting her in the face and head with his fists Mo hits her with a stick Again would say that she knew that she was to blame for not being stronger in attitude toward fa . . .[1]

In 1925 a Neapolitan family with six children lived with paternal relatives. Before marriage Mrs. Rienzi, as we will call her, had run her own restaurant. In Boston she was dependent on a store owned by these relatives, who, Mrs. Rienzi believed, provoked her husband to beat her. When she became ill in 1925, the oldest daughter, Silvia, dropped out of school and went to work in a factory. Mrs. Rienzi died in 1927, and seventeen-year-old Silvia became the housekeeper.

About 2 or 3 wks after mo's death one night fa came to the kitchen and locked the door, and made [Silvia] get on his lap, and had relations with her. This continued, sometimes in her room and sometimes in fa's usually when the chn were at sch, as after a while she left work staying at home. Said that fa used a safe and was careful so he told her not to get into trouble. Fa told her if she did not agree he would take the younger girls, and [Silvia] felt that mo would have wanted her to protect them. Said that pat. aunt had warned her about fa but this was after fa had assaulted her. Had wanted to tell the pastor[2] of her church, and had gone to see him but he had been out. One time she was angry with fa for a wk and he went in town, and later told her he had paid money for it, and threatened to spend all his money on it, if [Silvia] did not agree. Said that for the last few wks it was occurring 3 times daily.

Indicted for incest and rape, Mr. Rienzi denied the charges; the younger children at first lied in court to protect him against their older sister;

but were finally persuaded to admit their lies. The next daughter, whom I shall call Rita, said that

> one night after mo's death fa came into the room twice and one time got into bed between her and [Silvia who] then insisted on changing the room to the front of the house where fa could not get in. Said that fa was always quarrelsome, always abusive, and before her mo died tried to throw her down the cellar . . . abt 3 mos ago when she was alone in the store fa tried to kiss her, and wanted her to sit on his knee. [Rita] became suspicious because he never wanted to do this before, and ran away from him crying.

Mr. Rienzi was convicted and sentenced to ten to twelve years. He then made over his equity in the store to his sister and her family, and his children were committed to the Home for Destitute Catholic Children.[3]

Such cases were common in family-violence case records from the very beginning of the child-protection movement, constituting about 10 percent of the caseload. Yet by 1960 incest was conceived by experts, and described in textbooks on family problems, as a rare sexual perversion, a one-in-a-million occurrence.[4] In the last two decades incest has been "discovered" as if it were a new phenomenon. Part of this radical shift in the visibility of incest had to do with its different meanings, which need to be sorted out. For example, the cases described above were neither "innocent" sexual exploration nor illicit love affairs, but child abuse. This book discusses only the forms of incest that can properly be considered family violence, but in order to do so clearly we must first review some of the different forms that incest—in theory—can take, and clear them away, so to speak.

The mid-twentieth-century denial of incest resulted in part from certain influential scholarly reinterpretations of incest mythology. Myths of incest are, of course, among the most ancient artifacts of culture, functioning in an indeterminate and oblique relation to the near-universal prohibition on at least some forms of incest. Both psychoanalytic and anthropological interpretations, associated respectively with Freud and Lévi-Strauss, interpreted incest taboos as the bases of civilization. Both assumed, taking a particular interpretation of the role of mythology, that the taboos were effective and total, that incest was in fact extremely rare. Since mother-son incest figures predominantly in the mythology, it was assumed to be the most frequent in actual occurrence, sibling incest following next, with father-daughter incest the most rare. Neither psychoanalytic nor anthropological critique distinguished incestuous breeding from incestuous sex without reproductive consequences or potential. This proved a serious mistake, because the former have been effectively tabooed while the latter were condemned but tacitly permitted.[5]

Incest was brought out into the open only when a women's rights movement challenged assumptions that conventional family life was inherently superior. Several scholars argued that in developing his theories of infantile sexuality and Oedipal drives, Freud had used evidence that could more accurately have been interpreted to show the prevalence of intrafamily sexual abuse of children.[6] Other feminists showed how Lévi-Strauss's theory, that the incest taboo was a requirement of exogamy and the exchange of women, did not explain why it was women who were subordinated and exchanged, or the existence of gender, which is surely fundamental to our culture.[7]

Historically, Freudian thought did not so much *cause* social workers to deny children's complaints and hints about sexual mistreatment as it offered categories with which to explain away these complaints. As Boston psychiatrist Eleanor Pavenstedt commented in 1954, "Most of us have trained ourselves to skepticism toward the claims of young girls who maintain they have been seduced by their fathers . . . We must ask ourselves whether our tendency to disbelief is not in part at least based on denial. The incest barrier is perhaps the strongest support of our cultural family structure, and we may well shrink from the thought of its being threatened."[8] So did the dominant sociology of the family, which inverted Lévi-Strauss's functionalism to prove that the incest taboo was operative because it had to be.[9] The few historians to study incest have similarly studied public beliefs about incest, not behavior.[10]

The rediscovery of incest as a form of family violence has allowed the first historical consideration of incest as actual behavior. Evidence in child-protection-agency case records requires fundamental revisions in what had been the dominant views of incest. First, incest of a non-reproductive sort—creating new families—is not nearly so tabooed as was once thought. Second, several forms of intrafamily sexual activity are so different in their fundamental structure and meaning that classing them all as, simply, incest obscures their significance. For example, sibling sexual activity, or sex between other relatives of approximately the same age, is extremely common but difficult to identify. Woman-child incest, by contrast, is uncommon. Man-child incest is quite common, and it is, as we shall see below, the only type of incest that is regularly a form of family violence.[11]

The incest discussed here was virtually always an abusive relationship, a form of rape, between a man and a child.[12] There was less difficulty defining incest in this study than any other form of family violence, because sexual abuse perpetrators usually provided their own definition: as Dr. Judith Herman, a psychiatric expert on father-daughter incest, points out, when adults pressure children to keep their physical contact secret, that contact can safely be considered sexual abuse.[13] When sibling incest takes on this coercive nature, it too almost always involves an older male with a younger child, almost never an older female. This type of incest, incest as family violence, is a male crime. Women do not rape, are not often involved in sexual activity with children, and rarely commit incest with children.[14] Indeed, incest as a form of family violence is even more exclusively a male crime than marital violence, although the latter has traditionally been labeled as male, while the former has been seen primarily as a genderless sexual or psychological perversion. Just as in other forms of family violence, the occurrence and significance of incest is misunderstood without an analysis based on gender.

Because incest assailants are male does not mean that the female is a passive nonparticipant. One of the most complicated, and painful, aspects of incestuous sex—and all child sexual abuse, for that matter—is that it cannot be said to be motivated only by hostility or to be experienced simply as abuse. Understanding incest requires accepting ambiguity. The very definitions of acquiescence and resistance will be challenged, blurred, and perhaps reformulated in looking at particular cases.

GENERAL PATTERNS, 1880–1960

Incest patterns changed less than any other form of family violence over the last century. This does not mean that incest is a pathology uninfluenced by historical change, but that the social arrangements that give rise to it have been tenacious. There is no way to know whether its incidence remained the same. The proportion of incest cases found in family-violence agencies may tell us more about what social workers were noticing than about actual occurrence.[15]

The incestuous relationships in these records were predominantly heterosexual.[16] Forty-nine out of fifty of the older partners were male,[17] and they were on average twenty-five years older than their "partners."[18] Of the children involved, ninety-three out of ninety-seven were girls; all four boys were incestuously involved along with female siblings.[19]

The victims were children, not adolescents: their average age was ten. Furthermore, these figures overestimate ages, notably of the children, because the age of the child was noted at the time the incest was discovered. Most incest relationships continued for several years, and at the beginning of these relationships the children were younger. The once common view that incestuous men are attracted by pubescent girls is thus based on false assumptions.[20]

These incestuous relationships were not single occurrences, moments in which a man's ability to repress his sexual desires temporarily broke down. Being secret, the incestuous relationships were calculated and planned in advance to avoid detection. Furthermore, they were long-term. Sixty-seven percent continued for years—38 percent for three or more years, 29 percent for one to three years. Five percent continued for months, 17 percent occurred "several times," and only 10 percent "just once."[21] The sexual relationships were never ended voluntarily by the men. Usually the incest was terminated by the girl's moving away from the household, discovery by some other person, or, occasionally, by pregnancy or fear of it. When she reached fifteen, one long-term victim "told him if he ever got her into trouble she would make him pay for it and he has not been having relations with her since that time."[22]

Even if the perpetrator was not the girl's father, their relationship usually contained the power, authority, and dependency imbalance that characterizes filial bonds. Almost half of them *were* the biological fathers of the children, and the second largest group was "social fathers," that is, stepfathers, foster fathers, adoptive fathers, mothers' boyfriends. As the following table shows, nonbiological fathers were two to two-and-a-half times more often represented in sexual than in nonsexual abuse of children. Looking at it inversely, although biological fathers were less likely to abuse their children sexually than nonsexually, these fathers remain implicated in nearly half of all incest.[23]

7. INCEST ASSAILANTS' RELATIONSHIP TO VICTIM

RELATIONSHIP	TYPE OF ABUSE		
	Incest (N = 62)	*Child Abuse* (N = 110)	*Other Violence* (N = 478)
Biological Fathers	48.4%	74.5%	83.5%
Step-, Foster, and Adoptive Fathers	29.0	12.7	11.1
Other Adult Male Relatives	22.6	12.7	5.4

(N refers to number of cases.)

Some contemporary researchers argue that biological fatherhood creates a sociobiological taboo against incest which stepfathers do not internalize. These explanations assume that "inbreeding" reduces fitness and therefore survival rates; social groups which inhibit incest have survived. The anti-incest "imprinting" is pre-cultural.[24] However, the family violence data do not bear out this theory. There is no explanation of why the taboo would apply to nonreproductive sexual activity; and the proportion of biological fathers in these incest cases is still so high that it makes little sense to speak of a taboo. Since stepfathers are also overrepresented as perpetrators of nonsexual child abuse, sociobiologists would have to provide a separate explanation for that.

Another explanation fits all the facts better—that abuse is more likely to occur when the man feels little responsibility for the welfare of the child. "Social fathers," often in transient relationships with mothers and having only casual contact with the children, are less likely than natural fathers to have internalized a consciousness of the child's welfare. For example, consider this contradiction: fathers living with their children might be expected to have more opportunity for an illicit sexual relationship. But, in fact, incestuous fathers were less likely to live with their children than other types of abusive fathers. Ninety-five percent of male nonsexual child abusers lived in the same household with their children, as compared with 68 percent of incest assailants. The best explanation is that fathers living with their children had more responsibilities for and intimacy with the children than absent fathers. (The reason that nonsexual abuse rates remain higher among biological fathers is that it so often grew out of punishment, while sexual abuse did not.)

If there is an incest "taboo" that prohibits not only mating but also nonreproductive sex, that taboo grows from nurturant attitudes toward children, constructed through internalizing a conception of the child's own interest as distinct from the adult interest. This rendering of the "taboo" also explains why mothers do not often molest children sexually. Mothers who fail to internalize the child's interests are more rare than fathers.[25]

This redefinition of the incest taboo helps explain another consistent characteristic of incest situations: the relative powerlessness of the child's mother. In one fifth of cases there was no mother at all: 22 percent of incest episodes happened in male-headed single-parent households,[26] while such households constituted only 3.6 percent of the total sample. This absence of maternal protection gains in significance when associated with other cases in which the mother is present but weakened in her child-raising authority and confidence. In two-parent incestuous households, 78 percent of mothers had one or more characteristics of such weakening. The most common was that the woman herself was the object of her husband's or lover's violence—44 percent were beaten themselves. (By contrast, in our whole sample 34 percent of cases had wife-beating.) Thirty-six percent of the mothers were ill or disabled; 34 percent had other debilitating problems such as alcoholism, rejection by their own relatives, recent migration to the United States, inability to speak English, isolation as evidenced by infrequent trips outside the home.[27]

What was it about these "weakened" mothers that made their daughters more vulnerable?[28] Directly, it was the mothers' inability to stand up to men. They frequently tried to help their daughters but lacked the ability to take action that would have made a difference. For example, "Mo had told [daughter] to be careful about fa. before she died, but [daughter] did not understand . . ."[29] Indirectly, mothers' powerlessness prevented girls from internalizing the self-esteem they needed to resist sexual exploitation themselves. In principle this kind of self-esteem can be given to children by parents of both sexes. But in fact women did most of the mothering; and in their absence, the vacuum was not usually filled by fathers.

The incestuous men were remarkably nonparental. None expressed recognition of his capacity for hurting his children. Their defenses were of three types: most commonly they denied sexual acts; sometimes they blamed their wives for depriving them and/or the girls for seducing them; occasionally they claimed not to have known what they were doing, to be acting in a state of less than full consciousness. They refused to accept responsibility for their actions and attributed disproportionate power to the girls.

The fathers' denials or delusions notwithstanding, the narratives show that many of these men had suppressed girls' active resistance with violence or severe threats in order to get their way. There is still a legacy of incest mythology that questions the coercion in these relationships and suggests that girls seduced the grown men. Despite the mixed feelings many girls had (which will be discussed below), the evidence from this study shows conclusively that they found these sexual relationships undesirable and took considerable risks to get out of them. Indeed, they tried harder to resist than did victims of nonsexual abuse. Moreover, incestuous girls themselves initiated the contact with agencies in 50 percent of the cases; they were at least as likely to do so as victims of other forms of family violence.

In these findings our study differs from previous work, which has emphasized the powerlessness and/or acquiescence of incest victims.[30]

8. VICTIMS' RESISTANCE IN INCEST, CHILD ABUSE, AND NEGLECT

TYPE OF RESISTANCE	TYPE OF ABUSE		
	Incest	Child Abuse	Child Neglect
Attempts to Flee	38.9%	53.5%	25.3%
Any Resistance	85.2	71.4	46.0
Fought Back	22.2	6.6	3.6
Told Police	25.9	16.3	6.5
Told Others	74.1	65.1	43.9

The difference may arise from the fact that most of this previous scholarship drew its information from incest victims themselves, often speaking many years after the events. Moreover, these ex-victims were usually speaking to mental health clinicians to whom they came in distress, often expressing guilt feelings and self-blaming interpretations. Our information by contrast comes from case records in which there is evidence not subject to later reinterpretation from memory.

In one way incest resembles nonsexual child abuse. The child is treated badly, injuriously, by one who is supposed to be a caretaker. The dilemma for the child in both forms of abuse is that her molester is one on whom she must depend for love and sustenance. In other ways, sexual and nonsexual child abuse are different. Nonsexual abuse is never pleasant for the child, while incest may be, and may be interpreted as an expression of affection. Yet even very young children know that incestuous sex is, theoretically, forbidden, while nonsexual child abuse may develop out of punishment that is accepted as legitimate even by the child. Thus whatever gratification the child gets from parental attention in the incestuous relation is mixed with guilt.

The widespread and energetic resistance among incest victims was, therefore, confused, varied, and unsteady. Moreover, the resistance could not always be distinguished neatly from acquiescence, or desperation, or victimization itself. Temporary cooperation might be a form of defense; active resistance might be dangerous and for that reason a sign of lack of self-preservation drive. Children's resistance usually occurred on a terrain defined by the more powerful person and fell short of escape from paternal authority. Incest was a dynamic relationship in which assault and acquiescence, passivity and assertiveness, acceptance and resistance were merged and mutually influencing.

The leading problem in studying and treating incest is its secrecy. Parents have a great deal of leverage with which to enforce secrecy upon their children, and scholars who have studied incest in the past decade consider that the known cases are but a fraction of the actual practice. This secrecy is, however, only partly constructed by the perpetrators. It is also enforced, in part, by outsiders—family members, friends, neighbors, and even child welfare specialists who cannot or do not want to believe in the existence of this crime, who make it, literally, unspeakable. Faced with the incest victims' steady calls for help, skeptical clinicians did not so much ignore them as interpret them.

The original view of incest among child-savers contained the mixture of prudish, feminist, anti-immigrant, and anti-pauper attitudes that characterized all child-saving work. The MSPCC considered incest cases "too revolting to publish," but recognized that they were common and that they were quintessentially male crimes against girls.[31] Starting early in the twentieth century, incest was reinterpreted through a double process of reconstituting the victim and the assailant. Girl incest victims, even those as young as eight or nine, were labeled juvenile sex delinquents and blamed for their sexual activity. The culprits were redefined, first, as neglectful mothers, who failed to insulate their daughters from sexual experience, and, second, as men-in-the-street, sexual deviants, or "perverts," strangers to their victims. Both redefinitions served to withdraw scrutiny from family relationships and from what might be the cultural and social sources of this exclusively male crime.[32]

INCEST AS SOCIAL AND MORAL INFERIORITY, 1880–1910

The MSPCC's ability to recognize incest, if not to discuss it publicly, was in part based on its notion that it was exclusively a vice of the poor. The meanings of incestuous sex were constructed largely from a class ideology, pervaded also by anti-Catholicism. Conservative and progressive reformers spoke of the degradation of poverty as if its victims were animalistic, lacking in standards of family life. (There is a remarkable correspondence here to the common view in the United States that the slaves, and the Afro-American people after slavery, lacked commitment to family.[33]) Yet precisely this sense of superiority allowed the recognition of what was often denied. Since the MSPCC believed these perversions occurred mainly among the social "other," not in their own class, its agents did not see themselves in incestuous fathers, or their own daughters in the incest victims they met.

Although incest was identified by child protectors as a brutal male crime, still they did not view its victims as innocent. Child-savers noticed a connection, which contemporary scholars have also observed, between incestuous molestation in childhood and subsequent sexual misbehavior, and were pessimistic about breaking that connection. It was part of the mysterious and fetishized nature of sexual experience in the Victorian sexual system that the victim was herself polluted, however unprovoked the attack. The pollution, moreover, was seen as contagious, not only through the transmission of venereal disease, but also as behavior "catching" to other girls.[34] These fears were associated with childhood "precocity" or "sophistication," synonyms for sexual experience. The sophisticated could never again be naïve.

The permanence of the girl's ruin was symbolized and measured by her loss of virginity. There were no degrees, no nuances; it was an either/or matter. To determine whether this ruin had taken place, the MSPCC relied on vaginal examinations, which it required of any girl suspected of being the victim of sexual assault or of sexual delinquency. In these examinations the MSPCC physician was almost exclusively concerned with the condition of the hymen.[35] Thus sexual molestation of children was defined as intercourse, and other forms of sexual touching were considered less serious, a view which affected not only the judgment of the wrong done to the child but also the guilt of the alleged assailant.[36]

These pelvic examinations were done prior to and sometimes without any interview of the victim. Indeed, caseworkers doubted the reliability of children's testimony with regard to sexual abuse more than that concerning nonsexual abuse.[37] The doctors believed they could learn from physical examination not only whether the girl was a virgin but how extensive and how recent had been her sexual experience. The demand for physical evidence prevented some parents from being able to protect their children according to their own values, for without the parent's permission for a vaginal examination, the Society would not seriously consider any allegation of sexual molestation. The physical evidence was objective, "scientific"; the victim's statements were not.

There were some reasons for this approach. The MSPCC was besieged with false allegations of child abuse, and others which were uncertain. People carried on feuds with others by denouncing them to the MSPCC. Most cases offered two or more conflicting renditions of wrongdoing and little basis for determining which was more accurate. Children particularly were unreliable witnesses against their parents. In this context, bodily evidence was useful, and the Society pioneered in the use of photography and medical descriptions of contusions, scars, bruises, wounds, etc.

The reliance on pelvic examinations created many false conclusions, however. First, many girls have stretched or even torn hymens as a result of nonsexual activity, a fact not recognized by the MSPCC doctors.[38] Second, a great deal of incestuous sex, perhaps particularly that involving pre-adolescent girls, did not include penetration.[39] Indeed, precisely because of the widespread definition of "sex" as intercourse, many incestuous men refrained from intercourse, seeking other forms of satisfaction which they may have considered less "wrong." One stepfather, upon being told he was being reported for incest, begged his stepdaughter only to "say I have played with you with my hands."[40] Many allegations were disbelieved and/or dismissed entirely because of the girls' intact hymen.[41] There were of course also cases of disbelief without a physical exam, and occasional disbelief even where the girls' genitalia did suggest sexual intercourse. But the dismissal of allegations specifically because of the medical evidence was a particularly heavy blow to the accuser, as it provided a "scientific" basis for calling her a liar.

Although girls were blamed for polluting other girls, the agency did not conceive of girls as naturally sexual or seductive. Children, in their view, might become sexual, but only through a process of pollution which they called "moral contagion."[42] This view also prevented very young girls from being blamed for seducing men. A masturbator, it was assumed, had to be taught these bad habits by others. Sexuality in children was an aspect of ruin, a sign that they had been assaulted. Insistence on the sexual innocence of children was parallel to an overall view of children as pure, passive, and malleable. False accusations were not assumed to be fantasies, but the deliberate lies of girls made promiscuous and "hardened" through ill use.

The agencies' main tactic against incest assailants was prosecution. Arrests were made in 57 percent of cases, and convictions obtained in 36 percent of those. Victims might be asked to prepare affidavits against their fathers.[43] The MSPCC also expected other family members to testify against the accused, ignoring or overriding the ambivalence that so often characterizes children's and wives' response to abuse from those they depend on. When prosecution was not possible, little help was offered. Even when the victims were not blamed in the analysis of the problem, the solutions were left up to them.

However militant the agency's prosecution attempts, the victims were usually punished more than the culprits. At best they might be forced into foster care, almost certainly inadequate; they might be institutionalized; they would probably incur the anger, often leading to permanent estrangement, not only of the accused but of their mother and other relatives as well.

Useful preventive work against sexual abuse would have required analysis of its causes. Clinical contributions in this area were meager. Motherlessness was cited as a leading factor exposing girls to sex crimes by depriving them of "protection, special knowledge and general training."[44] In fact, as we have seen, most incest victims had mothers, but the experts did not seek other explanations for their inability to protect. Widowers were often blamed for the assaults, disproportionately to their actual numbers. Another common explanation was overcrowding,[45] but there is no evidence that this was correct. Only the minority of client families had one bed per person or couple; most were able to segregate the sexes by room, but even this was not always the case. Still, the crowding was not worse in the incest than in other cases. And crowdedness has mixed implications for incest: the traditional argument was that it caused exposure to the opposite sex, and thus temptation; but it also diminished opportunity for privacy. Indeed, one might guess that crowded families might be more likely to learn of these sexual infractions, and that in less crowded situations proportionately fewer incestuous relations would be discovered.

The agencies also blamed liquor. Their point of view is understandable, as drunkenness was so widespread among their clients. In 1887 the MSPCC estimated that two-thirds to three-quarters of its child-saving work was connected with intemperance.[46] But in associating drink specifically with sexual violence, however, the MSPCC was on less firm ground. Drinking figured less importantly in incest than in any other kinds of family violence.[47] Familial sexual abuse was rarely a crime of uncontrolled, momentary passion to which the lowering of inhibitions by alcohol might contribute; but a long-term, calculated relationship perpetuated during sober as well as drunken moments.

1910–1960: RECONSTITUTING THE VICTIM

About 1910, child-protection agencies sounded an alarm about sexual attacks on young girls. But these were a different variety of attack—

perpetrated by strangers—and their discovery coincided with the diminished visibility of incest. This was not a coincidence but a replacement of one crime by another. Often the girls assaulted "on the streets" had been incest victims whose problems were not noticed when they took place inside the family. Moreover, these girls, whether victims of street rape or willing participants in sex, were grouped in a single category: sex delinquents. In other words, the incest problem was virtually redefined as a problem of sex delinquency.

Child-protection workers became less active in seeking evidence against incestuous men; psychiatric caseworkers, such as those at the Judge Baker clinic, did not usually consider sexual abuse at all. Yet it was there: in 1920, although the Judge Baker therapists did not acknowledge it, 40 percent of sex-delinquency cases contained allegations of incest and another 20 percent allegations of nonincestuous rape.[48] Sociologists began to study delinquent or maladjusted girls at about this time, and several serendipitously uncovered evidence of the children's sexual victimization within their own families, but they did not make incest a topic of investigation or analysis.[49] A 1940 MSPCC record dismissed an incest complaint on the basis of a Boston Psychopathic Hospital diagnosis: "Patient is depressed, suspicious and tells a story of incest with fa which is not true . . . She hates her fa and the stories of incest apparently serve the purpose of getting her out of the home." This girl had tried complaining to her mother, her minister, the police, various neighbors, and an aunt and uncle, as well as the MSPCC, over a period of years.[50] A 1960 case showed direct conflict between a client's and the agency's interpretation of the relationships in an incestuous family. The client, mother of a five-year-old daughter, married to an alcoholic, had been victimized by her father. She articulated her anger clearly: "expresses anger at the community for not protecting herself and her sister from [their father], saying they knew and wouldn't let their children play with them. [She] doesn't blame [her mother] and doesn't know how she took it so long. [Father] once gave [her mother] a concussion in front of all the children . . . " This woman lived in the same building as her mother, and the social worker disapproved of the dependence between these women, complaining about both their fighting and the fact that they walked into each other's apartments without knocking. There was equal disapproval for the woman's unresolved relation with her father, whom she considered a menace to society and would not allow in her house. This client's resolute blaming of her father and acceptance of her mother did not fit the diagnostic categories.[51]

The theme of the girls' pollution overwhelmed that of their victimization. Locating this sexual delinquency on the streets shifted the blame onto girls' irresponsible presence in public and unrespectable spaces. This kind of problem was one for the police, who were not expected to contain predatory males but to control the girls. Throughout the United States after 1910, child-protector-supported campaigns for hiring women police officers arose, primarily in response to alarm about the white slave trade.[52] But the police orientation was also to delinquency, not to male sexual crime. The girls usually "fabricated" stories of why they left home, one policewoman wrote in her memoirs.[53]

In their turn toward victim-blaming, child protectors began to discover "feeblemindedness" in sexual assault victims.[54] In a more "modern" discourse than that about alcohol, feeblemindedness was a medical category, describing the presumably hereditary, fixed, and measurable nature of intelligence, as opposed to the moralistic view that alcoholism was caused by lack of "will." (Lagging a bit behind academic psychologists, the MSPCC adopted eugenical thought at its peak, around 1910, after it was already being subject to critique and modification.)[55] The feebleminded victims were allegedly morally retarded as well, and unable to maintain the resistance required of a good girl. Feeblemindedness thereby justified the incarceration of victims, for these girls could not be expected to look out for their own virtue. At the same time, the girls' alleged mental inadequacy made them bad witnesses and interfered with the prosecution of sex assailants.[56]

Wartime hastened the transformation of these girls from victims to villains. The panic about venereal disease was particularly intense in Boston, not only a major naval base but also, in World War II, an army base. With VD as the emphasis, soldiers and sailors became the victims, and their female sexual partners the disease-spreading sources.[57] Illogical as this implicit contagion theory was, "social hygiene" recommendations called for inspection, treatment, isolation, and prosecution of girls, never the soldiers and sailors they were sexually involved with. Prior to World War I, the *Journal of Social Hygiene*, the major publication of the anti-VD and anti-prostitution forces, referred often to sexual crimes against girls; during and after the war, it focused instead on the girls' sexual delinquency. In 1941 the Boston Committee on

Public Safety surveyed the "girl problem" through an intensified double standard:

> It is very difficult for the serviceman to meet the type of girl whom he was used to meeting in civilian life ... is therefore virtually compelled to seek his amusement in the cheaper commercial places where he meets girls of the prostitute or promiscuous type. It is easier and cheaper for the serviceman to meet one of these girls and spend the night with her than to hunt out inexpensive amusements less dangerous to his health.[58]

It would have been just as logical to discuss the difficulties of wholesome girls in avoiding boys of an inferior type, girls endangered by an influx of predatory strangers operating without normal familial and community controls. Moreover, the class analysis implicit in this perspective is wrong, since there is no reason to believe that these drafted men came from less "cheap" cultural backgrounds than the girls who now threatened them. In England in the 1870s the Contagious Diseases Acts, based on similar notions of women infecting men, were repealed by an organized women's movement. This experience suggests that a feminist influence among child protectors, as had prevailed previously, might have offered another interpretation of these sexual problems.

The absence of a feminist interpretation conditioned the disappearance of incest and the "discovery" of female sexual delinquency. That label blamed girls for things that boys could get away with. In a sample of Judge Baker cases from 1919 and 1920, nine girls and one boy were accused of sexual immorality, three girls and no boys of excessive sex interests, three girls and no boys of flirting, one girl of pregnancy and one boy of "bad habits [masturbation]."[59] Girls who stayed away from home, came home late, who used vulgar language, rode in cars, drank or smoked, walked or dressed "immodestly," were liable to be declared delinquent,[60] and thereby deprived of sympathy if they were sexually victimized. A medical expert in sex-abuse cases insisted that "we seldom find cases of rape in healthy, robust girls in possession of their faculties and who are above the age of fourteen"—those who were healthy are presumed to have been willing.[61]

Psychiatric clinicians diagnosed all female misbehavior or maladjustment sexually, and their diagnoses also discouraged investigation of girls' previous victimization. Rather, they emphasized girls' fantasies, and suggested that an emphasis on assault was an aspect of repression of desire. In 1940 one girl's incest allegations were interpreted as resulting from her jealous response to the fact that a boy she liked had married another girl.[62] To therapists of this period, the earlier child-savers' denunciations of male sexual depravity might have appeared as themselves the fantasies of a prudish generation. For example, here is a 1951 diagnosis regarding a sixteen-year-old delinquent girl:

> As far as the F [father] is concerned, I think there is an underlying rape fantasy at the very bottom [of the girl's behavior] but just above that is an attempt to be like the father instead of submitting to him, to be the man instead of the woman, as a kind of counteraction to that underlying fantasy. . . . She is very concerned about the fact that she hasn't got the genitals she is supposed to have if she is going to completely identify with the F. . . . when that is cleared up and the girl can accept the fact that she is a woman . . . [that will be] one of the first big steps to take . . .[63]

In another Judge Baker case from the early 1940s, a teenage girl was sexually involved with her foster father from the age of ten, becoming pregnant by him. The clinician reported, with some disapproval, that she became "very antagonistic and resentful" to him, "wishing he could be more severely punished and 'suffer as much as I have. He got out of it too easy.' " The clinician recorded that she had always liked her father better than her mother, was oriented toward getting love from men only, and was seductive toward her foster father. Her hints that she had been sexually victimized by her natural father prior to being placed out were ignored.[64]

RECONSTITUTING THE ASSAILANT

While incest victims were changed into delinquents, incest perpetrators became strangers. On the whole this was an incorrect interpretation: then as now, most sexual abusers of children know them well. There were some borderline cases. For example, for some poor children boundaries between incestuous and nonincestuous abuse were vague. Many lived with boarders who were also their mothers' lovers—that is, arguably, stepfathers; other boarders were relatives, especially among new immigrants to Boston. Social workers could define household sex abuse either as incest or as community crime and delinquency; from 1910 on, they increasingly chose the latter interpretation. Even more striking was the focus on street rape as opposed to household rape—an emphasis consistent with the widespread panic about the "white slave trade," i.e., the kidnapping of women into prostitution.

An important element in this reconstruction of child sexual abuse was the discovery of the "dirty old man." A police expert reported that "in almost all instances where the victim was very young and helpless the defendant was a sexually degenerated old man."[65] This particular stereotypical figure appeared with great frequency between 1910 and 1940. In 1910 fourteen out of sixteen MSPCC nonincestuous sex-assault cases, and in 1930 twenty out of twenty-two, involved such characters. (In several of these cases—for example, three in 1930—the agency labeled the problem exclusively as sex molestation by a stranger, even though it admitted there was also incest.) The accused were often small businessmen, craftsmen, or employees in shops which provided the physical space for secret activities with children—janitors, shopkeepers, cobblers, elevator operators. They were old from the children's point of view, usually over forty and often over fifty.[66] They often appeared as kindly, entertaining children and giving them treats; and it is important to remember the great attraction of small gifts for very poor children. It seems unlikely that the number of "dirty old men," or their opportunity, suddenly increased. Rather, the shift in agency interpretation brought these characters to attention.

A dirty old man had to have a private space, and he most frequently attracted his victims through their poverty. One typical culprit, in a 1910 case involving children from twelve families, was the Irish-American owner of a dye house in a prosperous working-class suburb. Children frequented this shop and were paid small amounts of money (5, 10, and 25 cents) for doing errands, as well as for submitting to sexual assaults. The sexual victims were girls ranging in age from nine to thirteen. Some of the children were actually raped and hurt badly; many managed not to return after a first experience; other children went freely, developing their own pretenses—bringing gloves to be cleaned, but not at their parents' request.[67] In another 1910 case an eight-year-old girl, born in Greece, speaking no English, accused her school janitor of assaulting her in the bathroom on several occasions. The first time he gave her a nickel; later he gave her bananas, a piece of chocolate, a doll. The MSPCC called in a Greek interpreter, who was skeptical and even hostile toward the girl, stating that she was convinced the story was trumped up, that the girl had been well coached and was "too clever for her years," a way of attributing sexual guilt of an unspecified nature to the girl. Because of the language problem, the girl had no means of communicating directly to the police or the MSPCC caseworker. (Typically fearful of telling, probably afraid that she would be punished, this girl attempted to hide her misfortune and was discovered because her mother found her washing out her bloomers and then discovered the gifts, hidden.)[68]

In focusing on the "perversion" of the culprits, child-protection agencies avoided confronting social patterns of male sexual privilege. For example, they ignored an important common thread in neighborhood sex-assault cases: many assailants were widely known in their communities as child molesters, yet maintained impunity. In 47 percent of the "dirty-old-men" cases, the accused already had community reputations for sexual misdeeds. Moreover, the assailants were neither strangers nor transients. In several cases they were family friends, in almost all they were well-known neighbors and community members, who had impunity for their molestation. In one extreme case from 1930, girls from at least four different families were involved with a fellow known as "Tom the Cat." That his nickname was known throughout the neighborhood suggests the common knowledge, even tolerance, of his seamy activity.[69] Once he had even been denied old-age assistance because of his immorality! In 1932 an investigator for the town solicitor uncovered a police conspiracy to refuse to prosecute Tom despite testimony against him by several girls.[70] Despite the "breaking" of these cases in 1930, Tom the Cat was still operating in 1941, when he was molesting his fifteen-year-old granddaughter. In case after case the girls were punished, never Tom. Even his granddaughter was sent to Lancaster (the state reform school for girls) after a physical examination proved she had "considerable sex experience."[71] In contrast to "Tom's" experience, of the three cases in which relatively quick legal action was taken against accused molesters, one was Chinese-American and one black, i.e., neither was a full member of the overwhelmingly white community.

The impunity of most neighborhood sexual abusers reveals not only the denial of children's experience, even by the victims' own parents, but also some tacit permission given these men to molest children (much as in incest cases). Certain girls were being sacrificed. To some extent the victims were chosen through maintaining an individual-family approach to public danger, in which parents restricted their own daughters but did not demand the prosecution of the culprit or organize pressure to stop his behavior. There was a class dimension to this approach too, for these men's adventures would not have been possible in prosperous neighborhoods. Most city dwellers at this time agreed that girls should remain domestic and that those who strayed into the streets were somehow fair prey; but only among poor girls was it assumed that some would always "go bad." Supporting these attitudes was an acceptance of male predatory sexuality as inevitable, which in turn required that some girls be sacrificed to protect the purity of other girls. In these neighborhood sex-abuse cases, the MSPCC attempts to prosecute offenders sometimes met community resistance, albeit passive resistance, by contrast with, say, nonsexual child-abuse cases in which there was more consensus for punishment of assailants.

The single incident of a contrary sort, a case in which neighbors took collective action against a molester, illustrates by its success that neighborhoods did have the power to stop molestation when they wished. In 1930 in East Cambridge, girls from two families, ages seven, eight, and ten, accused an elderly widower of taking them into a basement and molesting them. In fact, the complaint to the MSPCC originated with a neighbor (herself a mother of a daughter) whose kitchen overlooked the accused's and who saw him exposing himself and handling the children. She organized a trap: on a signal, two neighboring men went into the cellar pretending to look at the furnace and found the accused bending over the ten-year-old, with her bloomers removed. He was charged with assault and battery and being a lewd person and sent to Boston Psychopathic Hospital for thirty-five days' observation.[72]

Moving the locus of sexual abuse outside the home let fathers off the hook, but not mothers. "Incest" or "carnal abuse" was reclassified as moral neglect, which was by definition a mother's crime, as we saw in chapter 5. "While a mother cannot protect against the brute who attacks while the child is coming home from school, she can minimize the danger by not allowing the child to go out unattended except when absolutely necessary," wrote a police expert on sex abuse.[73] Mothers could be blamed even for their husband's sexual crimes: "using" their husbands' offenses to gain dominance.[74] The threat of sexual assault of girls was used to restrict the movements of the victims, tightening their confinement to domesticity. Not only public space in general, but modern popular culture in particular, was proscribed for girls:

> Certain moving-picture shows and the environment of the patrons in nearly all instances undoubtedly are provocative of sexual thoughts. The increase of picnics and excursions . . . The laxity of mothers in failing to inform their children in regard to sex forces the child to self-education.[75]

Caseworkers also reinterpreted the motivations of the male assailants. Psychologically oriented agencies looked for mental disease in sex offenders, blaming feeblemindedness, insanity, hormonal imbalances, "reduced power of inhibition caused by chorea, epilepsy, narcomania, alcohol, encephalitis, arteriosclerotic change, or senility" for their crimes.[76]

While some branded male sex offenders as sick, other experts simply became more indulgent toward male sexual aggression. In the nineteenth century, social workers were critical of male sexual excesses and sympathized both with feminist critiques of men as oversexed and with particular women who complained of their husbands' sexual demands. After the Progressive era it was more often the women who were labeled abnormal: frigid. The agencies in this study developed a new version of the "widower" explanation: citing men's chronic sexual deprivation as a factor.

In blaming women for men's sexual crimes, experts exempted the male offender from study, reform, or discipline. In the 1920s and 1930s, the child protectors emphasized "prevention," which meant casework and/or therapy. The object of agency work was the family unit, and in this work attribution of blame was considered destructive. Moreover, in therapy or counseling the woman of the family was usually the only adult "worked with." This pattern was most thoroughgoing in psychiatric social work. In none of the Judge Baker cases was the father or male assailant a participant in therapy.

THE ORDINARINESS OF INCEST:
THE VICTIMS' EXPERIENCE

There is no such thing as an individual response to incest. The responses of relatives, neighbors, and social workers—most often ignoring complaints and blinking at evidence—shaped the incest experience. Nevertheless, this social construction produced an intensely private experience which can be explored through these extraordinary case records, rich in detail precisely because the victims were trying so hard to get help. Their double bind—the condemnation of both resistance and acquiescence—produced self-blame. Moreover, their attempts to escape this double bind often sent them into street life and delinquent sexual activity, which further blurred the distinction between good and bad. Victims who were praised for being obedient and clung to a self-image as good turned out to have extensive sexual experience; others who became delinquent and harbored a deep sense of self as bad had struggled to protect themselves from their fathers' assaults. Dividing girls and women between the good and the bad has been a pervasive motif in the culture of male dominance, a means of enforcing women's sexual subordination, and it is understandable that rebellious girls sought to defy that dichotomy. For these girls, however, destroying their identification as "good" often meant deeply damaging their self-esteem.

In trying to negotiate a balance between good and bad, incest victims adapted to two alternative scripts. In the first, here called "domestic incest," girls became virtual housewives, taking over not only wifely sexual obligations but also housework, child care, and general family maintenance. This pattern was more common before 1930. The second pattern, "sex delinquency incest," produced girls precociously[77] active sexually, who "went with" boys on the streets, and became known as loose and available. In both patterns, the victim and her family were trying to assimilate the incest into conventional categories. This conventionalization of the experience contributed to the victim's bind, for she felt both terribly abused and also that she had no right to complain (another aspect of the way in which the incest experience merely exaggerates the situation of femaleness itself).

The two patterns, domestic and sex-delinquency incest, were not mutually exclusive. They categorize not different girls but different aspects of the incest experience, and many girls experienced both. Indeed, the domestic incest pattern tended to create the sex-delinquency pattern, by driving girls out of their parental home to the streets. In doing so, incest might be said to have been an extreme and grotesque case of a general deformation of domesticity which was creating a youthful female rebellion.

In 1910 the MSPCC was asked to help an Italian mother find her deserted husband in order that he pay child support for their six children. He was found but refused to pay. The mother nevertheless successfully resisted the agency's recommendation that her children be separated among different relatives, and also resisted the agency's pressure to take legal action against her husband. In other words, she did not have the characteristics of a typical incest mother, but displayed unusual spunk in her determination to manage as a single head of household. Some time in the next eight years her husband returned. In December 1918 she and her oldest daughter died in the influenza epidemic, leaving three daughters and two sons. Her dying request was that the next daughter drop out of school in order to keep the family together, and the daughter sadly complied. In February 1919, just two months later, this daughter telephoned to tell the agency that she had left home because of, she said, severe beatings by her father; instead, she would contribute financially, she said, and went to work at Magee Shirtwaist. A year and a quarter later, in March 1920, the next daughter came to the agency to complain, particularly about the father's beatings of the boys, and to refuse to continue the housekeeping. The father retaliated by bringing stubborn-child complaints against the younger children, whom she was trying to protect; these were dismissed by the court, however. The MSPCC, in investigating the home, complained that there were only two beds. The father responded, " 'What you think, rich man with so many beds?' " The minimal investigation done by the agency uncovered no incest allegation. Yet it hardly seems that the victims were reluctant to talk, as in 1922 a private attorney, relative of the dead mother, informed the agency that the children had engaged him to prosecute their father for incest with, now, an eleven-year-old daughter. At the trial it was revealed that the father had sexually assaulted three girls, one after another; the youngest now had gonorrhea. The father was sentenced to 8 to 10 years and the younger children placed with the City of Boston Child Welfare Division.[78]

This case shows how a domestic incest pattern might be imposed even on evidently assertive and self-confident girls. The first daughter had keenly sought education, and gave it up only to honor her mother's wishes. Ironically this mother's very strength and commitment to her family helped victimize her children. Despite the heavy pressure of a dying mother's wish, the first daughter escaped her victim position within two months. The next daughter, a mere ten at the time, was too young to resist her father. The older girls turned to the MSPCC because their mother knew of the agency, and in order to avoid creating a scandal among the relatives; but the youngest girl had to approach relatives, having gotten no help from the agency. It is not surprising that she ended up most alienated from the whole family. The older daughters' desire to protect their father despite his behavior re-emerged in 1926, when, in response to his self-pitying letters, they hired another lawyer to get him out of prison. The youngest daughter, far more seriously damaged by him (in 1926 she was again a victim of rape and VD, in other words a "sex delinquent"), was by contrast unforgiving and afraid of his revenge. Loyalty to this father had divided the sisters, just as in many cases with a living mother, loyalty to the father alienated mothers from daughters.

Every family is unique, and incestuous families are no exception, but many families shared certain classic lineaments of domestic incest: no mother; an older daughter who has become the mother, who feels great responsibility toward her whole family, particularly her younger siblings, and who is unusually disciplined and self-controlled; a father committed to and even dependent upon his family, yet rigid in his refusal to do housework and his expectation of being served.

Motherless girls were more vulnerable because they lacked a protector and became mothers themselves. Equally important is what did not happen: the father did not become a mother. Widows usually attempted to survive by becoming both mother and father to their children; widowers sought someone else to be mother. Similar patterns developed where the mother had been somehow debilitated. It was, of course, normal for men to dominate their families; but in the incestuous families the mothers were unable to fulfill even the traditional female familial role, that of sexual partner, housekeeper, and nurturer of children. In the domestic incest cases, the mothers' inability to function was so thorough-going that daughters were drafted to take over the housekeeping and child-raising, as well as the sexual duties of the wife. The drudgery of these girls was often substantial. They frequently did all the housework for large families, working very long hours and with little complaint. Many had internalized slave-like images of themselves.

The parents in incest families often held unusually conservative views about male supremacy and gender roles in domestic life.[79] Fathers complained about loose sexual morals in the community. These fathers were often especially tyrannical; the mothers, when present, unusually self-effacing. Frequently the mother had helped train and orient the daughter toward becoming the substitute housekeeper/mother/wife. This training produced in girls intense sisterly responsibility toward the family and a disapproving view of seeking education, career, or other egocentric achievement for oneself. The girls' housewifely role was also enforced by the pervasive view of femininity. To the younger siblings as well as the father, the housework and sexual services of the older sister appeared as part of the same, biological, "natural" female function. Often there were many younger children who depended on the older sister for care, although aspects of the domestic incest pattern remained when there was only one child, a daughter, whose obligations were exclusively toward her father. But in every case the victim, or the first victim, was the oldest daughter. Frequently, if an older daughter escaped the household, a younger daughter took her place, and protectiveness toward these younger sisters helped keep the older one in her place.[80] In one unusual case a father of eleven children had a sexual relationship with four of his daughters at the same time, while maintaining the domestic incest structure. He told them "that they could each be his wife for a week."[81]

The barb on this domestic hook in the flesh of the girl was that there were often emotional rewards for her, similar to the rewards of motherhood and wifehood. The younger children and the father appeared needy and loving, and were sometimes able to express their appreciation for the nurturance they received.

Mothers sometimes colluded in this domestic incest, although the degree and frequency of their participation has been exaggerated.[82] Several mothers (commonly, stepmothers) pressured girls to comply with men's sexual demands.[83] One daughter explained: "At times when I refused my mother would request me to do so for the sake of the rest of the family, as in the event that I did not submit to his wishes he would be very ugly to them. . . . My mother would coax me to give in to him."[84] The incestuous situation may have provided relief for the mother from her own exploitation, both as housekeeper and as sexual servant, without her having directly to defy the wishes of the father. One mother said, about the indecent demands of her husband, "if I can stand them you can too."[85] However, the high proportion of battered women among the mothers of incest victims suggests that the situation did not often provide freedom from marital abuse.

Another case history may illustrate these dynamics. In 1930 a fifteen-year-old girl (we will call her Agnes) claimed that her father had been molesting her since she was ten, when the family first came to the United States. She not only did housework, although there was a step-mother in the family, but her father had lied about her age to get her working papers and she had been employed in a rubber shop. The stepmother was much younger than the father, had married him at age sixteen, and reputedly cared little for the girl. Agnes claimed that the stepmother witnessed the father's advances and insisted that she obey him: "she was ironing clothes in the kitchen when fa. came in and took off his coat and hat and came up to her . . . and put his arms around her. She immediately got away from him and was rebuked by the stepmo." Or, "Several times she claimed that fa. came into her bedrm. at night time where she was sleeping with Ingrid [younger half sister, age nine] and insisted upon getting into bed with her, whereupon she wd. run out of the rm. . . . One night when the fa. came into the rm. stepmo. came in and took Ingrid from the bed into her own rm." When the victim was first removed from the home, Ingrid reported that "mo. was very anxious for Agnes to return to the home because mo. had already fainted four times from doing housework since Agnes had been gone."

Agnes was examined by an agency-appointed doctor, who concluded that there was no evidence that "any attempt had been made." No complaint was made against the father, therefore, although a psychologist concluded: "We are absolutely convinced that she has been sexually attacked . . ." Agnes went to stay with a maternal aunt. This determined girl felt responsible for her younger sister, still in the home, and repeatedly visited several agencies, demanding the prosecution of her father. On one occasion she arrived at the MSPCC with "a number of neighbors who were greatly upset because fa. had not been properly punished and they stated that they were going to see that further action was taken, and that a collection was being taken to raise funds to pay for a lawyer." Agnes had herself examined by another doctor, who found a ruptured hymen. An MSPCC district agent wrote in response: "It is my opinion, because of the natural vindictiveness of [these] people, that Agnes probably ruptured herself in an attempt to place serious charges against the father." In a sad epilogue to the case, in 1939, Ingrid, the younger half sister then eighteen, was pregnant by this father.[86]

It is difficult to avoid revulsion and incredulity toward mothers such as this. Surely there is no reason to excuse her responsibility. But many clues in the record hint at her powerlessness: she spoke English so poorly that she needed an interpreter, she answered all questions by referring the agent to the father, and she would not offer her own opinion on anything. One must assume that she was not self-supporting.

Mother-daughter relationships in these cases were often marked by mutually painful hostility and jealousy, often directly stimulated or intensified by the man. Daughters could be treated like classic "other women," their mothers' coldness, cruelty, and laziness the topic of repeated complaints to them by fathers. Sometimes the mother fled, in one instance explicitly deciding that the father and daughter should form the central couple around which the family was constructed.[87] In another case, the father gave all his wages to his fourteen-year-old daughter, deriding his wife, and said to the daughter, " 'You are my wife, not your mother.' "[88] In several cases stepfathers tried to marry their daughter-victims.[89]

Some daughters were rewarded by their incestuous fathers with affection and gifts, but other girls were beaten as well as sexually abused. The fathers were intensely concerned to prevent their daughters from telling, and used both rewards and threats to manage that. In some cases the physical abuse escalated as the sexual abuse stopped, either because the family had discovered it or the girl had become more firm in her refusal.[90] One contemporary clinical study found that incestuous fathers used unusual amounts of force in their families.[91] But beating children was more common fifty years ago than today; the incestuous fathers in this study were not more violent toward their children than nonincestuous ones. They were, however, more often wife-beaters, as we have seen.

The power of the fathers in the family, however, cannot be measured by or equated with physical violence. The violence might indicate the presence of a challenge to the father's power, and the most authoritarian may have been able to impose their wills without force. Victims may also have exaggerated the violence: in efforts to preserve some self-respect and to rationalize their acquiescence, they colluded in their vision of the father as irresistibly powerful. In general, the paternal power is better indicated by the family relationships, particularly the relative "weakness" of mothers, which was previously discussed. (This paternal power was usually stronger in the domestic-incest cases than in those which had "progressed" to the sex-delinquency phase—i.e., those in which the girl had left the family's control—or in cases which never had a domestic structure with a girl playing wife/mother.)

Probably the most striking indication of the father's power was his ability to create within the family an alternate psychosocial order, stable despite its contradictory relationship to larger community patterns. "Fa told her that it was all right for him to do such things . . . for all fas did so with their daus."[92] Could he have believed this? Indeed, perhaps the most extraordinary and frightening characteristic of domestic incest is its taking on the appearance of the ordinary, its experience within the family as normal. This is not to say that victims or other family members believed these incestuous relations to be legitimate. The secrecy would make that unlikely, as well as the response of any outsiders who sensed the existence of a family secret. However, the assimilation of the sexual relationship to other aspects of the family dynamics and division of labor created an alternative normality, logic, and order. It bears repeating that most incestuous relations continued for years. This deviant but quotidian order within the family was more stable when family members were relatively secluded, geographically and/or socially. Even in the highly urbanized locale of this study, semi-rural cases were prominent in domestic incest. Kept extremely isolated, sometimes hardly ever allowed out of the house, the daughters had no access to outside help or to outside verification of the possibility of escape. The family's deviant order operated as a further centripetal force, encouraging the girl to remain within the domestic scene, despite its drudgery, for there she felt understood, accepted, and possibly appreciated, while the outside world reminded her of her abnormality and sinfulness, and of the horror and revulsion her story would evoke in others.

The largest single factor in creating the aura of "normality" in these families was the father's attitude of entitlement. Not a single incest assailant expressed contrition for what he had done or guilt for having hurt his daughter—only denial, self-justification, and/or shame and humiliation at being discovered. This contrasts with the frequent expressions of guilt by fathers who abused their children nonsexually.[93] The most consistent "collusion" by mothers was their promotion within the family of a view of the fathers' needs, however brutal, as legitimate and deserving sympathy. Mothers' victimization by beatings reinforced the message to children that men's aggressions are to be submitted to.

"Domestic incest" occurred less often after than before 1930. Several structural social changes contributed to this decline. Compulsory education through high school, which became common in the 1930s, prevented adolescent girls from being kept at home. As children spent more, and more intense, time with their peers, they became aware of differences between their own and their acquaintances' familial experiences. New norms of children's rights to leisure and autonomy today made girls who were secluded, or who did many hours of housework every day, appear abnormal. Norms for children's household labor have changed not only quantitatively but also qualitatively: it became unusual to find girls accepting overall responsibility for tasks such as cooking, shopping, supervising younger children. And of course the expectation of unquestioning obedience to a father's orders has substantially lessened.[94]

However, if domestic incest once "fit" better into conventional family patterns than it does now, this does not mean that daughters entered into these relationships willingly or even with resignation. On the contrary, they were usually coerced, and they usually sought outside help when their own struggles failed. The pressure for secrecy, often including threats of mayhem, was so great that victims often tried to disguise their hints so they could claim not to have violated their assailant's demand for secrecy. In trying to get agency help, one common mode was to make some other complaint (say, of physical abuse), in the (perhaps unconscious) hope that the incest would be discovered without the victims taking responsibility for telling. Mothers reported their husbands for non-support, neighbors reported fathers for abuse of wife and children, children accused their father of beatings—and agency investigations then revealed incest.

Incest cases were often discovered when someone broke the family's façade of unity and privacy. In some cases the mother had left home, jealous of the girl-victim and/or unable to bear her own feelings of guilt toward her daughter and failure as a mother, and the family came to the agency's attention on suspicion of neglect due to the mother's absence.[95] Occasionally the father himself inadvertently exposed his own wrongdoing by reporting a child for stubbornness or incorrigibility. These "self-referrals" by incestuous men might be interpreted as one of the few examples of men asking for help, or alternatively as reflecting the incestuous fathers' great confidence in their own impunity.[96] A few times the victims became pregnant and sought help in arranging their confinements.[97]

The victims had good reason to fear breaking the secrecy of incestuous relationships. Even when they were believed, they would often have done better without intervention. The humiliation of exposure was by no means confined to the culprit, and the economic dependence of the mother and other children on the father usually meant that it was the victim who was sent away, deprived of her family, not the assailant. The majority of those who took action in their own behalf wanted to escape the situation without having the assailant prosecuted. They tried to get help in leaving home, or in rearranging household structure or even room assignments, in order to make the sexual demands on them stop, without revealing the truth.

One such method was to refuse to do housekeeping. In one 1930 case an older sister defied her father by taking a job, paying him $3 per week for board, but refusing to do any housework. She did not wish to move out of the house entirely, because she was protecting her two younger sisters from his advances. (She had brought first one and then the other to the MSPCC's attention, but their examinations had revealed the girls' "parts" to be normal, although there were "suspicious symptoms.") When her father steadily complained that he needed her housework, she raised her board payment to $4 and then $5 per week, but refused to do the work.[98]

But these girl housewives had the same problems as mother housewives in trying to resist their exploitation: their work involved caring for those they loved, particularly siblings. Leaving the family often appeared to these older sisters as "selfish" and "immoral"—just as it might to a mother contemplating leaving her children to escape an abusive husband. Doing so was called desertion by social workers, courts, and probably by peers. Particularly in families recently migrated to Boston from more rural environments, the commitment of siblings to each other was strong in comparison to that of today. For example, in the case summarized above, despite the stepmother's rejection Agnes developed a strong affection for the stepmother's own daughter, Ingrid, and tried energetically to protect Ingrid as she herself had not been protected. When domestic incest victims did try to leave the family, they often lacked the confidence or skills to find jobs. Already isolated and confident only at housework, they also absorbed from their conservative parents a fear of the outside world.

Thus many incest victims only made their move to get help when their younger sisters were threatened by the father's sexual demands.[99] In this respect, as in others, incest victims behaved like beaten wives, who often tolerated violence until it touched their children. This motherliness was both a strength and a weakness: it encouraged them to tolerate high levels of abuse "for the sake of the children," yet it helped them to limit what they would tolerate. The limits were hardly stringent ones, but the existence of some area of honor was strengthening and helped preserve sanity.

The relation of many incest victims to their siblings raises difficult questions about labels such as "passive," "acquiescent," and "resistant." Acquiescence, even self-abnegation in relation to a father, might be the mirror image of protective assertiveness toward a younger sister. Indeed, are not these either/or distinctions between passivity and aggressiveness biased against the particular work, familial roles, and strengths of women and children? The clients had reason to fear the breaking up of their families and being institutionalized themselves. In developing a strategy aimed at survival, maximum protection of others, and minimum physical and psychological damage to oneself, it is not clear that acquiescence was self-destructive.

The costs to a girl of escaping her incestuous exploitation could include denying her responsibility for other family members, and sacrificing her identity as a good daughter. A successful escape required great determination and a strong ego. One 1920 case involved an

American-born Chinese father who had imported a Chinese wife and their six children, including a newborn. The father owned and operated a laundry next to his residence, and the oldest daughter, sixteen, "Grace," the victim, worked there. She was beaten, badly overworked in the laundry, and raped by her father. The mother was extremely cowed. Also beaten by the father, in 1920 she was debilitated by a difficult birth (and five other children). She was aware of the incest, took no action to help her daughter, but said she lay awake nights worrying. She could hardly have avoided knowledge, according to Grace's story, for the noise must have been substantial—the girl said she put a trunk in front of her door and her father forced it aside. Yet Grace wrote at one point that she was willing to sacrifice herself to save her mother pain; and when she was taken from her home, she said she felt guilty at leaving her mother. From a contemporary perspective, there appears to be a role reversal here: the daughter felt she ought to be protecting her mother. In fact, in patriarchal families such an assumption of responsibility by a child was not a reversal at all. In working-class and particularly immigrant poor families, it was expected that children should work to spare their mothers; and mothers expected to be able to count on daughters for self-sacrifice. The incestuous pattern, again, is an exaggeration of the patriarchal pattern, not a reversal of it. And the patriarchal pattern defined mother-child as well as father-child relations.

In this case one might have expected the father to justify turning to his daughter for sex by his wife's confinement. He did not in fact say this, but claimed non-responsibility. He told a doctor that "he does not know what he does during the night and that he is perfectly surprised in the morning when his wife tells him of the things he has been doing." The doctor appeared to believe him, and so, perhaps, did Grace, but I did not. His behavior toward his daughter was calculating in other ways, and his exploitation of her systematic. For example, he secluded her from outside influences, trying to keep her from going to church or Sunday school (although he too was a Catholic); as soon as allegations against him were made, he tried to force her into a marriage he arranged; he successfully forced her to quit school; he opened her mail. Nor did he lose much. He kept his family together except for the one girl; there is no record of agency concern for the safety of the nine-year-old daughter or the mother; and no charges were filed against him.

Grace escaped her incest situation by writing to her Sunday-school teacher. While the whole family was Christian, the girl had become intensely religious in a manner resented by her father, suggesting that her religiosity was part of her resistance to his authority. (Rebellious women have often used religion, an appeal to a higher authority, against male domination.) Her letter is worth quoting at some length.

Dear Miss —————,

O, how heartbroken I am because of all these troubles I can't bear. You would not realize, I know, how many troubles I have because I try hard to be cheerful and happy. Now my heart is overflowing with grief. I have brought them to Jesus and I know he will make them right for me. I am telling you so that you may understand why I cannot be with you.

I have suffered since childhood my father's abuses. He hates me for what I am. I work for him and obeyed him as much as I can even if they are unjust. After school from two o'clock until seven or eight, I work in his laundry store, rolling collars, doing up bundles, act as book-keeper everything that can be done and yet he says that I am still a slave to him. I am willing to work if he gives me my freedom to do the right thing. He always did open my letters and if he didn't like them he would burn them. . . .

This last month father seemed to like me for he was very kind, but no, it didn't last long. He tried to make me sin [emphasis added by MSPCC social worker], I wouldn't do it so he made me promise not to tell anyone, but the week before last mother found out. I told her all. How many tears were shed, I can't say. Father is very angry and hates me worse than ever. He wants revenge and he torments me in every way. . . .

My Church envelopes are burnt and worst of all, he bought a horse-whip Saturday, threaten[s?] to whip me if I dared disobey him. I must, also, speak and talk to him as a daughter ought or I'd get whipped. I haven't spoken to him except answer his questions.

Don't you think this is hard? Cruelty cannot seem to rule me, only love can so I disobeyed him last Sunday.

I got dressed ready for S.S. [Sunday school], went downstairs and waited for a car in the door-steps. Father ran down, pulled me in, and knocked me about so that my head was in a whirl. My hat was off, my hair was down and o [sic], I thought my hair was torn by his awful treatment. He told me he would kill me with a knife, I answered and

told him I would be very glad to have him. I was ready to die, I couldn't
bear it any longer. . . .

The Sunday-school teacher helped her leave home and brought the
case to the MSPCC. To the caseworker, Grace at first expressed reluctance to leave her mother, guilt about creating a family scandal ("We
don't want . . . shame to our family"); yet ultimately leaving her home
was not only what she wanted but something she fought for. The social
worker, a Chinese-American, pressured Grace to return home.[100] Her
father threatened to send agents of a Chinese secret society after her for
running away. In fact, if one looks at what Grace did rather than what
she said, she was admirably effective at extricating herself from a difficult
situation, withdrawing her support from mother and siblings. She never
returned home but went to a seminary. Despite her serious accusations
against her father, she protected herself from becoming self-defined as
a bad daughter by defending him. "Don't be hard on father will you?"
she wrote, ". . . people talk because they cannot understand. . . . I
must be thankful for some of my parents' kindnesses so must not bring
trouble to them. It cannot be helped if the parents do not love their
children. . . . Of course, he is sorry for his sin even though he doesn't
say it[101] and he doesn't want me to go home to harm me, but he wants
me to go home because my family needs me." And, "We cannot hold
a sin against a man for life . . . father has sinned, but we all ought to
be merciful even as God is merciful . . ." Yet, underneath this rhetoric
of faith, she was rejecting paternal authority and family obligation in a
most secular manner. She used Catholicism as a route to modernization,
Americanization, and escape from patriarchy.

Since the escape from domestic incest required not only a way out
of an involuntary sexual relationship but also out of other "legitimate"
obligations of daughterhood in a patriarchal family (such as working in
the family laundry and marrying at father's direction), a girl's resistance
to incest in such families was often integrated into a general youthful
rebellion against parental authority. The feminine form of this youth
rebellion was flight from domesticity. Such rebellions were part of a
transition to more "modern," egalitarian family norms. This Chinese-
American girl wrote, "It is very wonderful to have such a society [the
MSPCC] to help the children. They don't have any in China and there
is no law to protect children. The parents can do what they please with

their children, some even killing them by drowning." Grace knew of course that the MSPCC loved hearing this, and her comments may also have displayed her Christian prejudices against the unconverted Chinese; on the other hand, she could hardly be expected to understand the limitations and mistakes of the society's activities. Still, in her belief that child and wife abuse were worse in patriarchal China than in the New World, she may have been right. (Certainly China was an extreme case, with great paternal impunity.) However, the closer communities in peasant societies had means of enforcing child-raising norms upon deviant parents, while in the impersonal, economically competitive city, kinship networks often having been disrupted by migration, there were fewer informal checks on intrafamily behavior. [102] In these circumstances each "patriarch" was more isolated, less subject to pressure from other family heads. Without community intimacy providing effective social sanctions against child-raising violations, and with the modern construction of family life as private, fathers' sins were more hidden. Ironically this very privacy helped explode families, for the victims had no resort short of running away, public exposure, and sometimes the disintegration of the entire household.

THE INCEST VICTIM IN REBELLION: SEX DELINQUENCY

"Sex delinquency" was an escape route not only of victims, but often of highly responsible victims, trying to avoid telling their secrets and exploding their families. Their disobedience was likely to begin by staying outside the house as much as possible, even running away or "bunking out." Their misbehavior might then extend to victimization by men or boys, and then to initiation of sexual adventures. Consider this 1930 case involving a Polish immigrant family, whom I call the Pucinskis. Mrs. Pucinski died in 1929 leaving sons eighteen and sixteen, factory workers, and girls thirteen and eight. The younger daughter was at first sent to maternal relatives in a nearby community; the older, Wanda, became housekeeper. At first she did a fine job of running the household, but some time in 1930 home conditions began to deteriorate drastically. The Depression cost her father his job, which he had held for twenty-five years, and forced him into the casual labor market; the girls began to appear ragged and undernourished to teachers and neighbors; the father was drinking heavily; the tenement was filthy, piled with garbage, dark: "No human family should be asked to occupy it," the social worker remarked. The sons quarreled with their father and began refusing to turn over their earnings to Wanda; rather, they bought a meal at a time from her!

Neighbors complained to the MSPCC that Wanda was "running" unsupervised in the streets, using bad language, and "entertaining" boys. Questioned, she hinted to the MSPCC worker that she had been sexually abused *in the past* (frightened victims often tried to be discovered without taking responsibility for telling by suggesting that they were talking about something no longer occurring), and she charged that her father and brothers beat and kicked her for not doing her housework well enough, and for refusing sexual demands. She had brought her younger sister back into the house, apparently to use as protection against her father's (and possibly brothers')[103] sexual advances, for she told a caseworker that she took her sister into her bed when her father approached. Wanda begged the MSPCC agent to remove her from the household. The MSPCC did not act until the case was reopened six months later by Mr. Pucinski's taking Wanda to court on stubborn-child charges. He was trying to defend his old-country patriarchal prerogatives with modern means—the juvenile court system. Wanda's medical examination revealed an intact hymen and no evidence of VD, so her accusations of sexual abuse were not pursued. Ultimately Wanda and her sister were adjudged neglected children and committed to institutions.[104]

Wanda's refusal of her housekeeping and sexual "obligations" may have been easier than for some other girls because she had only one younger sibling. Moreover, the Depression affected all the family dynamics: the father's economic fall provoked her brothers' defiance as well as her own. Wanda's "running in the streets" was her escape, and it did her no more harm than the MSPCC, which punished her and her sister and took no action against her father or brothers. For Wanda and many others like her, the old sexual morality, the good girl/bad girl distinction, provided no help for extricating themselves from incest.

In choosing street life, Wanda encountered the double standard not only of the social work establishment but also of the street kids themselves, who considered street girls polluted, appropriate targets for sexual molestation. The girls often accepted this "badness" as part of their identities and developed survival skills capitalizing on it. They truanted from school, loitering at the Sullivan Square station, Scollay Square in the old West End, the Charlestown Navy Yard, or Revere Beach, looking to pick up boys or men. They traveled in groups, covering for each other and soliciting for each other.

Like all victims of abuse, girls in incestuous situations appeared to have low self-esteem. In contrast to girls abused in other ways, incest victims had unusually sexualized self-images. The combination could be deadly. The incest victims had learned not only to expect little consideration from those closest to them but also that sex was their best means of gaining rewards or even acceptance.

Nevertheless, in their flight from home, incest victims may have been successfully preserving an autonomy vital to their survival. The behavior of the sex-delinquent incest victims seems puzzling at first, for they appear to be seeking to repeat that which has made them most miserable. It is no wonder that some observers have branded such girls masochists, suggesting that self-hatred and desire for punishment led them to acquiesce in the incestuous advances in the first place, and that guilt about the incestuous experience led them to seek punishment through further sexual humiliation and cruel treatment. My reading of the case records produced another interpretation, that sex delinquent girls were attempting to regain some autonomy. The girls who remained trapped in their homes, victims of domestic incest, were more passive and fatalistic than the delinquents who were using their sexuality—the only resource they "owned"—to manipulate others and accumulate some personal power. As Lenore Walker points out in her study of battered women, in situations of powerlessness, attempts to assert power may be deformed: thus women who appear to provoke beatings are not necessarily seeking pain for themselves, but may be trying to get an *inevitable* beating to occur at a time and place of their choosing, in a situation which will make it milder. [105] In one sense, the sex delinquents were "healthier" than the properly behaved girls.

Girls gained power in their sexual adventures by acting in groups. Seventy-nine percent of the MSPCC's sex assault cases from 1910 to 1930 involved groups of girls. [106] Solidarity among the girls was evident despite parents' attempts to defend their daughters by throwing the blame on another, a practice which social workers sometimes supported. One eleven-year-old, it was said, had done more to demoralize young girls in East Boston than any other person.[107] The girls' attachments to each other were so strong that the male offenders frequently molested them in each other's presence. In one 1930 case, the girls of the neighborhood were divided into two social networks, one that accepted the invitations of a "dirty old man" and one that wouldn't.[108] The group bonding increased the girls' bargaining power with men or boys, and reduced their vulnerability to force. On the other hand, the girls in groups were more daring and took more risks than they might have done singly, which increased their chances of getting into trouble. In groups, they went farther from home, stayed out later, and were more willing to defy authorities. This group behavior, of course, also raises the question, to what extent was "delinquency" produced by individual unhappiness and rebelliousness and to what extent by a different conformity, among peers? Particularly in the early twentieth century, with the erosion of parental and community discipline, peer acceptance was becoming increasingly important to children. Particularly for girls lacking reliable parental protection, the value of friends' approval must have been great.

Also evidence of the girls' initiative in their sexual adventures was the frequency with which they became prostitutes.[109] Sixty percent of the MSPCC sex assault cases from 1910 to 1930 involved the girls' taking payment.[110] Sexual delinquency then led to prostitution more quickly than today—because men and boys were more accustomed than they are today to pay for sex, and because the girls were so poor. At the standard of living—often beneath subsistence—of many of these client families, any pittance was of value—a nickel, a piece of food, a bag of coal. Furthermore, payment was of multiple value to the girls because it also provided them with a contribution to bring back to the family, enhancing their low status within their family, perhaps winning them approval from the person they usually felt most rejected by—mother.[111] In many cases, as soon as word got out that some man was willing to pay for sexual favors, the number of girls involved would snowball, so eager were they for the coins or oranges they might receive. Many poor parents did not ask the sources of contributions. Some knew the sources and raised no objections; in a few cases, it was alleged, parents participated in the prostitution arrangements.

Another reason for the girls' quick transition into prostitution was, ironically, the popular moral revulsion against it which had grown rapidly in the nineteenth century. Prostitution was the most pervasive symbol of female sin.[112] The female sexual world as it appeared in the moral discourse of the time had two continents: that of the respectable and that of prostitutes. Seeing their options in a strictly dichotomized way, and believing that they had definitively left the path of virtue, sex delinquent girls saw no reason not to explore the path of sin for profit.

Among these girl prostitutes one can distinguish between those who passively accepted rewards, usually the very young, and those who began actively to demand remuneration. Even the passive, for whom the size of the reward was set unilaterally by the man, *expected* payment. Some case records show a process in which girls became more demanding and began to set their own fees. The payments ceased being "tips" and became a piece rate. The rates were not always monetary, or standardized. Some girls engaged in aggressive bargaining. In cases between 1912 and 1920, girls were receiving payments ranging from five cents to five dollars.[113] Prostitution took on special importance when the girl's goal was to leave home permanently, given the lack of other jobs for young women.

In one way, these girls were becoming more assertive, less victimized, in becoming prostitutes. At least a prostitute was getting something for herself, as opposed to a girl who was raped or who allowed men and boys to use her sexually for free. These girls were not only attempting to get out of their victimizing homes, they were using their greatest strengths—their sense of women's sexual value to men. The power gained through such a flattened and instrumental view of the self could hardly have brought lasting self-esteem, and the girls must soon have learned about the risks that prostitution brought—legal trouble, disease, and violence. Nevertheless, the very manipulativeness of these girl sex delinquents suggests their refusal to accept victimization. When the police and social workers commented on the insolence, sauciness, aggressive dress, and foul language of girls picked up on the streets, they were accurately observing girls' rejection of an obedience that had been self-destructive, and that the girls knew to be self-destructive.

So, however, was their rebellion, which only put them in different situations of victimization. Furthermore, in one supremely important respect, all the sex delinquents, prostitutes or not, were worse off than those who remained domestic incest victims: the former were breaking the law and enraging the community moralists, while the latter were, in the eyes of law and community, good daughters. Sex delinquents were likely to be discovered by authorities and severely punished (even prosecuted by their molesters, when fathers brought stubborn-child charges against "sex-delinquent" daughters).[114] True, domestic incest victims who remained at home might be punished, *de facto*, if discovered, by being sent to institutions or otherwise losing their families. But they were less likely to be discovered. Furthermore, the molestors of girls who became delinquent were less likely to be punished, because these girls were less likely to be believed, and even if they were, the blame was their own. Indeed, the "delinquent" girls were less likely to try to denounce their incestuous assailants than girls who remained at home. The girls at home had more to lose in making an accusation, but the sex delinquents had a more powerful deterrent—they blamed themselves.

In interpreting their self-hatred and quest for punishment, one must question whether the legal punishment was worse than life on the street, and whether life on the street was worse than life in the home. Ambivalence pervaded the behavior of incest victims. Their search for freedom and power was produced as much by deprivation of security as by lack of restraint. Their aggressive manipulation of sex stemmed perhaps as much from search for love as from bitterness. These were, furthermore, often the needs of very young children. One six-year-old was accused of what amounts to pimping for her sister, and there were numerous full-fledged fallen women of ten.[115]

Let us look in greater depth at a case that illustrates the intricate relations between incest and sex delinquency. In 1930, at age eleven, Susan was already "promiscuous" and blamed for the ruin of a group of other neighborhood girls. She was sleeping with a boarder, who was also her mother's lover; indeed, Susan's mother had just had a baby by him. The family was financially dependent on this boarder, who helped Susan's mother with her home work (making catnip mice for $2 to $3 per week), as well as paying for room and board. Susan's father was at this time in jail for stealing from the school where he had been the janitor. Several social workers believed that Susan had also been sexually victimized by her father, who had previously admitted sexual molestation of a niece in their household. Susan had run away several times.

The mother's problems were characteristic of an incestuous family. An agency physician blamed the father's behavior on the mother: "Whole problem . . . started when mo refused to have any more chn. as fa. was unable to support them. . . . fa. went steadily down hill and started going out wi. other women." Meanwhile, the mother complained of the father's sexual demands, that he tried to get her to practice "perversions," and became violent if she refused. This type of complaint is common in these records; whatever her definition of perverse, it is clear that she experienced her husband as sexually coercive and was trying to resist him. Susan had witnessed the beating of her mother, but the joint victimization of the women in this family did not bring them together. Instead, their relationship was hostile. Susan told a therapist that her mother had not kissed her for two years, although she frequently hugged and kissed the other children—displaying the jealous hostility typical of the mother of an incest victim. Susan was required to stay home, do housework, look after her younger siblings, and pick up after her older brothers. "When bro comes into the house he drops his coat on the floor and Mrs. A. makes [Susan] pick it up instead of making him." The mother gave spending money to the younger children but not to Susan: "She says [Susan] should earn her money but [Susan] doesn't know how to do this." "She really wouldn't mind leaving home if she had a good home to go to . . ." Instead, Susan retaliated as best she could by threatening legal charges against her mother.

In this case, the incest assailants themselves led the victims into sex delinquency. Whether or not Susan's father molested her, her brothers did, beginning when she was eight. Her mother began refusing to leave the house; Susan concluded that the mother must have known about the incest; but it continued. One day one brother told Susan to come over to a store, "and the man in the store took her into the back room and stood her up against the wall and had partial intercourse with her. She thought he was going to give her some money and that was the reason she did it but he only gave her an orange. . . . Said that when the truth finally came out and her [mother] whipped her, she started to run off and go to him and risk the whipping." Susan also pimped for her brothers. She brought two neighborhood girls to her home and her two older brothers had sex with all three of them, also drawing in her younger sister and a younger brother. Susan frequently stated to agency interviewers that she thought her sexual adventures fun. She was jealous of her neighborhood friends for the sexual attention of the males involved with her; she was competitive with her mother for the attentions of the boarder; she complained not only when her brother preferred another girl to herself but also when her "dirty old man" did! But of course there should be nothing surprising about this when one recalls that this is a neglected eleven-year-old whose greatest longings were probably for parental love.

Susan enjoyed exaggerating, and her bravado offended and alarmed the social workers. "Money crazy, will do anything for money," her caseworker wrote. She was also concerned that Susan smoked, masturbated, and liked to read *True Story*. Professionals treated her as contagious. One psychiatrist wrote that she was "likely to be a great danger to other children." The record contains a detailed description of how she was taught to masturbate by a friend and, in turn, taught her sister. The fear and loathing of Susan displayed in the case notes must have been communicated to her, and she deeply believed in her own badness, saying about herself, "I was always a whore." Surely the outcome of the case confirmed her badness to herself: she and her sister were removed from their family and placed in foster homes, while no action was taken against her father, the boarder, or her brothers.[116]

Susan's case shows that sex delinquency is not necessarily or even usually distinct from domestic incest. Consider another example: In 1930 a Cambridge mother complained to the MSPCC that her husband had been "bothering" her fifteen-year-old daughter. The mother had been worried for some time, she said, but was afraid of him. The agency asked her to bring the girl in for a physical examination—the routine procedure; the mother agreed but then did not show up, a common behavior, caused by the qualms mothers had about vaginal examinations of their children, not to mention other fears (as of this husband). The agency did nothing until one year later. Then, in response to an MSPCC inquiry, the mother denied that it was going on any longer, giving as her reason that her daughter would have told her if it were. The case was closed. In 1933 the girl was in court on a stubborn-child complaint, having run away with some girlfriends, had numerous frightening sexual adventures in California and New York, contracted gonorrhea, which remained untreated, and earned a living through prostitution.[117]

It would have been difficult, perhaps, for the agency to have pursued the earlier allegations when the whole family was silent and hostile. But agency definitions and decisions had great power. For example, in 1910 Jane, an oldest daughter, was referred to the MSPCC by her teacher because she had nits, was filthy, and had just begun school at age ten. The family included five children, a drunken and abusive husband, and a battered mother declining rapidly into insanity. The agency defined this as a neglect case, ignoring wife-beating and hints about incest. Unusually, a women's organization, the Kings Daughter's Circle, became interested in this family and demanded action on behalf of the beaten woman. The MSPCC responded that her welfare was not its responsibility and that their doctor had determined she was not insane enough for committal, so there was nothing it could do. The three youngest children were removed from the family, but it was apparently assumed that the two older girls—ten and fifteen—could look after themselves. In 1912 the case was reopened, because the father, as he had done repeatedly, had deserted, the other daughter had left home, and the mother and Jane were reduced to begging.

By now, at age twelve, Jane was a sex delinquent. She was talking vulgarly on the streets; was "very wise for her age, and a bad influence with other girls." Interviewed about this new problem, the mother herself now hinted about incest. When taxed by the agency with spending the night away from home, considered a neglectful behavior, the woman misunderstood and responded, "'Oh she is all right, she is not afraid of fa." Another time she said her daughter has a " 'fondness for fa . . . [but] thinks she is not imm[oral].' " Yet the girl was not questioned directly until 1913; then, as soon as she was interviewed, she charged her father with sexually assaulting her, saying that she had told her mother, who promised to "speak to him." The police refused to prosecute this case, claiming they would only have the girl's word for evidence; and the Chief of Police said he would not question the father, "as it would be asking fa to incriminate himself." The daughter was committed through the State Board of Charities, and the father given six months for non-support. [118]

Most of the incest cases in this study had sad endings. They illustrate above all that so long as incest victims remained isolated, they were not usually powerful enough to escape their victimization without great damage to themselves, or to interpret it after the fact without self-blaming. They illustrate, by contrast, why victim-blaming interpretations of incest ceased only after incest survivors organized groups and situated their experience in the context of feminist critiques of male domination. Still, the roots of that transformation were evident in the resistance, however hopeless, of the victims in these historical cases. These cases disprove the theory of girls' willing participation in the incestuous relationships; they support recent discoveries of high rates of sexual victimization in the earlier lives of girls who become "delinquents"; and they lend support to contemporary analyses which relate incest to unusually male-dominant family structure.

Just as incest often occurs in families with exaggerated feminine subordination, so the girls' resistance to incest often assumed, perhaps had to assume, the form of resistance to the norms of feminine virtue, passivity, and subordination. Despite the revulsion incest has provoked, it opens a frightening but vital line of questioning about ordinary family relations. It identifies tensions between family solidarity and individual autonomy, between adult authority and children's rights, between women's status as victims and their responsibility as parents, tensions that one should not expect to resolve easily. It shows that many feminine virtues, not only those one might want to reject—obedience, quietness, obligingness—but also those one might want to preserve—discipline, responsibility, loyalty—can support victimization.

8

"THE POWERS OF THE WEAK": WIFE-BEATING AND BATTERED WOMEN'S RESISTANCE

Please call at 430 Cambridge St., E. Camb., Monday evening 7:30 or 8 o'clock. Kindly say you are just passing and thought you would call. [Letter to the MSPCC from a battered woman, 1922][1]

If I want I may clean my shoes on you. [Wife-beater, 1934][2]

I half to write this letter but my husband is not acting any better at all he is the man that know everything I went to [church] Sunday and the children had an awful time and now he hollers and he hit . . . the . . . children . . . I bought the newspaper on Sun he started on me because I got the paper he said all I do read the house is dirty . . . I can't go out he wont let any body mind the children for me I cant have my sister he tried funny business with my sister . . . I would like to speak with you write me a card saying you would like to see me so he went something will have to be done hoping to hear from you soon Your Truly [Battered wife, 1940][3]

The basis of wife-beating is male dominance—not superior physical strength or violent temperament (both of which may well have been effects rather than causes of male dominance), but social, economic, political, and psychological power. It is less useful to call male dominance the cause of wife-beating, because we usually mean something more specific when we speak of cause; after all, most men, including many very powerful and sexist men, do not beat women.[4] But it is male dominance that makes wife-beating a social rather than a personal problem. Wife-beating is not comparable to a drunken barroom assault or the hysterical attack of a jealous lover, which may be isolated incidents. Wife-beating is the chronic battering of a person of inferior power who for that reason cannot effectively resist.

Defining wife-beating as a social problem, not merely a phenomenon of particular violent individuals or relationships, was one of the great achievements of feminism. Women always resisted battering, but in the last hundred years they began to resist it politically and ideologically, with considerable success. While that success is far from complete, it is important to recognize the gains, and to give credit where it is due. Wife-beating is now not only illegal but also, to a majority of Americans, shameful. The contemporary alarm about wife-beating is an emblem of this achievement. The fact that many find it unacceptable that wife-beating continues at all is a sign of the greater respect that women have won, in large part as a result of 150 years of feminist consciousness-raising. Moreover, women have gained substantially, if unevenly, in the economic and psychological strengths needed to escape abusive men.

If the achievements of feminism in countering wife-beating have been inadequately recognized, those of battered women themselves have been practically invisible. It is not a denial of their victimization to notice also their bravery, resilience, and ingenuity, often with very limited resources, in trying to protect and nurture themselves and their children. Elizabeth Janeway has eloquently called such gifts the "powers of the weak."[5] This chapter argues that in the process of protecting themselves, battered women helped to formulate and promulgate the view that women have a right not to be beaten.

This chapter also examines *how* male dominance is enforced by, and produces, violence against women. Wife-beating usually arises out of specific domestic conflicts, in which women were by no means always passive, angelically patient, and self-sacrificing. To analyze these conflicts, and women's role in them, does not mean blaming the victim, a common distortion in the literature on wife-beating. That women are assertive in domestic power struggles is not a bad thing; women's suppression of their own needs and opinions is by far the greater danger. Victorian longings for women without egos or aggression should be understood as misogynist myths. Examining the construction of specific marital violence in historical context may contribute to understanding how male supremacy worked and is resisted.

CHILD PROTECTORS AND THE PROTECTION OF WOMEN

The child-protection agencies originally tried to avoid intervention between husbands and wives, but their clients, mainly mothers, virtually dragged the child protectors into wife-beating problems. Thirty-four percent of all the cases in this study had wife-beating. Indeed, throughout eighty years in which there were periods of strong professional disinclination to acknowledge the existence of wife-beating, battered women kept up a remarkably steady level of complaints to child-protection agencies.[6] The sensibility of nineteenth-century child-savers predisposed them to accept this larger jurisdiction. They believed, for example, that only a peaceful family was an appropriate environment for a child. Child-saving work was born of a radical environmentalism which took the form of parent-blaming; parents' behavior was at the diagnostic heart of child welfare work. The child-savers' commitment to the bourgeois ideal of domesticity, in many respects a conservative ideology in its implications for women, also predisposed them to taking responsibility for protection of women. Home was above all a space where women and children resided. Child protectors accepted the feminist interpretation of this domesticity, that women's and children's interests were closely connected. Elizabeth Cady Stanton, arguing for women's rights, considered it obvious that "the condition of the child always follows that of the mother . . ."[7] Mothers in any properly operating family were not conceived to have interests separate from, let alone antithetical to, those of children. A damage to one was a damage to both.

This is not to say that all women were considered perfect mothers. As was apparent in the case of single mothers, women who deviated visibly from the norms of maternalism, women who worked, drank, yelled, were dirty, remained unmarried—these women were not only considered bad mothers, they were cast outside the boundaries of true womanhood. They were denied sympathy, let alone help.

What determined whether victimized mothers were "deserving" in the eyes of child protectors? Agency clients, especially in the first fifty years, appeared to child protectors so overwhelmingly alien, poor, dirty, uncultured, that they might all have been considered unmotherly, undeserving. That so many of them were able to convince agency workers that they were deserving, even in early years when the caseworkers were male, was owing both to the ideology that made women into victims and working-class men into brutes, but also and especially to the efforts of the women themselves.

It seems at first surprising that the United States, with the most powerful women's rights movement in the world, never produced a major campaign specifically directed against cruelty to women. Historian Elizabeth Pleck has unearthed records of a Chicago group for the protection of both women and children, but it was exceptional.[8] Why was there never an SPCW?[9] This question has been indirectly addressed by several historians. William O'Neill has argued that the women's movement chose to focus on public rights such as suffrage and refused to challenge the family.[10] The very fact that the U.S. women's movement developed such a broad base and mass influence may have weakened its more radical factions. Or perhaps American women did not have an equally urgent need to challenge domestic patriarchy because they entered the nineteenth century with more social and cultural influence, and hence more domestic power, than European women. From the perspective of the child-protection movement, however, it becomes clear that the question was wrong. Since the brutalizer of women and children had the same face—the drunken, brutal, poor immigrant male— women were defended within the defense of children. The issue of wife-beating was influential throughout the nineteenth-century women's-rights movement, but it was addressed primarily indirectly, through temperance, child-welfare, and social purity campaigns, and only marginally through direct lobbying for legislative or judicial reforms regarding wife-beating.

Temperance in the nineteenth century had been in many ways a proto-feminist movement, reflecting the gradual development of a critique of male supremacy. The image of the beaten wife, the indirect victim of drink, was prominent in temperance rhetoric from the 1830s.[11] In the later half of the century, particularly in the work of the Women's Christian Temperance Union, drinking was a veritable code word for male violence.[12] Indeed, putting a temperance frame around criticisms of male behavior allowed feminists to score points obliquely, without attacking marriage or men in general. Male brutality, not male tyranny, was the target. The problem came from exceptional, "depraved" men, not the male gender as a norm.

Yet temperance agitation surely made drunkenness a gendered vice—male. And at the peak of the anti-alcohol agitation, there was no question but that Prohibition was considered a women's victory, and that political "wets" were expected to be hostile to women's rights. Considered as a veil thrown over challenges to male supremacy, temperance was a thin cloth indeed.

The feminist campaign for divorce also allowed the telling of shocking stories about wife-beating.[13] Some women's rights leaders took on wife-beating as a political struggle directly, primarily by publicizing particular cases involving victimized women of substantial social standing. Feminists sheltered runaway wives, agitated in particular divorce and child-custody cases, held a few public meetings on egregious cases of injustice—and used these cases to argue again for women's right to divorce and to vote.[14]

A small campaign for increased criminal prosecutions and severe sentences, including corporal punishment, for wife-beaters, beginning in the late 1870s, was led almost exclusively by men. Women and feminists were conspicuously absent, probably lacking in enthusiasm for violent remedies to violence. This campaign illustrates another source of the new opposition to wife-beating: a specifically male objection to this form of coercing women, as signifying an unacceptable pattern of masculinity. Historian Carroll Smith-Rosenberg has identified two mythic dramas competing for the power to define masculinity in the mid-nineteenth century. The more violent hero, the frontiersman Davy Crockett, in Smith-Rosenberg's symbolic analysis, was losing personal and public confidence in his physical contest with nature and with the "civilizing" influence of women. In the ascendant, bourgeois "script," adolescents achieved manhood by a Promethean struggle to channel sexual impulses into a "safe maturity of self-control and devotion to family."[15] The campaigns against child abuse and corporal punishment reflected the same goal. Middle-class reformers argued that brutality against the weak was "unmanly," cowardly. The new, bourgeois norms of masculinity required self-control, containment, rule through authority—i.e., symbolic force—which required no violence to impose itself. The new fatherhood, moreover, implied a distance from home and children which in turn entailed entrusting substantial autonomy over the household to women. Separate spheres—in other words, the new sexual division of labor characteristic of the urban middle class—should minimize conflict between husband and wife, and the latter should be in charge of domestic matters (which in a peasant economy had been more often shared).

The condemnation of wife-beating and child-beating had similar roots, and had made substantial progress by the late nineteenth century. Contrary to some common misconceptions, wife-beating was not generally accepted as a head-of-household's right at this time, but was considered a disreputable, seamy practice, and was effectively illegal in most states of the United States by 1870.[16]

Although wife-beating was not widely considered legitimate, neither was public discussion of it. If feminists as well as more conservative moralists preferred it to remain a hidden or at least whispered subject, it is not surprising that child-protection clients also opted for an indirect approach. In the strategies adopted by these battered women, we can see the outlines of a veritable history of the changing meanings of wife-beating among the immigrant working class. Many of the pre-industrial communities from which these clients, largely immigrants, had come tolerated a male privilege to hit ("punish") wives. However, one should not suppose that prior to modern feminism women never objected to or resisted beating. A better if rough paradigm with which to understand "tolerance" of wife-beating is as a tense compromise between men's and women's, patrilineal and matrilineal interests. Unlimited family violence was never tolerated, and there were always standards as to what constituted excessive violence. Recently such notions as the "rule of thumb"—that a man might not use a stick thicker than his thumb to beat his wife—have been cited as evidence of the extremes of women's humiliation and powerlessness. On the contrary, such regulation was evidence of a degree of women's power, albeit enforceable mainly through the willingness of others to defend it. But women often did have allies within the patriarchal community. If that much abused word "patriarchy" is to have any usefulness, it must be used to describe a system larger than any individual family, a system which required regulation even of its privileged members. While patriarchal fathers could control their households, they in turn were subject to sanctions—social control—by the community, whose power brokers included not only fellow patriarchs but also women, particularly senior women. The agency clients were accustomed to appealing to fathers as well as mothers, brothers as well as sisters and friends, for support against abusive husbands.

Nevertheless, in the nineteenth and early twentieth centuries, many women clients did not seem to believe they had a "right" to freedom from physical violence. When social workers expressed disgust at the way they were treated, the clients sometimes considered that reaction naïve. They spoke of the inevitability of male violence. Their refusal to condemn marital violence in moral terms must be interpreted carefully. It did not mean that these women were passive or accepted beatings. They often resisted assault in many ways: fighting back, running away, attempting to embarrass the men before others, calling the police. And they did express moral outrage if their men crossed some border of tolerability. There is no contradiction here. The language of absolute "rights" is only one legitimate approach to self-defense. In a patriarchal system there were neither institutions nor concepts defending absolute rights, but rather custom and bargaining. Because the client women did not conduct a head-on challenge to their husbands' prerogatives does not mean that they liked being hit or believed that their virtue required accepting it. (Failure to make this distinction is the result of flat and ahistorical conceptions of what patriarchy and female subordination have been like. There was no society in which women so "internalized" their inferiority, to use a modern way of explanation, that they did not struggle to improve their situation.)

What was new in the nineteenth-century middle-class reform sensibility was the notion that wife-beating was entirely intolerable. Family reformers proposed, like abolitionists toward slavery and prohibitionists toward drink, to do away with physical violence in marriage altogether. This differed from their attitude toward child abuse, because they did not propose to do away with spanking. By contrast, many poor battered women had a more complex view of the problem than their benefactors: welcoming all the help they could get in their individual struggles against assault, they also needed economic help in order to provide a decent family life for children. Given a choice, they might have preferred economic aid to prosecution of wife-beaters.

Feminist reformers also avoided women's violence toward men, whether offensive or defensive. The Victorian sensibility made them feel they should offer charity only to "true women," peaceful and long-suffering. There were political advantages to their myopia: they kept the focus on battered women and declined to redefine the problem as mutual marital violence; they knew that it was a whole system of male power, not just physical violence, that made women battered.[17] On the other hand, their view of women's proper role ruled out the possibility that women could create independent lives and reject violent husbands. To these nineteenth-century child-savers, women's victimization meant virtue more than weakness; women who submitted to abuse were more praised than those who left their husbands. For example, in the random sample of this study, battered women frequently left or kicked out their husbands, then repeatedly reconciled or reunited with them.[18] In the 1960s such a record would probably have made a social worker question a woman's sincerity and doubt the point of continuing to offer help. In the nineteenth century these women's ambivalence was interpreted as evidence of their commitment to fulfilling wifely duties.

A "RIGHT" NOT TO BE BEATEN

The best articulated definitions of what counted as abusive were, of course, those of the social workers, who wrote the case notes and who determined what constituted a "case." But the clients' definitions were also visible. In their complaints against husbands we see women's implicit construction of a "right," an entitlement to protection. It was a claim women began to make only when they had some reasonable expectation that they could win—otherwise strategies other than head-on confrontation with a husband's prerogatives were more effective.

Women's invention of a right not to be beaten came from a dialectic between changing social possibilities and aspirations. When women's best hope was husbands' kindness, because they were economically dependent on marriage, they did not protest violations of their individual rights but rested their case on their importance as mothers. As women's possibilities expanded to include wage-earning, remarriage after divorce, birth limitation, and aid to single mothers, their best hopes escalated to include escape from marital violence altogether.

For example, in the earlier decades of this study, several women clients complained bitterly about their husband's obscene language. A 1916 wife who had left her husband agreed that she would "keep his house if he would treat her respectfully and use decent language before the chn."[19] A 1920 mother thought her husband's "dirty mouth" was "the hardest thing we have to bear in this house, harder even than [his] not working."[20]

By far the most striking and consistent women's complaint, however, through the 1930s, focused on their husbands' non-support rather than abuse. (Non-support cases involved not single mothers but married women whose husbands did not adequately provide, for reasons which might include unemployment, illness, drunkenness, hostility, negligence.) In 1910 a mother who was permanently crippled by her husband's beatings, who had appeared to the police and her priest so badly bruised that they advised her to have him arrested, complained to the MSPCC only about his failure to provide.[21] In 1901 a young mother complained only about non-support; the abuse then uncovered was so severe that an MSPCC agent began making secret plans to sneak the mother and two children out of the house after the father had gone off to work![22]

In approaching child-saving agencies, the mothers had to present evidence of mistreatment of children. Many women calculated that foul language was a violation of norms of respectability that social control agents could be expected to defend. They emphasized non-support not because they considered it more unbearable than beating, but because they thought it was a more criminal and therefore actionable grievance to social workers. These women believed that they had a claim on the community, as represented by the social-work agencies, for their support by husbands, but not to protection from physical violence in marriage. Nineteenth-century women also used the courts to bring wife-beating charges, but with little success; the likelihood of conviction was high only in egregious cases or in cases including also non-support and/or intemperance.

Women tried to get support from social control agencies without directly challenging male authority. In 1893 a wife complained that she had left her husband "with his permission," but that he broke his word. He had been extremely abusive and frighteningly deranged: he threatened to shoot her and slept with a pistol and cutlass [sic] at his pillow. His "permission" meant that he had allowed her to take some furniture when she left, and that he promised to provide for their children, but he did not deliver.[23] In 1917, a wife and children were beaten for not fulfilling the father's work demands; but the woman complained only about his demands, not about the beatings. She asked the caseworkers to persuade him to take in fewer boarders, as the work was too much for her. Her logic differed from that of the agency, which was willing to investigate the violence but told her that the "agency was not in [the] business" of regulating his labor demands.[24]

Surprisingly, women's complaints about wife-beating escalated just as feminism was at its nadir. The 1930s were the divide in this study, after which the majority of women clients complained directly rather than indirectly about wife-beating. In 1934, for example, a young mother of three, married through a matchmaker at sixteen to an Italian-born man, repeatedly made assault-and-battery complaints against him. He was also a non-supporter, but her logic differed from that of earlier clients, and it was the beating that appeared actionable to her. It should not be surprising that this was an American-born woman much younger than her immigrant husband, a woman who may have had higher or perhaps less conventional aspirations than was the average among family-violence clients. Her husband's probation officer described her as a "high-type Italian," and the caseworker thought she expected "people to do things for her."[25] Women continued to allege child abuse in order to get agency help, but in the investigations they tended to protest about their own abuse more strongly. One MSPCC agent complained in 1940 that the mother was not really very interested in her son's problem but only wanted to talk about herself.[26]

In other cases in that year, women rationalized their battering in new ways: not as an inevitable part of the female condition, as a result of the male nature, but as something they individually deserved. One woman said, "This is my punishment for marrying against my mo.'s wishes."[27] Even in blaming themselves women expressed a new sensibility that wife-beating should not be the general lot of women.

Wife-beating accusations stood out even more because of the virtual disappearance of non-support complaints. This striking inverse correlation between non-support and wife-beating complaints stimulates an economistic hypothesis: economic dependence prevented women's formulation of a sense of entitlement to protection against marital violence, but it also gave them a sense of entitlement to support; by contrast, the growth of a wage labor economy, bringing unemployment, transience, and dispersal of kinfolk, lessened women's sense of entitlement to support from their husbands, but allowed them to insist on their physical integrity. It is a reasonable hypothesis that the Depression, by the leveling impact of its widespread unemployment, actually encouraged women regarding the possibilities of independence.

An oblique kind of supporting evidence for this process of consciousness change is provided by wife-beaters' defenses. Men did not often initiate complaints to agencies, but they frequently responded with counter-complaints when they were questioned. Their grievances were usually defensive, self-pitying, and opportunistic. They remain, however, important evidence of a consensus among men about the services they expected from wives—or about what complaints might be effective with social workers. Men accused of wife-beating usually countered that their wives were poor housekeepers and neglectful mothers, making themselves the aggrieved parties. The men's counter-accusations were, of course, a means of seeking to reimpose a threatened domination. Yet they simultaneously expressed a sense of an injustice, the violation of a traditional and/or contractual agreement, and their dismay at the historical changes that made women less able or willing to meet these expectations.

Often male and female expectations of marital responsibilities were consonant. Women as well as men professed allegiance to male-supremacist understanding of what relations between the sexes should be like. These shared assumptions, however, by no means prevented conflict. Women's assumptions of male dominance did not mean that they quit trying to improve their situations. Husbands expected dominance but also expected women's resistance to it. Clients of both sexes expected marriage and family life to be conflict-ridden—they did not share the bourgeois denial of family disharmony—and demonstrated no shyness in exposing their family hostilities to social workers. Female clients often both "accepted" that men were violent—that is, they did not approve but expected it—and also tried to stop it.

By emphasizing mutual conflict as the origin of wife-beating, I do not mean to suggest an equality in battle. Marital violence almost always resulted in the defeat of women and served to enforce women's subordination. Nor did every act of marital violence emerge from an argument. Contestation could be chronic, structured into the relationship. Male violence often became a pattern, virtually normal, appearing regularly or erratically, without relation to any particular interaction. One man who eventually murdered his wife beat her because their children "had no shoe lacings."[28] Some men simply came home drunk and angry enough to hit anyone in the way. But their drinking, as we shall see below, was often an assertion of privilege, as was their violence an assertion of dominance.

Women's assertiveness against battering was both strengthened and limited by child-raising. Most wife-beating victims are mothers—even more so in the past than today, for women using birth control to defer child-bearing were unusual in this study. They negotiated living with their husbands not as individuals but as mothers responsible for children. We can see the impact of this double position of women—as themselves victims and as guardians of children—in the connections between wife-beating and violence against children. Wife-beating was most highly correlated with incest, as we have seen. It was often correlated with child neglect—28 percent of battered women were also allegedly child neglecters. Only 13 percent of wife-beating victims were child abusers, but 41 percent of wife-beaters were also child abusers.[29]

Let us consider what these abstract correlations meant in real cases. One native-born family, recently moved to Boston from Utica, New York, was reported by neighbors for the father's great brutality. He was fifteen years older than his wife; married in 1903, they had six children at the case opening date in 1917 and were to have three more. Mr. Schmidt, a hard-working boilermaker, claimed that he chose to move his family to Boston because his mother-in-law and neighbors gave him a hard time; whatever his experience with the relatives, the result was that the family was isolated from kin. In 1917 we meet an abusive father, trying to accumulate enough money to buy the house they live in; his ambition escalates his abuse, and he overworks his children and turns over all but two rooms of the house to boarders. The social worker described Mr. Schmidt as energetic, industrious, wanting to get ahead; these qualities are valued and they serve to mitigate the condemnation of his violence. His ability to tyrannize his family members must have been extraordinary, because on one occasion when he claimed to have found his wife and visiting mother-in-law "a little drunk," he called his wife upstairs and she returned with a black eye! By 1922 the MSPCC agent sensed some deep exhaustion in Mrs. Schmidt and recommended that she take a vacation!—hardly a possibility for a woman with, by now, eight children. In 1924 the oldest daughter had married "a shiftless character" and Mr. Schmidt, holding his wife responsible, had beaten her for it; she came to the MSPCC trying to get this marriage annulled. Then in 1926 a male boarder was arrested for the rape of another daughter, sixteen. This girl, in telling her story, claimed that her father had often tried to force sexual relations with his wife in front of the children; the father alleged that his wife and daughter had jointly been having immoral relations with boarders. When asked about these things, Mrs. Schmidt could not speak but only cried. In 1928 the MSPCC filed a neglect complaint: the father and children were living in filthy conditions; Mrs. Schmidt was spending nights at home but leaving early in the morning and staying away from home, no one knew where, all day. When Mr. Schmidt lost his license to keep boarders because of the terrible conditions, she returned to housekeeping. The family re-entered the agency records again in 1935, when Mrs. Schmidt was arrested for breaking and entering and was sent to the psychopathic hospital for observation; she was classified as an imbecile; the remaining children were committed to state guardianship.[30]

This case illustrates how a battered woman was transformed into a neglectful mother. Indeed, the process virtually deconstructed the woman's ego: a grown woman, about whom there is no hint of incompetence in 1917, is called an imbecile, with a mental age of 6.6 years, in 1934.

She has no way of defending herself except to leave her children and becomes increasingly depressed and slack.

In some cases the child neglect was clearly a symptom of depression, even derangement. In 1916, a twenty-two-year-old mother was reported by neighbors: she had stomped on and ruined her husband's vegetable garden, made suicide attempts, and she left her children (three and eighteen months) alone at night while she went out with men. The children had urine blisters and boils from unchanged diapers. She had boarded the children in several homes, failed to pay the boarding costs, visited erratically and unexpectedly. Her marital experiences had been unusually brutal from the beginning: forced into marriage by her pregnancy, the husband had been resentful from the beginning. He had beaten her when pregnant and during childbirth, striking her again and again on the face in an effort to stop her screaming during labor, until the birth attendant got help to have the father removed. When she became pregnant a second time, he attempted to create an abortion, "bent her backward so violently that flow was induced . . ." Her husband was stingy and rigid, trying to force her to run the home in an exacting, systematic fashion; he had locked her in the house. Nor did her suicide attempt bring her help: after being rescued when she turned on the gas in her bathroom, "the landlord then insisted [she] move so as not to endanger the landlord's family in such a fashion again."[31]

The relationship between wife-beating and child abuse was different. "Triangular" conflicts involving parents and children often escalated marital conflict. Women were beaten for protecting children. Men also beat their wives in anger at their mothering: because the men considered them too lenient, or were jealous of the attention paid to children, for women were often more intimate with their children than with their husbands. One man threw a bread knife at his wife for "indulging" a baby by giving it milk in the middle of the night.[32] The structure of the family and, indeed, the whole sexual division of labor created implicit alliances of women and children against men. Many women got beaten because their husbands perceived their alliance with children as insubordinate; and children were beaten because of their attempts to defend their mothers.

While alliance with children made women vulnerable to male abuse, it also strengthened women, because defense of children against abuse was the factor most likely to increase women's resistance to battering.

Women resisted the abuse of their children more than their own abuse, in the past as well as today. In 1930 a woman abused throughout her marriage came to the MSPCC demanding a divorce and placement of her fifteen-year-old daughter when her husband tried to molest her.[33] In 1920 an immigrant Jewish mother, normally obedient to her "quick-tempered" husband (one of the many euphemisms used by caseworkers who did not "see" wife-beating), would interfere when the father beat their delinquent son, thereby receiving more punishment herself.[34] This pattern reveals another aspect of the clients' own expectations. They believed that they were obligated to protect their children and that they could expect help from outsiders in doing so, even when they did not seek or expect help for themselves. As mothers they felt entitled; as women, not.

THE CAUSES OF WIFE-BEATING

Today as in the nineteenth century, many people blame wife-beating on drinking.[35] It is not widely understood that the second wave of anti-wife-beating work was also affected by "temperance": the first U.S. battered women's shelters, opened in 1973 to 1974, were for wives of alcoholics, funded by Al-Anon and state money; the English Chiswick Women's Aid, which developed at about the same time but was the first shelter to "go public," also emphasized alcoholism as a causal problem.[36]

It is only very recently that experts and activists have challenged this temperance orientation, and it is a radical challenge indeed. Associating wife-beating with drinking placed it in a male culture of recreation—or depravity, depending on the perspective—and kept it defined in trivial and fatalistic terms. It was a male foible, not a crime against women. By the twentieth century a man did not often claim the right to punish a wife; more often, the story was that he had lost control; it was a plea from weakness, not from authority.[37] Liquor provides the evidence of loss of self-control.[38]

But there is anthropological evidence that liquor does not in itself cause aggressive behavior, or even loosen inhibition against it; in different societies the conventional drunken behavior varies widely, suggesting that drunken behavior is itself learned.[39] Interviews with batterers conducted by EMERGE, an organization dedicated to reforming wife-beaters, show that they are enough in "control" to regulate the amount of injury they cause. Arresting and jailing wife-beaters has been shown to create immediate reductions in battering, providing evidence that when there are definite costs to the assailant, he can usually control his aggression.[40] Still, drinking and wife-beating are correlated. For example, in 67 percent of our cases, social workers or victims believed that drinking was a cause of wife-beating incidents. Does drunkenness cause wife-beating or do batterers drink in order to assault?[41] Our case records provide an opportunity to look closely at the relation between drinking and wife-beating.

These cases supplied little evidence that the physiological, chemical effects of alcohol were causes of wife-beating (or other forms of family violence). Rather, the social relations involved in drinking escalated hostilities. For example, liquor "caused" wife-beating because of its cost. Many couples fought about the sums spent, usually by the husband, on drink—i.e., drinking up the pay envelope instead of turning it over to the woman for housekeeping needs.[42] It is not that the women in these cases did not drink, although they appear to have drunk less than men. Rather, the major difference is that the women—mothers, it must be remembered—felt responsible for feeding their families. Sometimes the wife-beating emerged out of a husband's attempts to insist upon his drinking privileges and to silence his wife's resistance. In 1880 a woman explained, "We had trouble because I would not get him beer."[43] Among the most wretched families were those with both parents alcoholic, because then even the woman had lost the incentive or ability to worry about providing for the children.[44] These cases suggested, by contrast, that the "nagging" wife was sometimes more responsible, even if she "provoked" violence, than the patient one.

A related source of dispute was that men often drank in taverns, while women—again, mothers—were bound at home. Women were doubly enraged when the men not only drank but did so out of reach of remonstrance, enjoying a mobility which women did not have. Moreover, saloon camaraderie tended to escalate men's hostility to women, or at least consolidated and encouraged it. Anthropologist Ann Whitehead has given us an incisive participant-observer's view of that process in a British pub of the 1960s. She described how "firm" treatment of wives was encouraged, and how individual men who gave their wives "privileges," such as the right to go out with women friends, were ridiculed by their bar mates.[45] At the same time, women's drinking seemed to enrage men, particularly when it was social. Since women did not as often go to bars, they tended to congregate with friends in houses. Several husbands attacked their wives because they found them socializing in this way, even when their friends were women.[46]

Another major source of marital conflict was money. We have seen that women's frequent complaints of non-support reflected the area in which they felt entitled. At the same time, conflicts *about* non-support detonated wife-beating. Just as many charity workers did not understand the structural unemployment inherent in an industrial capitalist economy, so too many wives interpreted their husbands' failure to support as willful. Women had few resources other than their husband in the task of supporting children. They simultaneously resented their dependency and the failure of those on whom they were dependent to make good their side of the presumed wage-labor bargain between the sexes. This is one of the reasons, along with the anger and depression it created in men, that unemployment intensified marital tensions.[47]

Mothers agitated to get more money from their husbands. In 1930 an Italian-born father who had worked as a watchman and plasterer was trying to sell vegetables from a cart. His wife was furious because he was spending virtually all the $15 a week he earned to board his horse, and "on pleasure," she said.[48] Many cases involved in-laws. In 1932 a couple was living with the husband's mother. He treated her as the female head of household, turning over to her his entire paycheck, which infuriated his wife.[49] Women frequently complained of inconsistency between what their husbands should have earned and what they were given for housekeeping. Even though few women had direct knowledge of the size of their husband's pay packet, most were clever at computing its approximate size. Another Italian-American mother figured her husband made 80 cents an hour as a construction worker and counted his hours of work; she complained to the MSPCC that despite his good income she had only bread to eat and not enough coal all winter.[50] Another wife knew that her husband earned $25 a week as a bank guard, plus a $45 monthly navy pension, yet she had to depend on her neighbors for food and could not afford ice for the baby's milk.[51]

Men not only felt persecuted by these complaints, and perhaps by the reminders of their inadequacy, but often blamed their wives. In 1910 a Jewish immigrant family was referred to the MSPCC because of abject poverty: the children were "almost naked" and there was only a small amount of bread in the house. The wife said her husband worked two weeks, then drank two weeks. But he claimed she "wanted to have things as wealthier people have."[52] Other husbands accused their wives of poor budgeting—not only an obvious defensive maneuver, but an accusation designed to pique the interest of caseworkers. One man responded to agency criticism of his violence by demanding that his wife be required to turn in accounts of what she had done with his money.[53] Others were enraged as women "stole" money of contested ownership: in 1895 a battered wife left home, then came back to curse the "housekeeper" her husband was living with and to steal some of his money;[54] in 1893 a husband accused his wife of stealing $285 of his savings—she claimed it was money she had earned caning chairs.[55]

If liquor and money were two of the major sources of marital conflicts leading to violence, they were closely followed by work and sex. Indeed, all four were connected. Both men's and women's senses of their spouses' inadequacy as workers were of course escalated by poverty, and their sexual antagonisms were in part reflections of hostility provoked by other aspects of their relations.

Men's and women's discontent with each other's work took different forms for the reason that men were primarily engaged in wage labor, and in labor outside the home, while women were usually exclusively responsible for children. Men's adequacy as workers was therefore measured exclusively by their earnings, and women's anger at men's poor support was intensified by their responsibility for children. Women's and children's work was, by contrast, task-defined. Particularly immigrant men, accustomed to a family economy, sometimes claimed patriarchal powers to deploy their family's labor. For example, in 1917 a man forced his older children to work and turn over their wages, the younger children to work in a vegetable patch, and his wife to care for many boarders, beating them all if he was dissatisfied with their performance.[56]

Women's work, moreover, because it consisted primarily of housekeeping and mothering labor, had intense emotional meanings for other family members. Men's dependence on that labor, and its symbolic affirmation of his domination and her submission, made them vulnerable to extreme disappointment and frustration if it was not forthcoming. Women's rage at non-supporting husbands could be substantial, but, on the evidence of these case records, it never approached in intensity, bitterness, and self-pity the rage of men at wives they considered inadequately caring. In 1916 one man wrote to the MSPCC:

> From the beginning of our married life things have been unbearable. A bed of thorns, instead of roses, has been my lot. As a poor housekeeper and cook my wife has no equal. Many nights I had to sleep on the floor tired and hungry, because she could not during the day find time to do the cooking and the housework. As much as I love to be clean I put up with everything, but I could not bear to see my poor children swimming in dirt and full of vermin. . . . Sir, as a family man and a lover of liberty, I ask you what can a peaceful person do in such a case to keep out of the State Prison?"[57]

Husbands' laments were often very specific. One 1916 father described his wife as putting dirty clothes to soak in the sink and leaving them there for weeks until they "rotted" and she threw them away.[58] Moreover, it is clear that the men were complaining not only on their children's behalf but also on their own. "She cooks only when she is hungry";[59] "She refuses to put up lunches for him in the morning so he is forced to buy his lunch. Sometimes he is forced to buy his breakfast. He comes home nights and she refuses to cook meals."[60] The intensity of these complaints suggests the men's sense of entitlement to wives who took care not only of children but also of husbands.

Despite the common cultural image of the shrewish wife, violent husbands did not cite wives' nagging in their defense until after World War II. The word "nagging" had been in use since the early nineteenth century, and its synonyms for many centuries. But in comparison to the intensity of men's anger at women's failure to fulfill labor, sexual, and reproductive duties, these poor men did not display much demand for harmony in marriage.

In many ways marital battles about sex took a form similar to those about work. Spouses had conflicting—and changing—ideas of their obligations and entitlements. The single most common sexual grievance expressed in the case notes was wives' charges that their husbands made excessive and/or perverse sexual demands. From 1917 to 1934 (the period after detailed record-keeping began, and before modern "sexual-liberation" ideas came to dominate social work interpretation), over one-fifth of wife-beating cases contained such accusations by wives.[61] "Excessive sexual demands" was the usual code in which social workers noted the complaint, but occasionally the women's insistence led to the inclusion of specifics in the notes, usually referring to demands for anal intercourse, fellatio, sex in front of witnesses, and enforced prostitution.[62] In some cases the men's controlling motivations could be distinguished from their sexual ones. For example, a 1934 Italian man told his wife whenever he saw her dressed up, "it's time for you to have another baby."[63] More often, the different motives were conflated. Women's allegations that they had been forced into exhibitionist acts were not uncommon—in front of children or other men. Alternatively, several husbands had humiliated their wives by bringing other women into their very bedrooms, even their own beds. One of the most extraordinary power plays was described by a 1930 single mother with six children: she was introduced to a man by a friend; he had insisted upon calling and asked her to marry him, which she refused. Then: "One day [he] came into the house and refused to go. He stayed there for sometime until finally one of the neighbors told the O.P.W. when mo. was forced to marry him." A "sex pervert," the father made advances toward the woman's daughters and "is constantly demanding sexual intercourse, unnatural acts and immorality."[64]

Fear of pregnancy was only rarely articulated as part of women's resistance to these sexual demands. As one woman in 1931 said, "she does not have anything to do with fa as she has all the chn she can handle now on the amount of money he gives her to run the house on." But her emphasis was on money, and she implied that if he would give her more housekeeping money, she would sleep with him—a fairly direct exchange of money for sex.[65]

Before about 1934 there was also a marked conflict of standards between male clients and social workers. The latter did not accept the assumption that wives owed sexual availability to their husbands, but retained a rather Victorian suspicion of male sexual demands and sympathy for women's right to refuse. Thus husbands were not able to defend their violence on the grounds of sexual frustration or deprivation. This lack of sympathy from social workers may help explain why so many husbands accused of sexual excess responded by accusing their wives of "immorality." Most frequently, these were allegations of un-specified "running around," not accusations of specific liaisons with specific lovers. It appears that they were, however, not only responses to agency workers but also expressive of intense jealousy, as they were often accompanied by wives' complaints of their husbands' attempts to seclude and imprison them. We have no way of knowing, of course, the truth of these allegations of immorality. It is striking that some of the most abject, helpless women were so accused, as, for example, the woman described above whose husband beat her during her childbirth. At first thought it seems not credible that such terrified wives would defy or taunt their husbands in such a major way, but analysis of the meaning of immorality, and the situation of these women, tells us otherwise. Immorality usually meant any nonmarital relationship, and the more powerless the wife, the more likely that only another lover could provide an escape route. Some beaten wives in these records did in fact leave their husbands with a "boarder," including a woman beaten severely for fourteen years by the husband, who had bragged, " 'If I want I may clean my shoes on you.' "[66] Another meaning of the im-morality charge may have been desertion. In the past as today, many women were attacked because they had left or were threatening to leave, their husbands wanting to force them to stay or return.

A remarkable change in the nature of these sexual recriminations was evident after the 1940s. The very complaints that had previously been recorded as allegations of "sexual excess" were now rendered as evidence of female frigidity and sexual withholding. For example, in one 1950 case we meet exactly the same frank articulation that marriage entailed an exchange of sex for money that we met in the 1931 case. The client said that "she used refusal of intercourse as a weapon so that he would turn over his paychecks to her . . . it seemed to be the only way." For this she was condemned and his non-support ignored, as were her allegations that he was a drunkard, an abuser, a non-supporter, intensely jealous and unnaturally suspicious, and had threatened her with a knife.[67] An MSPCC social worker wrote the following analysis of a marital problem in her 1960 case notes:

[Father began] to act out a good deal, drinking, getting into trouble, killing a pedestrian [sic]. According to mo, fa was quite insistent sexually.

(It is my feeling that mo is probably very frigid.) He used to have to beat mo down to have intercourse with her . . .[68]

Denial of work and sex converge when one partner in a relationship threatens to leave. Such threats may have been the most dangerous acts of all for women in battering relationships: much of the marital violence in this study was aimed at forcing a wife to remain.[69] As employment, welfare provisions, and custom made it more possible for women to leave their husbands, the proportion of violence representing attacks on women trying to leave marriages may have increased. In a study of domestic murder in Australia, Judith Allen showed a steady increase in the citing of women's "desertion" as a precipitating factor in homicides by men: 40 percent of 1880's cases, 56 percent of 1900–1909 cases, 77 percent of 1920's cases, 81 percent of 1930's cases.[70]

VICTIMS' RESISTANCE

While the first-wave women's movement had asserted women's rights to personal freedom even in marriage, it had not provided any organized, institutional means for poor women to secure and defend that right, a power which was necessary for women really to believe in their own entitlement. Until the revival of feminism and the establishment of battered-women's shelters in the 1970s, wife-beating victims had three resources: their own individual strategies of resistance; the help of relatives, friends, and neighbors; and the intervention of child-welfare agencies. None was adequate to the task. The first two were easily outweighed by the superior power of husbands and the sanctity of marriage itself, and the last did not well represent the interests of the women themselves. Still, on some occasions victims were able to use these inadequate resources to construct definite improvements, if not permanent solutions.

Women in abusive relationships with men still face great difficulties in extricating themselves. These difficulties in turn weaken their ability to insist that the men's behavior change, since the woman's threat to leave is often her most powerful lever and his only incentive to change.

Such difficulties were greater fifty or one hundred years ago, and greater for the poor and uneducated women who dominated in these cases. Their difficulties were essentially those faced by single mothers. The biggest obstacle for most women facing abusive men was that they did not wish to lose their children; indeed, their motherhood was for most of them (including, it must be emphasized, many who were categorized as abusive or neglectful parents) their greatest source of pleasure, self-esteem, and social status. In escaping they had to find a way simultaneously to earn and raise children in an economy of limited jobs for women, little child care, and little or no reliable aid to single mothers. They had to do this with the often low confidence characteristic of women trying to take unconventional action. Moreover, these women of the past had the added burden of defying a social norm condemning marital separation and encouraging submission as a womanly virtue.

Mrs. O'Brien, for example, changed her mind repeatedly about how she wanted to deal with her problem, and her seeming ambivalence reflects the lack of options she and so many others had. Living with a husband so brutal even the police advised her to have him arrested, she told them, speaking for thousands, "She does not want to lose her chn. however and the little money which she does receive from fa. enables her to keep her home together." Instead, she tried to get the MSPCC agent to "scare" him into treating her and her children "right." This was, arguably, impossible, since previous jail terms had not "reformed" him. She agreed to another prosecution at one point of rage—"would rather starve than endure the treatment"—then changed her mind and agreed to let him return to live with her if he would give her all his wages. The MSPCC then got her to agree that it would collect $10 per week from him and give it to her. When he agreed to this, she raised her demand to $11 per week, evidently dreading taking him back. But he agreed to this too, and three months later he was sentenced to six months for assaulting her; she was pregnant and soon began campaigning to get him out of jail. This pattern continued for years; in 1914 and again in 1920 she was threatening to murder him, describing herself as in a "desperate state of mind."[71]

Mrs. O'Brien's ambivalence was a rational response to her situation. Her children, numbering six by 1920, literally forced her into submission to her husband. Her problems illustrate the limited usefulness of prosecution as a remedy in the absence of economic provisions for single mothers. (It also suggests why prosecution might have different meanings today, when greater employment opportunities, ADC, and shelters offer women somewhat more chance of survival alone with their children.) But Mrs. O'Brien, like many victims, believed in the potential benefit of prosecution as a deterrent; this was not an option forced on her by social control agents. The resulting contradictory behavior was common. Many women prosecuted and then withdrew their complaints or petitioned for pardons for their husbands. In January 1870 John K. was sentenced to three months for assault and battery on his wife; but she soon petitioned for his pardon, explaining that she was partly blind and needed him home for planting season.[72] Michael B., sentenced to three months in May 1870, was pardoned, at the request of his wife, in one month: she said she needed his support and admitted to having provoked him. Eugene D., sentenced to four months, was pardoned in two months, also because his wife (who was illiterate and could only mark X for her name) needed his support—she did not even bother to say she had provoked him.[73] Arnold W., a second offender, whose wife had testified that she was afraid for her life, was sentenced to five months in 1870 by a judge who considered him "incorrigible." But Mrs. W. returned within two months to say she had testified against him "while angry" but now needed his release on grounds of poverty; the District Attorney, supporting her petition, wrote that "certainly she is right, if the starved appearance of her children is any indication."[74] Elizabeth Pleck's tentative conclusion that black and immigrant women were more likely than other women to complain to the police for wife-beating may indicate that prosecution was a weapon of last resort, and that native-born women, with more resources, more likelihood of being adequately supported by husbands, and more respectability to protect, feared the stigma of dealing with police and courts.[75]

Batterers also knew women could not seek prosecution for fear of losing economic support. One husband threatened that "if she ever sues for divorce or separation or if she ever has him brought into court . . . he will throw up his job and then she will be without support . . ."[76] Others derided their wives' chance for independence: ". . . if you want to come back, all right, if not all right, we will see who wins out in this deal. . . . I work for W. C. Hill, when you want me arrested," one wife-beater wrote in 1911 to his wife, who had left.[77]

Mrs. O'Brien's ultimate desire, having rejected prosecution as a solution, was for a "separation and maintenance" agreement, as such provisions were then known: she wanted the state to guarantee her the right to a separate household and require her husband to pay support. Such plans were the most common desire of the beaten wives in this study. As another woman explained to a caseworker, also in 1920, "She did not wish him to be put away as he is a steady worker but wd. like the case arranged so that he wd. live apart and support her and the chn.[78] Mrs. O'Brien managed to get aid from the new Massachusetts mothers' pension program in 1920, but only after she had been struggling against her husband's abuse for at least ten years, he having built up a record of convictions and jail terms for assault and non-support.

Failing to get separation-and-maintenance agreements, and unable to collect support even when it was promised, the remaining option—called desertion—was taken only by the most depressed, disheartened, and desperate women. A moralistic nomenclature no longer common, desertion meant a woman leaving a husband and children. Female desertion was extremely uncommon in these cases, especially in contrast with the prevalence of male desertion. The low female desertion rate revealed the strength of women's attachment to their children. Moreover, the guilt and stigma attached to such action usually meant that women "deserters" simultaneously cut themselves off from friends and kin. All in all, it was unlikely that ridding themselves of the burdens of children would lead to better futures for wife-beating victims.

Another response to beatings was fighting. For differing reasons, both feminists and sexists have been reluctant to recognize or acknowledge women's physical aggression. Yet fighting was common and accepted among poor women of the past, more so than among "respectable" women and contemporary women.[79] Fourteen percent of the marital violence cases contained some female violence—8 percent mutual violence and 8 percent husband-beating.

Most of the women's violence was responsive or reactive. This distinguished it from men's violence, which grew out of mutual conflict, to be sure, but was more often a regular tactic in an ongoing power struggle. Some examples may help to illuminate this distinction. Women's violence toward husbands in these records fell into three typical patterns. The most common was mutual violence. Consider the 1934 case of an Irish Catholic woman married to a Danish fisherman. He was gone at sea all but thirty days a year, and there was violence whenever he returned. One particular target of his rage was Catholicism: he beat his sons, she claimed, to prevent them going to church with her and loudly cursed the Irish and the Catholics—he was an atheist. The neighbors took her side, and would hide her three sons when their father was in a rage. The downstairs tenants took his side. They reported that she swore, yelled, hit him, and chased him with a butcher knife; that she threw herself down some stairs to make it look as if he had beaten her. Amid these conflicting charges it was certain, however, that she wanted to leave her husband, but he refused to let her have custody of the children; after a year of attempted mediation, the MSPCC ultimately lent its support for a separation.[80] In this case the woman responded with violence to a situation that she was eager to leave, while he used violence to hold her in the marriage. Her violence, as well as her maintenance of neighborhood support, worked relatively effectively to give her some leverage and ultimately to get her out of the situation. An analogous pattern with the sexes reversed could not be found— indeed, probably could not occur. Women's violence in these situations was a matter of holding their own and/or hurting a hated partner whom they were not free to leave. The case records contain many plaintive letters from wife-beaters begging for their wives' return: "The suspense is awfull at times especially at night, when I arrive Home, I call it Home yet, when I do not hear those gentle voices and innocent souls whisper and speak my name."[81]

A second pattern consisted of extremely frightened, usually fatalistic wives who occasionally defended themselves with a weapon. In 1960, for example, the MSPCC took on a case of such a woman, underweight and malnourished, very frightened of her profane, abusive, alcoholic, and possibly insane husband. One day she struck him on the head so hard he had to be hospitalized.[82] This is the pattern that most commonly led, and leads, to murder. Female murderers much more commonly kill husbands or lovers than men do; the overwhelming majority (93 percent) claim to have been victims of abuse.[83]

In a third pattern, the least common, women were the primary aggressors. One 1932 mother, obese, ill, described as slovenly, kicked and slammed her six children around, locked them out of the house, knocked them down the stairs, and scratched them, as well as beating her husband and forcing him and an oldest daughter to do all the housework. His employer described him as "weak and spineless, but very good-hearted."

Ultimately this woman was committed to a state mental hospital at her own request on the basis of a diagnosis of an unspecified psychosis.[84]

Of the three patterns of female violence, the latter two usually involved extremely distressed, depressed, even disoriented women. The fighting women in mutual violence cases were not depressed, and may have been better off than more peaceful ones. Over time there appeared to be a decline in mutual violence and women's aggression.[85] The apparent decline in women's violence was offset by an increase in women's leaving marriages. A likely hypothesis is that there is a trade-off between women's physical violence and their ability to get separations or divorces.

Although women usually lost in fights, the decline in women's violence was not a clear gain for women and their families.[86] Condemnation of female violence went along with the romanticization of female passivity which contributed to women's participation in their own victimization. Historian Nancy Tomes found that a decline in women's violence in England between 1850 and 1890 corresponded to an increase in women's sense of shame about wife-beating, and reluctance to report or discuss it.[87] In this area feminism's impact on women in violent families was mixed. The delegitimization of wife-beating increased battered women's guilt about their inability to escape; they increasingly thought themselves exceptional, adding to their shame. First-wave feminism, expressing its relatively elite class base, helped construct a femininity that was oppressive to battered women: by emphasizing the superiority of women's peacefulness, feminist influence made women loathe and attempt to suppress their own aggressiveness and anger.

NEIGHBORHOOD AND KINSHIP RESPONSE

Few battered women kept their problems to themselves. This was the case despite the fact that people with close support networks were probably less likely to appear in this study because they did not become agency clients at all.[88] The population represented in these records was, as we have seen earlier, disproportionately poor, transient, and unstable, not a population rooted in old communities and kinship networks.

Nevertheless, they tried hard to get help. Beaten women often asked for places to stay, the minimum condition for escape. One 1910 incest and wife-beating case developed in part *because* of a woman's lack of a place to live. She had previously left her abusive husband to stay with her mother but was left homeless when her mother died; she returned to her husband in 1911; in 1914 he was convicted of assault and battery on her, and in 1916 of incest with their oldest daughter.[89]

Or women might ask for money to help maintain their own households. Close neighbors, landladies, and relatives might be asked for child care, for credit, or for food. One very young wife, at age twenty-one already a four-year veteran of an extremely abusive marriage, had at first displayed the typical ambivalent pattern, leaving several times to stay with her relatives and always returning. Taking a firm decision only when she discovered that her husband had infected her and her young daughter with venereal disease, she left for good, able to return to a household that still contained a mother, sister, and brother who supplied child care as well as a home. Four years later she was managing on her own, her daughter cared for by her sister while she worked as a stenographer.[90] This sort of kinship support was, of course, no guarantee of a woman's safety. In Charlestown in 1917 a beaten wife stayed with her parents and took a job. But whenever her payday came, the estranged husband would arrive to demand her money; her father refused to let him in, but the wife would meet him secretly and give him money.[91] In a 1940 case, a battered wife had already left her husband and gone to live with her mother, but he threatened and attacked his mother-in-law too, until she became frightened to have her daughter with her; he also terrorized the welfare workers, who were, in his view, supporting his wife's defiance.[92]

There were occasional cases of more direct intervention by relatives, more frequent in the first half of this study. Mr. Amato, whom we met in chapter 1, had tried to stop his son from assaulting his wife.[93] In 1893 a woman's brother came to another part of Boston to stay with her at night to protect her from her husband, "who would lie in wait for her with a club."[94] But relatives also set clear limits on their involvement. In 1917 an Italian-born husband had battered his wife for years, ending their relationship by forcibly committing her to a mental hospital (despite the attempts of a thirteen-year-old daughter to convince a caseworker that abuse was her mother's main mental problem). Her parents lived close by and had been very involved with the family; the wife had fled to them on several occasions and they vociferously condemned her husband in speaking to a social worker; when the wife's mother died they blamed it on her anguish at her daughter's abuse. But they were unwilling to interfere with his authority so far as to shelter her when he demanded her return. Moreover, having committed his wife, he retained his right to be accepted by her relatives as a member of the family.[95]

The close involvement of parents, when they lived nearby, was expected. More unusual to the contemporary observer was the importance of sisters. In friendship, the provision of child care, and material aid, sisters and sisters-in-law were called upon almost as often as parents, until the most recent decades. Sisters were the relatives most likely to complain to agencies about abuse and the most likely to accompany women asking agencies for help. This phenomenon reveals, by contrast, the relative decline in the importance of sibling relationships among adults in the more recent period. It also reveals the gender difference in sibling relationships. Brothers might take protective or financial responsibility for siblings, particularly in Italian-American families, but they did not involve themselves personally.

The role of relatives is not necessarily distinct from that of neighbors, since many relatives *were* neighbors. In Boston, relatives often shared the same two- or three-family house: typically parents owned and rented to children, siblings, or other close relatives.[96] Despite the overlap between kin and neighbors, however, there were differences in their involvement: neighbors were more likely to be hostile, relatives to be supportive.[97]

More important than material help was the influence of others on how victims defined the standards of treatment they would tolerate. In these crowded urban conditions there was little privacy from neighbors, who were therefore well informed about the nature of next-door intrafamily relationships. Indeed, agency workers regarded them as reliable witnesses, unless loyalty prevented them from snitching. Their reactions affected the responses of victims and assailants. Some responded with shrugs, words of resignation, or homilies about female destiny and the inevitability of male violence; others responded with disapproval or even outrage. Even loving parents like those above, who took their daughter in but deferred to her abusive husband's ultimate authority, were telling their daughter that beatings should be tolerated. By contrast, in another Italian-American family, the mother and sister of a battered woman not only took her in with her six children but brought her to complain to the MSPCC.[98]

In many cases outsiders gave mixed messages. In 1918 a doctor's wife reported the abuse of her maid, having seen her bruises. The victim's relatives offered very different evaluations: her sister said she would not live with the man and was surprised that the woman had stuck it out so long; the husband's sister admitted he abused her but said the trouble started because the woman interfered with his punishment of the children and suggested that she should keep quiet when he was "correcting" them. (In fact, he was a child abuser.) These relatives lived in the same building.[99] In the Amato case, the message to the victim was mixed in another way: her father-in-law would attempt to discipline her abuser but would not tolerate her autonomous action.[100] Being "told on" by neighbors also had numerous meanings: hostility to the assailant or the whole family; a preference against personal involvement; but also a message about community norms.

Several historians have described traditional community sanctions against unacceptable marital violence. Rituals of public shaming, known as charivari, skimmington rides, rough music, and misrules, among many other names, involving costumes and floats, dancing, singing rude songs, and, sometimes, physical punishments, were common from the fifteenth through the nineteenth century. These were most commonly directed at women who upset the proper sexual order through their insubordination, but occasionally were used to discipline men who overstepped the acceptable limits of their authority.[101] Most of this evidence of community enforcement of marital standards comes from Europe, and from preindustrial times, in situations of relatively stable old communities. Some similar activity in the United States in the nineteenth and twentieth centuries has been discovered. Some vigilante groups, including the Ku Klux Klan, punished wife-beaters.[102] At least one Afro-American church conducted trials of members for domestic disharmony.[103] But in the Boston cases, and probably in most big cities, such informal sanctions were clearly inadequate to control domestic violence.

SOCIAL-WORK RESPONSE

Battered women turned to child-welfare agencies when their informal networks could not protect them, adding these agencies to their reservoir of resistance strategies.[104] Women not only initiated complaints to agencies, but their friends and relatives helped and urged them to do so. One 1910 downstairs neighbor of an abused wife was pleased to see the caseworker because "she had been taking care of chn. more or less, but could not do much for them as her men folks worked nights and had to sleep during day."[105] In 1930 two women friends came together to the MSPCC to seek intervention in behalf of a third friend, whose battering husband was an ex-policeman, with friends on the force.[106] They were enlisting one social-control agency against another. Opposition between community and professional social control developed when professionals tried to prevent the "interference" of friends and relatives, wanting exclusive control of treatment. The "community" did not necessarily accept that prohibition.[107] Its offers and denials of support, opinions, and emotions continued to influence not only the family members but also the experts.

Before the development of charity or professional agencies devoted to family conflict, another agency had already long been active in such cases: the police. In Boston they were frequently involved in domestic disturbances in the nineteenth century, and these cops who walked their beats knew most of the residents of their districts, including their secrets. When MSPCC agents inquired at local stations about complaints, the police almost always knew the people involved; if they did not, the people were likely to be transient.

The police were to some extent replaced by social-service agencies in child abuse and neglect cases, but not in marital violence. Police were called in 49 percent of wife-beating cases, a rate almost constant throughout this study. Women had no other agency to call for emergency help, but what they got was almost always unsatisfactory. Their stories sound familiar: the police implicitly (and sometimes explicitly) identified with the husband and, while urging him to moderate his violence and to sober up, sympathized with his frustration and trivialized his assaults. They did often remove the angry men from their homes for a while, calming them, and this service was of some limited value to women. Sometimes the police threatened men with arrest and jail. Often, too, the police knew that little they could do would be useful to the women, who could not survive without these men. At times the police were worse than useless: in one 1910 case a woman who went to the station to complain about her husband was arrested herself instead, for drunkenness.[108] Often the police simply refused to respond to domestic disturbance calls. In 1930 one officer told a social worker, "she is always calling on the Police for the slightest things and the Police will no longer go to the home when [she] requests them to."[109] At most the police would only charge an offender with drunk and disorderly conduct.[110] Or, as another woman reported, the police pacified her husband in another room and did not talk with her at all.[111]

Battered women turned to child-protection agencies in part because of the inadequacy of police protection.[112] Women not only expected more sympathy from social workers but also wanted something beyond the powers of the police, particularly separation and maintenance agreements. But such agreements, establishing female-headed households, provoked opposition (as we have seen in chapter 4). Caught in a contradictory set of constraints—attempting to shore up two-parent families, failing to find levers with which to reform violent men—many social workers and their supervisors tried to ignore wife-beating. When it could not be ignored, caseworkers, especially those of a therapeutic orientation, began to define it as a problem for the woman to work on.

For several reasons a woman-blaming response to wife-beating became more pervasive after the 1930s. Changes in social work procedures created a structural imperative to map the problem onto the client who was present and influenceable. In the early years of child protection, caseworkers tried to reform men. The unembarrassed moralism of the earlier period, combined with the wider range of pre-professional techniques, gave agency workers a choice of tactics to influence male behavior: they hectored, threatened, and cajoled; they used short jail sentences, frequent home visits, including surprise visits, visits to employers and relatives; and they dunned non-supporting men for money. As professionalized casework concentrated on office visits, fewer men were seen. Moreover, women were more introspective and self-critical—more productive in casework. Men infrequently originated cases, were rarely willing to meet with caseworkers, and were more defensive about their own behavior. In search of any ways to influence troubled families, social workers not unnaturally focused on those most open to influence.

More fundamentally, blaming family problems on women was part of a change in family and gender ideology evident by the 1930s. The caseworkers were more affected by the decline of feminism than their clients were, apparently. Ironically, these social-work attitudes were also conditioned by gains in sexual equality. Women were no longer pictured as helpless in the manner of the nineteenth-century victim, and indeed, women were not so helpless, having greater ability to divorce and create separate households or new marriages than they had had earlier. As child neglect became, virtually by definition, a sign of maternal inadequacy, so did marital violence become a sign of wifely dysfunction. "Instead of aligning our agency with the mother," the MSPCC reported in 1959, "we felt it only proper to have the father present his side of the picture. . . . The mother was seen and, instead of encouraging her laments about her husband, efforts were made to help her to understand his needs and the strains he was under."[113]

After World War II a particularly intense anxiety about wifely sexual and gender maladjustment became evident. Nor was there parallelism: if men suffered similar maladjustment, no one noticed. Freudian thought influenced many caseworkers in this direction, with its story that women's maturity required self-sacrifice and renunciation. But the social workers' concern about maladjusted women was also an observation of the stresses of actual social and economic change, the conflicts women were experiencing between earning and housekeeping, raised aspirations and continued constriction of opportunity, public rights and continued subordination. They had to counsel women to perform in contradictory ways.

This was the era of the "feminine mystique," not of Victoria. Divorce was a common occurrence. The marital counsel offered by the child protectors and marriage experts combined woman-blaming with toleration for marital separation. A standard social work manual on women in marital conflict categorized problems under the headings: excessive dependence, the need to suffer, rejection of femininity, sex response, interfering relatives, cultural differences, and economic factors; four of the seven referred to women's faults, none to men's faults, and three to extramarital pressures. A classic "feminine mystique" document, the book expresses the contradictions of the age, condemning both excessive dependence, a quality acknowledged to be culturally encouraged—

"combines well with femininity"—*and* women's employment. It blamed women for provoking abusive men and then for staying with them; indeed, suspicion is expressed that dependence created battering.[114]

Caseworkers frequently offered analyses that deepened women's double binds. For example, although accepting the necessity for marital separation at times, both child-protection and psychiatric social workers communicated to women their convictions that being single was always undesirable, not only for children—"no man in the house with whom he can identify"—but also for adult women. A caseworker might support a separation but expect and even encourage the woman to suffer.[115] A woman who had left her husband was criticized for enjoying her job too much, allegedly putting it ahead of her child.[116] Some caseworkers remained intolerant of divorce in any situation. An MSPCC agent in the 1950s repeatedly urged a battered wife to reconcile with her husband despite her long struggle to leave. The story is consistently written in terms critical of her. For example, "fa had social disease before married of which he informed mo but she willingly accepted him and later she contracted same from fa . . . Mo finds fault w fa bec he is not gay and does not want to go places. . . . refuses to associate w her friends." The wife agreed to reconsider her current plan to separate if the agent would "restrain fa from using his fists. Agt warned mo that she places emphasis on the wrong values and that she should learn to distinguish between undesirable acquaintances and the genuine love of a devoted husband."[117] Other workers continued to ignore marital conflict. In 1950 an anonymous neglect complaint (almost certainly made by the husband) revealed a terrified fifteen-year-old wife, badly bruised from her husband's beatings, waiting for her mother to wire her some money so she could return to her parents' home in Texas. Meanwhile, she was deathly afraid that her husband would learn about her plans to flee and would try to stop her and to seize their baby. The agent responded only with legalisms, reiterating that she had legal custody and was free to leave. In fact, the husband did just what she feared—went to the train station and took the baby. The agent closed the case, saying this was a marital, not a child welfare, problem.[118]

Not all social workers were so narrow-minded and insensitive. In another MSPCC 1950s case, also originated by a husband's neglect complaint against his wife, the caseworker was originally hostile to the wife because she drank. Within four months this analysis was revised to the diagnosis that wife-beating was the root of the problem, of which her drinking was a symptom.[119] In every period there were caseworkers who listened well and helped clients to value their own resources, both personal and social. But the success stories usually involved exceptionally tenacious, determined clients.

The denial of wife-beating was expressed in the language. By the 1940s gender-neutral euphemisms like marital discord and marital disharmony began to dominate.[120] Where the violence was directly named by the women, social workers sought to probe "deeper." For example, in 1960, a woman told the worker that "fa had thrown her onto the floor. Worker said that she did not believe that mo had to accept this from fa but that if mo removed the cause for fa's doing this, namely mo's excessive drinking, and inability to get along with fa [sic], perhaps this would never have happened."[121] This language not only places onto the woman the responsibility for "getting along" with a violent man but, through use of the passive, makes it appear as if the violence just "happens"; there is no attribution of responsibility. Women's attribution of responsibility to their husbands was an infantile "blaming," a denial of adult responsibility.[122]

These analyses became psychologized, or psychiatric, not only at the Judge Baker clinic, but also at the traditional casework agencies. Masochism was a repeated diagnosis.[123] An MSPCC agent wrote in 1956,

> She did say he was very abusive to her when he was drunk and it was difficult to ascertain if mo derived masochistic pleasure in the abuse or if she is too limited because of physical disabilities and emotional difficulties to do anything about the situation.[124]

These kinds of diagnoses emerged even in cases in which workers were obviously sympathetic to the women. A Polish-American woman from a rigid and religious family was seduced with a promise of marriage by a Protestant man twelve years her senior, who then refused to marry her. She had three out-of-wedlock children with him and was distraught with guilt. His non-support finally sent her to the Catholic Charity organization, which forced him to marry her. He had beaten her severely throughout their relationship and she retaliated by refusing to sleep with him as soon as they were married, using sex as a lever to get money from him: "that was one thing she didn't like to do but it seemed the only way." In 1950, in a drunken rage, he had beaten their son so badly that she overcame her fears and left, returning to her parents. Her caseworker said of her, with sympathy as well as condescension, "I think it becomes quite a problem just how one can make life have more meaning for these women . . . bitter for having to return home with the children and live with their parents with no husband . . ." (One might suspect, on the contrary, that she would be feeling elated.) Working part-time as a dishwasher, she was diagnosed as a "woman who doesn't like making a home and probably didn't want children." (One might surmise, on the contrary, that her work reflected her concern to support her children decently.) Worried that men made "passes" at her, she expressed her characteristic sexual guilt, wondering "if she looks tough or hard or if she in some way unconsciously encourages without really meaning to." The social worker responded, "I tell her that the latter is possible." The clinicians were concerned about the "feminization" of her seven-year-old son, his "castration fear . . . given frightening reality by the accidental loss of his eye. . . . I wonder if this so-called accident—this loss of the eye—wasn't provoked by him." His mother, of course, is the castrator, because she "banished" the father from the home. (In fact, she had to leave the home, lacking the power to banish him.) The fact that the boy reportedly told his mother, "Mummy I won't chase you with a knife like Daddy did," might suggest an alternative explanation for the boy's castration fears, if they existed, but this alternative was not explored. [125]

WIFE-BEATING, GENDER, AND SOCIETY

This chapter has been an extended demonstration that wife-beating is a social problem. It has been sanctioned and controlled through culture—religious belief, law, and, most importantly, the norms of friendship, kinship, and neighborhood groups. One assault does not make a battered woman; she becomes that because of her socially determined inability to resist or escape: her lack of economic independence, law enforcement services, and, quite likely, self-confidence. Battering behavior is also socially determined, by a man's expectations of what a woman should do for him and his acculturation to violence. Wife-beating arose not just from subordination but also from contesting it. Had women consistently accepted their subordinate status, and had men never felt their superior status challenged, there might have been less marital violence. To focus on women's "provocations," and to examine men's grievances against their wives, is not to blame women but, often, to praise them. It is to uncover the evidence of women's resistance.

To some extent the female gender itself has been influenced by mil-lennia of violence, and a socialization toward passivity. But the rela-tionship between battering and femininity is more complex. Women have been as aggressive, irrational, and self-destructive as men in marital conflict. But by and large, because women had the most to lose in relationships structured by coercion, women developed greater coop-erative, socially manipulative skills. Their much-reputed wicked tongues were evident in these case records. Indeed, women's verbal skills were often honed to sharpness precisely to do battle against men's superior power, including violence. Their verbal style was a better tool for creating familial and community cohesion than was violence. This superi-ority was not, however, a result of moral superiority, as the nineteenth-century reformers believed; rather, it was a collective characteristic developed as a result of the structural position of the gender.

Wife-beaters' behavior was also highly gendered. Accustomed to su-premacy, acculturated to expect service and deference from women, and integrating these expectations into the ego itself, men were under-standably disoriented to encounter resistance and unskilled at negotiating compromises. Within this context, some men have a smaller range of responses to anger, less constructive responses to stress and frustration than others. Wife-beaters are by no means commonly crazy or even temporarily disoriented, but they may indeed have more self-destructive behaviors than less violent men. We have seen how wife-beating was commonly associated with heavy drinking, desertion, and sexual abuse of children. Men's plea of loss of self-control as an extenuating factor was not convincing, as I have argued above, but it expressed a subjective experience of weak ego.

The batterers I have described were not ideologues defending the dominance of their sex. Neither were they necessarily insecure. They were using violence to increase their control over particular women, defending real, material benefits. Beatings kept women from leaving, kept them providing sexual, housework, and child care services (or were intended to do so).[126] Wife-beating was not usually a mere emotional expression of annoyance, or a symbolic display of power. It did not result from an individual man's "need" to demonstrate masculinity; if masculinity was threatened, that threat arose in a struggle with another person. Some beatings resulted from demands for deference or from conflicts about status, apparently symbolic issues. But in these relationships the symbolism of power functioned to organize and reinforce real power relationships, which in turn provided real benefits and privileges to the "boss."

Sociologist William Goode's "resource" theory has some useful explanatory elements regarding wife-beating. It identifies the sources of power, or resources, with which people try to win benefits. Using a market metaphor, it considers violence a more "costly" resource which will not be spent unless "cheaper" resources, such as love, approval, or money, are absent or depleted. This theory would explain why poor and low-status men, who lack other resources, may use violence more readily than rich and prestigious men. (The fact being explained, however, has been challenged: as with all family violence, it is difficult to distinguish reported incidents from actual incidence.) A problem with this theory is the assumption that violence is somehow more "expensive," a tactic of last resort; it is evident that many, mainly men, turn to violence quickly, long before they have exhausted other tactics.[127] Nevertheless, the metaphor of resources reminds us that violence is a tactic in a struggle for an end, not merely a ritual behavior which could be altered by retraining.

Batterers were not necessarily conscious of their goals. Often they felt so wounded by women's behavior, and so desperately longed for a wife's services, that they experienced their violence as uncontrollable; they felt they had no recourse. Their sense of entitlement was so strong it was experienced as a need. Their wives did not feel so entitled. And when, stimulated often by responsibility for children, they gave up trying to wheedle and pacify, and tried to escape, they found what they had always suspected: a set of obstacles, any one of which might have been definitive—poverty, motherhood, isolation, and the hostility or indifference of social control agencies. When the context is supplied, many seemingly ineffective responses to wife-beating, including resignation, pandering, and changes of mind, are revealed to be rational, trial-and-error, even experienced and skilled survival and escape tactics.

Battered women's defeats are losses for everyone. Wife-beating molds not only individual relationships but also the overall social definitions of heterosexual relations. Wife-beating sends "messages" to all who know about it or suspect it; it encourages timidity, fatalism, manipulativeness in women. Men's violence against some women (extra- as well as intrafamilial) reinforces all women's subordination and all men's dominance. This does not mean that wife-beaters got what they wanted. On the contrary, wife-beating, even more than nonfamily violence against women, is often dysfunctional even for the assailants. In many of the cases reviewed here, men longed for the impossible, for sycophantic service and selfless devotion, which they would have hated had they gotten it, and their violence brought them no gain. On the contrary, in most marriages, even in extremely patriarchal societies, men's and women's interests have been complementary as well as adversary, especially because their economic futures were joined. This contradictory nature of marriage and the family—requiring cooperation among unequals—helps explain why wife-beating is not universal. Men benefited more from camaraderie, mutual respect, and friendship. Cooperation, especially in work, promoted men's as well as women's values: prosperity, health, calm, leisure.

If battered women's failures were costly to all, their successes were beneficial to all. The victims' own struggles were hard to see until the last two decades, when battered women organized themselves as part of a feminist movement. In fact, battered women's self-image, interpretation of their problem, and strategies of resistance had always been influenced by organized feminism. In turn, they also influenced social and legal policy, particularly through their interactions with social workers and other authorities: at worst they kept the issue from being completely forgotten, at best they provided a pressure for such solutions as we have today—liberalized divorce, AFDC, prosecution. Even women who have never been struck have benefited from the "disestablishment" of marriage that is now taking place, the process of transforming it from a coercive institution, inescapable and necessary for survival, to a relationship that is chosen.

9

CONCLUSION: SOCIAL CONTROL AND THE "POWERS OF THE WEAK"

"Whether I shall turn out to be the hero of my own life, or whether that station will be held by anybody else, these pages must show."
—Charles Dickens, *David Copperfield*.

Most of this book is sad. Most of the individual stories had bad endings. Family violence has not been stopped. Moreover, there is more wretchedness than heroism in this study. There has been a tendency, in telling the histories of the poor, to render survivors as heroes, to romanticize forbearance. The family-violence stories do not allow this because in them many who did not survive were equally brave, including the alcoholic, the delinquent, the depressed. Few of the victims were without some moment of complicity or resignation that lessened their resistance, at least temporarily. And many who were victims were also aggressors.

But this history is not finished. Both the struggle against family violence, and the interpretation of its history, are continuing. In the short period since the end of this study—in the 1960s and 1970s—the situation has changed markedly. The recent rediscovery of family violence was accomplished in part by pressure from the victims themselves. A much greater proportion of the contemporary response to family violence has been empowering to its victims, notably through battered women's shelters and other self-help groups. Moreover, as better histories of women, children, and social policy are written, they will reveal, I think, that these recent developments built on earlier achievements: the original exposure of crimes against women and children, including previously denied and unspeakable sexual crimes; the campaigns that focused on child welfare, such as pensions for single mothers, anti-child-labor legislation, laws against the adulteration of milk and other foods, for examples. These accomplishments, all critical to the protection of women and children, have been obscured by the long period of the quiescence of feminism between 1920 and 1960.

The rediscovery of family violence in the last two decades is no evidence that the problem is actually increasing. No one can know the *per capita* occurrence of family violence prior to the last few decades. The potential of publicity to increase reports of such problems is great. The definitions of what constitutes family violence suggest that less violence is tolerated as acceptable punishment today.

Moreover, even in the worst of times, there were many family-violence victims attempting to become the heroes of their own lives, as Charles Dickens put it. Using the "powers of the weak," to cite Elizabeth Janeway again, attempting to replace with creativity and stubbornness what they lacked in resources, they manipulated every device at their disposal to free themselves from abuse. The people I knew from these case records were often isolated, poor, and sick, depressed and angry, but they did not appear to have done worse than I might have done under the same circumstances.

In exercising these powers of the weak, the family-violence clients contribute to an understanding of the dilemmas of all social control and social helping. Conflicts between privacy and social control, between individual rights and public responsibility, affect not only family violence but many aspects of "personal" life. In this study, despite the fact that I considered only cases in which criminal violence or neglect was proved, the violent families seemed ordinary, not alien.

Moreover, the very definition of family violence is by no means established. Ultimately we may all have to define for ourselves, for our own lives, the border between acceptable and unacceptable attempts to coerce. In Jean Thompson's extraordinary short story "The People of Color," a woman comes to question her own marriage from listening to beatings and screams from the next apartment. Considering the violence of others, instead of congratulating herself on the superiority of her relationship, she begins to question what might be called the institutionalized violence of her own marriage, a relationship that "works" only because of her acquiescence to her husband's infantile need for domination and ego support. The boundaries of family violence are openly in dispute among child-abuse experts, some of whom would declare all physical punishment to be abusive, although the majority of Americans use it.

This study made the variability of definitions of family violence a central part of its subject. It also encompassed, moreover, not only the changing experience of family violence, but also the strategies of both its participants and social control agents in responding to it. It has been necessary to show that family violence is not the unilateral expression of one person's violent temperament, but is cooked up jointly—albeit not equally—by several individuals in the pot of the family. There are no objects, only subjects, in this study. Out of this complex perspective, three general conclusions have emerged. First, family violence is a political issue. It has been defined and policies about it formed under the influence of changing political contexts since the 1870s. Second, domestic violence itself, as experienced by its participants, was also affected by historical change as it entered gender and generational relations. Third, the participants in family violence, both victims and assailants, were by no means passive recipients of social-control policies. Rather, they struggled actively to get help they considered useful from charity and social-work agencies as well as kin and neighbors.

Awareness of family violence has been shaped by several reform movements of which the most important was feminism. It promoted critique of the conventional family and social responsibility for the welfare of children. During the period of this study, before 1960, it legitimated state intervention in behalf of children, but not for women. Nevertheless, the close connection, in ideology and in material circumstances, between women's and children's well-being meant that women gained much from child-protection agencies. Indeed, the inadequacy of means of caring for children outside their original families has meant that women may well have gained more, because children gained so little, from child-protection work.

The decline of feminist influence in social work, particularly after World War I, meant not only the decreased visibility of family-violence problems altogether but also their redefinition in ways that were disadvantageous to victims. For example, the definitions of child neglect from the Progressive era tended to hold women exclusively responsible for the welfare of children; to emphasize economic deprivation but not gender domination; and, through the maintenance of a punitive approach without complementary social services, to intensify poor women's vulnerability to neglect allegations and to loss of their children. When child-welfare workers lost their familiarity with critiques of male domination as an overall social problem, they also lost their ability to "see" the particularly male types of family-violence, wife-beating, and sexual abuse. A more continuous feminist influence might have encouraged a search for alternative responses to child abuse other than removal of children. Only in the past few decades has a women's movement been again strong enough to direct attention to wife-beating and incest; there is need for a stronger feminist influence in the analysis of child abuse and neglect.

Family violence has been political not only in its definitions but also in its causes. It usually emerged from power struggles in which family members were contesting for material, and often scarce, benefits. Moreover, the goals of the individuals were affected by historical change, particularly that influencing the aspirations of women and children, or frustrating the expectations of men. This study encountered less evidence of the contribution of individual, psychological factors to these struggles, but we know they were there. Structural, "social" analyses do not contradict the importance of individual temperament. (The psychological categories for personality and mental disorders have been so shifting over the years that it is best to remain here with vernacular categories such as "temperament.") But very few of the victims or assailants in these family-violence cases were mentally ill. Moreover, to call family violence political is not to deny that each subjective experience of it is wholly personal and unique.

Despite psychological and social disabilities, many agency clients were far from despairing or resigned. The women clients, whether victims or assailants, were not only resourceful in seeking help for themselves and their families but also self-critical about their own behavior. Their aspirations thus contributed to social definitions of their own deviance. In these efforts they helped others beyond themselves, because they collectively influenced the responses of individual social workers and, ultimately, the policy of the agencies.

SOCIAL CONTROL

These conclusions, especially with respect to the activity of clients of child-protection agencies, call into question much of the legacy of scholarship about social control. Ever since E. A. Ross first used the phrase "social control" in 1901, two traditions have dominated appraisals of the growing social regulatory side of the state. One, the liberal interpretation, that of Ross himself and Talcott Parsons after him in the 1940s and 1950s, considered such intervention a sign of progress. They viewed the replacement of family functions—such as socialization—by professionals as beneficial. A contrasting, more pessimistic interpretation of social control has been advanced since the 1930s by both Marxists and conservatives, from the Frankfurt School to Ortega y Gasset. The former were concerned with the suppression of class consciousness, the latter with individual autonomy, but both joined in a condemnation of professional intervention. [1] These condemnations, not only of regulatory agencies but also of the controlling aspects of much of the apparatus of the modern welfare state, were continued by scholars influenced by the New Left in the 1960s and 1970s.

Neither positive nor negative appraisals of social control had gender or generational analyses. Both, in fact, continued a patriarchal usage in identifying "the family" that was being invaded with a male-dominated, father-dominated form of family. If one uses family violence as the key instance of social control, an issue that contained an inherent critique of patriarchal domination, then new questions arise and the evaluation of intervention must be more complex.

For example, the critique of social control, both left and right, frequently points to the violation of civil liberties as evidence of the dangers of intervention into family privacy. We have seen many instances of such violations in this book, but before condemning the very enterprise of intervening into the family, one must ask: Whose privacy? Whose liberties? The conception of liberties dominant in the nineteenth century was one of individual rights against the state, which was in fact an attribution of rights to heads of households. These rights functioned to enshrine the home as private and inviolable, and the champions of these rights were naturally adult men, particular those with the privilege and wealth to maintain independent households. (Many poor and working-class people were not able to achieve these independent households.) Such rights did not protect subordinate members of families against intrafamily oppression or violence. On the contrary, privacy rights have been invoked to remove some individuals from the public guarantees of these liberties. Until recently it was customary for law enforcement officials to decline to guarantee such liberties to battered women, for example. Children did not usually even get as far as telling their story to law officers, so removed were they from access to their "rights." Thus one man's loss in privacy was often another's (frequently a woman's) gain in rights.

Of course the control of family violence guaranteed no victories for victims, and may often have hurt them further. Once social-control agents, whether public or private, entered families, all family members lost their privacy. The victims often had their "rights" defined for them in ways that they did not always recognize, let alone want. Yet what privacy or control did they have without these interventions? The clients' problems were defined not only by their own faults, not only by their interaction with the larger economy and social structure, but also by a range of very personal and very invasive other relationships. A family-violence case is constructed by children and their parents, in-laws and grandparents and cousins, caseworkers, judges, probation officers, relief officials, school counsellors, doctors, psychologists. Behind the fear of invasion of privacy is also the myth of an isolated nuclear family.

Nor is it true, as several scholars have argued, that these interventions by "outsiders" are a modern piece of deviltry destroying a traditional family autonomy. On the contrary, no family relations have been immune from social regulation.[2] Certainly the modern form of social control exercised by child-protection agencies is qualitatively and quantitatively different from that of traditional societies. The child protectors were "outsiders," lacking investment in local community values and traditions, uncaring about the individuals involved. But traditional forms of social control—community gossip or private interventions—were no more tolerant of individual liberty or deviance than the modern bureaucratic state and its professionals.

Furthermore, we have seen that clients often wanted this intervention. While the definitions of family violence and its remedies have reflected the biases of dominant groups—have been unfair, discriminatory, and oppressive—family violence remains as a problem experienced *by its participants*. The clients did not consider their sufferings inevitable. The power of labeling, the representation of poor people's behavior by experts whose status is defined through their critique of the problematic behavior of others, coexists with real family oppressions. In one case an immigrant father who sexually molested his thirteen-year-old daughter told a social worker that that was the way it was done in the old country! He was not only lying but also trying to manipulate a social worker, perhaps one he had recognized as guilt-ridden over her privileged role, using his own fictitious cultural relativism. His daughter's victimization by incest was not the result of oppression by professionals.

The "interventions" of professionals, bureaucrats, or even upper-class charity workers were, as often as not, really invitations by family members. This does not mean that the inviters kept control of the relationships, or got what they wanted. The guests did not usually leave upon request. Moreover, collectively the interveners and the establishment they represented had much more power than the clients individually or collectively. But it is a mistake to see the flow of initiative in these social-control relationships in only one direction, from top to bottom, from professionals to clients, from elite to subordinate. In fact, the clients were not usually passive but, rather, active in arguing for what they wanted.[3] And sometimes they got what they wanted: single mothers got relief, battered wives got separations, abused children got, at least, attention. More frequently, the clients did not get what they wanted, but their cumulative pressure affected the agencies' definitions of problems and proposals for help.

In historical fact, most of the invitations for intervention came from women and secondarily children. In other words, the inviters were the weaker members of family power structures. Social work intervention has not been a process that can be expressed simply in class terms, as the rich against the poor. In their struggles to escape the control of a patriarchal family, women not only used the professions and the state but helped build them. The social work/social control establishment did not arise out of the independent agenda of the ruling class, or even of the middle class. Rather it developed out of conflicts that had gender and generational as well as class "sides."

When critics of social control perceive social work simply as unwanted intervention, and fail to recognize the active role of agency clients, it is in large part because they conceive of the family as a homogeneous unit. There is an intellectual reification here which expresses itself in sentence structure, particularly in academic language: "The family is in decline," "threats to the family," "the family responds to industrialization." Shorthand expressions attributing behavior to an aggregate such as the family would be harmless except that they often impose particular cultural norms about what "the family" is, and mask intra-family differences and conflicts of interest. Usually "the family" becomes a representation of the interests of the family head, if it is a man, carrying an assumption that all family members share his interests. (Families without a married male head, like single-parent or grandparent-headed families, are, in the common usage, broken, deformed, or incomplete families.) Among the clients in family-violence cases, outrage over the intervention into the family was frequently an outrage over a territorial violation, a challenge to male authority; or, expressed differently, an outrage at the exposure of intrafamily conflict and of the family head's lack of control. Indeed, the interventions actually *were* more substantive, more invasive, when their purpose was to change the status quo than if they had been designed to reinforce it. The effect of social workers' involvement was sometimes to change existing family power relations, usually in the interest of the weaker family members.

In the legitimation of charitable and professional intervention into domestic problems, an important political leadership was contributed by the women's rights movement. Feminist consciousness was largely responsible, not only for the several waves of sensitivity to women's and children's domestic victimization, but also for public assumption of responsibility for defending them against abusive husbands and parents. Indeed, the whole welfare state, including particularly its regulatory organizations, derived to a significant degree from the feminist agenda of the late nineteenth and early twentieth centuries. The influence of these women activists and their vision is only slowly being recognized. Their vision reflected, of course, their class as well as their sex position, and most of them were elite. Feminist influence as well as male leadership and professional social work were guilty of disdain for non-Wasp cultures, arrogance toward the poor, failure to understand the impact of structural unemployment, and refusal to defend the rights of single mothers, to name but a few examples.

But that enthusiasm for state regulation was not strictly a middle-class maneuver, nor was it on balance disadvantageous to poor women.[4] Furthermore, many family oppressions were problems shared by women across class lines. Opposition to wife-beating did not need to be taught to the working class by middle-class women; poor mothers did not lag behind prosperous mothers in their desire for kindness, safety, education, and nutrition for their children; and the rebellion of both women and children against paternal tyranny was easily as sharp in the working class as elsewhere. In other words, family violence was not a middle-class or "bourgeois" issue. The women who called upon the child protectors knew the risks they were taking. Despite the fact that fathers were more often outraged at being investigated and possibly maligned, the mothers had more to lose: by far the most common outcome of agency action was the removal of children, an action dreaded least by fathers and most by mothers. But these fears did not stop women from attempting to manipulate social workers in their own interest—both because they had confidence in their own purposes and because they wanted help so badly. Nor was it only victims who appealed: abusive and neglectful mothers, distressed that they were not able to raise their children according to their own standards, were among the complainants. These people were finding the traditional informal methods of social controls, which may have prevailed in agrarian societies, inadequate to their needs in modern, impersonal urban society.

The usual critique of social-control-as-domination also ignores the fact that the controllers often preferred not to act. Chronically underfunded and under-staffed, agencies frequently disregarded complaints and repelled requests for help. Most cases led to no action; indeed caseworkers more often disappointed clients by their inactivity than by their activism.

Despite patterns of class and cultural domination, family casework agencies were often helpful to clients. This was mainly because individual caseworkers were usually better (although sometimes worse) than the official agency policies they were supposed to follow. This superiority, in turn, came in part from the casework approach itself, and the attention paid to all aspects of clients' family context. Even more it came from the fact that individuals brought flexibility, creativity, and empathy beyond the strictures of agency policy.[5] The most helpful caseworkers were those who understood family-violence problems to be simultaneously social/cultural and personal in origin, and who therefore offered help in both dimensions. Good caseworkers might help a family get relief, or medical care, or a better apartment, and build a woman's or child's self-esteem by legitimating their complaints and aspirations.

Social work interventions in family-violence cases rarely changed assailants' behavior, but they had a greater impact on victims. The main factor determining the usefulness of casework was the activity of clients: those who sought help and knew what they wanted were more likely to get it. This is why, ironically, the child-protection agencies contributed more to help battered women, defined as outside their jurisdiction, than abused children. Modern urban society gave women some opportunity to leave abusive men because they could earn their own living. In these circumstances, even a bit of material help—a referral to a relief agency, a positive recommendation to the courts regarding child custody—could turn their aspirations for autonomy into reality. Moreover, women could get this help despite class and ethnic prejudices against them. Italian-American women might reap this benefit even from social workers who held derogatory views of Italians; single mothers might get help in establishing independent households despite charity workers' suspicions of their morals. Children would need more than money to escape abusive parents.

At the same time, in this society of great inequality, interventions against family violence have been and continue to be discriminatory. Class privilege brings with it immunity from discovery and/or intervention. Not only have poor, working-class, immigrant, and black people been discriminated against, but so too have women, despite the feminist influence in stimulating anti-family-violence intervention. The disrespect and victim-blaming of many professionals toward clients was the worst, because they were proffered by those defined as "helping." Loss of control was a debilitating experience for many clients, including those who may have gained some material aid. Often the main beneficiaries of professionals' interventions hated them most, because in wrestling with them one rarely gets what one really wants but, rather, is asked to submit to another's interpretation of one's needs.

In these complexities, anti-family-violence work is emblematic of the entire welfare state. Its unfairness is true of every aspect of the welfare state, from which, despite much popular myth to the contrary, the rich and privileged benefit more than the poor. But the abolition of such interventions would not better protect the subordinate groups from discrimination. The dichotomous argument, between those who applaud the welfare state as a sign of progress and those who condemn its oppressiveness, is not useful. The very inequalities of power that make the state oppressive create the need for state responsibility for welfare, and these inequalities include gender and age as well as class. Integrating gender and generational conflicts along with class and economic conflicts into our understanding of the welfare state will demonstrate the need for a more complex appraisal.

I do not wish to discard the cumulative insights offered by many critiques of social control, and by contemporary revelations of the unfairness and violence of many accusations of family violence. Rather, I want to insist that an accurate view of this "outside" intervention into the family must consider, as the clients so often did in their strategic decisions, both external and familial forms of domination. This is a complexity that women particularly faced, struggling as they so often were not only for themselves but also for children. But I do not see any way to circumvent this contradiction. There is no returning to an old or newly romanticized "family autonomy." An answer to problems of family violence, indeed to the whole question of public responsibility for private welfare, must contain and wrestle with, not seek to eradicate, this tension.

APPENDIX A
RESEARCH AND
ANALYSIS METHODS

Finding Sources

Searching for data for this study, I identified three potential sources: (a) legal records, from criminal and civil court proceedings, records of the medical examiner (coroner), and gubernatorial pardon files; (b) public charity records, including those from institutional homes run by the State Board of Charities and state and local relief programs; and (c) private social-work-agency files.

The first proved the least fruitful. Most criminal records in Boston-area family-violence cases consisted only of docket books and other official lists; other papers either never existed (i.e., there was no court recording, and no affidavits were ever gathered) or had been destroyed.

Records of homicide investigations by the state medical examiner covered only the most extreme cases of family violence, those resulting in murder; they could not be used for a representative study of family violence. The pardon files were significant in one respect—since pardons were most frequently applied for, in family-violence cases, by those who originally prosecuted the offense, they reveal the ambivalence of family-violence victims toward their assailants. Nevertheless, since pardons were applied for only in cases ending in jail sentences, by definition the more serious, they could not provide a representative sample.

State agency records were also disappointing. The older records, of almshouses, asylums, and early foster care arrangements, located in the Commonwealth of Massachusetts Archives, included mainly ledgers of how and where the children were kept once in state hands, with no histories of previous family problems. More recent welfare records, which would be fuller, have been routinely destroyed after a certain lapsed time.

Private social-work agencies in Boston (and those dealing with family-violence problems were exclusively private during the time period of this study) turned out to be the repositories of rich collections of records. Many of these agencies were not themselves aware of what records they actually held. In cellars and attics of seven agencies I found several hundred boxes of case records, in one case dating back to 1803. In several agencies the files were badly deteriorated—chewed by mice and rats, disintegrating from hostile temperature and humidity conditions; in virtually all the agencies, the old records were disorganized. In addition to case notes, one agency had an invaluable collection of old glass slides, used to document child abuse cases at the turn of the century, from which the pictures in this book were reproduced.

I selected the three agencies whose records provided the richest and most representative data:

The Massachusetts Society for the Prevention of Cruelty to Children (MSPCC), established in 1878. MSPCC records, through 1939, are at the University of Massachusetts/Boston Archives; the remainder in the MSPCC offices.

The Boston Children's Service Association (BCSA), an umbrella group representing a merger of many private Protestant non-sectarian child-service institutions and agencies. Specializing in foster care and adoption services, the BCSA handled many cases of children removed from their natural parents due to abuse or neglect. Its current title came into existence only in 1960, and its subsidiary agencies, whose records were used for this study, included the Boston Children's Aid Society (1863–1922), the Boston Children's Friend Society (1833–1960), the Children's Aid Association (1922–1960), and the Boston Society for the Care of Girls (1910–1946). Also ultimately merged into the BCSA were the Boston Female Asylum (1800–1922), the Rebecca Pomeroy House, the Gwynne Temporary Home for Children (1888–1915), the Temporary Home for the Destitute (1847–1888), the Massachusetts Infant Asylum (1868–1916), the Society for Helping Destitute Mothers and Infants (1874–1918), and the North End Mission (1868–1926). For simplicity's sake, in discussing cases in this book I referred to all of them as coming from the BCSA. The records of most of these subsidiary organizations are at the University of Massachusetts/ Boston Archives, the remainder at the BCSA offices.

The Judge Baker Guidance Center (JBGC), established in 1917, was a clinic providing psychotherapy for problem children, particularly juvenile delinquents. A high proportion of these children had abuse in their backgrounds. The JBGC case records through 1950 are at the Countway Library of the Harvard Medical School, the remainder at the Judge Baker clinic.

Before research began, agreements for confidentiality and the protection of the subjects of the case records were negotiated with each agency. In this book, not only are all names fictional, but the case record numbers used are not the actual agency case numbers, but part of a code system developed for this research. Any researcher who has permission of the relevant agency to see the records can get the actual case numbers by writing to me.

Preservation and Organization

The first tasks were to preserve these records from further deterioration, and to organize and inventory them. In some cases the discovery of the records was in itself a prod toward their preservation, since agency staff members were thereby appraised of the historic value of their records. One agency, the Judge Baker Guidance Center, had already arranged the transfer of the older records to the Harvard Medical School Library; for the MSPCC and the BCSA, placement of the older records, including photographs and glass slides, in the University of Massachusetts Boston Archives was arranged. Records of these child-welfare agencies were inventoried and reorganized.

Coding and Analysis

From these three agencies, we considered only cases from the Boston metropolitan area, which we defined as Suffolk and Middlesex counties. This area includes Cambridge and Somerville as well as some smaller towns and more rural areas. Case records were sampled from every tenth year between 1880 and 1960, and for four additional years chosen because they marked times of economic and social stress: depression years 1893 and 1934, and war years 1917 and 1944. From each sample year, case numbers were chosen with the use of a random number table. Approximately 1,500 cases were read and 502 were coded, from which 2,274 incidents of family violence were analyzed. Every case was coded for information pertaining to each important individual, to the family history, to the economic and social situation of the family, to agency action in relation to the problem. Over six hundred variables were coded for each case, although many were not useful for statistical analyses because the information was so uneven in quantity and reliability. We used the SPSS program to analyze the data.

Five researchers worked on coding these records, their work tested by having all five code the same case and comparing the results. During the research, frequent meetings helped us compare our judgments and standardize coding decisions.

In addition to the computer coding, notes and summaries were prepared for approximately half the cases. These were chosen not because they were representative but because they had rich detail and/or because the problems and their handling by agencies were particularly interesting.

After the random sample was completed, I wanted to learn more about some of the types of family violence least common in these case records—i.e., precisely those that were unrepresentative—particularly wife-beating and sexual abuse of children. I looked for additional cases of these types and included them in discussions of those particular problems. These non-random cases were not included, of course, in any of the statements about general patterns. In the footnotes these non-random cases are indicated with an "A" following the case code number.

The size and quality of the case records varied greatly. In the 1880, 1890, 1893, and 1900 samples, they were handwritten entries in ledger books, ranging from a sentence or a few short phrases to several pages. Entries from this period contained little information. The charity organization of Boston, Associated Charities, kept a central name index, and late in the nineteenth century the MSPCC began a card file of client names. These two indices helped agencies prevent duplication of records and connect individuals who were related. Starting with the sample year 1910, case records were typed and placed in folders so that new material could be added. Simultaneously, professional casework standards began to influence the agencies and basic social information was collected more systematically. A standard "face sheet" was developed which collected certain basic information for each case. These were not, however, filled out consistently: caseworkers were often overloaded, clients were close-mouthed, translators were not available. Case records also varied between agencies. Judge Baker records consisted primarily of psychiatric caseworkers' interpretations and notes from case conferences, but contained little social information. BCSA and MSPCC records did not contain case conference notes but did contain summaries of records from other agencies.

On the whole, I consider the qualitative evidence in this book more reliable than the quantitative. There are several reasons for this. One is that different cases contain different types of information, making comparison misleading; another is that covering a long period of time meant choosing only a few cases from each year. Reporting only those patterns which occurred in numerous enough cases to make a quantitative statement reliable would mean losing the most interesting information. For example, although 502 cases were coded, the number of cases from each agency from each sample year was often less than twenty, less than ten for six agency yearly samples, not enough to make a numerical statement useful. Moreover, the lack of mention of a particular factor in a case record does not mean the absence of that factor. The quantitative information collected was often less interesting and less revealing that the qualitative. To make different factors in different cases comparable, the variables had to be extremely simplified. In the most basic of categories, for example, child abuse, are included as many different ways of attacking children as there are parents. Some factors could not be simplified enough to form categories large enough for quantitative analysis.

In reporting quantitative findings, I have eliminated the results of significance tests. The SPSS program frequently calculated acceptable, even good significance rates, where I knew the data were so few and so uneven that reporting such rates would be misleading.

In relying on qualitative evidence, and sacrificing often the possibility of specifying how many cases were similar, I am acting in the belief that what is revealing of deeper patterns is more significant than what is representative. For similar reasons, I have chosen often to tell whole case stories, instead of citing specific aspects of cases. As I have argued in the Introduction, family violence is always constructed as a social problem by a process in which the values of those doing the defining interact with family behaviors; in this process I am similar to the social workers I wrote about in redefining a social problem. There is no "objective" family violence.

APPENDIX B
CLIENT CHARACTERISTICS
Further Detail on Methods
and Data Used in Chapter 1

Poverty

Because exact figures about earnings and expenditures were not available, five imprecise categories for standard of living were established: deprivation, i.e., lacking necessities for health, e.g., shoes, fuel, food; subsistence, maintaining life and health at a minimal standard and with chronic insecurity and uncertainty; competence, living without chronic insecurity or uncertainty about ability to keep family members adequately housed, warmed, clothed, and fed, and with at least some items defined as non-necessary, e.g., a watch; middle-class, those with standards, aspirations, or employment that set them above manual laborers; prosperous, those who could afford substantial luxuries.

9. HOUSEHOLD ECONOMIC STATUS, BY YEAR[1]

	YEAR			
	1880–1909	1910–29	1930–43	1944–60
Deprivation	41.6%	18.6%	16.8%	15.9%
Subsistence	44.2	46.6	43.9	56.1
Competence	11.7	27.1	34.8	22.4
Middle class	2.6	5.9	3.2	3.7
Prosperous	0	1.7	1.3	1.9

Welfare

The growth in the importance of welfare over the period of this study can be seen below:[2]

10. CLIENTS' WELFARE HISTORY, BY YEAR

	YEAR		
	1910–29	1930–43	1944–60
Never received welfare	35.2% (N = 32)	34.8% (N = 46)	25.8% (N = 24)
Chronically on welfare	31.9 (29)	32.6 (43)	41.9 (39)
Once received welfare	14.3 (13)	13.6 (18)	18.3 (17)
Agency helped client get welfare	18.7 (17)	18.9 (25)	14.0 (13)

(N = number of cases.)

Contributors to the Family Economy

The historical impact of welfare can be traced also through another question: Who was the main contributor to the clients' family economies? The answer, as illustrated below, includes a declining proportion of fathers *and* mothers, an unchanging small proportion of other relatives, and a tripled dependence on welfare.

11. MAIN CONTRIBUTORS TO THE CLIENTS' FAMILY ECONOMIES, BY YEAR

	YEAR		
	1910–29	*1930–43*	*1944–60*
Father	58.8% (N=67)	54.7% (N=82)	48.5% (N=50)
Mother	20.2 (23)	16.0 (24)	12.6 (13)
Relatives	12.3 (14)	14.0 (21)	12.6 (13)
Welfare	8.8 (10)	15.3 (23)	26.2 (27)

(N = number of cases.)

Even more striking evidence about the poverty of the clients emerged in examining secondary contributors to the family economy. In the period 1880 to 1909, as one might expect, the most common answer was children (in 40.5 percent of cases). Yet in the period 1944 to 1960, children were still the main secondary contributor in 31.3 percent of cases, a pattern found only among the very poor.

Transience

Forty-one percent of clients had lived at their present address less than two years; that proportion went up to 49 percent between 1910 and 1929, and down to 37 percent thereafter. Only 18 percent of clients had lived more than five years at their address, a figure relatively constant across the years.

Sociability

Looking for a way to measure the clients' experience of community, I formulated four levels of sociability—isolation, moderate relationships, amicable friendships, and intensely supportive social networks. These were impressionistic and fallible measures, and the evidence was thin, but the results are suggestive. Thirty-one percent were extremely isolated—that is, there was no evidence of any social relationships with other than household members—not even with siblings or grandparents. Only 30 percent were in the two most sociable categories. These findings fit the view of contemporary experts that social isolation contributes to family violence.[3]

Ethnicity and Migration Status

In the first half of this study, disproportionate numbers of clients were foreign-born; this ratio fell off in recent years.[4]

12. PROPORTION OF FOREIGN-BORN CLIENTS, BY YEAR

	YEAR		
	1890	1920	1950
Family violence clients	71	65.5	20
Boston population	35	32	16

The following table summarizes the representation of the main ethnic groups in this study. Among the groups with smaller representation in the records, mainly due to the small representation in the Boston area, were Syrians, Portuguese, Latin Americans, and Jewish, Catholic, and Orthodox Eastern Europeans.

13. REPRESENTATION OF ETHNIC GROUPS, BY YEAR

	YEAR			
	1890	1920	1950	All years
Italians	13.6% (N = 3)	29.6% (N = 27)	17.7% (N = 11)	14.9% (N = 126)
Irish	68.0 (15)	20.8 (19)	21.0 (13)	25.2 (213)
Canadians	18.1 (4)	3.3 (3)	3.2 (2)	10.7 (90)
Blacks	0	5.5 (5)	8.1 (5)	13.8 (65)
"Americans"	4.5 (1)	19.8 (18)	24.2 (15)	NA

(N = number of cases.)

In 1890, only 1.8 percent of the city's population was black, and no blacks appeared in our random sample of cases; by 1920, when blacks constituted 5.5 percent of our sample, they were only 2.2 percent of the population; but in 1950 they were overrepresented by a ratio of 8:5.[5]

Family and Household Size

Family-violence clients had smaller than average families and households in the first half of this study, larger in the second half. Neither difference, however, was significant enough to suggest any substantive influence on family violence.[6]

14. AVERAGE FAMILY AND HOUSEHOLD SIZE, BOSTON RESIDENTS AND AGENCY CLIENTS, BY YEAR

	YEAR			
	1880	*1910*	*1930*	*1950*
Boston census	5.0	4.8	3.43	3.63
Agency clients	4.0	4.56	5.0	5.66

NOTES

Explanatory Note:

Specific cases are referred to simply by a code number, such as #2065. These numbers are not the actual case numbers assigned by the agencies, but part of a coding system devised by the author. Case numbers followed by an A refer to cases which were not a part of the random sample but among those read in addition after the random sample was complete. (See Appendix A for more detail on research methods.) A few very early cases, dating from before the random sampling began in 1880 or before the agencies began systematic case numbering, are referred to by their actual number or date; these are always followed by reference to their location in the agency ledger book.

Most quotations from case records are verbatim. This means that even when the client is quoted, her or his words have been recorded by the caseworker so that one must assume some inaccuracy in the representation. I have changed these quotations occasionally in one respect: translating into English words the abbreviations used by caseworkers (e.g., "mo" for mother) when I thought they might be misunderstood. I did this in order to avoid burdening the quotations with brackets and *sics* so that they could be read fluently.

The following abbreviations are used to describe various other sources:

AC: Associated Charities

AR: Annual Report. Unless otherwise specified, these are published pamphlets.

BCSA: Boston Children's Service Association. Papers located at the BCSA office in Boston.

CAA: Children's Aid Association, now part of BCSA.

JBGC: Judge Baker Guidance Center. Case records located at the Countway Medical Library, Harvard University Medical School.

MSPCC Mss.: Papers of the MSPCC other than case records, located at the University of Massachusetts/Boston Library Archives and at MSPCC offices.

NCCC: National Conference of Charities and Corrections.

Pardon files: Commonwealth of Massachusetts, Executive Council, Pardon, Commutation and Parole Files, located in Commonwealth Archives, Boston.

Chapter 1

1. By a social problem I mean an issue that is of concern even to those who do not directly experience it, one which creates an experienced threat to the social order and is deemed to require collective action in response.

2. Various data are summarized in Mildred Daley Pagelow, *Family Violence* (New York: Praeger, 1984), chapter 2.

3. See W. Norton Grubb and Marvin Lazerson, *Broken Promises. How Americans Fail Their Children* (New York: Basic Books, 1982), e.g., p. 5, chapter 1, passim, for an insightful but incomplete analysis, lacking incorporation of the importance of gender to issues concerning children.

4. I have developed this argument in my article with Wini Breines, "The New Scholarship on Family Violence," *Signs* 8, 3 (Spring 1983), pp. 490–531.

5. A more detailed critique of contemporary family-violence scholarship can be found in Breines and Gordon. Examples of the psychological diagnosis can be found in the work of pediatricians and psychiatrists C. Henry Kempe, Brandt Steele, and Carl Pollack; articles by all three are in Ray Helfer and C. Henry Kempe, eds., *The Battered Child* (Chicago: University of Chicago Press, 1968). The leading sociological interpreters are Murray Straus and Richard Gelles, whose approach can be sampled in Suzanne K. Steinmetz and Murray A. Straus, eds., *Violence in the Family* (New York: Harper & Row, 1974); David Finkelhor et al., eds., *The Dark Side of Families* (Beverly Hills: Sage, 1983); and Murray A. Straus, Richard J. Gelles, and Suzanne K. Steinmetz, *Behind Closed Doors. Violence in the American Family* (Garden City, N.Y.: Anchor/Doubleday, 1980). For an example of the debate among service-providers, see American Humane Association, *Neglecting Parents—A Study of Psychosocial Characteristics*, pamphlet #37, n.d. but probably 1968.

6. A notable and excellent exception is *Defining Child Abuse*, by Rosina Becerra and Jeanne Giovannoni (New York: Free Press, 1979).

7. In the last several decades, child-protection experts have begun to use the phrase "non-accidental injury," abbreviated NAI, instead of child abuse. This oddly euphemistic definition arises from the fact that many injuries to children are in fact the result of child neglect, that is, of parental negligence, rather than of actual attack, and that experts make allegations of assault warily because they are hard to prove.

8. Recently several other categories of family violence have been added to the purview of such agencies: abuse of the elderly; sibling violence. As these did not appear as social problems until the last two decades, they did not appear as problems in my case records. This does not mean that they did not occur. It means only that they were visible to outsiders or experienced by participants not as *social* problems but as personal troubles.

9. The research used 1880 as a starting date because in the previous few years the relevant agencies were still in an organizational phase, including rapid shifts in patterns of work. By stopping in 1960, I limited myself to "closed" case records, thereby minimizing the violation of privacy involved in this research. See Appendix A regarding procedures used to protect the confidentiality of records.

10. The term "client" came into use only in the early twentieth century, as part of the professionalization of child-protection work. Technically, the agencies' clients were the children only. However, for the sake of simplicity and continuity, I refer to all members of client families as clients.

11. For a discussion of this discrimination today, see, for example, Robert L. Hampton and Eli H. Newberger, "Child Abuse Incidence and Reporting

by Hospitals, Significance of Severity, Class, and Race," in *American Journal of Public Health* 75, 1 (January 1985), pp. 56–60.

12. What follows is a summary for which the evidence and more detail can be found in Appendix B.

13. Frederick A. Bushee, *Ethnic Factors in the Population of Boston*, Publications of the American Economic Association, Vol. 4, May 1903 (New York: Macmillan), p. 113; Perry R. Duis, *The Saloon: Public Drinking in Chicago and Boston 1880–1920* (Urbana: University of Illinois Press, 1983), pp. 34, 73; Kate Holladay Claghorn, "The Italian under Economic Stress," reprinted in Lydio F. Tomasi, ed., *The Italian in America* (New York: Center for Migration Studies, 1972), p. 132; Hasia R. Diner, *Erin's Daughters in America. Irish Immigrant Women in the Nineteenth Century* (Baltimore: Johns Hopkins University Press, 1983), pp. 112–13, for example.

14. Diner, pp. 112–13

15. Diner, pp. 59–60; Zilpha D. Smith, *Deserted Wives and Deserting Husbands. A Study of 234 Families . . . of the Associated Charities of Boston* (Boston: Associated Charities, 1901), pp. 5–6; Bushee, pp. 33, 85, 113–14; Stephan Thernstrom, *The Other Bostonians* (Cambridge, Mass: Harvard University Press, 1973), p. 166.

16. Diner, passim.

17. Thernstrom, p. 136 and passim; Bushee, pp. 33, 40–45.

18. Bushee, p. 85.

19. Smith, p. 4.

20. Claghorn, *loc. cit.*

21. The total number of Canadians was probably underestimated in this study, because of the religious and ethnic similarity of many of them to what caseworkers would call "Americans." For example, in Bushee's famous study of the 1890s, Canadians were not considered as a separate group, neither in ethnicity nor in birthplace. Between 1860 and 1900 alone, approximately 600,000 French Canadians migrated to New England; the numbers of non-French Canadians, uncounted, may have been as high. Many were drawn to the Merrimack Valley textile mills, just north of Boston. On French Canadians, see Frances H. Early, "The French-Canadian Family Economy and Standard-of-Living in Lowell, Massachusetts, 1870," *Journal of Family History* 7, 2 (Summer 1982), pp. 180–99.

22. Thernstrom, pp. 210, 179–81.

23. A more detailed description of my methods of finding and interpreting data for this study is in Appendix A.

24. The history of the BCSA is complex, involving a series of mergers which ended with the uniting of at least ten private child-saving agencies into the BCSA in 1960. Appendix A depicts this history in more detail. To spare

the reader confusion, all case records of these agencies will be identified as BCSA cases; since they appear only as coded numbers, the reader would not be able to consult them directly in any case. The actual agency and case number can be obtained from the author if the researcher has the agency's permission to use the records.

25. As a result of these referrals, many of the cases sampled for this study contained records in two or more agencies, partly repetitive but also partly different.

26. #2085A.

27. #2781, 3560A, 6081, 6086, for just a few of many examples.

28. #2059A.

29. #3860.

30. #6087.

31. #3786.

32. #3559A.

33. #3041, report done for the MSPCC by the Boston Psychopathic Hospital in 1921.

34. For an excellent investigation of these client-caseworker misunderstandings, see John E. Mayer and Noel Timms, *The Client Speaks. Working Class Impressions of Casework* (New York: Atherton Press, 1970). On the responses of MSPCC clients at a later date, see Edith Varon, "The Client of a Protective Agency in the Context of the Community: A Field Study of the MSPCC," Ph.D. diss., Florence Heller Graduate School for Advanced Studies in Social Welfare, Brandeis University, 1961.

35. All names of clients used in this book are fictitious.

36. Eli Newberger and Richard Bourne, "The Medicalization and Legalization of Child Abuse," in *Critical Perspectives on Child Abuse*, eds. Bourne and Newberger (Lexington, Mass.: Lexington Books, 1979), pp. 139–56.

Chapter 2

1. On the "discovery" of child abuse, see Joyce Antler and Stephen Antler, "From Child Rescue to Family Protection: The Evolution of the Child Protective Movement in the United States," *Children and Youth Service Review* 1 (1979), pp. 177–204.

2. A revulsion against urban life was fundamental to the conception of all crime and violence in the nineteenth century. See Anthony M. Platt, *The Child Savers. The Invention of Delinquency*, 2nd ed. (Chicago: University of Chicago, 1977), pp. 36–43.

3. For an excellent discussion of these social control movements, see Paul Boyer, *Urban Masses and Moral Order in America, 1820–1920* (Cambridge, Mass.: Harvard University Press, 1978), p. 130.

4. On child protection in Europe, see George K. Behlmer, *Child Abuse and Moral Reform in England 1870–1908* (Stanford: Stanford University Press, 1982).

5. Robert Archey Woods, ed., *The City Wilderness. A Settlement Study by Residents & Associates of the South End House* (Boston: Houghton Mifflin, 1898), chapters 2 and 3; Robert A. Woods and Albert J. Kennedy, *The Zone of Emergence. Observations of the Lower Middle and Upper Working Class Communities of Boston, 1905–1914*, ed. Sam Bass Warner, Jr. (Cambridge, Mass.: Harvard University Press, 1962), Introduction; Nathan Huggins, *Protestants Against Poverty: Boston's Charities 1870–1900* (Westport, Conn.: Greenwood, 1971), p. 12.

6. Thernstrom, pp. 112–13.

7. An initial movement of the Wasp elite into the new South End never consolidated, perhaps because it was begun so late (1830s and 1840s) that immigrants were soon competitors for the territory. As the need for more middle-class housing grew, the filling in of Back Bay began in the late 1850s, and this area did become a more homogeneous Protestant neighborhood. See *A Picture of the South End* (Boston: South End Historical Society, 1968).

8. Boston Female Asylum, Board of Managers, Proceedings and Annual Reports, "Constitution and Rules of the Society," September 26, 1800; in Massachussetts State Library Manuscripts Collection.

9. Bowlby, *Child Care and the Growth of Love*, abridged and ed. Margaret Fry (London: Penguin, 1953), p. 136.

10. Lyman Cobb, *The Evil Tendencies of Corporal Punishment as a Means of Moral Discipline in Families and Schools* (New York: M. H. Newman, 1847); Mary Blake, *Twenty-six Hours a Day* (Boston: D. Lothrop, 1883); Mrs. C. A. Hopkinson, *Hints for the Nursery* (Boston: Little Brown, 1863); Herbert L. Costner, *Changing Folkways of Parenthood* (New York: Arno, 1980). Elizabeth Pleck calculated that six out of seven child-raising manuals published in England or America in the first half of the century favored limiting corporal punishment. See her *Domestic Tyranny. The Making of American Social Policy Against Family Violence from Colonial Times to the Present* (New York: Oxford, 1987), p. 34.

11. Despite the argument of Kathleen W. Jones in her "Sentiment and Science: The Late Nineteenth Century Pediatrician as Mother's Advisor," *Journal of Social History* 17, 1 (Fall 1983), pp. 79–96, about L. Emmett Holt, I found that doctors' child-raising manuals of the nineteenth century limited

themselves to advice on health, feeding, and perhaps toilet training and did not take on issues of discipline and punishment.

12. Blake; Hopkinson.

13. MSPCC AR 1885, p. 21; Myra C. Glenn, "The Naval Reform Campaign Against Flogging: A Case Study in Changing Attitudes Toward Corporal Punishment, 1830–1850," *American Quarterly* 35, 4 (Fall 1983), pp. 408–25; N. Ray Hiner, "Children's Rights, Corporal Punishment, and Child Abuse. Changing American Attitudes, 1870–1920," *Bulletin of the Menninger Clinic* 43, 3 (1979), references, pp. 246–48; Carl F. Kaestle, "Social Change, Discipline and the Common School in Early Nineteenth-Century America," *Journal of Interdisciplinary History* IX, 1 (Summer 1978), pp. 1–17.

14. On animal protection, see James Turner, *Reckoning with the Beast. Animals, Pain, and Humanity in the Victorian Mind* (Baltimore: Johns Hopkins University Press, 1980).

15. Arthur Mann, *Yankee Reformers in the Urban Age* (Cambridge, Mass.: Belknap Press of Harvard University Press, 1954), p. 213; Mary Margaret Huth, "Kate Gannett Wells: A Biographical Study of an Anti-Suffragist," typescript, M.A. thesis, University of Rochester, copy in Schlesinger Library, p. 213.

16. Kate Gannett Wells, "Women in Organizations," *Atlantic Monthly* XLVI, CCLXXV (September 1880), p. 360.

17. Wells, "Women on School Boards," *North American Review* DLXXXVI (September 1905), p. 428.

18. Historian John Cumbler has argued from the example of two smaller industrial cities in Massachusetts that upper-class women active in charity might actually subvert the class goals of their husbands, who provided the funds. The women in these projects broadened the goals of their charitable work, examined the actual conditions of their clients, reduced the victim-blaming, moralistic judgments of the poor, and lent their support to reform programs that were in some sense adversarial toward their husbands' factories. See Cumbler, "The Politics of Charity: Gender and Class in Late 19th Century Charity Policy," *Journal of Social History* 14, 1 (Fall 1980), pp. 99–111. No such separation of gender and class interests appeared in the MSPCC.

19. Tom Appleton, quoted in Mann, p. 208.

20. E.g., Phillips Brooks to R. E. Apthorp, MSPCC president, January 26, 1880: "If you think that I can serve the Consolidated Society by being one of its Vice-Presidents I will gladly serve. I ought not to be a Director for I have almost no time . . ." MSPCC Mss., Mt. Vernon Street.

21. See Otis to Apthorp, February 16, 1880, MSPCC Mss.

22. "Preliminary Report to the Social Agencies of Boston by the Special

Committee on Financing of Social Agencies of the Boston Chamber of Commerce," 1924. Pamphlet, author's possession.

23. 'AR 1882, pp. 33-34.

24. See top photos opposite p. 51.

25. For a study of similar attitudes in another charity, see Marion Hunt, "Women and Childsaving: St. Louis Children's Hospital 1879-1979," in *Bulletin, Missouri Historical Society* XXXVI, 2 (January 1980), pp. 65-79. For an example from among many MSPCC descriptions of their home, see AR 1900, pp. 8-9.

26. His style was so arrogant and crude that he antagonized many supporters he needed, including his own board of directors. For examples, see Loring Moody to Henrietta S. L. Wolcott, September 25, 1879, MSPCC Mss. Forced to resign, he started a rival organization, the Society for Lost, Stolen or Abused Children, which, unable to win support, dissolved by 1881.

27. AR 1881, p. 17.

28. E.g., #2997, 3103, 3410, from Vol. 11 of the MSPCC ledger books.

29. This figure includes only cases of known origin; since the cases of unexplained origin were likely to have been agent-originated, the proportion may well have been as high as 52 percent.

30. Handwritten address of Dixwell to MSPCC Directors, June 1878, MSPCC Archives.

31. Ledger book, Vol. 2, p. 72, December 29, 1878.

32. Ledger book, Vol. 2, p. 6, December 14, 1878.

33. Ledger book, Vol. 2, p. 5, December 14, 1878.

34. Ledger book, Vol. 2, no page number, December 20, 1878.

35. Ledger book, Vol. 2, p. 278, January 31, 1879.

36. This figure includes only cases for which the sources of complaint was known, still the minority of cases.

37. #0501A.

38. #0521.

39. MSPCC Mss., folder 3, August 14, 1879.

40. Bremner, "The Children with the Organ Man," *American Quarterly* 8, 3 (1956), p. 279. See also Humbert S. Nelli, "The Italian Padrone System in the United States," *Labor History* V (Spring 1964), pp. 153-67.

41. Catherine J. Ross, "Society's Children: The Case of Indigent Youngsters in New York City, 1875-1903." Ph.D. diss., Yale University, 1977, pp. 30-31.

42. See Joseph F. Kett, "Curing the Disease of Precocity," *American Journal of Sociology*, Vol. 84 Supplement, reprinted as *Turning Points, Historical and Sociological Essays on the Family*, eds. John Demos and Sarane Spence Boocock (Chicago: University of Chicago Press, 1978), pp. S183-84.

43. In fact, Brace remarked that the organ-grinders could not "be reproached with intoxication, prostitution, quarreling, stealing, etc.," as could the "other nationalities." See Charles Loring Brace, *The Dangerous Classes of New York and Twenty Years' Work Among Them* (New York: Wynkoop and Hallenbeck, 1872), p. 195.

44. AR 1881, p. 27.

45. Bremner, pp. 277–82.

46. Elbridge T. Gerry, president of the New York SPCC, letter to the *Boston Transcript*, dated December 15, 1881, clipping, n.d., in MSPCC clippings scrapbook.

47. AR 1881, p. 26.

48. AR 1893, pp. 10–11.

49. Letter from P. E. Apthorp, MSPCC director, in *Boston Transcript*, n.d., MSPCC clippings scrapbook.

50. Wells to Fay, January 27, 1882, MSPCC Mss., folder 25.

51. # 2977 and 2993, 1883.

52. Ledger book, Vol. 2, 1878, pp. 18, 214–25.

53. *Revised Manuals of Laws of Massachusetts Concerning Children*, MSPCC pamphlets, 1882 and 1890.

54. #2991, 1883 ledger book.

55. #1023, 1895 ledger book.

56. #1028, 1894 ledger book.

57. #2980, 1883 ledger book.

58. #3000, 1883 ledger book.

59. Eric H. Monkkonen, *Police in Urban America 1860–1920* (Cambridge, England: Cambridge University Press, 1981), pp. 109–28 and Appendix D, Table D2. Monkkonen, the only historian who has studied this police practice, assumed that the number of lost children was a constant, pp. 118–19. In fact, that hundreds of children (half under the age of three) and parents depended on the police to reunite them suggests substantial change in the conditions of children's play and supervision over village or small-town life.

60. E.g., in a few pages of MSPCC ledger book, Vol. 11, # 3013, 3015, 3019, 3031, 3048, 3064, 3065, 3067, 3068, 3080, 3099, 3104, 3126.

61. Behlmer, pp. 25ff. A similar campaign arose in Australia: see Judith Allen, "The State and Domestic Violence," typescript, MacQuarie University, n.d., 1980s.

62. In one case of a twenty-one-month-old boy, the doctor who signed his death certificate stated, "I suppose there is no remedy. Mrs. M. . . . [the boarding mother] has done nearly as well as she knew how with this child," although the boy had been given only water with a bit of condensed milk in it for nourishment. *New York Times*, July 28, 1874, p. 8.

63. *New York Times*, September 24, 1873, p. 8 and October 7, 1873, p. 8.

64. Ibid., July 2, 1876, p. 12, for example; see Frank Fay's testimony at International Congress of Charities, in *The Care of Dependent, Neglected and Wayward Children*, eds. Spencer and Birtwell (Baltimore: Johns Hopkins University Press, 1894), p. 132.

65. *Boston Globe*, January 10, 1890, p. 6; evening edition, p. 1; January 11, p. 5.

66. Mary Boyle O'Reilly, "The Daughters of Herod. A Plea for Child-saving Legislation in New Hampshire," *New England Magazine* XLIII (1910), 2-3, pp. 137-48 and 277-90.

67. A good general review of both types of baby farming was offered by Benjamin Waugh, "Baby Farming," *Contemporary Review* (London), Vol. 57 (May 1890), pp. 700-14; see also Frances Low, "A Remedy for Baby-farming," *Fortnightly Review* (London), Vol. 69 (New Series bound volume 63) (1898), pp. 280-86; for examples, see *New York Times* July 28, 1874, p. 8; July 22, 1880, p. 5; July 2, 1876, p. 12.

68. *New York Times*, July 17, July 19, and July 20, 1905.

69. *New York Times*, February 7, 1877, p. 8.

70. *New York Times*, August 2, 1874, p. 8.

71. Rosalind Pollack Petchesky, *Abortion and Woman's Choice. The State, Sexuality, and Reproductive Freedom* (New York: Longman, 1984), pp. 73-78; James Mohr, *Abortion in America* (New York: Oxford University Press, 1978), p. 86; Linda Gordon, *Woman's Body, Woman's Right: A Social History of Birth Control in America* (New York: Viking Penguin, 1976), pp. 57-60.

72. It may be that baby farming was replacing infanticide and abandonment done by the mother herself. Several factors could have accounted for this: fear of detection (in some press reports the baby farmers' main service seemed to be their ability to get rid of the babies' bodies discreetly), or an increased sentimental or moralistic sensibility about doing the deed oneself, and a preference for the disguised and hypocritical contract with the baby farmer. If so, the spread of baby farming might reflect, in a grotesque way, a greater tenderness toward infancy.

73. Viviana A. Zelizer, *Pricing the Priceless Child. The Changing Social Value of Children* (New York: Basic Books, 1985), p. 118.

74. See the MSPCC AR, 1891. Such accusations had been common in Europe for several decades. See Behlmer, p. 121; Zelizer, pp. 118-20; M. Loane, *Neighbors and Friends* (London, 1910), pp. 281-82.

75. Zelizer, p. 116.

76. Ibid., p. 129.

77. Ibid., chapter 5.

78. AR 1907, pp. 20–21.

79. For examples, see ARs 1893, pp. 13–14; 1894, p. 10; 1914, p. 33; 1916, p. 28.

80. Duis, *The Saloon*, pp. 11–12, 97–99. There was local prohibition in Massachusetts until 1875. Then sumptuary legislation was revived, "dramshop acts," which made sellers of liquor responsible for the criminal actions of forbidden customers (e.g., children and drunks).

81. #3041 and 6087.

82. Ledger book, Vol. 12, January 22, 1879 ff.

83. #2975, 1883 ledger book.

84. #3053, 1883 ledger book.

85. AR 1902, p. 13; the "society" refers to the MSPCC.

86. E.g., 2051.

87. This proportion of "no action" cases is the more striking when one remembers (a) that cases found to be without evidence have already been excluded from the sample and (b) that these are data from the most litigious, punitive period of MSPCC activity, before its early twentieth-century emphasis on casework and prevention.

88. E.g., #2978, 1883.

89. #2976, 1883.

90. Ledger book, Vol. 11, p. 47, March 17, 1883.

91. AR 1883, p. 16.

92. #3018, 1883 ledger book.

93. # 3027, 3079, 3082, in a few days of the 1883 ledger book.

94. #2994, 1883 ledger book.

95. MSPCC Mss., folder 3, dated June 15, 1889.

96. MSPCC Mss., folder 3, agreement of January 14, 1885, with the Shakers of Grafton County, New Hampshire.

97. Agreement dated January 11, 1882, signed by mother with an X and by MSPCC Temporary Home Matron, MSPCC Mss., folder 3.

98. Ledger book, Vol. 2, 1879, p. 193. In Dixwell's short period of leadership, his high-handedness seemed headed to create resistance from judges. E.g., in the course of a woman's suit against her husband for cruel and abusive treatment and non-support, the husband went to her home, took their four-year-old son, and brought him to the MSPCC. Here he arranged to pay $3 per week for the child's support and got an agreement from the society that the mother should not be allowed to see the child! As the *Boston Herald* reported it, "Dr. Dixwell . . . gave as a reason . . . that . . . they could not allow 'free and promiscuous visitation' . . . He also stated that the father alleged that the mother was not a proper person to have charge of the child; that she was a loose character, and that the actions of the child when admitted to the institution

corroborated that assertion. . . . Judge Lord told Dr. Dixwell that . . . pending the libel, both parties were to be presumed to be in the right . . . Judge Lord told the doctor that he had made use of the expression 'legal guardian' three times, and that he didn't want him to repeat it again, as the court knew quite as much about that matter as he did." August 22, 1879, *Boston Herald* clipping in MSPCC clippings scrapbook. But in the 1880s and 1890s, General Agent Fay's diplomatic style brought great legal influence to the agency.

99. Acts of 1882, chap. 270, *Revised Manual of Laws of Massachusetts Concerning Children* (Boston: MSPCC, 1882), p. 24; Acts of 1889, chap. 309, *Amended Manual of Laws of Massachusetts Concerning Children* (Boston: MSPCC, 1890), pp. 19–20.

100. Acts of 1887, chap. 446, in *Amended Manual*, 1890, p. 34.

101. Acts of 1884, chap. 99, in Ibid., p. 26.

102. Acts of 1886, chap. 72, in Ibid., p. 27.

103. Acts of 1884, chap. 78, in Ibid., p. 30.

104. Acts of 1889, chap. 229; Acts of 1887, chap. 422; in Ibid., pp. 33–34.

105. Acts of 1888, chap. 391; Acts of 1886, chaps. 305 and 1329; in Ibid., pp. 39–43.

106. Acts of 1889, chaps. 249, 422, 464; Acts of 1890, chaps. 384 & 309; in Ibid., pp. 49–52 and 56–60.

107. AR 1881, p. 18.

108. Letter by Lothrop, February 10, 1913, in #2059A.

109. AR 1881, p. 20.

110. AR 1884, p. 12.

111. AR 1885, pp. 12–13.

112. For an explicit expression of this double identity, see James R. Garfield, "A Program of Action for a Children's Protective Society," *Proceedings*, National Conference of Charities and Corrections, 1912, p. 33.

113. On the notion of the state as including private agencies, see Tove Stang Dahl, "State Intervention and Social Control in Nineteenth-Century Europe," *Contemporary Crises* 1, 2 (April 1977), p. 170.

114. Edith Varon, "The Client of a Protective Agency in the Context of the Community: A Field Study of the MSPCC," Brandeis University Ph.D. dissertation, p. 88.

115. Robert H. Bremner, ed., *Children and Youth in America* (Cambridge, Mass.: Harvard University Press, 1971), Vol. II, p. 190; Gerry, "The Relation of Societies for the Prevention of Cruelty to Children to Child-saving Work," *Proceedings*, 1882 National Conference of Charities and Corrections, Madison, 1883, p. 129.

116. AR 1881, pp. 5, 9.

117. MSPCC Mss.

118. On the romanticization of the family as a result of the decline of the material cohesion of the family, see Ilene Philipson, "Child Rearing Literature and Capitalist Industrialization," *Berkeley Journal of Sociology* XXVI (1981), pp. 57–74.

119. For a fuller argument on this point, see my article "Family Violence, Feminism, and Social Control," in *Feminist Studies* 12, 3 (Fall 1986), pp. 453–78.

Chapter 3

1. "Down the Memory Lane," a typescript reminiscence by MSPCC clerk Maggie B. Blake, 1947, pp. 10–13, MSPCC Mss.

2. For a similar judgment, see Lee E. Teitelbaum and Leslie J. Harris, "Some Historical Perspectives on Government Regulation of Children and Parents," p. 28, in *Beyond Control. Status Offenders in the Juvenile Court*, eds. Lee E. Teitelbaum and Aidan R. Gough (Cambridge, Mass.: Ballinger, 1977).

3. Huggins, pp. 59–60.

4. Being a statewide organization, in smaller Massachusetts towns the MSPCC did the AC's work.

5. Boston's AC, for example, campaigned for vaccinations, kindergartens, better police, and other public reforms, and for the enforcement of tenement codes. "Laws Applying to Tenements in the City of Boston," pamphlet No. 51, Associated Charities of Boston, 1889, Schlesinger Library.

6. For example, in its First Annual Report, Boston AC specified as its goals:

I. To aid every private person to give alms only to worthy poor, or rather to give with knowledge.

II. To lessen the labors of relieving agencies, by giving to each the knowledge of the others.

III. To stop imposture so that the occupation of living on alms may cease. Registration notifies every lazy tramp to quit Boston or go to work.

IV. The main object is to make sure that relief is adapted to real needs. This will lessen relief for the unworthy. But for the really worthy and most suffering poor it should make relief more full and prompt and tender.

7. Amos Griswold Warner, Stuart Alfred Queen, and Ernest Bouldin

Harper, *American Charities and Social Work*, 4th ed. (New York: Thomas Y Crowell, 1930), pp. 37 and 538.

8. The Denison House papers, in the Schlesinger Library, relating to Boston's leading settlement, are noticeable for their lack of reference to the MSPCC.

9. ARs 1888, p. 10; 1889, p. 8; 1900, p. 5, for examples.

10. There had been a virtual coup in the MSPCC, as General Agent Charles K. Morton was fired due to his "lack of sympathy" with the new reformist currents in social work thought.

11. AR 1906, pp. 4–7.

12. William J. Shultz, *The Humane Movement in the United States 1910–1922* (New York: Columbia University Studies in History, Economics, and Public Law CXIII, 1, No. 252, 1924), chapters X & XI.

13. AR 1914, p. 24.

14. AR 1908, p. 10.

15. AR 1913, p. 20.

16. As Carstens's stenographer recalled, "In Mr. Carstens' mind dwelt the fact that every child handled by our Society . . . should be a subject of record. . . . That at no time could it ever be said that the Mass. S.P.C.C. took away a human being and neglected to record the place to which it took him." Carstens had to begin virtually from scratch an adequate filing system, having inherited from the previous regime only "a card filing box which was purchased by some ladies. . . ." Blake, pp. 13–14.

17. AR 1928, p. 16.

18. In 1946 there was still only one caseworker with professional training. AR 1956, p. 1. This is because after the Progressive era, for several decades the MSPCC, and child-protection agencies in general, fell behind other sectors of social work in their degree of professionalization.

19. "Outline of Plan for Training New Agents," typescript in MSPCC Mss., n.d., date attributed by the author from the context as 1929–31.

20. Quoted in Emma Octavia Lundberg, *Unto the Least of These. Social Services for Children* (New York: D. Appleton-Century Crofts, 1947), pp. 249–50.

21. Lundberg, esp. chapters V, IX, X; Clarke A. Chambers, "Women in the Creation of the Profession of Social Work," *Social Service Review* 60, 1 (March 1986), pp. 1–33; Lela Costin, *Two Sisters for Social Justice. A Biography of Grace and Edith Abbott* (Urbana: University of Illinois Press, 1983); Dorothy E. Bradbury, *Five Decades of Action for Children: A History of the Children's Bureau* (Washington, D.C.: Department of HEW, Social Security Administration, Children's Bureau, USGPO, 1962).

22. Blake, pp. 10–13.

23. Ibid., pp. 67–71.

24. This study focuses only on Boston.

25. AR 1911, pp. 45–46; MSPCC clippings scrapbook, 1908–12, passim.

26. Blake, *loc. cit.*

27. Ibid.

28. He had been a "Friendly Visitor" for the Children's Aid Society and, in 1895, secretary of a conference of child-helping societies in Boston. As a judge he took an unusual degree of responsibility for children, often personally visiting them if they were placed in institutions, and conducting regular conferences with probation officers. See Roy M. Cushman, "Harvey Humphrey Baker, Man and Judge," in Judge Baker Foundation, *Harvey Humphrey Baker, Upbuilder of the Juvenile Court* (Boston, n.d.), pp. 1–10.

29. Ellen Ryerson, *The Best-Laid Plans. America's Juvenile Court Experiment* (New York: Hill and Wang, 1978), p. 88.

30. William Healy and Augusta F. Bronner, "The Work of the Judge Baker Foundation," in Cushman, p. 123, emphasis in original.

31. The Judge Baker clinicians did not approach their work with sensitivity to family violence: they did not seek it out in interviews with clients, and they were primarily interested in intrapsychic, not interpersonal, conflict. Nevertheless, because so many of their patients were delinquents, a high proportion of their case records contained evidence of family violence.

32. This and the following list from MSPCC Mss., Early Correspondence folder.

33. A change since the previous decade cannot be identified with certainty: neglect cases increased between 1880 and 1890 only from 45.3 percent to 47.4 percent.

34. E.g., AR 1898, p. 12.

35. AR 1911, p. 16. In addition to Carstens's active work in various child welfare programs and committees, he repeatedly called for community responsibility and greater state expenditures on child welfare, e.g., in AR 1915, p. 31.

36. AR 1910, p. 13.

37. AR 1907, p. 17.

38. AR 1909, p. 31.

39. In this regard I disagree with Paul Boyer's implication of a lessening of the moral/social control orientation in social work. A look at agency practice casts doubt not only on the moralist-environmentalist distinction, but also on the distinction Boyer also draws between negative and positive environmentalism, that is, between coercive attempts to mold behavior and the use of

positive inducements. See Boyer, pp. 233–74. Michael Katz also noticed the inappropriateness of these distinctions, to child-saving at least, in his *Poverty and Policy in American History* (New York: Academic Press, 1983), p. 193.

40. From 1914 on, when the MSPCC began tabulating and ranking causes of child mistreatment, it consistently gave high marks to "separation of parents." There were no earlier tabulations, so we cannot compare earlier diagnostic analyses numerically, but in general in the nineteenth century marital separation was viewed with greater resignation as an attribute of lower-class life.

41. AR 1913, p. 18.

42. AR 1914, p. 31; see also NCCC *Proceedings* XLI (1915), p. 168.

43. W. I. Thomas and Florian Znaniecki, *The Polish Peasant in Europe and America* (Chicago: University of Chicago Press, 1918); Thomas, *The Unadjusted Girl* (Boston: Little Brown, 1923).

44. MSPCC Hampshire District, ARs, 1913–21, passim; Carstens, "New Methods in Rural Work for Children," NCCC *Proceedings*, 1914, pp. 160–71.

45. AR 1919; Elizabeth Ewen, *Immigrant Women in the Land of Dollars. Life and Culture on the Lower East Side, 1890–1925* (New York: Monthly Review Press, 1985), chapter 12.

46. See my *Woman's Body, Woman's Right: A Social History of Birth Control in America* (New York: Viking Penguin, 1976), chapter 6, on environmentalist hereditarian thought.

47. ARs 1910 ff, passim; case records, 1910 ff, passim. Massachusetts was in the vanguard of the study and training of mental defectives. See Martin W. Barr, MD, *Mental Defectives, Their History, Treatment and Training* (Philadelphia: P. Blakiston's Son & Co., 1904), pp. 63–64. The agencies in this study were slow to adopt more refined calibrations of mental deficiency, and as late as the 1940s, even in the "scientific" Judge Baker clinic, clients were labeled with untested categories, such as "low mentality," "low-grade individual," "feeble-minded," "ignorant type."

48. AR 1915, p. 27.

49. AR 1910, p. 10.

50. NCCC *Proceedings*, 1915, p. 95; AR 1920, p. 28; "The Development of Social Work for Child Protection," in *Annals of the American Academy of Political and Social Science* XCVII, 187 (November 1921), pp. 139–42.

51. AR 1922, p. 20; see the next chapter for a discussion of the implications of the exemption of adults from the state's welfare responsibility.

52. AR 1914, pp. 27–31.

53. AR 1914, p. 28.

Chapter 4

1. The definition of neglect will be discussed further in the next chapter.

2. A good summary of such expectations of family life, with many references, can be found in Lee Teitelbaum's "Family History and Family Law," University of Wisconsin–Madison Institute for Legal Studies Working Papers, Series 1, #1.

3. Between 1880 and 1910, 19 percent; in 1930, 19.8 percent; and between 1940 and 1960, 21.2 percent. These figures are census averages. Figures are not available for other years. The census changed its category to "household" instead of "family" in 1950. These figures are probably underestimates because many married women were single heads of household for substantial but nevertheless unrecorded periods of time. For example, in our case records, 15 percent of individuals were classified as "married and living together off and on," but not counted as single household heads.

4. #2503.

5. #3041.

6. These figures come from all three agencies studied. Fractional figures result from apportioning cases in which the single mothers fell into more than one category.

TABLE 15. SINGLE MOTHERS IN CHILD-NEGLECT CASES

	1880–1930		1934–60	
Never married	7.8%	(N = 2.5)	9.2%	(N = 6)
Widowed	35.9	(11.5)	7.7	(5)
Divorced	7.8	(2.5)	13.8	(9)
Deserted	10.9	(3.5)	6.2	(4)
Separated	37.5	(12)	63.1	(41)

(N *refers to number of cases.*)

7. The figures given here refer to cases in which social workers categorized the women clients as deserted. Although the proportion of desertion in these family-violence records was not apparently higher than that in a comparable population of the poor—an estimated 9.33 percent of families asking for relief contained deserted wives in the 1890s in Boston, for example (see Smith, *Deserted Wives and Deserting Husbands*, p. 3)—desertion was a causal factor in 16 percent of all family violence and 25 percent of all child-neglect incidents.

8. #2042, 2053, 3041, for examples.

9. There was no legal recognition of common-law marriage in Massachusetts.

10. It is also possible that in the more recent decades single fathers gained more impunity from the intervention of child-protection agencies, and less often appeared in the case records. See chapter 5 for more on this question.

11. Precisely 25.4 percent. The slight difference between this figure and the 28 percent reported in my "Single Mothers and Child Neglect," *American Quarterly* 37, 2 (Summer 1985), p. 178, results from the fact that the article used figures only from the MSPCC; this figure is from all three agencies studied. From 1880 through 1934, the average was 23 percent; after 1940, 30 percent.

12. The overrepresentation of single mothers was not confined to immigrants. The proportion of foreign-born women who headed households was larger than the overall average—12 percent of foreign-born women headed households between 1880 and 1910, as compared to 8 percent of all Boston women—but not equal to the proportion in the case records. Similarly, after 1940, while black households were more likely to be female-headed (29 percent), the nonwhite population of Boston was relatively small and excluding it would not substantially reduce the proportion of female household heads. I am indebted to Leslie Reagan for some of these computations.

13. There were many cases containing both abuse and neglect; these were counted in both categories.

14. Many cases included several types of violence. Thus:

TABLE 16. TYPES OF FAMILY VIOLENCE AFFECTING SINGLE MOTHERS, BEFORE AND AFTER 1934

	PERCENTAGE OF SINGLE-MOTHER CASES INCLUDING:			
YEAR	MOTHER AS ASSAILANT			MOTHER AS VICTIM
	Neglect	*Abuse*	*Sexual Abuse*	*Wife-Beating*
1880–1930	84.3	15.6	21.9	18.8
1934–1960	83.0	50.7	24.6	60.0

15. This diagnosis was applied 68.9 percent of the time to women, 31.1 percent to men. The figures in this paragraph pertain only to the years 1880 to 1920; after that, caseworkers became more circumspect in their written labeling and their attitudes were thus impossible to quantify.

16. 43.9 percent women, 56.1 percent men.

17. For a spelling out of this double standard, see Anna Ely Moorehouse, "The Neglected Children of Widowers," in *Children in Need of Special Care. Studies Based on Two Thousand Case Records of Social Agencies,* eds. Lucile Eaves and associates (Boston, 1923), p. 55; or consider Mary Richmond's comment, "The danger of family disintegration is much greater where the mother, rather than the father, is the weak member," in her *The Long View: Papers and Addresses by Mary E. Richmond,* ed. Joanna Colcord (New York: Russell Sage Foundation, 1930), pp. 450–51.

18. See chapter 5.

19. 77 percent mothers and 23 percent fathers.

20. Police were drawn into 76.6 percent of all cases and into 87.4 percent of single-mother cases.

21. Afterward the agencies stopped ranking the severity of cases, so a controlled comparison was not possible.

22. I can suggest two hypotheses to explain why single mothers, despite their greater poverty, were more committed to keeping their children at all times: (1) single women gained in social status and self-respect from having children more than women in couples did; (2) single women knew that they were more likely to lose custody of their children permanently if they gave them up even temporarily.

23. The legal procedure in neglect cases was to have the child adjudged neglected and given over into the custody of an agency, or returned to the parents with a continuance under the supervision of an agency. Parents were not convicted or sentenced for child neglect; their punishment was *de facto*, the loss of the child. Parents prosecuted for drunkenness or non-support did not necessarily or even usually lose their children.

24. There are not enough cases to support this statistically.

25. Pardon files, Box 16, #516.

26. See Appendix B for explanation of the economic categories used in this study.

27. See Carol Brown, "Mothers, Fathers, and Children: From Private to Public Patriarchy," in *Women and Revolution*, ed. Lydia Sargent (Boston: South End Press, 1981), pp. 242–47.

28. See, for example, Mimi Abramovitz, "The Family Ethic: The Female Pauper and Public Aid, Pre-1900," *Social Service Review* (March 1985), pp. 121–35. For an example from another locale, see Elizabeth Gaspar Brown, "Poor Relief in a Wisconsin County, 1846–1866: Administration and Recipients," *American Journal of Legal History* 20 (April 1976), pp. 79–117.

29. Carroll D. Wright, *The Working Girls of Boston* (Boston: Wright and Potter Publishing, 1889), p. 81 and passim.

30. Mary E. Richmond and Fred S. Hall, *A Study of Nine Hundred and Eighty-five Widows Known to Certain Charity Organization Societies in 1910* (New York: Russell Sage Foundation, 1913), p. 22; Irene O. Andrews, *The Relation of Irregular Employment to the Living Wage for Women* (New York: New York State Factory Investigating Commission, 1915); Emily C. Brown, *Industrial Home Work* (Washington, D.C.: U.S. Women's Bureau Bulletin #79, 1930); Louise C. Odencrantz, *Italian Women in Industry* (New York: Russell Sage Foundation, 1919); Mary Van Kleeck, *Artificial Flower Makers* (New York: Survey Associates, 1913).

31. Helen Glenn Tyson, "The Fatherless Family," in Frank D. Watson,

ed., *Social Work with Families. Social Case Treatment,* Vol. LXXVII and Supplement of *Annals,* American Academy of Political and Social Science (Philadelphia), May 1918, p. 85.

32. Included here are allegations made by MSPCC workers, relatives, or neighbors. One should not assume, however, that these were boarders who became lovers, thereby proving the moral dangers of taking boarders. They may as well have been lovers, or common-law husbands, whom the women were trying to disguise to social workers as boarders.

33. That is, they sold liquor not only by the bottle by also by the drink.

34. In one 1917 case two rooms of a four-room tenement were sublet to a peddler who stored his fruits and vegetables there. Yet the two children were malnourished.

35. #0814A.

36. Richmond and Hall, chapter X.

37. E.g., #2001, 2500, 3302. See the excellent description of the worker-client relationship producing dishonesty in Jane Addams's *Democracy and Social Ethics* (New York: Macmillan, 1902), chapter II.

38. In fact, as historian Michael Grossberg has shown, the maternal custody victories actually delegated power to decide children's guardianship to the state, which was to decide the child's best interests. See Michael Grossberg, *Governing the Hearth. Law and the Family in Nineteenth-Century America* (Chapel Hill: University of North Carolina Press, 1985).

39. Gordon, "Family Violence, Feminism, and Social Control"; Eileen Boris and Peter Bardaglio, "The Transformation of Patriarchy: The Historic Role of the State," in *Families, Politics, and Public Policy,* ed. Irene Diamond (New York: Longman, 1983), pp. 70–93; Carol Brown; Sylvia Law, "Women, Work, Welfare, and the Preservation of Patriarchy," *University of Pennsylvania Law Review* 131 (May 1983), pp. 1250–61; Grossberg.

40. MSPCC AR 1908, p. 17; Mary Conyngton, *How to Help. A Manual of Practical Charity* (New York: Macmillan, 1906), pp. 150–51; Helen Foss, "The Genus Deserter: His Singularities and Their Social Consequences—A Study of Local Fact and Interstate Remedies," *Charities* X (May 2, 1903), pp. 456–60; Charles Zunsser, "Family Desertion (Report on a Study of 423 Cases)," in *Annals, American Academy of Political and Social Science* CXLV, 234 (September 1929), pp. 98–104.

41. Smith, *Deserted Wives and Deserting Husbands,* pp. 9–13.

42. Richmond, *The Long View,* p. 80; this essay orig. 1897.

43. Eliot, "Deserted Wives," *Charities Review* X (October 1900), p. 347.

44. The policy is explained in AR 1894; examples of actual agreements between the Society and fathers are in MSPCC Mss., Early Correspondence, e.g., agreement with Jeremiah Doherty, November 25, 1892, folder 27.

45. ARs 1894, 1908, 1911; State Rep. William T. Forbes to Theodore A. Lothrop, General Secretary of MSPCC, letter of August 12, 1930, MSPCC Mss.

46. #3041.

47. #0305, 0314A, 1080.

48. #2042, 2053, 3041, for example.

49. #2565.

50. #2042.

51. #3361.

52. #0501, 0524, 0815A.

53. A good view of this contradictory impulse is in *The First Massachusetts Conference of Charities*, 1903, pamphlet, reprinted from *Charities* (November 28, 1903), pp. 8–11, 23–31; see also MSPCC AR 1892.

54. This change in the manner of dealing with illegitimacy created a differential treatment for the poor, since prosperous girls who got "in trouble" continued to be moved away during the later stages of pregnancy, to deliver their babies in private homes, to surrender the babies and return to normal life without damage to their futures. See Joan Jacobs Brumberg, " 'Ruined' Girls: Changing Community Responses to Illegitimacy in Upstate New York, 1890–1920," *Journal of Social History* 18, 2 (Winter 1985), pp. 247–72.

55. Boston Conference on Illegitimacy, untitled article, *Survey* 30 (September 13, 1913), pp. 707–8; Anna T. Wilson, "Foundlings and Illegitimate Children," in International Congress of Charities, Corrections and Philanthropy, *The Care of Dependent, Neglected and Wayward Children*, eds. Anna Garlin Spencer and Charles Wesley Birtwell (Baltimore: Johns Hopkins University Press, 1894), pp. 57–68; *First Massachusetts State Conference of Charities*, p. 11.

56. Alberta S. B. Guibord and Ida R. Parker, *What Becomes of the Unmarried Mother? A Study of 82 Cases* (Boston, 1922), p. 37, for example.

57. Ida R. Parker, *A Follow-up Study of 550 Illegitimacy Applications* (Boston: Research Bureau on Social Case Work, 1924). Of course this low figure reflects the fact that unmarried mothers who had supportive relatives were less likely to need agency help and would not appear in the records.

58. The peak number of babies were with grandparents and illegitimate mothers at age nine months. Emma O. Lundberg and Katharine F. Lenroot, *Illegitimacy as a Child-Welfare Problem*, Report of the U.S. Department of Labor, Children's Bureau (Washington, D.C.: GPO, 1920), II, p. 144.

59. Wilson, "Foundlings and Illegitimate Children"; Tilley, in *First Massachusetts Conference*, p. 9; George L. Jones, "How Does Our Treatment of the Unmarried Mother with the Second Child Differ from Our Treatment of

the Unmarried Mother with Her First Child?" NCCC *Proceedings*, 1919, pp. 81–85.

60. Lynn Y. Weiner, *From Working Girl to Working Mother. The Female Labor Force in the United States, 1820–1980* (Chapel Hill: University of North Carolina Press, 1985), pp. 124–26.

61. E.g., #2024, 3041; MSPCC newsletter, *The Square Deal* II, 1 (February 1919), p. 8. In one case of a non-supporting husband, from an agency similar to the MSPCC, the record reads: "The woman was willing to work— had applied for day nursery care, but [the agency worker] had persuaded the nursery not to accept their children." Quoted approvingly by Joanna Colcord in her *Broken Homes. A Study of Family Desertion and Its Social Treatment* (New York: Russell Sage Foundation, 1919), p. 189. The objections to women's employment stemmed from deep convictions about women's domesticity. This view was not a "sexist" attitude. Seeing women's employment as, at best, a misfortune was common among feminists as well, a result of the nearly universal understanding of motherhood as women's unique and essential calling. For example, Florence Kelley, "The Family and the Woman's Wage," NCCC *Proceedings* 1909, pp. 118–21; Jane Addams, Presidential Address, "Charity and Social Justice," in ibid., 1910, pp. 6–7. George Mangold, a nonfeminist, makes exactly the same argument in his *Child Problems* (New York: Macmillan, 1910), pp. 89–90, as does Conyngton, p. 185.

62. #3565A.

63. #4800.

64. Colcord, chapter II; Conyngton, p. 185; Earle Eubank, *A Study of Family Desertion* (Chicago: Department of Public Welfare, 1916), p. 13.

65. Colcord, p. 154.

66. On the opposition, see Grace Abbott, "Mothers' Aid in the Modern Public Assistance Program," in *From Relief to Social Security. The Development of the New Public Welfare Services and Their Administration* (New York: Russell & Russell, 1966), pp. 265 ff. Many contemporary commentators, following the rhetoric in the debate, also neglected gender aspects of the mothers' pension controversy, e.g., Mark H. Leff, "Consensus for Reform: The Mothers' Pension Movement in the Progressive Era," *Social Service Review* 47 (September 1973), pp. 397–417; James Leiby, *A History of Social Welfare and Social Work in the U.S.* (New York: Columbia University Press, 1978); Muriel W. Pumphrey and Ralph E. Pumphrey, "The Widows' Pension Movement, 1900–1930: Preventive Child-Saving or Social Control," in *Social Welfare or Social Control? Some Historical Reflections on "Regulating the Poor,"* ed. Walter I. Trattner (Knoxville: University of Tennessee Press, 1983), pp. 51–66; Michael Katz, *Poverty and Policy*, chapter 3. More recently, feminist scholars have noted the gender dimensions of this controversy: Ann Vandepol, "Dependent Children,

Child Custody, and the Mothers' Pensions: The Transformation of State-Family Relations in the Early 20th Century," *Social Problems* 29, 3 (February 1982), pp. 221–35; Barbara Nelson, "The Gender, Race, and Class Origins of Early Welfare Policy and the Welfare State: A Comparison of Workmen's Compensation and Mothers' Aid," forthcoming in *Women in Twentieth Century Politics*, eds. Pat Gurin and Louise Tilly (New York: Russell Sage).

67. Carstens, *Public Pensions to Widows with Children* (New York: Russell Sage Foundation, 1913), p. 28.

68. NCCC, *Proceedings*, 1914, p. 453. She added that pensions were not "virile"!

69. Devine, "The Breaking Up of Families," *Charities Review* X, 5 (October 1900), p. 461.

70. Devine, "Pensions for Mothers," from *American Labor Legislation Review* 3 (June 1913), reprinted in *Selected Articles on Mothers' Pensions*, compiled by Edna D. Bullock (New York, 1915), p. 177.

71. #0314A.

72. #4584.

73. #2564.

74. #2540.

75. Homer Folks, *The Care of Destitute, Neglected and Delinquent Children* (New York: Macmillan, 1902), p. 134.

76. Despite the enunciation of a policy of family placements for children, up through 1920 the vast majority were institutionalized; see Andrew Billingsley and Jeanne M. Giovannoni, *Children of the Storm. Black Children and American Child Welfare* (New York: Harcourt Brace Jovanovich, 1972), pp. 69–70.

77. Larry Bumpus, "Children and Marital Disruption: A Replication and Update," *Demography* 21, 1 (February 1984), pp. 71–82. I am indebted to Sara McLanahan for this reference and for general orientation on this issue.

78. Of course these case records capture the experience of the least fortunate, by definition; those with stronger social support networks were much less likely to come to the attention of social agencies. But our subject *is* the least fortunate.

79. #4061.

80. #2044, 2540, 2542, 3361. Similarly, mothers' parents often complained about their sons-in-law, but the latter rarely had the children and did not so often retain contact with their in-laws. In the rare cases in which single fathers did have custody, the intensity of their conflicts with in-laws suggests that maternal relatives may typically have been even more controlling in relation to children. E.g., #4300.

81. #3541.

82. #4003, 4303.

83. #5600, 5740.

84. #4021, 4285.
85. #4282, 4541, 4583, 4760.
86. E.g., #2783, 4300, 5784, 5862.
87. #2783, 4300, 5784.
88. #4541, 4583, 4760.
89. #4583.
90. #4501.
91. #5061.
92. #6201.
93. #4285.
94. #5781.
95. #5784.
96. #5782. Parents' overwork has been noted as a stress contributing to child abuse in contemporary research: e.g., Claire Justice and David F. Duncan, "Child Abuse as a Work-Related Problem," *Corrective and Social Psychiatry and Journal of Behavior* 23 (1977), pp. 53–55.

Chapter 5

1. #3044.
2. #3555A.
3. By the 1930s, in fact, neglect was often the general rubric under which all mistreatment of children was categorized—quite a change from "cruelty." See, for example, *Correction and Prevention of Neglect of Children*, prepared by Theodore A. Lothrop, Chairman, and the Committee on the Correction and Prevention of Neglect of Children, White House Conference on Child Health and Protection, pamphlet (New York: D. Appleton-Century, 1933). Of course child neglect is not necessarily violent at all, but became included because the family-violence agencies were, at root, child-protection agencies. Neglect accounted for 37.1 percent of all the cases in this study's random sample. These included only those neglect cases serious enough to require court action or child removal. Had the less serious neglect complaints been included, the figures from this study would have been consonant with those of the MSPCC, which in the 1950s estimated its proportion of neglect cases, variously, as 10:1, 20:1, or 86 percent. See ARs 1958 and 1959. (Its earlier calculations use non-parallel categories, which did not distinguish abuse from neglect; see chapter 2.) These high proportions resulted, however, not only

from increased agency sensitivity to neglect but also from the decreased emphasis on physical abuse and the virtual invisibility of sexual abuse. By contrast, in this study, where researchers were trained to notice all four categories of family violence, and to discard the unproven and relatively minor cases, neglect never accounted for more than 50 percent of cases in a given year.

4. #2561. This material, and that in the case following, is not quoted but paraphrased from the case record.

5. #5585.

6. *Correction and Prevention of Neglect of Children*, p. 355.

7. #4080.

8. #3052A.

9. #3101.

10. #3584.

11. "Types of Cases Accepted by the MSPCC for Investigation," typescript, MSPCC Mss., n.d., date attributed by author.

12. The domestic standard for women has been widely discussed by historians, for example, Barbara Welter, "The Cult of True Womanhood," *American Quarterly* 18, 2 (1966), pp. 151–74; and Nancy Cott, *The Bonds of Womanhood. "Woman's Sphere" in New England, 1780–1835* (New Haven: Yale University Press, 1977). Children's domesticity has been rarely noticed, a major exception being Christine Stansell, "Women, Children, and the Uses of the Streets: Class and Gender Conflicts in New York City, 1850–1860," *Feminist Studies* 8, 2 (Summer 1982), pp. 306–35.

13. *New York Mirror*, 1831, quoted by Stansell, p. 314.

14. AR 1901, p. 17.

15. Philip Davis, *Street-Land. Its Little People and Big Problems* (Boston: Small, Maynard, 1915), p. 33; Viviana Zelizer, *Pricing the Priceless Child. The Changing Social Value of Children* (New York: Basic Books, 1985), esp. pp. 32–50; MSPCC AR 1901, pp. 15–18. (Other street dangers to children's welfare fell into the moral neglect category, to be examined below.)

16. Stansell, pp. 310–11. Paul Boyer has a more generous interpretation of these motives. In his discussion of Charles Loring Brace, the most well known of the savers of children on the streets, Boyer comments on Brace's admiration for the children's spunkiness and self-help. See Boyer, pp. 96–97.

17. Stansell, pp. 309, 319, 326.

18. Zelizer, p. 145 and fn. 18.

19. Quoted in Stansell, p. 325.

20. Mornay Williams, *The Street Boy*, pamphlet reprint from NCCC *Proceedings* 1903.

21. Ibid., p. 3.

22. Boston was one of the first cities to impose compulsory school attendance, and had a system of truant officers after 1873. See David Tyack and Michael Berkowitz, "The Man Nobody Liked: Toward a Social History of the Truant Officer, 1840–1940," *American Quarterly* 29, 1 (1977), pp. 38 and 41.

23. Zelizer, chapter 3.

24. *The Square Deal*, MSPCC publication, I, 3 (June 1918), pp. 5–7; AR 1921, p. 27, for example.

25. #2541.

26. #2044.

27. #2523.

28. E.g., #5082.

29. Hon. Harvey H. Baker, "What Constitutes a Neglected Child under the Massachusetts Statutes," pamphlet, 1910, MSPCC.

30. CAA AR 1922, p. 35.

31. #2500.

32. E.g., #2001, 2053, 3302.

33. The record reads "cycloric stenosis," but I am considering this an error of the caseworker or typist.

34. #3500.

35. No such case appeared in the random sample after 1930.

36. #6062.

37. MSPCC ARs 1921–29, passim. In these years the MSPCC ranked the forms of child mistreatment, and immorality ranked second and sometimes third. In the random sample of this study, parental immorality was cited as the form of neglect in 16 percent of cases. It peaked in the war year 1917, at 20.5 percent. (The impact of the war on fears of immorality will be discussed below.) It had declined as a neglect category by 1930 and did not escalate again during the Second World War.

38. Memo in MSPCC Mss., unsorted files, initialed RAH, date attributed by author.

39. See, for example, MSPCC ARs 1951–59, passim.

40. E.g., #5542, 6085.

41. #3026.

42. #3061.

43. See discussion of this in Ellen DuBois and Linda Gordon, "Seeking Ecstasy on the Battlefield: Danger and Pleasure in Nineteenth-Century Feminist Sexual Thought," *Feminist Studies* 9, 1 (Spring 1983), pp. 7–25.

44. The only exception was a few cases in the latest two decades of this study in which Judge Baker experts treated boys who were rapists.

45. CAA AR 1927–28, p. 4.

46. For a compendium of examples, see John S. Haller and Robin M. Haller, *The Physician and Sexuality in Victorian America* (Urbana: University of Illinois Press, 1974), pp. 197–211; Ronald G. Walters, ed., *Primers for Prudery. Sexual Advice to Victorian America* (Englewood Cliffs, N.J.: Prentice-Hall, 1974), chapter 2.

47. E.g., B. G. Jefferis and J. L. Nichols in *Safe Counsel or Practical Eugenics*, 39th ed. (Chicago: J. L. Nichols, 1928), p. 256, pronounced that self-abuse was more common among girls than boys.

48. MSPCC AR 1917, p. 28.

49. MSPCC AR 1921, p.15. Quoting from General Baden-Powell, the MSPCC insisted: " 'The war will be decided in 1935 . . . in the quality of the men who have to carry on.' " *The Square Deal* I, 1, p. 1.

50. ARs 1917–19.

51. *Journal of Social Hygiene*, passim during war years.

52. MSPCC AR 1918, pp. 23–24.

53. MSPCC AR 1918.

54. Ruth True's *The Neglected Girl* (New York: Russell Sage, Survey Associates, 1914) contributed to this perspective.

55. E.g., CAA ARs 1924, p. 5; 1925–26, p. 5; 1927–28, p. 4. For a brief general statement of views on deliquency, see Eleanor T. Glueck, "The Family, the School, and Crime," *Vital Speeches of the Day* I, 16 (May 6, 1935), pp. 516–20.

56. Or at least defined as sexual; see chapter 7.

57. J. Adams Puffer, *The Boy and His Gang* (Boston: Houghton-Mifflin, 1912); Joseph F. Kett, *Rites of Passage. Adolescence in America, 1790 to the Present* (New York: Basic Books, 1977), pp. 256 ff.

58. Philip Davis, influential Boston settlement leader, joined Jane Addams in calling for more public recreational programs and spaces for children. See his *Street-Land: Its Little People and Big Problems*, chapters VIII and IX. Edward Clopper, Secretary of the National Child Labor Committee for the Mississippi Valley, argued the pointlessness of trying to repress children's peddling when it was so necessary to their families' budgets. See his *Child Labor in City Streets* (New York: Macmillan, 1912), pp. 20–21.

59. *Boston Evening American*, February 25, 1931, in clippings scrapbooks, MSPCC Mss.

60. MSPCC AR 1919, pp. 27–28.

61. MSPCC AR 1921, p. 21.

62. MSPCC AR 1923, p. 20.

63. CAA AR 1922, pp. 10–11. I use a case cited in the published report

rather than from the random sample in order to get a concise statement of the agency's analysis; similar cases were common in the files.

64. CAA AR 1924, p. 5.

65. E.g., #3561, 3581, 3801, 4220.

66. #3284.

67. #3280.

68. #3241.

69. See chapter 7.

70. For examples, see MSPCC ARs 1893, pp. 13–14; 1894, p. 10; 1914, p. 33; 1916, p. 28. In 1899 MSPCC reports cited intemperance as causal in 75 percent of its cases, and continued to list it as the primary factor until Prohibition. This causal analysis was confused and contradictory because the drunkenness was usually blamed on immigrant groups, among which were nationalities without patterns of high alcohol consumption, such as Italians, Portuguese, and Southeast Europeans. See, for example, AR 1907, pp. 20–21.

71. Local prohibition was common in Massachusetts until 1875. Then sumptuary legislation was revived, the dramshop acts, which made sellers of liquor responsible for the criminal actions of its forbidden customers (e.g., children or drunks), but these required lawsuits and were rarely enforced. In the 1880s, with MSPCC support, a Citizens' Law and Order League tried to enforce various anti-drinking acts, but with little success. See Duis, *The Saloon*, pp. 11–12, 97–99.

72. E.g., *Christian Science Monitor*, January 17, 1928, "Liquor Ban Proves Help to Children," quoting Lothrop; Cora Frances Stoddard (Executive Secretary of the Scientific Temperance Federation), "More Massachusetts Records and Prohibition," pamphlet, n.d., probably 1926.

73. Mark Edward Lender and James Kirby Martin, *Drinking in America: A History* (New York: Free Press, 1982), p. 196. Since beer and cider, which is often categorized as beer, had a higher alcoholic content early in the nineteenth century than it does today, the comparison over time is based on amount of alcohol, not amount of beer. The fact that arrests for drunkenness were increasing indicates not more drinking but, in Boston and most large U.S. cities, an increase in the number of professional police and in their hostility to drunkenness. See Roger Lane, "Urbanization and Criminal Violence," *Journal of Social History* II, 2 (December 1968), pp. 156–63.

74. Figures are as follows:

TABLE 17. DRUNKENNESS IN THREE TYPES OF FAMILY-VIOLENCE CASES, BY YEAR

Year	All Violence	CASES IN WHICH ASSAILANTS WERE ALLEGED DRUNK		
		Child Abuse	Child Neglect	Adult Violence
1880	87.0%	100	88.9	Na
1890	83.3	57.1	95.7	100
1893	78.7	75	87.5	60
1900	85.9	78.9	93.1	71.4
1910	68.8	41.9	82.4	76
1917	55.0	44.8	58.5	51.9
1920	28.0	21.5	27.3	59.1
1930	53.7	46.9	55	63.2
1934	46.1	39.1	50.8	55.8
1940	42.5	27	49.1	69.6
1944	50.7	41.9	53.3	72.7
1950	66.4	52.3	66.1	80
1960	60.5	44.4	65.7	75
All years	56.6	42.1	65.7	45.7

The MSPCC also reported a low point in drunkenness in AR 1921, p. 20. Correlation of drinking with sexual abuse is discussed separately in chapter 7.

75. AR 1921, p. 20.

76. ARs 1924, 1927.

77. Andrew Sinclair, *Era of Excess. A Social History of the Prohibition Movement* (Boston: Little Brown, 1962); James H. Timberlake, *Prohibition and the Progressive Movement, 1900–1920* (Cambridge, Mass.: Harvard University Press, 1963), esp. pp. 115–19, for examples.

78. Lane, "Urbanization and Criminal Violence."

79. Ibid., although Lane cautions that increases in arrests for drunkenness were also a product of professional police forces. Furthermore, many middle-class people took up the use of patent medicines, which were high in alcohol content and contained opiates. Judith Leavitt, chair, Department of the History of Medicine, University of Wisconsin, private communication, December 1985.

80. Most notably by Barbara Leslie Epstein in her *The Politics of Domesticity. Women, Evangelism, and Temperance in Nineteenth-Century America* (Middletown, CT: Wesleyan University Press, 1981); see also Ruth Bordin, *Woman and Temperance. The Quest for Power and Liberty, 1873–1900* (Philadelphia: Temple University Press, 1981).

81. See chapter 8.

82. Lender and Martin, p. 179, report that the male-female ratio among heavy drinkers today is 28:8.

83. Duis, pp. 106–8.

84. #4084.

85. Duis, pp. 95–96.

86. Mirra Komarovsky, *The Unemployed Man and His Family. The Effect of Unemployment upon the Status of the Man in Fifty-nine Families* (New York: Institute of Social Research, Dryden Press, 1940); Ruth Shonle Cavan and Katherine Howland Fanck, *The Family and the Depression. A Study of One Hundred Chicago Families*, Vol. XXXV in *Social Science Studies* (University of Chicago, 1938).

87. AR 1931, typescript, unpublished that year due to lack of funds; AR 1932.

88. AR 1933. This defense was repeated in 1934 and 1935.

89. MSPCC clippings scrapbook 1933–38; minutes of Exec. Comm., February 20, 1934, pp. 3–4, MSPCC Mss.

90. #4362.

91. MSPCC ARs 1933, 1934, and 1935. In this study child abuse declined as a proportion of all family-violence cases from 48.2 percent in 1920 to 33.1 percent in 1934.

92. Alida C. Bowler, "The Problems of the Transient Boy—In Relation to a Community's Social Hygiene Program," *Journal of Social Hygiene* 19, 4 (April 1933), pp. 188–93.

93. Readers should be reminded that these case records provided no possibility of measuring poverty objectively. This data is presented in tabular fashion in Appendix B.

94. #4082.

95. #4501.

96. John Ehrenreich, *The Altruistic Imagination: A History of Social Work and Social Policy in the United States* (Ithaca: Cornell University Press, 1985), p. 142.

97. #4080. See chapter 2 on burial insurance.

98. #4005A.

99. #4502.

100. In many state laws, the distinction between poverty and neglect was weak until very recently. As of 1975, sixteen states still allowed poverty as an explicit basis for declaring a child neglected. See Areen, p. 926.

101. 1932, Report of the General Secretary, typescript, p. 1, MSPCC Mss.

102. E.g., #5001, 5040, 5042.

103. #4806.

104. #4301.

105. During the Depression married women's proportional representation in the labor force had actually declined; in the next decade it grew from 29 to 36 percent. Twelve percent of married women worked in 1940, 25 percent in 1950, and this included the temporary postwar decline in married women's work. See Wiener, *From Working Girl to Working Mother*, p. 6.

106. #3802.

107. ARs 1941, 1942.

108. On working mothers and delinquency, see Sheldon and Eleanor Glueck, "Working Mothers and Delinquency," in *Ventures in Criminology*, eds. S. and E. Glueck (Cambridge, Mass.: Harvard University Press, 1964), pp. 31–59, orig. 1957; for a critical view, see Joyce Cowley, "Working Mothers and Delinquency," from *The Militant*, September 12, 1955, in *America's Working Women*, eds. Baxandall et al. (New York: Random House, 1976), pp. 318–19.

109. U.S. Children's Bureau, *Controlling Juvenile Delinquency*, publication #301, 1943. See also Susan B. Anthony II, *Out of the Kitchen—Into the War* (New York: Stephen Daye, Inc., 1943), pp. 6–9.

110. ARs 1942 and 1943, repeated in 1945.

111. "A Study of the Relation of the Employment of Mothers to the Neglect or Delinquency of Their Children as Seen by the Massachusetts Society for the Prevention of Cruelty of Children," Part II, typescript, MSPCC Mss. This startling lack is in fact typical of the low level of social science in child-protection work at that time.

112. #5255.

113. #5263.

114. "A Study of the Relation of the Employment of Mothers . . . ," p. 6.

115. It may be that the Judge Baker therapists seem more ideological than the MSPCC and BCSA caseworkers because of the different nature of therapeutic case notes. These customarily contain therapists' summaries and commentaries on individual sessions as well as notes from periodic case conferences, therefore allowing a better view of the therapist's attitude; in addition, the client files usually contain copies of summaries from other agencies as well as of documentation regarding previous records, thereby allowing comparison of the JBGC perspective with that of other agencies and with some of the facts of the clients' situation.

116. See, for example, Francis Ivan Nye and Lois Wladis Hoffman, *The Employed Mother in America* (Chicago: Rand McNally, 1963), especially articles by Hoffman, Douvan, Nye and Nye, Perry and Ogles.

117. MSPCC AR 1944.

118. MSPCC AR 1943.

119. MSPCC Mss. Presidential and Departmental Reports, folder for 1939–45, Temporary Home report for 1943. Remember that the term "sophisticated" was entirely negative in this usage, connoting the feared "precocity" of children learning about sex too early.

120. MSPCC AR 1941, p. 2.

121. E.g., #5062, 5257, 5304.

122. E.g., #5257, 5302, 5580.

123. Memorandum, "Subject: Dealing with World War Veterans," May 1945, MSPCC Mss.

124. Glen H. Elder, Jr., Tri Van Nguyen, and Avshalom Caspi, "Linking Family Hardship to Children's Lives," typescript, Cornell University, 1984; Jeffrey K. Liker and Elder, "Economic Hardships and Marital Relations in the 1930's,"*American Sociological Review* 48 (June 1983), pp. 343–59; Liker and Elder, "Hard Times in Women's Lives: Historical Influences Across Forty Years," *American Journal of Sociology* 88, 2, 1982, pp. 241–69.

125. Could the awareness of military violence and the fascist threat have diminished the apparent importance of family squabbles by contrast? Perhaps, but in the 1960s and 1970s, concern with public and media violence intensified the critique of family violence.

126. #6240.

127. #5784.

128. #5785.

129. E.g., MSPCC AR 1955, citing a commissioned study by a psychiatrist.

130. American Humane Association, *Neglecting Parents—A Study of Psychosocial Characteristics* (Denver: American Humane Association, 1968), pamphlet, p. 18.

131. There were many possible reasons for this: she was an Irish Catholic; divorce was rare among the working class of any religion; she may have wanted to avoid even the possibility of remarriage.

132. #5781.

133. One controlled study of contemporary child neglect found that social contacts with other adults and frequency of getting away from children were the factors most consistently differentiating non-neglectful from neglectful mothers. Joan M. Jones and R. L. McNeely, "Mothers Who Neglect and Those Who Don't: A Comparative Study," *Social Casework* 61 (November 1980), pp. 559–67.

134. #5500.

135. #5560.

136. #5562.

137. E.g., CAA AR 1924, p. 5; 1925–26, p. 5; 1927–28, p. 4.

138. Categories used in check sheet, 1950 JB cases.

139. For example, a BCSA caseworker spoke of "manifest neglect and rejection both physical and psychological" in describing a child's situation in 1950, #5601; *Standards for Child Protective Services* (Child Welfare League of America, pamphlet, 1960), p. 10, referring to a definition by Robert Mulford of the MSPCC. In the journal *Social Work* between 1956 and 1960, emotional neglect was the most common category of child mistreatment mentioned.

140. For a critique of the use of bonding and attachment theory in the child abuse and neglect field, see Breines and Gordon.

141. E.g., #6085.

142. Apparently a balance between too little and too much sex-role stereotyping is required.

143. Norman A. Polansky, Christine DeSaix, and Shlomo A. Sharlin, *Child Neglect: Understanding and Reaching the Parent* (New York: Child Welfare League of America, 1972), pamphlet; the questionnaire was reprinted in Norman Polansky, Mary Ann Chalmers, Elizabeth Buttenwieser, and David P. Williams, *Damaged Parents. An Anatomy of Child Neglect* (Chicago: University of Chicago Press, 1981), appendices.

144. *Damaged Parents*, p. 115.

145. Polansky et al., *Child Neglect*; the mother-blaming, I am glad to say, was somewhat reduced by the 1981 publication of *Damaged Parents*.

146. Louis Jacobucci, "Casework Treatment of the Neglectful Mother," *Social Casework* (April 1965). Jacobucci was an MSPCC District Executive.

147. Ibid.

148. Polansky, *Damaged Parents*, pp. 245–47.

149. #6081.

150. For an interesting discussion of how the Thatcher government in England has used the child-abuse issue to support conservative social policies, but one which unfortunately is entirely blind to gender, see Nigel Parton, *The Politics of Child Abuse* (New York: St. Martin's Press, 1985).

151. #4640.

152. #3041.

Chapter 6

1. #1596.

2. #2781.

3. #3766.

4. Let me repeat here that throughout this book I have adopted the common contemporary usage in which "child abuse" means exclusively *non-sexual* abuse.

5. Sue Gronewold, *Beautiful Merchandise. Prostitution in China 1860–*

1936 (New York: Institute for Research in History and the Haworth Press, 1982).

6. Breines and Gordon; Robert L. Burgess and James Garbarino, "Doing What Comes Naturally? An Evolutionary Perspective on Child Abuse," in *The Dark Side of Families. Current Family Violence Research*, eds. David Finkelhor et al. (Beverly Hills: Sage, 1983), pp. 88–101.

7. Child-abuse expert David Gil argues, for example, that child abuse has been virtually eliminated from Israeli kibbutzim, in his "The Political and Economic Context of Child Abuse," in *Unhappy Families: Clinical and Research Perspectives on Family Violence*, eds. Eli H. Newberger and Richard Bourne (Littleton, MA: PSG Publishing, 1985), p. 15.

8. Ingleby, "The Psychology of Child Psychology," in *The Integration of a Child into a Social World*, ed. Martin P. M. Richards (London: Cambridge University Press, 1974), p. 296, quoted in Anna E. Yeatman, "Where Are Children Today? A Sociology of Child/Parent Relations," typescript, 1979, p. 10.

9. Regarding the role of children in provoking abuse, see Alfred White Franklin, ed., *Child Abuse. Prediction, Prevention and Follow Up* (Edinburgh: Churchill Livingstone, 1977), articles by Harold Martin, Pamela Howat, Margaret Lynch and Jacqueline Roberts, and Ruth Hanson, J. W. McCulloch, and Susan A. Hartley; William N. Friedrich and Jerry A. Boriskin, "The Role of the Child in Abuse: A Review of the Literature," *American Journal of Orthopsychiatry* 46, 4 (October 1976), pp. 580–90.

10. For references and a critique of the "cycle of violence" theory, see Breines and Gordon; Evan Stark and Anne Flitcraft, "Woman-battering, child abuse and social heredity: what is the relationship?" in *Marital Violence*, ed. Norman Johnson (London: Routledge, Kegan & Paul, 1985), pp. 147–71.

11. For summaries of references on these findings, see David Finkelhor, "Common Features of Family Abuse," *The Dark Side of Families*, pp. 17–28; Breines and Gordon.

12. Good examples of contemporary work on this topic include Carolyn M. Newberger, "Parents and Practitioners as Developmental Theorists," in *Unhappy Families*, pp. 131–44; C. M. Newberger and S. Cook, "Parental Awareness and Child Abuse: A Cognitive Developmental Analysis of Urban and Rural Samples," *American Journal of Orthopsychiatry* 53, 3 (July 1983), pp. 512–24.

13. In these data cases are counted more than once, where several kinds of stress were present. In interpreting these figures one should not assume that identical factors are being compared. For example, the contribution of unemployment to child abuse is different than that of neglect. In child abuse, unemployment was correlated with male violence at twice the rate as with

female violence, because men were more often at home and more angry, leading to greater paternal violence against children. In child neglect, by contrast, male and female rates were closer, because unemployment created poverty and depression in both parents. For a useful report on the role of these factors in contemporary child abuse, see Blaire Justice and David F. Duncan, "Child Abuse as a Work-Related Problem," *Corrective and Social Psychiatry and Journal of Behavior* 23 (1977), pp. 53-55. Drinking also had different influences in different types of violence. In wife-beating, one or both participants was often drunk during the violence. In child abuse and neglect cases, drinking was often a long-term contributor to family poverty, anger, and irresponsibility, not necessarily responsible for individual incidents.

14. Judith Martin, "Maternal and Paternal Abuse of Children," in *The Dark Side of Families*, pp. 293-304. These figures, moreover, exclude cases in which both parents were abusive; including those further reduces the proportion of women child abusers, because women are more often violent together with a spouse and less often violent on their own. The proportion of mothers among abusers tended to go down over time: they were 62 percent of assailants from 1880 through 1900, 41 percent from 1910 through 1934, 47 percent from 1940 through 1960. This decline may follow from men's slightly increased responsibilities in child care and from women's greatly increased employment outside their homes; it may also result from agencies' increased willingness to hold fathers responsible for children's welfare.

15. This perspective is being challenged. Many battered women's shelters now focus directly on child abuse, including violence by mothers. It is also being challenged in scholarly work: see, e.g., Sandra M. Gilbert, "Soldier's Heart: Literary Men, Literary Women, and the Great War," *Signs* 8, 3 (Spring 1983), pp. 422-50; Carolyn Kott Washburne, "A Feminist Analysis of Child Abuse and Neglect," in *The Dark Side of Families*, pp. 289-90.

16. In this study women's share of severe abuse cases—7.1 percent—was slightly greater but not significantly different than men's, 6.3 percent.

17. #5145.

18. #2003, 2044, 2081, 2560, 3024, 3040, 3242, 3585, 4085, 4261, 4262, 4284, 4702, for examples.

19. Varon, "The Client of a Protective Agency in the Context of the Community," 1961, chapters V, VII, and VIII.

20. Margo I. Wilson, Martin Daly, and Suzanne Weghorst, "Differential Maltreatment of Girls and Boys," *Victimology*, Vol. 6, 1981, pp. 249-61.

21. We have reliable data only for older children. These records contained few infant abuse, as opposed to neglect cases. The scarcity of infant abuse cases in this study resulted from the referral process. Medical personnel are responsible for most infant abuse cases today, while (a) this study relied exclusively

on social-work agencies for its cases and (b) fewer medical workers were concerned with child abuse altogether before 1960, so that fewer infant-abuse cases were discovered.

22. Due to the inclusion of Judge Baker records, which, by focusing on delinquency, overrepresent teenagers.

23. This discrepancy would be even greater if one controlled for the overrepresentation of teenagers.

24. The distribution of types of violence in our sample looked like this:

TABLE 18. INCIDENCE OF FOUR TYPES OF FAMILY VIOLENCE, BY YEAR

YEAR	CHILD ABUSE	MARITAL VIOLENCE	SEX ASSAULT	CHILD NEGLECT
1880	41.5%	3.8%	0%	45.3
1890	40.4	10.5	1.8	47.4
1893	28.4	24.5	5.9	38.2
1900	20.0	24.6	5.4	50.0
1910	21.9	23.7	5.3	46.7
1917	22.7	18.6	6.2	40.2
1920	48.2	15.3	5.3	24.1
1930	36.3	19.9	8.0	28.3
1934	33.1	23.5	10.8	28.3
1940	34.3	17.9	6.3	35.3
1944	32.9	21.3	7.2	27.5
1950	27.3	22.7	8.1	32.8
1960	29.2	24.6	5.4	33.8

25. AR 1884, pp. 11–12, 16.

26. AR 1891, p. 8.

27. AR 1914, p. 31.

28. E.g., George B. Mangold, *Problems of Child Welfare* 3rd ed. (New York: Macmillan, 1936), p. 457; White House Conference on Child Health and Protection, Report of the Committee on the Socially Handicapped, pamphlet (New York: D. Appleton-Century, 1933), p. 23.

29. Catherine J. Ross, "The Lessons of the Past: Defining and Controlling Child Abuse in the United States," in *Child Abuse. An Agenda for Action*, eds. George Gerbner et al. (New York: Oxford University Press, 1980), p. 75.

30. Police involvement in marital violence declined much less, from 46.5 percent to 40 percent, a phenomenon to be explained in chapter 8.

31. MSPCC AR 1900, facing p. 16.

32. E.g., Murray Straus, "The Changing Status of Children and Changes in the Incidence of Child Abuse," typescript, 1979, pp. 6–7.

33. Indeed, both advocates and opponents of spanking tend to hold their

opinions intensely and moralistically. In teaching and lecturing about family violence for several years, I have found that the consistently most controversial issue was not wife-beating, as I had expected, but whether or not spanking children is a good idea.

34. Daniel R. Miller and Guy E. Swanson, *The Changing American Parent. A Study in the Detroit Area* (New York: John Wiley & Sons, 1958); Urie Bronfenbrenner, "Socialization and Social Class Through Time and Space," orig. 1958, in David Gil, ed., *Child Abuse and Violence* (New York: AMS Press, 1979), pp. 441–83.

35. Seymour M. Lipset, *Political Man. The Social Bases of Politics* (Garden City, NY: Doubleday, 1960), chapter 3.

36. Arnold W. Green, "The Middle Class Male Child and Neurosis," *American Sociological Review* II, 1 (1946), pp. 31–41; Howard S. Erlanger, "Social Class and Corporal Punishment in Child Rearing. A Reassessment," in Gil, *Child Abuse and Violence*, pp. 484–515; Martha C. Ericson, "Social Status and Child-Rearing Practices," in *Readings in Social Psychology*, eds. Theodore M. Newcomb and Eugene L. Hartley (New York: Henry Holt and Co., 1947), pp. 494–501; Allison Davis and Robert J. Havighurst, "Social Class and Color Differences in Child-rearing," *American Sociological Review* 11, 6 (December 1946), pp. 698–710.

37. Richard Gelles, "Violence Toward Children in the United States," *Family Violence* (Beverly Hills: Sage, 1979), p. 74.

38. Straus et al., *Behind Closed Doors*, chapter 3, for one popular example of this point of view; for more scholarly presentations, see *Violence in the Family*, eds. Steinmetz and Straus (New York: Harper & Row, 1974), chapter V; Gelles, *The Violent Home* (Beverly Hills: Sage, 1974), pp. 62–70 and chapter 6. For a critique of this perspective, see Breines and Gordon.

39. E.g., #3785.

40. #5700.

41. See Straus et al., *Behind Closed Doors*, pp. 55–57.

42. This information was only available for thirty-four cases in the earlier, and fifty cases in the later, period.

43. #4261.

44. #3241.

45. #5200.

46. #3647.

47. #1825A, 2044.

48. #2523.

49. #2560.

50. For a summary of evidence on this point, see Ewen, chapter 5.

51. #2027.

52. #3240

53. #5082.

54. #5700.

55. #3785.

56. ARs 1887, pp. 10–11; 1898, p. 11.

57. Overwork was not one of the seventeen categories of cruelty to children listed in MSPCC statistical tables, as were physical neglect, moral neglect, intemperance, non-support, medical neglect, physical cruelty.

58. #3763, 4262, 4761.

59. #6201.

60. #5145.

61. E.g., #6041.

62. Approximately 20 percent of the child victims of abuse were bed-wetters, and this is a low estimate because it includes many teenagers in whom bed-wetting was an uncommon symptom. Bed-wetting appeared more common as a provocation for abuse in the period before about 1930, but we were unable to measure this, since the earlier case records contain less detail than the later ones.

63. #5252.

64. #1502.

65. #4262. See also #4761, 5700, for other examples of the violent reactions of fathers to boys' stealing.

66. As Margaret Mead put it, the child "will never be, as an adult, a member of the same culture of which his father stands as the representative during his early years." See her "Social Change and Cultural Surrogates," *Journal of Educational Sociology* 14, 1 (September 1940), p. 103. My argument here is a version of that made by John and Virginia Demos in "Adolescence in Historical Perspective," *Journal of Marriage and the Family* XXXI, 4 (1969), pp. 632–38, and Joseph F. Kett, "Adolescence and Youth in Nineteenth-Century America," *Journal of Interdisciplinary History* II, 2 (Autumn 1971), pp. 282–98.

67. Kett, *Rites of Passage*, p. 227.

68. Steven L. Schlossman, "Before Home Start: Notes toward a History of Parent Education in America, 1897–1929," *Harvard Education Review* 46, 3 (August 1976), pp. 436–67.

69. Another historian who has actually studied some case records, those of the Judge Baker clinic, came to a similar conclusion regarding the reality of new problems of adolescence. See Nancy J. Tomes, "Dynamic Psychiatry and the Female Delinquent," paper at 1983 OAH, typescript.

70. Paula Fass, *The Damned and the Beautiful. American Youth in the 1920s* (New York: Oxford University Press, 1977).

71. #3260.

72. #4243.

73. #2021.

74. #2800A.

75. Tomes, pp. 18–19.

76. Teitelbaum and Harris, p. 33.

77. #3043.

78. #3260.

79. #3043, 3585.

80. #2008.

81. #2560.

82. #3785.

83. #2800A.

84. #4806.

85. E.g., #2047.

86. Children sometimes did go to agencies, particularly the MSPCC, on the basis of rumor about their powers and services, but they were more likely to go to relatives or individual friends if they had no previous connection with social workers.

87. #3860.

88. #3021.

89. #4240.

90. In this study I was forced to exclude the general topic of child-initiated family violence for lack of information: it had not yet emerged as a recognized social problem, social workers did not ask about this kind of violence. Violence of adults against the elderly may have been less widespread than it is today.

91. #4200.

92. E.g., #4060, 6201.

93. #5259.

94. #5082.

95. This is consistent with the relative lower visibility of lesbianism until the last few decades.

96. #3284.

97. #4702.

98. #4760.

99. #3280.

100. #6062.

101. #3809.

102. #3809.

103. #3280.

104. Nor did changes in average family size over time correlate with any changes in proportion of child abuse to other forms of family violence in this study.

105. #6061.

106. #4262.

107. #4284.

108. The most often cited contemporary study, from 1981, showed stepfathers implicated in child-abuse cases at one-third the rate of natural fathers. However, this figure is not necessarily higher than the proportion of stepfathers in the sample population. See Jean Giles-Sims and David Finkelhor, "Child Abuse in Stepfamilies," typescript, December 1983; Richard J. Light, "Abused and Neglected Children in America: A Study of Alternative Policies," *Harvard Educational Review* 43, 4 (November 1973), 556–98. Among those who argue that stepparents are disproportionately abusive, some have invoked sociobiological theories to account for the overrepresentation. Starting from the theoretical postulate that parents make an "investment" in a child that increases that child's chance of survival, they argue that stepparents have a lesser investment and are therefore less constrained from abusing; e.g., Robert L. Burgess and James Garbarino, "Doing What Comes Naturally? An Evolutionary Perspective on Child Abuse," in *The Dark Side of Families*, pp. 88–101. This theory overlooks the predominance of natural parents among child abusers, and offers no way to differentiate the great "investment" of some parents from that of others. Giles-Sims and Finkelhor have pointed out that child abuse usually results in injury, not death, and that injury increases the cost of child-raising to the parent.

109. Giles-Sims and Finkelhor.

110. Bruce Bellingham, "Waifs and Strays: History of Childhood, Abandonment and the Circulation of Children Between Households in the Mid-Nineteenth Century," paper for Davis Center, Princeton University, 1986, pp. 16–17; for the same phenomenon in Europe, see Louise A. Tilly and Joan W. Scott, *Women, Work and Family* (New York: Holt, Rinehart and Winston, 1978).

111. Mothers and daughters, by contrast, expressed frequent suspicion of stepfathers with regard to sexual abuse. Mothers often warned their daughters against stepfathers, or covertly attempted to prevent their being left alone with stepfathers.

112. #4261.

113. #4300.

114. Herman, *Father-Daughter Incest* (Cambridge, Mass.: Harvard University Press, 1981), pp. 1–3.

Chapter 7

1. #4301.
2. This is probably a caseworker's mistake, as the Rienzis were Catholic.
3. #3047A.
4. For example, S. Weinberg, *Incest Behavior* (New York: Citadel Press, 1955). For a summary and other references, see Carolyn Moore Newberger and Eli H. Newberger, "Sex with Children: A Moral Analysis," *Scientific American*, forthcoming.
5. Florence Rush, *The Best-Kept Secret. Sexual Abuse of Children* (Englewood Cliffs, NJ: Prentice-Hall, 1980).
6. Rush; Herman, *Father-Daughter Incest*; Jeffrey Moussaieff Masson, *The Assault on Truth. Freud's Suppression of the Seduction Theory* (New York: Farrar, Straus and Giroux, 1984).
7. Gayle Rubin, "The Traffic in Women: Notes on the 'Political Economy' of Sex," in Rayna R. Reiter, ed., *Toward an Anthropology of Women* (New York: Monthly Review, 1975), pp. 157–210.
8. Addendum to Irving Kaufman, Alice L. Peck, and Consuelo K. Tagiuri, "The Family Constellation and Overt Incestuous Relations between Father and Daughter," *American Journal of Orthopsychiatry* 24 (1954), pp. 266–79.
9. For example, "No known human society could tolerate much incest without ruinous disruption," write Paul Gebhard, J. Gagnon, Wardell Pomeroy, and C. Christenson, *Sex Offenders* (New York: Harper and Row, 1965), p. 208. See also Kingsley Davis, *Human Society* (New York: Macmillan 1949); Norman Bell and Ezra Vogel, eds., *A Modern Introduction to the Family* (New York: The Free Press 1963), for examples.
10. Several reversed the functionalist denial into an assumption that incest existed wherever outside observers feared its existence, incest being a practice commonly attributed to the social and economically "backward"; e.g., Anthony S. Wohl, "Sex and the Single Room: Incest among the Victorian Working Classes," in *The Victorian Family: Structure and Stress*, ed. Wohl (New York: St. Martin's Press, 1978), pp. 197–216; Bryan Strong, "Toward a History of the Experiential Family: Sex and Incest in the Nineteenth-Century Family," *Journal of Marriage and the Family* 35, 3 (August 1973), pp. 457–66. This

article is called an "experiential" study, although it has no evidence of experience in it whatsoever.

11. The existing anthropological, psychological, and sociological scholarship differs in its recognition of the non-symmetrical occurrence of these various types of incest. Some, like Robin Fox, recognize the greater incidence of father-daughter incest but do not analyze it in terms of family and gender politics. See his *Kinship and Marriage* (London: Penguin, 1967), p. 71. In the family-violence field, this blindness to gender is well represented by the work of C. Henry Kempe, e.g., "Incest and Other Forms of Sexual Abuse," in *The Battered Child*, eds. Kempe and Helfer (Chicago: University of Chicago, 1980), pp. 198-214. Others carry on the discussion as if all types of incest were equally prevalent. For example, John Money's introduction to the incest section in Gertrude J. Williams and John Money, eds., *Traumatic Abuse and Neglect of Children at Home* (Baltimore: Johns Hopkins University Press, 1980), pp. 411-14. Others find ingenious ways of explaining away actuality with speculation about possibility. Thus Kate Rist argues that "society has created a stronger prohibition against mother-son incest" because "it is most likely to occur. . . . This has led to the intriguing situation in which father-daughter incest appears to have a lower natural probability of occurrence, is therefore less strongly prohibited, and in practice occurs more often." See her "Incest: Theoretical and Clinical Views," *American Journal of Orthopsychiatry* 49, 4 (October 1979), p. 682.

12. Virtually all contemporary studies of family-violence incest find the same pattern. There is a good summary in Pagelow, *Family Violence*. Other kinds of incestuous relationships may not have appeared because they did not trouble those who knew about it—but this absence of anxiety precisely suggests that these cases are not properly considered family violence.

13. Herman, p. 70.

14. Kee MacFarlane, "Sexual Abuse of Children," in *The Victimization of Women*, eds. J. R. Chapman and M. Gates (Beverly Hills: Sage, 1978), pp. 87-88.

15. Diana Russell has argued, based on interviews with 930 women, that incest as well as extrafamily sexual abuse has radically increased—quadrupled. See her *The Secret Trauma. Incest in the Lives of Girls and Women* (New York: Basic Books, 1986), chapter 5. I am not convinced, however, that she has adequately accounted for the factors that might have created a proportional overreporting in more recent cases.

16. The generalizations that follow are based on approximately one hundred cases. Of these, exactly fifty were among the random sample used for our statistics; in other words, 10 percent of the randomly selected family-violence

cases had incestuous episodes. These fifty cases we call Sample A. All statistics cited refer to (random) Sample A unless otherwise noted. Approximately fifty additional case records were read in a search for more incest cases. The larger group of one hundred cases (Sample A plus fifty more) is called Sample B, and it is not random. Nevertheless, since the extra cases were not selected for any particular features, and include every incest case in the order in which they occurred in examining all cases from a given year in numerical order, there is no reason to suspect that Sample B is less representative than Sample A. All statistical tables and graphs are based on the random sample.

17. The one exception was a fifteen-year-old mother who was accused of sexually molesting her infant son.

18. The mean age of the forty-nine male incest perpetrators was 35.2, the median age 38. The underrepresentation of younger men and boys does not necessarily mean that they were not involved in incestuous relations, but that these did not appear so often as major problems.

19. Sample B.

20. Note too that these cases come from as long ago as 1880, when puberty occurred later than it does today. (One estimate places the mean age of female puberty at 15.1 years in the period 1850–1899 and 14.4 years during 1900–1949.) See Edward Shorter, *The Making of the Modern Family* (New York: Basic Books, 1977), p. 294n.

21. Sample B.

22. #4301.

23. Contemporary figures collected by the National Incidence Study of 1981 show even higher proportions of stepfathers in incest cases; in this survey, stepfathers actually outnumbered fathers as sexual abuse perpetrators, 30 percent to 28 percent. See the discussion in Jean Giles-Sims and David Finkelhor, "Child Abuse in Stepfamilies," typescript, December 1983. Diana Russell's work also shows disproportionately high numbers of stepfathers: *The Secret Trauma*, chapter 16.

24. P. van den Berghe, "Human Inbreeding Avoidance: Culture in Nature," *The Behavior and Brain Sciences* 6 (1983), pp. 91–123.

25. For a philosophical discussion of this aspect of maternalism, see Sara Ruddick, "Maternal Thinking," *Feminist Studies* 6, 3 (Summer 1980), pp. 343–67.

26. Sample B.

27. Sample B. Similar findings regarding the relative powerlessness of mothers have been reported by Herman; David Finkelhor, *Sexually Victimized Children* (New York: The Free Press, 1979); and Pagelow, *Family Violence*, p. 385.

28. Let me re-emphasize that by "weakened" I do not refer to a defect in the women but am describing their victimization in a male-dominant family and society.

29. #3047A.

30. Herman; Ann Wolbert Burgess, Lynda Lytle Holmstrom, and Maureen P. McCausland, "Divided Loyalty in Incest Cases," in *Sexual Assault of Children and Adolescents*, eds. Burgess et al. (Lexington, MA: Lexington Books, 1978); Louise Armstrong, *Kiss Daddy Goodnight: A Speak-Out on Incest* (New York: Hawthorn Books, 1978); Sandra Butler, *Conspiracy of Silence: The Trauma of Incest* (San Francisco: Glide Publications, 1978); Susan Forward and Craig Buck, *Betrayal of Innocence: Incest and Its Devastation* (New York: Penguin, 1978).

31. ARs 1902, p. 11, and 1914, p. 29.

32. I would hypothesize a similar transformation of the representation of adult rape from an intrafamily problem to a problem of violent strangers, with the resultant tendency to blame women for being public and unprotected. The recent feminist arguments against marital rape are a rediscovery of something commonly discussed, albeit in other terms, in the nineteenth century.

33. Herbert G. Gutman, *The Black Family in Slavery and Freedom 1750–1925* (New York: Pantheon, 1976).

34. The themes of permanence and contagion of moral ruin were tenacious at the MSPCC, from its first *Annual Report*: ". . . worse than . . . danger to . . . physical health . . . immorality and degradation . . . becomes an inheritance, and generations are polluted" (1881, p. 19), to its forty-second: "Moral neglect is far more serious than physical neglect, because it leaves scars which time cannot heal" (1922, pp. 13–14), to its report on sixty-five years of work, published in 1943, containing a description of the contagion of group sex delinquency, *Crusading for Children, 1878–1943*.

35. The following description of medical procedure is taken from notations in MSPCC case records. For a physician's prescription regarding focus on the hymen in such examinations and a general description of how examinations should be done, see Gurney Williams, M.D., "Rape in Children and in Young Girls," *International Clinics* (Philadelphia and London), 2nd series, 23 (1913), pp. 251–63, esp. p. 260.

36. A man who had *only* used his hands, or who was incapable of erection, or "crippled in any way which would make the act particularly difficult" was less culpable. See Williams, pp. 248–50.

37. Again this is substantiated in published instructions: "It is always a good working rule to be guided only by the physical conditions that present themselves to your eye and finger, and to forget what the sense of hearing has suggested." Williams, p. 247.

38. Williams, perhaps typically, acknowledged the unreliability of hymen condition as evidence of sexual activity even as he continued to view it as the main evidence to which a doctor should testify in sexual abuse cases.

39. This continues to be the case today; see Finkelhor, *Sexually Victimized Children.*

40. #2590A.

41. E.g., #3549A, 3552A.

42. Carstens, special report in MSPCC AR 1910.

43. Sample B. The chilling impact of reading one suggests why this may have been hard for girls. For example, from #3046A: "At the age of thirteen . . . my father had sexual intercourse with me on many occasions, such acts taking place at night in the presence of my mother in their bed and also in my own bed. . . . "

44. Carstens, special report, p. 25.

45. Overcrowding was the most common connection drawn by reformers between poverty and incest. For use of this explanation in England, see Anthony S. Wohl, "Sex and the Single Room."

46. AR 1916, p. 28.

47. Only 28 percent of incest cases had drunkenness as a significant factor, as compared to 50 percent of nonsexual abuse, 70 percent of neglect, and 75 percent of wife-beating cases. See Linda Gordon and Paul O'Keefe, "Incest as a Form of Family Violence: Evidence from Historical Case Records," *Journal of Marriage and the Family* 46, 1 (February 1984), pp. 27-34.

48. Based on reading all Judge Baker sex delinquency cases from 1920. Another researcher, Nancy Tomes, also found that the caseworkers never cited sexual abuse but rather "early sex knowledge" as a cause of 25 percent of the girls' and 14 percent of the boys' delinquency. See her "Dynamic Psychiatry and the Female Delinquent," table 4. I also suspect incest in many sex delinquency cases where there was no such allegation. Contemporary scholarship on teenage sexual promiscuity and sexual assault of children abounds with evidence for the connection between incest and sex delinquency. A desire to stay away from home was, and still is, a common symptom of incest victimization. See Herman, Finkelhor.

49. Sophonisba Breckenridge and Grace Abbott found 47 out of 157 girls in the State Training School in Chicago to have been sexually attacked by a family member, in *The Delinquent Child and the Home,* pp. 74 and 105. W. I. Thomas in his study *The Unadjusted Girl* (New York: Little Brown, 1923) repeated evidence from Sidney and Beatrice Webb and Katherine Bement Davis on the proportions of incest victims among delinquents, pp. 117–18. Similar references are in Sheldon and Eleanor T. Glueck, *Five Hundred Delinquent Women* (New York: Knopf, 1934), chapters III and V; Jacob and Rosamond

Goldberg, *Girls on City Streets. A Study of 1400 Cases of Rape* (New York: American Social Hygiene Association, 1935), pp. 164–65; Mabel Ruth Fernald, *A Study of Women Delinquents in New York State* (1920, repr. Montclair, N.J.: Patterson Smith, 1968), chap. XII.

50. #4301.

51. #6242.

52. For example, in 1919 the Boston Society for the Care of Girls (predecessor of the BCSA) organized a mass meeting demanding women police, and in response, in 1920 the city of Boston hired six policewomen. See Chloe Owings, *Women Police* (New York: F. H. Hitchcock, 1925), pp. 124–27; Sabina Marshall, "Development of the Policewomen's Movement in Cleveland, Ohio," *Journal of Social Hygiene* 11, 4 (April 1925), pp. 193–214.

53. Mary Sullivan, *My Double Life. The Story of a New York Policewoman* (New York: Farrar & Rinehart, 1938), pp. 259–60.

54. This diagnosis was also common in explaining prostitution in this period. See Allan M. Brandt, *No Magic Bullet. A Social History of Venereal Disease in the United States since 1880* (New York: Oxford University Press, 1985), p. 91.

55. E.g., the 1926 AR, pp. 20–23, contained both an emphasis on feeblemindedness and a citation to a recent study by Bronner and Healy which debunked that problem as a cause of delinquency.

56. MSPCC ARs 1914, p. 29, and 1922, p. 12.

57. Brandt, chapter II.

58. This report published in part in *Journal of Social Hygiene* 28, 7 (October 1942), pp. 403–18.

59. Tomes, p. 28a.

60. Steven Schlossman and Stephanie Wallach, "The Crime of Precocious Sexuality: Female Juvenile Delinquency in the Progressive Era," *Harvard Educational Review* 48 (1978), pp. 65–94. They were also treated more harshly than boys, a higher proportion sent immediately to reformatories, without probation, even on first offenses.

61. Williams, p. 259.

62. #4301.

63. #5784.

64. #5252.

65. Williams, p. 245.

66. According to census statistics from 1936, convicted sex offenders were disproportionately in the age group over forty-five. See *Prisoners in State and Federal Prisons and Reformatories: 1936*, quoted in Ira S. Wile, "Sex Offenders

Against Young Children: What Shall Be Done About Them?," *Journal of Social Hygiene*, Vol. 25, 1 (January 1939), p. 34.

67. #2330A.

68. #2321A.

69. #2322A.

70. #3642.

71. #3642. The girl and her parents—her father was Tom's son—were bribed into agreeing to the physical exam by offering her free dental work for front teeth which were completely rotted out and gums which were infected.

72. #3830A. The outcome is not known to me.

73. Williams, p. 246.

74. Thomas B. Garrett and Richard Wright, "Wives of Rapists and Incest Offenders," *Journal of Sex Research* 11, 2 (May 1975), pp. 149-57.

75. Williams, p. 245.

76. Wile, pp. 35, 41.

77. The use here of words such as "precocious" is similar to that of "delinquency." I am not suggesting any biological age at which sexual activity or leaving home is appropriate, but am referring to the social and cultural standards of the period. It bears notice, however, that these standards were not necessarily identical for all social groups, and indeed they were themselves contested.

78. #3043.

79. A finding corroborated by Dr. Judith Herman, private communication.

80. E.g., #3088A, 3564A.

81. #3564A. See also #3051A.

82. Breines and Gordon.

83. If the stepmother is notoriously exploitive of daughters (see Herman), as Cinderella and other fairy tales warn us, the reasons may be connected to certain family-structural characteristics of remarriage. (See the discussion on stepparents in the chapter on child abuse.) In many cases, particularly with relatively new stepmothers, the women may not have experienced the responsibility and the rewards of nurturing a child, thereby establishing a mutual love. Furthermore, the child may have responded to the stepmother with jealousy and rejection, thereby not encouraging positive feelings. In relation to the father the stepmother may have been in a weak position. Particularly in poor and immigrant communities, marrying a man who already had children may have been a sign of low value on the marriage market.

84. #3065A. See also #3046A.

85. #3088A.

86. #3559A.
87. #3644.
88. #3361.
89. E.g., #3302.
90. E.g., #3561A, 3566A.
91. Herman, pp. 73-74.
92. #2058A.
93. In the early decades of this study, when so many of the incestuous families were immigrants from more rural and patriarchal environments, the absence of guilt recalls David Riesman's distinction between shame and guilt cultures. In his *The Lonely Crowd* (New Haven: Yale University Press, 1950), p. 24, Riesman distinguished between tradition-directed, inner-directed, and other-directed character structure, each accompanied by a characteristic emotional sanction: guilt, shame, and anxiety respectively. Guilt, an internalized shame which one feels even when alone and undiscovered, and which in Riesman's formulation was characteristic of modern individualized societies, was not expressed. However, the assailants' response upon discovery did not change in the more recent decades. They did not begin to express guilt or contrition in relation to their victims. If the guilt/shame distinction has meaning, and I think it does, one must hypothesize that for some men the assumption of entitlement continues in individualized society. Dr. Judith Herman also found both the sense of entitlement and the lack of remorse among incestuous fathers. (Private communication.)
94. It would be most useful to have a class and cultural analysis of domestic incest. If this hypothesis about change over time is right, one would expect to find this type of incest less common in groups which were less patriarchal in their expectations of girls. Conceivably, incestuous fathers in more permissive, middle-class and/or "modernized" families would be more likely to feel guilty. But these families were much less likely to become clients of social-work agencies, so we have no records about their handling of deviance.
95. E.g., #3644.
96. E.g., #3044 or #3051A; sometimes also, fathers brought stubborn-child charges as a means of defending themselves against the girls' accusations.
97. Incestuous pregnancies were not very common in these cases, partly owing to the young age of many of the incest victims, and perhaps also to the nature of the sex (often not intercourse) they had been involved in. By contrast case records from agencies specializing in helping unwed mothers show considerable proportions of incest, proving that pregnancies did occur. Joan Jacobs Brumberg in a private communication reported that 7.5 percent of the pregnancies in the home for unwed mothers she studied were incest cases, a high

proportion considering how few such cases would have been identified as such. See her " 'Ruined' Girls: Changing Community Responses to Illegitimacy in Upstate New York, 1890–1920," *Journal of Social History* 18, 2 (Winter 1984), pp. 247-72.

98. #3556A.

99. #3047A, 3556A, 3558A, 3559A, 3840A.

100. It is not clear what the social worker's motives were in this. She may have been responding to the girl's own ambivalence; she may have been fearful of the strong disapproval of the Chinese community for splitting up the family. She offered to get a lock for the girl's room!

101. To repeat, in all the incest cases there was not one statement of apology by the man.

102. E.g., W. I. Thomas, *The Unadjusted Girl*, pp. 49, 69, 81.

103. It is not clear from the record whether the brothers were sexually using Wanda themselves, or whether their beatings of her were part of a system of reinforcing the father's authority and access.

104. #3585.

105. Walker, *The Battered Woman* (New York: Harper & Row, 1979).

106. Thirty out of thirty-eight.

107. #2322A.

108. #3826A.

109. I use this term to mean any acceptance of money or goods in exchange for sex, although even in this wide definition one must be cautious. Many girls were wrongly labeled prostitutes. Estimates of the numbers of prostitutes in nineteenth- and early- twentieth-century cities were often inflated, in part because any women who engaged in casual sex, or were on the street, or looked disrespectable, or lived with men out of wedlock, might be thus labeled. See DuBois and Gordon, "Ecstasy on the Battlefield." Furthermore, there is no clear line between prostitution and other sexual intercourse when women are economically dependent. A variety of exchanges of goods, services, favors, or kindnesses between people in a sexual relationship might be defined alternatively as affection, help, or pay.

110. Twenty-three of twenty-eight.

111. As we have said earlier, children in poor families were expected to contribute to the family economy. With families no longer working together (as on farms), and wage labor not available or not allowed, children were encouraged to contribute through casual bits of paid labor, "gleaning," begging, or stealing.

112. DuBois and Gordon.

113. #2082A, 3042, 3644.

114. E.g., #3049A.
115. #3543, 3085A, for examples.
116. #3642.
117. #3557A.
118. #2057A.

Chapter 8

1. #3242.
2. #4242.
3. #4541.
4. No studies to date have identified characteristics which distinguish wife-beaters from other men. The reason may be the either-or approach, some scholars looking for psychological disorders and others for social-stress factors. E.g., Frank A. Elliott, "The Neurology of Explosive Rage: The Dyscontrol Syndrome"; John R. Lion, "Clinical Aspects of Wifebattering," M. Faulk, "Men Who Assault Their Wives," and Natalie Shainess, "Psychological Aspects of Wifebattering," all in Maria Roy, ed., *Battered Women. A Psychosociological Study of Domestic Violence* (New York: Van Nostrand, 1977); Evan Stark and Anne H. Flitcraft, "Violence Among Intimates: An Epidemiological Review," forthcoming in *Handbook of Family Violence*, eds. Vincent B. Van Hasselt et al. Some might hypothesize that batterers are men who think they can get away with it. This study did not provide the evidence to study violent men. In these case records, women were virtually the only adults interviewed. This tilt was overdetermined: the caseworkers considered women the responsible parents and consulted with them primarily; the women were voluble in complaining about marital violence—and all personal problems—while the men were not; as aggressors, the men felt it in their interest to make themselves scarce.
5. Elizabeth Janeway's *Powers of the Weak* (New York: Knopf, 1980) is an important and underrated contribution to feminist theory. In the tradition of Eugene Genovese's and Herbert Gutman's understanding of slave resistance, and of many labor historians' accounts of workers' resistance, it is followed now by James Scott's *Weapons of the Weak: Everyday Forms of Peasant Resistance* (New Haven: Yale University Press, 1986), an analysis of peasant resistance.
6. Incidents of marital violence were distributed as follows:

TABLE 19. PROPORTION OF MARITAL VIOLENCE IN ALL FAMILY VIOLENCE, BY YEAR

	MARITAL VIOLENCE INCIDENTS	
YEAR	%	N
1880	4.1	2
1890	10.5	6
1893	25.2	25
1900	24.6	32
1910	24.2	40
1917	21.2	36
1920	16.4	26
1930	21.5	50
1934	24.5	59
1940	19.1	37
1944	23.9	44
1950	25.	45
1960	26.4	32

This chart counts incidents, not cases; there were often several different violence incidents in one case; however, repeated assaults of the same type are recorded as one incident. About the low proportions in 1880 and 1890, one might hypothesize that it took some time for victimized women to develop the strategy of using the new child-saving agency—of the three agencies studied here, only the MSPCC existed at that time—against wife-beating, or for the Society to agree that this form of violence impinged upon children. It is not certain that there is statistical significance in the declines in percent of wife-beating cases in 1920 and 1940, but if there is, one might seek to explain it in terms of the fact that these were years of relative prosperity and optimism.

7. "Address to the Legislature of New York on Women's Rights," 1854, in *Elizabeth Cady Stanton, Susan B. Anthony, Correspondence, Writings, Speeches*, ed. Ellen Carol DuBois (New York: Schocken, 1981), p. 49.

8. See her "Feminist Responses to 'Crimes against Women,' 1868–1896," *Signs* 8, 3 (Spring 1983), pp. 465–69. By contrast, the movement against wife-beating in England was more substantial. See, for example, Nancy Tomes, "A 'Torrent of Abuse': Crimes of Violence between Working-Class Men and Women in London, 1840–1875," *Journal of Social History* 11, 3 (Spring 1978), pp. 328–45; Margaret May, "Violence in the Family: An Historical Perspective," in *Violence and the Family*, ed. J. P. Martin (Chichester: John Wiley & Sons, 1978), esp. pp. 137–50; Carol Bauer and Lawrence and Ritt, " 'A Husband Is a Beating Animal'—Frances Power Cobbe Confronts the Wife-Abuse Problem in Victorian England," *International Journal of Women's Studies* 6, 2 (March/April 1983), pp. 99–118; and ibid., "Wife-Abuse, Late Victorian English Feminists, and the Legacy of Frances Power Cobbe," 6, 3 (May/June 1983), pp. 195–207.

9. Society for the Prevention of Cruelty to Women.

10. William L. O'Neill, *Everyone Was Brave. The Rise and Fall of Feminism in America* (Chicago: Quadrangle, 1969).

11. Jerome Nadelhaft, "Domestic Violence in the Literature of the Temperance Movement," unpub. paper, University of Maine, 1986.

12. Ruth Bordin, *Woman and Temperance. The Quest for Power and Liberty, 1873-1900* (Philadelphia: Temple University Press, 1981), e.g., p. 162; Barbara Leslie Epstein, *The Politics of Domesticity. Women, Evangelism and Temperance in Nineteenth-Century America* (Middletown, CT: Wesleyan University Press, 1981), e.g., p. 114.

13. For an early example of this propaganda, see *The Una* I, 6 (1855), p. 84. That the divorce advocates harped more on marital rape than on wife-beating suggests that they considered the latter to have criminal remedies, while the former had none; e.g., Debates on Marriage and Divorce, 10th National Women's Rights Convention, 1860, in *The Concise History of Woman Suffrage*, eds. Mari Jo and Paul Buhle (Urbana: University of Illinois Press 1978), pp. 170-89.

14. DuBois, p. 95; Pleck, op. cit.

15. Smith-Rosenberg, *Disorderly Conduct: Visions of Gender in Victorian America* (New York: Knopf, 1985), p. 92.

16. Elizabeth Pleck, "Wife Beating in Nineteenth-Century America, *Victimology* 4, 1 (1979), pp. 60-74. This did not mean that courts reliably found against wife-beaters. The nineteen most often cited precedents from 1823 to 1876 defy a generalization that there was steady motion toward women's rights to physical protection from their husbands: People v. Winters, N.Y. 1823; Bradley v. State, Miss. 1824; Perry v. Perry, N.Y. 1831; Poor v. Poor, N.H. 1836; The State v. Buckley, Del. 1838; People v. Mercein, N.Y. 1842; Commonwealth v. Fox, Mass. 1856; Richards v. Richards, Penn. 1856; Gholston v. Gholston, Ga. 1860; Joyner v. Joyner, N.C. 1862; State v. Black, Ala. 1864; Commonwealth v. Wood, Mass. 1867; Adams v. Adams, Mass. 1868; State v. Rhodes, N.C. 1868; State v. Mabrey, N.C. 1870; Fulgham v. State, Ala. 1871; Knight v. Knight, Iowa 1871; Commonwealth v. McAfee, Mass. 1871; Shackett v. Shackett, Vt. 1876. (Research by Kathy Brown.) The uneven development was partly because there is such variation among the states, and partly because the relevant decisions were responding also to custody contests. But opinions were common that specifically denied that men had *any* right to physical chastisement of wives. For example, in Commonwealth v. McAfee, Mass. 1871: "A man has no right to beat or strike his wife even if she is drunk or insolent." Or, in Fulgham v. State, Ala. 1871: "The husband can not commit a battery upon his wife, by way of inflicting

upon her 'moderate correction' in order to enforce obedience to his just commands."

17. The few cases of beaten husbands were not used, as they might have been later, to call attention to women's culpability, but the men were portrayed as "of low type," drunken, immoral. #2008, 2561.

18. For just a few examples, #0315A, 0813A, 2003, 2008, 2054A, 2058A.

19. #3646.

20. #3240.

21. #2027.

22. #3363.

23. #1040.

24. #2523.

25. #4007A.

26. #4584.

27. #4284.

28. #1825A.

29. Altogether 34 percent of all the cases of child mistreatment contained wife-beating. Contemporary research about the connection between wife-beating and child abuse has produced mixed findings. Evan Stark and Anne H. Flitcraft, "Violence Among Intimates," pp. 31–33, and Elaine Hilberman and K. Munson, "Sixty Battered Women," *Victimology* 2 (1977–78), 3–4, pp. 460–70, argue for a high correlation; M. Levine, "Interparental Violence and Its Effect on the Children," *Medicine, Science and the Law* 15, 3 (1975), p. 172, found a low correlation.

30. #2523.

31. #3101. Some husbands claimed, in opposition to what I have argued, that they beat their wives *because* they were neglectful toward their children. This seems improbable, because it would assume that fathers had higher standards for child care than mothers.

32. #3363.

33. #3553A.

34. #3280.

35. Margaret Borkowski, Mervyn Murch, Val Walker, *Marital Violence. The Community Response* (London: Tavistock, 1983), pp. 57–59.

36. Marlena Studer, "Wife Beating as a Social Problem: The Process of Definition," *International Journal of Women's Studies* 7 (November–December 1984), p. 417; Susan Schechter, *Women and Male Violence: The Visions and Struggles of the Battered Women's Movement* (Boston: South End Press, 1982), pp. 55–56, 127; Del Martin, *Battered Wives* (New York: Pocket Books, 1976), pp. 207–9.

37. The source of these particular records, of course, made that particular justification more popular, as the wife-beaters knew that social workers would be unreceptive to their claims of a right to hit a woman.

38. James Ptacek, "Wifebeaters' Accounts of Their Violence: Loss of Control as Excuse and as Subjective Experience," M.A. thesis, University of New Hampshire, 1985.

39. Craig MacAndrew and Robert B. Edgerton, *Drunken Comportment: A Social Explanation* (Chicago: Aldine, 1969); Richard J. Gelles, *The Violent Home: A Study of Physical Aggression Between Husbands and Wives* (Beverly Hills: Sage, 1974), p. 114.

40. Lawrence W. Sherman and Richard A. Berk, "The Specific Deterrent Effects of Arrest for Domestic Assault," *American Sociological Review* 49, 2 (1984), pp. 261–72.

41. Murray Straus, Richard Gelles, Suzanne Steinmetz, "Violence in the Family: An Assessment of Knowledge and Research Needs," paper for AAAS, 1976, typescript, p. 32; Gelles, *The Violent Home*, pp. 116–17; Martin, pp. 56–58.

42. E.g., #2027, Richard Gelles found the same fighting about drinking in his contemporary study; ibid., e.g., pp. 161–63.

43. #0315A.

44. E.g., #2001, 2561.

45. Whitehead, "Sexual Antagonism in Herefordshire," in *Dependence and Exploitation in Work and Marriage*, eds. Diana Leonard Barker and Sheila Allen (London: Longman, 1976), pp. 169–203.

46. #2047, 2520, 2523.

47. For recognition of this influence of unemployment by other social observers, see, e.g., Mary C. Blehar, "Family Adjustment to Unemployment," summarizing Louis A. Ferman's research, in *Families Today: A Research Sampler on Families and Children*, ed. Eunice Corfman (Washington, D.C.: NIMH, 1979), pp. 413–39; Ruth Shonle Cavan and Katherine Howland Ranck, *The Family and the Depression. A Study of One Hundred Chicago Families*, vol. XXXV in Social Science Studies (Chicago: University of Chicago, 1938), e.g., pp. 120–37.

48. #3260.

49. #3545.

50. #3551. Her husband's brother's testimony, incidentally, supported her: he had given his brother $200 to start his own business but it had been gambled away.

51. #3560A.

52. #3640.

53. #2008.

54. #0813A.
55. #1040.
56. #2523.
57. #3646.
58. #3101.
59. #3821A.
60. #3560A.
61. Eleven out of fifty-one.
62. #2523, 2548A, 3554A, 3560A, 3585, 3643, 4000, 4004A, 4100, 4141, 4284, 5560, 5601, 5740, 5743A, 6000, 6200, for examples.
63. #4284.
64. #3554A.
65. #6040.
66. #4242.
67. #5740.
68. #6000. The naming of marital rape as a serious problem in the last decade has reclaimed a nineteenth-century feminist understanding of these problems which was temporarily eclipsed. Yet at the same time the separation of marital rape as a problem distinct from wife-beating has analytic disadvantages: it hides the role of men's sexual demands and women's resistance to them in creating nonsexual violence, and equally disguises the function of rape as an enforcement of nonsexual domination. See, e.g., Walker, *The Battered Woman*, chapter 5, for example.
69. Contemporary studies of wife-beaters reveal the same pattern; in fact, separated and divorced women today are more often victimized by their estranged husbands than are women living with their husbands; e.g., Leroy G. Shultz, "The Wife Assaulter," *Journal of Social Therapy* 6, 2 (1960), pp. 103–12; Patsy A. Klaus and Michael R. Rand, *Family Violence* (Washington, D.C.: U.S. Department of Justice, Bureau of Justice Statistics, 1984).
70. Allen, "The State and Domestic Violence," typescript, n.d.
71. #2027.
72. Pardon Files, unnumbered box 12-1-69 to 3-1-70.
73. Ibid., 6-2-70 to 7-30-70.
74. Ibid.
75. Pleck, "Wife Beating in Nineteenth-Century America," p. 65.
76. #6040.
77. #2024.
78. #3040.
79. These case records contain, for example, instances of fights among women, particularly among neighbors, but also among family members.
80. #4060. See also, e.g., #2008, 2561, 3541, 3546, 5085.

81. #2024.

82. #6042. See also, e.g., #3363, 5543.

83. Jane Totman, *The Murderess. A Psychosocial Study of Criminal Homicide* (San Francisco: R. and E. Research Associates, 1978), pp. 3, 48.

84. #3024. See also #4261, 4501, 6086. I cannot resist the only partly humorous observation that if there is a pattern of "masochism" in violent marriages, it describes male better than female behavior, since it is mainly the men who appear to want to continue the violent relationships.

85. Particularly noticeable was the disappearance of women attacking other women. In the first decades of this study the random sample turned up several cases like that of a 1910 Irish-American woman who had "drinking parties" with other women, not infrequently ending in name-calling and fights; she and her daughter fought physically in front of an MSPCC agent; and her daughter was arrested for a fight with another girl. (See #2047.) As previously, we do not have enough data on women's violence to support this impression statistically. Several experts on contemporary marital violence have found, contrary to my impression, continuing high rates of mutual violence and women's violence—e.g., according to Murray Straus, as much as 49.5 percent, of couples reporting any violence, although women remain the more severely victimized. See Murray Straus, "Victims and Aggressors in Marital Violence," *American Behavioral Scientist* 23, 5 (May–June 1980), pp. 681–704. The studies reporting female-to-male violence have been sharply criticized for producing misleading data; see, for example, Elizabeth Pleck, Joseph H. Pleck, Marlyn Grossman, and Pauline Bart, "The Battered Data Syndrome: A Reply to Steinmetz," *Victimology* II, 3–4, 1977–78, pp. 680–83.

86. It is possible that there was no decline in women's violence but only in the reporting of it.

87. Tomes, "A Torrent of Abuse."

88. They may have been better able to cope with or solve domestic violence problems without recourse to professional intervention. See, for example, Jeanne M. Giovannoni and Andrew Billingsley, "Child Neglect Among the Poor: A Study of Parental Adequacy in Families of Three Ethnic Groups," *Child Welfare* 49, 4 (April 1970), pp. 196–204; Noel A. Cazenave and Murray A. Straus, "Race, Class, Network Embeddedness and Family Violence: A Search for Potent Support Systems," *Journal of Comparative Family Studies* X, 3 (Autumn 1979), pp. 281–99.

89. #2054A.

90. #2058A.

91. #2520.

92. #4502.

93. #2042.

94. #1040.

95. #2800A.

96. Boston's housing stock, which included many buildings of three to six apartments, intensified the typical pattern of ethnically homogeneous neighborhoods characteristic of poor urban living at this time. This was in contrast not only to single-family homes but also to the larger tenements characteristic of, e.g., New York.

97. There is of course a sampling bias here: these unhappy clients were more than normally likely to have poor social relationships. Many had even antagonized close relatives. Still, the predominant pattern was unquestioning support, at least passive, from any nearby kinfolk.

98. #6300.

99. #3040.

100. #2042.

101. See, e.g., Natalie Zemon Davis, "The Reasons of Misrule: Youth Groups and Charivaris in Sixteenth Century France," *Past and Present* 51 (February 1971), pp. 51–75; E. P. Thompson, "Rough Music: Le Charivari Anglais," *Annales (Économies, Sociétés, Civilisations)* 27, 2 (1972), pp. 285–312.

102. Pleck, "Wife Beating in Nineteenth-Century America," pp. 69–70.

103. Carol V. R. George, *Segregated Sabbaths: Richard Allen and the Rise of Independent Black Churches, 1760–1840* (New York: Oxford University Press, 1973), p. 95. Thanks to Jean Humez for this reference.

104. Contrary to what Russell and Emerson Dobash have argued in "Community Response to Violence Against Wives: Charivari, Abstract Justice, and Patriarchy," *Social Problems* 28, 5 (June 1981), pp. 563–81, this professional intervention did not cut women off from other community supports.

105. #2024.

106. #3560A.

107. Literature about professionalization often assumes a sharp, sudden "takeover." I am indebted to Judith Leavitt's much more subtle interpretation of the consequences of physicians' involvement in childbirth, in her *Brought to Bed. Child-bearing in America, 1750–1950* (New York: Oxford University Press, 1986).

108. #3040.

109. #3560A.

110. #6040.

111. #6041.

112. Martin Rein, unpublished paper, quoted in Judith Areen, "Intervention Between Parent and Child: A Reappraisal of the State's Role in Child Neglect and Abuse Cases," *Georgetown Law Journal* 63, 3 (1975), p. 919.

113. AR 1959, p. 9.

114. Florence Hollis, *Women in Marital Conflict: A Casework Study* (New York: Family Service Association of America, 1949), pp. 33, 84, 86–87, and passim.

115. E.g., #5585.

116. #5781.

117. #5040.

118. #4042.

119. #5560.

120. E.g., #6041.

121. #6041.

122. E.g., #6081.

123. E.g., #6200, 6201.

124. #5585.

125. #5740.

126. Two works that make this argument are Susan Schechter's *Women and Male Violence*, chapter 9, and Emerson R. and Russell Dobash's *Violence Against Wives: A Case Against the Patriarchy* (New York: The Free Press, 1979).

127. For a fuller discussion of resource theory and references, see Breines and Gordon, pp. 514 ff.

Chapter 9

1. A fuller version of this argument can be found in my "Family Violence, Feminism, and Social Control," *Feminist Studies* 12, 3 (Fall 1986), pp. 452-78.

2. Nancy Cott, for example, has identified some of the processes of community involvement in family life in eighteenth-century Massachusetts, in her "Eighteenth-Century Family and Social Life Revealed in Massachusetts Divorce Records," *Journal of Social History* 10 (Fall 1976), pp. 20–43; Ann Whitehead has described the informal regulation of marital relations that occurred in pub conversations in her "Sexual Antagonism in Herefordshire."

3. Social work scholarship and textbooks commonly call attention to the relational quality of worker-client contacts, the influence of social workers' personalities and personal reactions to individual clients, implicitly thereby recognizing the influence of clients' personalities and actions. See, for e.g., Alfred Kadushin, *Child Welfare Services*, 3rd ed. (New York: Macmillan, 1980) or James W. Green, *Cultural Awareness in the Human Services* (Englewood

Cliffs, NJ: Prentice Hall, 1982). Historians have been less attentive to these factors.

4. Some contemporary feminist theorists, speaking of "state patriarchy" or "public patriarchy," make the mistake of concluding that women are no better off today, because they are controlled by the state instead of individual men. A better interpretation can be found in Jane Lewis, "Feminism and Welfare," about England, in *What Is Feminism*, eds. Juliet Mitchell and Ann Oakley (London: Basil Blackwell, 1986).

5. The question also arises, were women caseworkers better than men, because they were more empathetic, because their gender commonality helped them to transcend their class differences? This study could not answer that question.

Appendix B

1. Note that significance rates will not be reported for this or any other statistical evidence in this book. See Appendix A for an explanation. N's are given for those charts in which the number of cases or episodes were particularly small, making the statistical findings less significant.

2. So few clients could get any relief before 1910 that earlier figures would be meaningless.

3. E.g., Richard J. Gelles, "Family Violence: What We Know and Can Do," in *Unhappy Families.*, eds. Newberger and Bourne, p. 5; Noel Cazenave and Murray A. Straus, "Race, Class, Network Embeddedness and Family Violence: A Search for Potent Support Systems, *Journal of Comparative Family Studies* X, 3 (Autumn 1979), pp. 280–99; James Garbarino, "The Human Ecology of Child Maltreatment: A Conceptual Model for Research," *Journal of Marriage and the Family* 39 (1977), pp. 721-35.

4. The 1890 figure is an underestimate because 90 percent of the remainder had no ethnic designation. Figures on Boston are from Thernstrom, p. 113.

5. These figures include both clients identified by ethnicity and clients for whom ethnicity was deduced from names and other information. For that reason, there may be some underestimation of blacks, since they are rarely identifiable by name; on the other hand, agency caseworkers virtually always identified them as "colored" or Negro. The phrase "Americans" was used by agency workers in a number of ways: in the early years to mean those of Anglo-Saxon stock; later, to mean the native-born; often to indicate merely that the clients did not appear alien. Thus this figure has no meaning in the aggregate,

but is included for specific years merely to give an indication of the caseworkers' judgment about ethnic balance of clients.

6. Unfortunately, the census shifted its units of measurement several times during this period. From 1880 through 1910 it measured the mean size of households, including unrelated lodgers and also including single-person households. In 1930 it measured "private families," i.e., people related by blood or marriage, including single-person families, and offered a median instead of a mean. In 1950 and thereafter, it offered a mean size of private families without including single-person families. In this chart I have tried to develop figures from this study that would match the census figures as exactly as possible. These figures are not completely reliable, because neither census-takers nor agency workers collected accurate information, and the information was particularly inaccurate among the poor, the foreign-speaking, and those who were suspicious of such questioning. The household sizes (1880 and 1910) are the more accurate, because measuring family size meant identifying, for example, children no longer living with their parents. For example, in our study, households, through at least 1930, were smaller or only slightly greater than nuclear families, despite the presence of many boarders and non-nuclear relatives in households. This is because the mothers in this study had many children, and they were not always all in the household at the same time. Many older children had left the household while young ones remained; children were sometimes living with various relatives, especially when marriages were broken by separation or death. I am indebted to Leslie Reagan for getting the Boston census figures.

INDEX

Boston, birth of anti-child-abuse campaign in, 32–37
Boston, characteristics of, 32–37
Boston Children's Aid Society, 123
Boston Children's Friend Society, 32
Boston Children's Hospital, 128, 129
Boston Children's Service Association (BCSA), 13, 102, 128, 140, 302–303, 304, 305, 316n–17n, 358n
origin of, 12, 32
Boston City Hospital, 129, 197
Boston Committee on Public Safety, 220–21
Boston Daily Globe, 37
Boston Family Welfare Society, 87–88
Boston Female Asylum, 32
Boston Herald, 38, 323n, 324n
Boston Psychopathic Hospital, 219, 225
Boston School Board, 125
Boston Society for the Care of Girls, 358n
Bowlby, John, 32, 318n
Brace, Charles Loring, 33, 40, 321n, 337n
Bremner, Robert, 39–40, 320n, 321n, 324n
British Medical Journal, 43
Broken Homes (Colcord), 65, 334n

Carstens, Carl C., 104, 328n, 335n, 357n
MSPCC under, 63–66, 69–70, 73, 74, 76–77, 79, 104, 326n
square deal of, 74–75, 338n
on state responsibility, 76–77, 80, 327n
Carter, James S., 60
Case Records (Sheffield), 65
case records, 12–18, 301–306
caseworkers:
anti-feminism in, 73, 282
clients misunderstood by, 16–17, 101, 123, 317n
clients' neighbors and, 278
economic stresses and, 149
Freudian thought and, 282
judgmental attitudes of, 160, 298–99
non-supporting husbands and, 101
professionalization of, 62–63, 65, 73, 76, 281, 305
racism and class bias in, 3, 11, 14–

16, 21, 46, 47, 92, 131–32, 164–165, 298
record-keeping of, 12, 13, 17, 73, 305
services offered by, 17, 48, 67, 151, 298
women, 66–68, 371n
see also child-protection agencies; clients
Chardon Street Home, 49
charity organization societies (COSs), 61–63
child abuse, 1–2, 6, 9, 27–115, 168–203, 295
adolescence and, 187–93
baby farming as, 43–45, 322n
bed-wetting and, 186, 350n
child labor as, *see* child labor
child neglect vs., 21, 69–75, 78, 315n
class differences and, 177–80
corporal punishment and, 177–81, 255, 291, 319n, 348n–49n
cruelty to children vs., 6, 20
definitions of, 5, 21, 39, 42, 69–78, 82, 177–81, 291, 315n
delinquency and, 140–41
discipline and, 175, 178, 179, 180, 192
discovery of, 27, 317n
familial power struggles and, 171, 172, 191–93, 200, 202
gender roles and, 5, 114–15, 175–176, 196, 203, 255, 314n
as historical and cultural issue, 172, 177–203
as male crime, 73
misbehavior and, 185–87
as non-accidental injury, 315n
patriarchal families and, 56
patterns of, 172–73
poverty and, 23, 28, 29, 83, 179–80
public denial of, 158
racism and, 195–96
rediscovery of, in 1960s, 171
running away and, 187, 191
sexual, *see* sexual abuse
star boarders and, 97
in stepfamilies, 200–202, 352n, 355n
stress factors and, 158, 173, 179, 200
stubborn-child law and, 190–93, 228, 241

husbands' non-support and, 258–
259, 260, 266, 267, 268, 270,
281, 323n
illegality of, 255
immorality and, 269–70, 323n–324n
incest and, 160, 212, 233, 234, 236,
242, 246, 248, 261, 277, 286, 330n
in-laws and, 266
lack of specific campaign against, 253
male dominance as basis of, 251,
252, 260–61, 285–86, 288, 291,
292
marital rape and, 1, 7, 364n, 367n
money conflicts and, 265, 266–67,
269, 284–85
MSPCC and, 258, 260, 262, 264,
266–68, 270–72, 275, 279, 280,
282–84, 323n–24n
murder and, 275
neighborhood and kinship response
to, 276–79
police and, 280–81, 294
prosecution for, 254, 272–73, 281,
288
psychiatric therapy and, 23–24
public denial of, 21–22, 117, 158
separation-and-maintenance agreements and, 273–74, 281, 295
sexual antagonisms and, 199, 267,
268–71, 284–85, 287

shelters for victims of, 25, 254, 271,
273, 290, 347n
as social problem, 251, 285–86, 288
temperance and, 254
tolerance of, 255–57, 279
victim-blaming in, 159, 252, 260,
276, 281–84, 286
victims' responses to, 271–76, 286,
287–88
violent remedies proposed for, 254–
255
women's power and, 255–56
women's violence and, 274–76, 368n
work conflicts and, 267–68, 271
Women's Christian Temperance
Union, 254
women's-rights movement, see feminism, feminists
Wood, E. S., 42
World War I, 146, 292
child-protection work and, 136–38
VD and, 137
World War II, 9, 159, 181, 184, 199
child-protection work and, 23–24,
80, 137, 146, 152–58
VD and, 220–21
women employed during, 154–55
Wrentham State School, 64

youth movements, 20